Interneurons

THEIR ORIGIN, ACTION, SPECIFICITY, GROWTH, AND PLASTICITY

A Series of Books in Biology

Interneurons

THEIR ORIGIN, ACTION, SPECIFICITY, GROWTH, AND PLASTICITY

G. Adrian Horridge

University of St. Andrews, Scotland

W. H. Freeman and Company

London and San Francisco

Preface

This is mainly a work of compilation addressed to postgraduate students, research workers, and teachers whose work is concerned with nerve cells, the brain, or behaviour. The scope is largely limited to recent developments, and for that reason it may soon be found that certain judgments in it are hasty or that the material may pass out of date. However, the nature of the new discoveries in this field suggests that, like anatomy, the descriptions of what nerve cells actually do will remain relevant if they have been described accurately in detail. It also seems likely that the revolution of ideas that has followed the use of the new techniques will not be reversed. Part of the intention of this work is to see how far these new results lead to an understanding of the brain and to what extent models of brains can be tested within the range of possible experiment and observation.

The writing has been eased considerably by the recent appearance of a number of reviews and symposia, which are listed at the end of the book. However, the increasing numbers of works of this kind by multiple authors, each upon their own specialist topic, leads to a situation in which students and outsiders can find no coherent account. The topic is, then, like a glacier, broken into isolated parts, and for a single author the problem is to thread the maze of crevasses. The path that I have followed must largely reflect my own confusions and struggles to bring together different aspects of the subject and to rationalize often-conflicting views.

Some authors may find that I have but slightly paraphrased their words, others may find their exact words are recognizable in sentences here and there. In chapters based upon reviews and papers by others, it is almost inevitable that the most concise and accurate way of expressing the facts has already been used. I suggest that works of extraction and summary by single authors still have a place among symposium volumes, but at the same time I would like to acknowledge my debt to the cited editors and reviewers who have previously brought the subject together.

A major part of my intention is to present detailed findings by tables and illustrations. Without a great deal of solid factual evidence the subject cannot be presented, except in vague generalizations. Moreover, for a long time the subject will remain in the state of accumulating more facts of the same kind. There are many, many nerve cells of almost infinite diversity.

Most readers will have access to reference works which explain standard terminology at the level of the advanced student in medicine, neurobiology, physiology, cybernetics, or zoology. In the present account, in the interests of brevity, standard terms and experimental situations have been introduced without explanation, with the expectation that reference works will be used. I have consciously overestimated the ability of the reader to catch on, and sometimes the illustrations have been designed with this in view.

Reference citations have been reduced to the minimum number of recent, critical, or review articles, which will allow an entry into the literature, and the text has been left reasonably clear. With modern aids it is easy to cite a great number of references and to fill the text with them; it is much more difficult for the writer—but far more valuable to the student—to quote only a small number of relevant ones, which then present a much less formidable obstacle to the newcomer. At the same time it is my hope that a perusal of the titles of the references will lead to the discovery of the source of factual information.

To a considerable extent the level is the same as that of an earlier book written with T. H. Bullock: *Structure and Function in the Nervous Systems of Invertebrates* (W. H. Freeman and Company, San Francisco and London, 1965). That work contains an extensive glossary and introductory chapters of general principles that do not require duplication; what is to be found here is often a pointer to recent findings that modify the earlier account. Most of the first nine chapters would serve to bring up to date the equivalent parts of *Structure and Function*, but my aim is to introduce the properties of interneurons and not to produce a work of general reference.

Some of the material has been selected around topics in which I have been personally interested in the last few years, mainly on lower animals, nerve nets, and coordination in ctenophores, annelids, and arthropods. Many topics of interest have had to be omitted, and I for one am sorry that the neurons of the outstandingly convenient mollusc *Aplysia* could not be treated in full. The electric organs and electrical location mechanisms of fish are also omitted. My only excuse for these omissions is that they deserve separate books of their own. Nor would they contribute any new facet to my principal theme, which is the relation between the connectivity patterns and the natural activity of nerve cells.

G. Adrian Horridge

Acknowledgments

My very grateful thanks are due to the numerous friends, colleagues, and especially students who have contributed by discussion and criticism, often in places far from St. Andrews. We can often never retrace the steps by which trains of thought and the determination to set them down become established, but my debt to others extends far beyond what is suggested by the reference lists. Much of the initial work was completed while I was the guest of Yale University in the academic year 1965–1966, where I found the necessary isolation and access to excellent libraries. I would also like to take this opportunity of thanking the following assistants and secretaries who have patiently carried out my exacting demands: Mrs. D. Hunter, Mrs. E. Stickney, A. Ioannides, S. R. Shaw, and J. Stevenson. Finally, the greatest debt is to my wife, without whom the book would never have been completed.

For permission to reproduce illustrations, I owe thanks to the following journals and institutions.

Academic Press, Inc., New York and London
Experimental Neurology
The Physiology of the Insect Nervous System. J. E. Treherne and J. W. L. Beament (Eds.)

American Association for the Advancement of Science, Washington, D.C.
Science

American Physiological Society, Bethesda, Md.
Journal of Neurophysiology

The American Society of Zoologists, Chicago
The American Zoologist

Annals Publishing Company, St. Louis
Annals of Otology, Rhinology and Laryngology

University of Pisa, Italy
Archives Italiennes de Biologie, Pisa

Baillière, Tindall and Cassell, Ltd., London
Animal Behaviour

Cambridge Philosophical Society, London
  Biological Reviews
J. and A. Churchill, Ltd., London
  Ciba Symposia Series
The Company of Biologists, Ltd., Cambridge
  Journal of Experimental Biology
  Quarterly Journal of Microscopical Science
  Symposia of the Society of Experimental Biology
Elsevier Publishing Company, Amsterdam
  Progress in Brain Research
Excerpta Medica Foundation, London
  Information Processing in the Nervous System. R. W. Gerard and J. W. Duyff (Eds.)
W. H. Freeman and Company, San Francisco and London
  Structure and Function in the Nervous Systems of Invertebrates. T. H. Bullock and G. A. Horridge
The Johns Hopkins Press, Baltimore
  Bulletin of the Johns Hopkins Hospital
Little, Brown and Company, Boston
  Reticular Formation of the Brain. H. H. Jasper (Ed.)
Long Island Biological Association Inc., Cold Spring Harbor
  Cold Spring Harbor Symposia on Quantitative Biology
Macmillan and Company, Ltd., London
  Nature
Masson et Companie, Editeurs, Paris
  Annales des Sciences Naturelles
North-Holland Publishing Company, Amsterdam
  Acta Physiologica Pharmacologica
Pergamon Press, Ltd., Oxford
  Comparative Biochemistry and Physiology
  Comparative Neurochemistry. D. Richter (Ed.)
  Nervous Inhibition. E. Florey (Ed.)
  Olfaction and Taste. Y. Zotterman (Ed.)
The Physiological Society, London
  The Journal of Physiology
The Rockefeller University Press, New York
  Journal of Cell Biology
  Journal of General Physiology
The Royal Microscopical Society, London
  Journal of the Royal Microscopical Society
The Royal Society of London, London
  Philosophical Transactions
  Proceedings
The Society of Protozoologists, Urbana
  Journal of Protozoology
Springer-Verlag, Berlin and Heidelberg
  Kybernetic
  Protoplasma

Zeitschrift für Anatomie und Entwicklungsgeschichte
Zeitschrift für vergleichende Physiologie
Stanford University Press, Stanford
Neural Theory and Modeling. R. F. Reiss (Ed.)
The Wistar Institute of Anatomy and Biology, Philadelphia
Journal of Cellular and Comparative Physiology
Journal of Comparative Neurology

Contents

13

14

15

16

List of figures

10

11

12

16

List of tables

Introduction

Descriptions of interneurons are based upon the technique of sampling hundreds of nerve cells. The action of each is recorded individually to discover how each nerve cell is most readily excited or inhibited. The most effective types of stimulus and the most frequent receptive fields for large numbers of nerve cells are then used to construct a theory of how they interact. The theory is compared with the behaviour of the whole animal, and the integrative activity of the nervous system may be thereby explained. The theory of interaction must of course be compatible with the actual anatomical connexions of the nerve fibres.

This method of establishing what actually goes on in each of the nerve cells has led to a quiet revolution in many important concepts about the analysis of peripheral stimuli and the control of behaviour. It is as if conversations of individuals in a city of long ago were to become separately observable to a modern historian by a new technique that allowed him to probe blindly back in time into an immensely complex historical situation. The individual speakers would be identifiable only by their words, and they would mostly seem irrelevant to the main course of events. After much patient labour, however, theories derived from these studies might throw a great deal of light on causes and interactions of the past which could be reached by no other method. This is the process that is now being actively pursued for the nervous system of many animals, and some of the problems and modifications of major concepts have already emerged. We cannot yet tell how far the revolution will proceed before a new plateau is reached in our comprehension of what actually goes on when animals or men perceive and respond, or act apparently spontaneously.

Startling recent results of neurophysiology now demand more definite supporting facts from all kinds of related fields. Some of the best research in anatomy, behaviour study, electron microscopy, and analytical biochemistry is now being done because neurophysiological problems pose definite questions. Many of those problems are still concerned with membranes, synapses, and transmitter substances, even though we have just passed through a golden decade of these studies.

The new period is one of intense survey of the features and properties of interneurons, in the hope of discovering laws that govern the receptive fields of neurons: how do they abstract the relevant features of their inputs? what exactly are the "well-formed phrases" that induce neurons to respond? The quoted phrase is from the logic game called *WFF'N PROOF*, which is played with the five operations of the conditional, alternation, conjunction, exclusion, and negation; a well-formed phrase is like a stimulus or key that fits the logical system of any one game. As will be seen, the nervous system uses the same rules in abstracting generalities from a pattern of external stimuli. Hard-edged rules of logic are all-or-nothing, however, and are inapplicable to the abstracting properties of neurons until the quantities, properties, and dimensions of excitation in different neurons can be weighted and treated with different degrees of emphasis. At this borderline neurophysiology puts in a valid claim for a new type of mathematics that will be a multidimensional, statistical, partial logic.

This book also emphasizes another theme—that the evolution of progressively more complex functions has been made possible by the evolution of more complex connectivity patterns and greater differences between individual neurons. In the lower animals or in simpler situations we find nervous systems with many equivalent cells. In some of the higher forms in each major group, many of the neurons are anatomically different and appear to be "recognizable" to each other at their terminations. Although little is known of the mechanisms controlling their growth, the neurons follow certain rules that decide their connectivity. From lower to higher animals there is a scale of increasing complexity in connectivity patterns, and this is made possible by progressively greater specificity and resolution in the morphogenetic mechanisms by which neurons avoid some contacts and form others. The nature of these mechanisms is almost entirely unknown, and an initial barrier to advance in their understanding is that diversity of the individual cells has proceeded to such an extent that one can almost say that every neuron is uniquely different from all the others in an advanced adult animal such as a mammal or a crayfish. In arthropods, every muscle fibre may be unique as well. Even for the analysis of behaviour, this sets a formidable problem in which the method of recording does not permit the individual identification of the cells that are studied, except by their responses.

This topic of forming connexions is related to that of learning, because animals that can make a new discrimination, or act differently when a new stimulus becomes significant, behave as if they have changed some connexions between their nerve cells. Whether they have in fact done so remains a topic for the future.

What is written here is a group of signposts and a general itinerary rather than an exhaustive guide for travelers. At the present time we venture into obscure regions when we try to formulate the mechanisms by which neurons grow into the fantastic patterns of connexions that bring about their remarkable properties, which in turn make possible the richness of behaviour. I hope that the signposts point in the right direction, towards the elaboration of specific chemical differences between individual neurons, passed on at contacts with other higher-order neurons. If my emphasis, perhaps misplaced, leads any of my readers to devise experiments of their own, my efforts will not be wasted.

1

Transmission within cells: protozoa, cilia, muscle, neurons

We begin with a consideration of communication within cells because, as will be shown, processes within nerve cells are important in the long-term control of interactions between them. Furthermore, if obvious lines of communication and stores of information within any cell can be utilized in rapid processes that involve the electrical response of the membrane, they are of immediate interest, whether or not we yet have evidence that they are important in the activity of neurons. Unfortunately, at the present time a large number of isolated examples of intracellular communication cannot be explained by established general principles.

The peculiarity of Protozoa is that they have such diverse and adaptive behaviour, yet with apparently inadequate means of coordination. Undoubtedly there is still much to know about different species in the diversity of their abilities, especially about the degrees of independence of the different types of coordination that can go on simultaneously. Analysis of mechanisms is extremely difficult on this small scale. Cilia are the most intensively studied organelles, primarily because they are conveniently observed.

TRANSMISSION ALONG THE SHAFT OF A SINGLE CILIUM

When a flagellum beats, the wave of movement along the shaft may be symmetrical or the forward stroke may be quite different from the backward stroke (Fig. 1.1, A). The wave may die away as it travels along or it may be sustained by an equal energy production all along the shaft. These rather typical waves can be explained as mechanical propagations along the shaft. One acceptable suggestion is that the movement of one region excites the next region, which responds by its own characteristic movement. When extracted with glycerine, isolated cilia and flagella

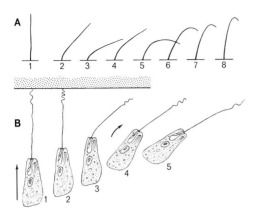

Figure 1.1

Types of transmission along cilia.

A. Wave of change of curvature running along a typical cilium from base to tip, in successive positions 1–8.

B. Startle response and change of direction in *Peranema*. This animal is normally drawn along by waves that move for only a short distance away from the tip. When the tip crashes into a stationary object, a different kind of signal is conveyed right to the base, which then bends and causes a change in the direction of movement.

beat if supplied with ATP. That each region is mechanically sensitive is clear, but the mechanism of the movement in response is unknown. One theory suggests that one side of the cilium contracts; another theory, that the component tubules of the cilium slide upon each other. There are, however, many exceptional examples—one readily available in the laboratory is *Peranema*, in which only the tip of one flagellum beats and, in doing so, pulls the animal along. The waves start at the tip, apparently spontaneously, and as they move away from it they pull the animal forward. When the flagellum bumps into a stationary object, it bends at its base, but such bending also occurs spontaneously at other times. This shows that excitation is in some way transmitted (perhaps mechanically) from the tip to the base of the cilium. Consequently the animal turns, and the subsequent movement of the tip of the flagellum takes it off in a new direction (Fig. 1.1, B). The whole action is one of numerous examples of avoidance responses that are achieved *without nerves* in Protozoa.

INITIATION OF BEAT IN A CILIUM

The mechanical sensitivity of cilia and flagella has been exploited in numerous mechanoreceptor sense organs of higher animals. In several examples among Protozoa and Metazoa the normal beat is triggered by the movement of a neighbouring cilium, as in *Paramecium* and *Opalina*. In addition, any cilium can apparently beat spontaneously, so that when several lie side by side the fastest becomes a pacemaker and drives its neighbours. Mechanical coupling of this type can be inferred when an increase in the viscosity of the medium reduces both the amplitude of the beat and the velocity of the waves that pass over the animal, because the mechanical coupling is increased even though at the same time the amplitude of each wave is reduced [19]. Some multicellular gill filaments of the clam *Modiolus* continue to show metachronal waves that are passed from cell to cell when reactivated with ATP after being extracted with ethylene glycol and glycerine [6]. Experiments on the normal gills of other lamellibranchs also show that transmission from cilium to cilium can be effected through the water by virtue of the mechanical sensitivity of cilia to the movement of their neighbours. Clearly the membrane of the cell is not essential for the mechanical sensitivity or for the movement.

CONTROL OF THE RATE OF BEATING

Most cilia are under control, but usually only with regard to the frequency, not to the direction of their beat. The nature of the control is not known, but in ctenophore comb plates the beating is faster in depolarized cells. The ciliary beat of many Protozoa is all-or-none; either they beat at full speed or they are inactive. It is curious that in many electron micrographs of cilia the cell membrane approaches the basal body closely at one point; thus, if the cilium is accessible to control by current flow through the membrane, we might expect the sensitive point to be at the base, since this is where movement begins. Between their numerous basal bodies the macrocilia of *Beroë* [10] have a system of tubules that have a structural and perhaps a functional similarity to the sarcoplasmic tubules that carry excitation into muscle fibres. Inhibition of cilia in some Metazoa certainly occurs via nerves, but the only synapses so far known upon ciliated cells are in ctenophore comb plates; even there it is not clear how the message crosses the cell from the synapses at one end to the cilia at the other [9] unless the membrane potential controls the rate of beat.

CONTROL OF DIRECTION OF BEATING

Most cilia and flagella always beat in a direction that is fixed in relation to their position in the animal, but among some Protozoa and a few Metazoa the direction is clearly controlled by factors that spread from elsewhere across the cell. Sometimes there is only a plain reversal of the direction of the power stroke, as in the pharnyx of sea anemones. On the other hand, the somatic cilia of many Protozoa beat under control in any plane, which is one way they determine the direction of locomotion. In a few cases investigated, principally in the flat, leaflike frog parasite *Opalina*, the change in direction can be artificially controlled by the membrane potential (Fig. 1.2). The latter can be recorded directly with a microelectrode while the cilia are observed. There is no clue to how the membrane potential is controlled, but we can draw a useful concept from

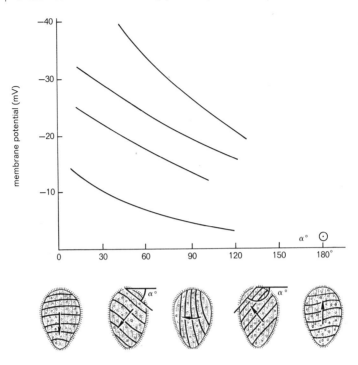

Figure 1.2

The direction of ciliary beat in *Opalina* as related to the membrane potential. The arrows show the directions of the metachronal waves across the surface of the animal and also the direction of the power stroke of the beat. The angle is that plotted in the graph. The four curves show measurements on four different individuals. [Modified from Kinosita, in Bullock and Horridge, 1965.]

the ctenophores. These animals apparently have, at one place, sensory cilia that modify the membrane potential of the cells that bear them, and, elsewhere, motor cilia that, by a single beat, depolarize adjacent cells. Sensory cilia of protozoans or movement of the motor cilia themselves might well control the membrane potential in such a way as to effect a sensible relation to the immediate environment. With suitable arrangement of directions and polarities the animal might steer out of trouble with this simple equipment, but there is no evidence that this theory provides an adequate explanation.

The behaviour of some Protozoa suggests that different mechanisms of coordination coexist side by side in the same animal; however, few lines of conduction are available, and those that are known seem inadequate. The most complicated conduction, in the flat uniform ciliary fields on each side of *Opalina*, shows only two independent mechanisms. Here a cut stops the metachronal wave by blocking the smooth course of the mechanical transmission between adjacent cilia, but fails to prevent the coordination of the direction of beat between the two sides of the cut, because this second aspect is controlled by the potential of the membrane of the whole cell. Apart from subsurface structures there is little else to coordinate the animal, and yet some protozoans appear able to coordinate several simultaneous actions.

COORDINATION OF CILIA BY SUBSURFACE STRUCTURES

There are no known examples of transmission of a wave between ciliated cells that is achieved by nerves. The closest approximation is in ctenophores, in which the ciliated cells themselves have electrically excitable properties similar to those of nerves. In Protozoa, however, it has long been suspected that fibrils in the cytoplasm may transmit the signals that set off the beat of a distant group of cilia. In his experiments in 1920 on *Euplotes,* Taylor cut through the bundles of fibres which run from the gullet region to certain isolated tufts of cilia at the aboral end, and he found that control or coordination of the small tufts disappeared when their own bundle was cut [21]. In a review twenty years later Taylor did not mention his own work, and a careful attempt to repeat it failed [14], but curiously there is one recent confirmation of it [7]. There is no conclusive evidence that internal tubules or fibrils are conducting elements: they may exert some effect by tension. A suggestion that subsurface structures are important comes from work on the large cilia of the oral membranelles of the ciliate *Stentor*. Along the row of membranelles there runs a metachronal ciliary wave that is not modified by a small increase in viscosity of the medium. The velocity of the metachronal wave is independent of its amplitude, even under the influence of agents as varied as temperature, viscosity, magnesium ions, and drugs. The inference is that the transmission process is not via a mechanical coupling through the water, and is presumably via a subsurface structure. Nervelike transmission along the membrane would be much too rapid. Subsurface fibres form loops between membranelles, and these probably have a conducting function, perhaps exerted by tension. However, no-one has yet tested whether subsurface fibres here or elsewhere work by mechanical pulling on the basal bodies or whether they conduct in some other way. Of the various proposed conducting mechanisms in protein fibrils, none have survived real tests on the animals themselves.

COORDINATION OF CHANGES IN CELL FORM

Many protozoans, especially flagellates and ciliates, change their shape in locomotion, in protective retraction, and in twisting around sharply curved surfaces. Only seldom is the movement clearly caused by fibrous structures. One exception is the stem of the peritrich ciliate *Vorticella*, in which there are thin solid fibrils and membrane tubes. This stem shortens to a fraction of its original length, but the exact mechanism is not known. Many protozoans have fibrils (defined as solid and of diameter 5 to 10 nm) or tubules (defined as hollow and of diameter 20 to 30 nm), running in definite patterns parallel to their surface. Sometimes both are present, and there may be fibrils and tubules deep in the cytoplasm as well as associated with the membrane. Roots of cilia are commonly clusters of fibrils, but in many forms there are single tubules, or bundles of them, that spread out from the basal bodies of some cilia. In no instance is it possible to identify a fibril or tubule as a transmission line, and in only a few instances is it possible to identify a fibril or tubule as a likely driving source of mechanical movement. There are, however, some clues to their function; as more favourable situations are discovered, the capabilities of fibrils and tubules will become more thoroughly documented.

Figure 1.3

A. A living suctorian, *Tokophyra,* with numerous tentacles (*t*) and a stalk (*s*), which leads down to an attachment disc (*d*).

B. Cross section of a tentacle, which is not feeding, showing the pellicle (*p*), the plasma membrane (*pm*), the scalloped lumen of the inner tube (*it*), with its wall of 49 tubular fibrils arranged in 7 groups of 3, and 7 groups of 4.

C. Cross section of a tentacle with food contents in the centre and the tubules displaced towards the periphery. [Rudzinska, 1965.]

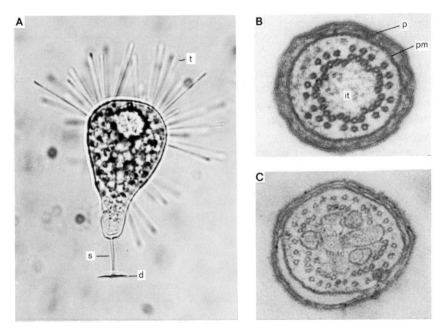

Some tubules are clearly skeletal—for example, those that are sprung inside the rim of blood platelets, where they presumably maintain the shape as a disc. We also find a variety of situations in which there is movement (including cytoplasmic streaming) and where tubules (diameter 20 nm) are present. Spindles in dividing cells are composed of tubules that are rather easily dissolved and reformed from the soluble state. Throughout the animal kingdom, from cnidarians to mammals, many axons and dendrites of nerve cells have tubules in the axoplasm; others, such as the squid giant axon, have neurofilaments that are thinner and less obviously tubular. The one-way or two-way movement of particles and axoplasm along axons is perhaps attributable to the neurotubules.

The carnivorous flagellate *Peranema* bites fiercely with skeletal rods of the gullet. These rods are composed of tight bundles of tubules, but how they move is not clear. When a suctorian feeds, the contents of the *Paramecium* that it "sucks out" stream down the centre of the tentacle that makes the capture. These tentacles consist of an inner tube, down which the cytoplasm of the prey flows, surrounded by a curious pattern of 49 tubules (Fig. 1.3). Outside these tubules the cytoplasm of the suctorian flows outwards along the tentacle, carrying particles that presumably are involved in digestion [18]. The undulating membrane of sporozoans also contains small bundles of tubules, which by sliding upon each other could cause the animal's slow oscillatory movement (Fig. 1.4, A); indeed it is difficult to see how else the movement could arise [13]. A similar sliding of tubules is the basis of one theory of the origin of movement in sperm tails, cilia, and flagella, especially in several curious instances where there are far more than the usual number of tubules within one membrane. The long stiff arms of the heliozoans catch food particles that adhere to them, and then the particles slide down the arms to the cell body (Fig. 1.4, B). This movement may be caused by the bundle of tubules that form a spiral pattern in the arm [22]. The flagellate *Euglena*, which makes sinuous bending movements in all directions, has in its surface numerous parallel strips arranged as a spiral over the whole animal. Each fold where these strips meet contains a small group of regularly arranged tubules in just the appropriate position to cause sliding of each strip against its neighbour [12]. The 20-mm microtubules commonly occurring in mechanoreceptors, especially of arthropods, perhaps "take up the slack" and so adjust the mechanical threshold.

In all these instances, usefully applied movement is possible only if the tubules are appropriately attached, but the pattern of attachments is poorly known. The movement is along the line of the tubules, and does not rule out movement by sliding. The relevance of all these comparative observations is that similar tubules, and streaming in both directions, are typical of all neurons that have been observed by appropriate methods.

Another approach has led to the finding that a number of different

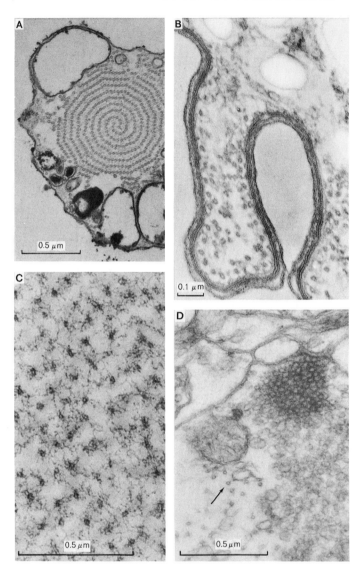

Figure 1.4

Tubules in two protozoans and in neurons.

A. Section through the base of an arm of a heliozoan, *Actinosphaerium,* showing two intertwined spiral arrays of microtubules.

B. Section through the wall of a gregarine, *Selenidium,* showing tubules that run in the raised ridges and folds.

C. Section through the axon of a locust retinula cell.

D. Section through the axon of the worm, *Harmothoë,* showing neurotubules. In all these cases it is probable that the tubules cause a flow of other cytoplasmic components along their length and so give rise to movement. [A from Tilney and Porter, 1965; B from MacGregor and Thomasson, 1965; D courtesy J. Lawry.]

cytoplasmic particles in cultured mammalian cells move short distances in a saltatory fashion and that such movements usually occur along one particular path in either direction. Treatment with 0.001 M colchicine destroys the tubules in the cells and also halts movement [2]. Tubules in other cells are sometimes surrounded by a clear region, as though particles had been wafted away. The pigment grains in the melanophores of the fish *Fundulus* move along predetermined channels that are lined with microtubules 22 nm in diameter [4]. Perhaps the tubules provide a basic intracellular mechanism of transport by sliding; if so, we have two fundamental questions. How do they work? Does their presence in nerve cells mean that we have to consider intracellular transport as their principal function in nerve fibres?

MECHANISM OF AMOEBOID MOVEMENT AND ITS CONTROL

Neurons move in tissue cultures, and some grow by an advancing tip, which resembles an amoeba (see p. 290). Whether filaments account for the flow patterns in amoeboid movement is unknown. Filaments, but not microtubules, can generally be found where such movement occurs, but it is still not certain whether they are artefacts [1]. Various evidence suggests that cytoplasmic flow originates in the area of movement and is not impressed from the outside, but whether filaments slide over each other or whether they contract in situ, or both, is not clear. Velocities are very low; 1 to 5 mm/hr is typical, although the flow appears faster under the microscope. Currents of a different speed and direction can occur side by side; therefore, a simple theory according to which the gel contracts and squeezes the sol is not adequate for all motions. There is no obvious difference, even under the electron microscope, between the solid outer "gel" region and the inner "sol," which does the moving. The particles at the surface stand still relative to the surface, and the centre of a pseudopodium flows forward. Streaming cannot be caused by pressure from behind, for it is not stopped when two-thirds of the contents of an *Amoeba* are removed by suction through a pipette inserted at the hind end. Growth of axons, of course, may be quite different, and depend on pressure, but this is more likely to be generated in the axon than in the distant soma. Any part of the ectoplasmic gel layer can contract in *Amoeba*, usually when stimulated either on its outside or inside; normally it is presumably relaxed. Streaming does not depend upon the outside membrane, for droplets of an *Amoeba* that is broken up under oil will continue to stream without their membrane [1]. Cytoplasm can be observed to stream in many plant cells, where cell walls cannot push. A curious feature is that measurements of the refractive index of *Amoeba* show 40% more solids in the tail end than at the front, and water being continually moved out from the tail region. Therefore, the self-stirring mechanism is more efficient at moving water than in moving the particles and proteins. Perhaps moving water strokes the sol along the central region, but flows back alone in the clear zone under the cell wall outside the gel layer, so that the net movement of solids is forward. We have no idea whether water transport occurs along axons or glial cells, but much will be said about the transport of proteins along axons.

Difflugia, which is related to *Amoeba* but covers itself with a coat of sand grains, extends transparent pseudopodia. As soon as one of these attaches to the substrate a mass of fibrils develops in the ectoplasm between the attachment region and the cytoplasm in the shell. The pseudopodium then contracts, whereupon the fibrils disappear. Apparently the fibrils are connected firmly to the cell membrane and they cause the contraction, but how they extend and how contraction is controlled remains a mystery. Streaming in the slime mould *Physarum* seems attributable to 7 nm filaments that contain ATP-ase.

In the internode and leaf cells of the alga *Nitella*, the endoplasm streams continuously past stationary ectoplasm, which contains the chloroplasts. At this interface, where the movement appears to be generated, are bundles of 50 to 100 microfilaments, each 5 nm thick and many microns long, in bundles 100 nm thick and 500 nm apart [2].

CONTRACTION OF MUSCLE

That the sliding of fibres within the cell can be controlled from the cell membrane is illustrated best in muscle, where the process obviously occurs. Such sliding has been well studied, but its exact mechanisms are unknown. The giant striated muscle fibres of a large Pacific barnacle are each up to 2 mm in diameter and 2 cm long, with two types of filaments and with H and I bands similar to those of typical mammalian muscle (Fig. 1.5). The I band becomes longer on stretching the muscle, and disappears on contraction. The thick filaments, 15–18 nm in diameter, form a hexagonal array and often appear hollow. Thin filaments of diameter 6 nm, attached to dense bodies in the Z membranes, are distributed between the thick filaments; at rest those from adjacent Z membranes almost meet in the middle of the A bands (Fig. 1.5, A). During contraction the thick filaments do not shorten, but they slide closer to the Z membranes until the I bands are obliterated. If neurally stimulated to further contraction, the thick filaments move through holes in the Z membranes into the adjacent sarcomere, and consequently the muscle can contract to a third of its length even in situ in the animal (Fig. 1.5, B). In contrast, when contraction is caused by ATP in fibres extracted in glycerine, the holes in the Z membranes fail to open and, as soon as contraction exceeds 50% of the resting length, the thick fibres are curled over and doubled back on themselves (Fig. 1.5, C). This is one of several evidences that thick and thin fibres generate contraction by sliding actively over each other in opposite directions. Apparently this also happens in smooth muscle, except that the attachments of the thin filaments to the cell membrane are distributed evenly and not arranged in Z bands [11].

How the control operates on the inside of the cell from the membrane is largely a mystery for most effector cells, such as glands and photophores, although it is partly understood in muscle. When the muscle fibre membrane is excited, it changes its permeability and lets in calcium (and perhaps other) ions, which somehow set off the contraction. A decrease in latency is achieved in larger striated muscle fibres of vertebrates and

Figure 1.5

The sliding of thick and thin filaments in a striated muscle of the giant barnacle. Contraction to less than half the extended length is brought about by two different means.

A. Maximum passive extension, thick and thin filaments hardly overlapping.

B. Contraction caused by nerve impulses; the thick filaments pass through the Z membranes.

C. Contraction caused by ATP; the Z membranes have not opened and the thick filaments crash and crumple against them. Both the contraction and the opening of the Z membranes are ultimately controlled by the outer membrane of the muscle fibre. [Adapted from Hoyle, McAlear, and Stevenson, 1965.]

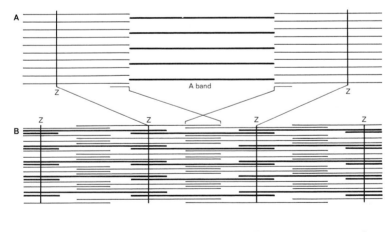

crustaceans by a system of channels that are extensions of the outer membrane permeating the muscle fibre. The membranes of these channels concentrate calcium ions, which are released when the channel membranes are depolarized along with the outer cell membrane. These channels therefore bring a signal from the outer membrane deep into the muscle fibre. When current flows from inside the muscle fibre to its outside, apparently only about 10% is carried through the outer membrane, most going via the transverse channels, which are selectively permeable to chloride ions. In at least two separately evolved types of striated muscle there is a second system of endoplasmic tubules that are closed off from the outside (see Fig. 1.6); it is not, however, clear how excitation is passed to this second system, if at all. No internal conducting system is known in any nerve cell.

CONCLUSION

One comprehensive suggestion that accounts for many of the various movements discussed is that certain fibrils can fold themselves, and that tubules have the property of being able to transfer material along their

Figure 1.6

Reconstruction of the sarcoplasmic reticulum that runs across the myofibrils within a striated muscle fibre of the frog. The transverse tubules (*tt*) are continuous with the outer membrane of the cell, and their membrane is thought to be the route by which excitation is conducted rapidly to the myofibrils at the centre of the fibre. The terminal cisternae (*tc*) are thought to concentrate calcium ions, which cause contraction when suddenly released by the arriving electrical excitation. [Peachey, 1965.]

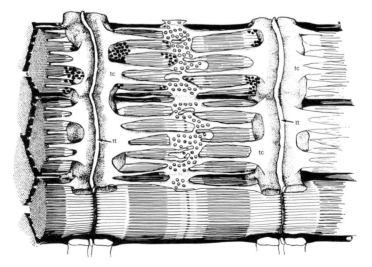

outside surface by some physical process such as electro-osmosis. Sometimes this carries particles along; sometimes we find a movement of water; sometimes there is a sliding of a fibril or tubule over its neighbour. Tubules around water-excreting contractile vacuoles seem to be one specialization of this ability, and perhaps striated muscle and cilia are also highly evolved modifications.

When we consider how changes within the cell, whether they be contraction or secretion, are controlled from the membrane in the above examples, we find almost nothing around which to plan neuron studies. In later chapters it will be inferred that the contents, growth, memories, and secretion of nerve cells are influenced by their membrane activity, but unfortunately no principles of explanatory value are available from studies at the cellular level. In fact, there is only the inward movement of ions to account for the inward transmission of information from the membrane. Similarly, if nerve terminals move on a fine scale, we have almost no general principles from which we could infer how such movements are brought about or controlled. Useful and certainly interesting models, however, might be found in the control systems of a variety of effector cells, such as those that secrete or become luminous.

The neurotubules seen in some nerve fibres are apparently constructed like those associated with movement. Present research indicates that in vertebrates the neurotubules are more typical of dendrites than of axons, and that throughout the invertebrates they are characteristic of certain neurons but not of others. Although time-lapse films show quite rapid movements in both directions in nerve fibres at rates of 0.5—2 mm/hour, the net movement of axoplasm is slow and similar to the rate of regeneration of cut fibres—about 2mm/day. Despite the wealth of comparative evidence to suggest that neurotubules may be a transport system, their incidence has not been correlated with the amount of particle movement inside nerve fibres, and it has even been suggested that the weak peristalsis observed in frog axons is responsible for the flow of axoplasm. However, neurofilaments, 10 nm in diameter, which are abundant in young fibres and in the growing tips of axons, might play an important part in the elongation of the growing tip. In the light of what has been summarized in this chapter, the part played by neurotubules and neurofilaments in intracellular transport of signals in neurons deserves intense investigation in a wide variety of animals. The general conclusion is that mechanisms of subcellular communication are a topic for the future; the examples so far known are from specialized cells, and the findings are not applicable to nerve cells. When more is known of subcellular communication, the control of secretion will be more relevant to the control of long-term changes within nerve cells. At present it cannot be too strongly stressed that movement of substances along the axon plays a most important part in the control of long-term relations, in the formation and maintenance of connexions, and in individual differences between neurons.

REFERENCES FOR CHAPTER 1

1. Allen, R. D., and Kamiya, N. (Eds.). 1964. *Primitive Motile Systems in Cell Biology*. New York, Academic Press.
2. American Society of Cell Biology. 1965. Abstracts of papers. *J. Cell Biol.* **27**:1A–149A.
3. Anderson, W. A., Weissman, A., and Ellis, R. A. 1966. A comparative study of microtubules in some vertebrate and invertebrate cells. *Zeit. Zellforsch.* **71**:1–13.
4. Bikle, D., Tilney, L. G., and Porter, K. R. 1966. Microtubules and pigment migration in the melanophores of *Fundulus heteroclitus* L. *Protoplasma* **61**: 322–345.
5. Bullock, T. H., and Horridge, G. A. 1965. *Structure and Function in the Nervous Systems of Invertebrates*. San Francisco and London, W. H. Freeman and Company. Chapter 7.
6. Child, F. M., and Tamm, S. 1963. Metachronal ciliary coordination in ATP-reactivated models of *Modiolus* gills. *Biol. Bull. Woods Hole* **125**:373.
7. Gliddon, R. 1965. Ciliary activity and coordination in *Euplotes eurystomus*. 2nd Internat. Conf. E. M. London, Excerpta Medica Series No. 91. Paper 307.
8. Hagiwara, S. 1966. Membrane properties of the barnacle muscle fiber. *Ann. N.Y. Acad. Sci.* **137**:1015–1024.
9. Horridge, G. A. 1965 [Papers on cilia of ctenophores; see p. 32.]
10. Horridge, G. A. 1965. Macrocilia with numerous shafts from the lips of the ctenophore *Beroë*. *Proc. Roy. Soc. B* **162**:351–364.
11. Hoyle, G., McAlear, J. H., and Stevenson, A. 1965. Mechanism of supercontraction in a striated muscle. *J. Cell Biol.* **26**:621–640.
12. Leedale, G. F., 1964. Pellicle structure in *Euglena*. *Brit. Phycol. Bull.* **2**: 291–306.
13. MacGregor, H. C., and Thomasson, P. A. 1965. The fine structure of two archigregarines; *Selenidium fallax* and *Ditrypanocystis cirratuli*. *J. Protozool.* **12**:438–443.
14. Okajima, A., and Kinosita, H. 1966. Ciliary activity and coordination in *Euplotes eurystomus*. I. Effect of microdissection of neuromotor fibres. *Comp. Biochem. Physiol.* **19**:115–132.
15. Peachey, L. D. 1965. The sarcoplasmic reticulum and transverse tubules of the frog's sartorius. *J. Cell Biol.* **25**:209–232.
16. Peachey, L. D. 1966. The role of transverse tubules in excitation contraction coupling in striated muscles. *Ann. N.Y. Acad. Sci.* **137**:1025–1037.
17. Robinson, W. G. 1966. Microtubules in relation to the motility of a sperm syncytium in an armored scale insect. *J. Cell Biol.* **29**:251–266.
18. Rudzinska, M. A. 1965. The fine structure and function of the tentacle in *Tokophrya infusionum*. *J. Cell Biol.* **25**:459–477.
19. Sleigh, M. A. 1962. *The Biology of Cilia and Flagella*. Oxford. Pergamon Press.

20. Taylor, A. C. 1966. Microtubules in the microspikes and cortical cytoplasm of isolated cells. *J. Cell Biol.* **28:**155–168.

21. Taylor, C. V. 1920. Demonstration of the function of the neuromotor apparatus in *Euplotes* by the method of microdissecton. *Univ. Cal. Publ. Zool.* **19:**403–471.

22. Tilney, L. G., and Porter, K. R. 1965. Studies on microtubules in Heliozoa. *Protoplasma* **60:**317–344.

2

Ctenophores

Ctenophores are a group of marine planktonic animals that bear some resemblance to medusae. They have no consolidated organs except for an apical sensory region, which is a group of spontaneously active ciliated cells arranged around an otolith. Ctenophores feed mainly on zooplankton and grow quickly by addition of highly hydrated mesogloea or jelly. They differ from coelenterates in having nerve and muscle fibres in the mesogloea and in having explosive cells called colloblasts, which are quite different from the nematocysts of anemones and jellyfish. The similarities to medusae, including transparency and independence of locomotion from other responses, are examples of convergence that can be related to the similarity of habitat and feeding tactics (Fig. 2.1).

Ctenophores illustrate, par excellence, a diversity of functions in which cilia participate. Apart from a few curious genera (such as *Cestus*, the straplike Venus' Girdle, which undulates like an eel), they swim through the water by metachronal waves of rows of giant cilia, arranged in a series of plates that form eight meridional combs (Fig. 2.2). These animals illustrate how a few simple responses, coordinated by two or three pathways, ensure survival.

ANATOMY OF THE NERVE NET

The neurons of the superficial ectoderm are mostly tripolar, with processes that run as far as the next neuron, forming a polyhedral primary net uniformly over the body surface (Fig. 2.3). In at least two situations a lateral compression and directionality is imposed on this net, so that it forms a kind of tract. First, most ctenophores have tentacles that can be withdrawn into a tube, and in the floor of the tube there is an area where the fibres run in a preferred direction, forming a tract that continues along the tentacle. Second, a part of the same net is concentrated along

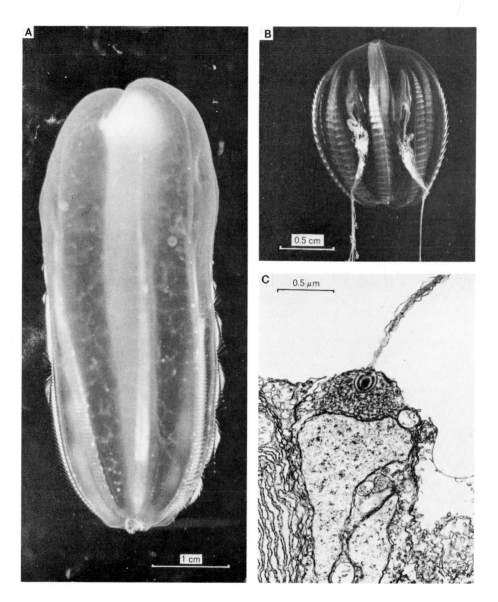

Figure 2.1

Two ctenophores—**A**, *Beroë* and **B**, *Pleurobrachia*—swimming upwards with mouth uppermost and apical organ below. The *Beroë*, with more comb plates active on the right, is turning towards the left. The comb plates are at rest in the *Pleurobrachia*.

C. A sensory neuron of the ctenophore *Eucharis*, bearing a nonmotile cilium with a peculiarly modified basal body; this is a receptor of underwater vibrations. In *Eucharis* it releases the responses of the extensile fingers; similar nonmotile cilia occur on the tentacles and epithelium of other ctenophores. [A and B photographed by M. S. Laverack; C from Horridge, 1965.]

the ciliated groove, which is a line of ciliated cells running down from the apical organ to the comb plates, and nerve fibres run beneath the ciliated cells (Fig. 2.4). All fibres of this primary net lie near the mesogloea, among the bases of the epithelial cells [1].

The question of transmission by motoneurons or interneurons across the mesogloea is as controversial in ctenophores as it is in sea anemones.

Figure 2.2

A series of sections at different magnifications showing the structure of the comb plates.

A. Whole animal, with a square round the region illustrated in **B**.

B. Three comb plates from above, showing a section transverse to the comb plate and longitudinal to the comb row.

C. A single ciliated cell.

D. Section along the line in **B**, showing cell boundaries and the mass of cilia.

E. Detail from the basal regions of the polster cells as shown by the square in **D**, showing nerve endings between the ciliated cells which are dotted.

F. Transverse section of a cilium showing the direction of the power stroke in relation to the pattern of nine fibrils, the third central fibril, and the compartmenting lamellae. *ap*, apical organ; *b*, direction of power beat; *cg*, ciliated groove from apical organ to comb row; *cil*, cilia; *cl*, compartmenting lamellae; *fi*, fibrils in ciliated cell; *l*, lipidal droplet; *m*, mitochondrion in nerve; *mo*, mouth; *mp*, mitochondrion in ciliated cell; *n*, nucleus; *nv*, axon sections; *s*, synaptic cleft. [Horridge and Mackay, 1964.]

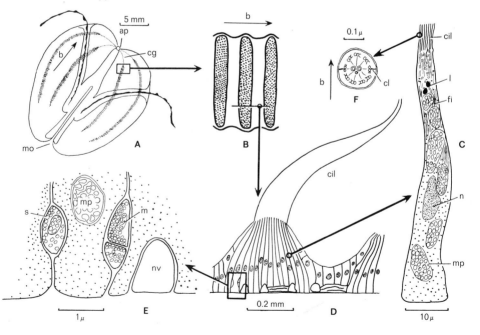

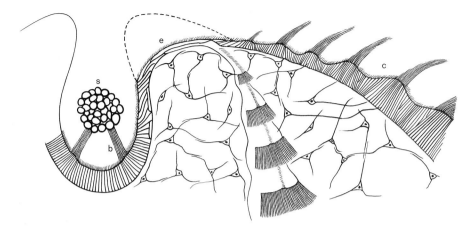

Figure 2.3

The arrangement of the principal elements of the ctenophore coordinating system. The statolith (*s*) stands upon groups of balancer cilia (*b*), whose frequency of beating depends on the loading as modified by tilting the animal. Each time the balancer cilia give a beat, a wave of excitation spreads from them along elongated cells of the ciliated groove (*e*) to the comb plates (*c*). Transmission in this system is presumed to be from cell to cell. Elsewhere on the surface is a net of bi- and tripolar nerve cells, in which a wave of excitation stops the beat of the comb-plate system and causes contraction of tentacles and other muscle systems. [Horridge, 1965.]

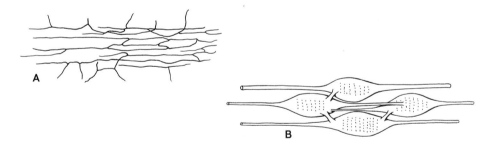

Figure 2.4

The two types of elongated fibres in the ciliated groove of ctenophores as first found by vital methylene blue staining of *Beroë* and confirmed in *Pleurobrachia*.

A. Fine fibres, which are a part of the general ectodermal nerve net that inhibits the ciliary beats.

B. A second system of bipolar ciliated cells. The cilia of these cells beat when a wave of excitation passes down the ciliated groove to the comb plates. Conduction and beating are not blocked by excess magnesium ions, which in ctenophores anaesthetizes all other responses, including the inhibition of the ciliary beat. The insensitivity to magnesium ions suggests that the fibres in B are not nerves but are elongated ciliated cells. The bridges, drawn as seen in the original description by Heider (1927), may represent tight junctions. [Horridge, 1965.]

Thick muscle fibres with branched ends are easily distinguished in ctenophore mesogloea. Intermingled with them, as seen under the light microscope, are thinner fibres, having the appearance and staining properties
of nerve fibres, which make contacts with the muscle fibres and connect
with the superficial nerve net. For a historical reason (concerning an
earlier controversy about nerve fibres in mesogloea of anemones), the
onus of proof is on those who wish to demonstrate that fibres in mesogloea
are in fact nervous. For ctenophores, light microscopists (on their criteria)
have concluded that the ectodermal net continues into the mesogloea and
makes contact with the muscle fibres. However, the electron microscopists
ask that this be demonstrated on their criterion, which is an undeniable
neuromuscular junction in the mesogloea. Thus far, neuromuscular junctions, with cleft and presynaptic vesicles, have appeared in sections of
ordinary epithelium and comb plates, but even if they are found in the
mesogloea, there still remains the possibility of an additional means of
transmission from muscle fibre to fibre.

Ctenophores have no concentrations of nerve cells or fibres having the
appearance of neuropile or ganglia. The apical organ is essentially an
epithelial cup bearing modified cilia on cells that are presumably sensory,
together with cells that are secretory and others that conduct excitation
to the ciliated grooves. This organ cannot be called a ganglion because
there is as yet no anatomical or behavioral evidence of neuropile, synapses,
or nervous interaction.

RESPONSES INVOLVING THE SUPERFICIAL NET

A touch to any part of a ctenophore causes the sudden arrest of the waves
of ciliary action. This happens in small pieces of any part, or after any
pattern of cuts, so that the conducting system has the properties of a
ubiquitous inhibitory net. There is a single sharp threshold to electrical
stimulation, and the velocity of transmission is 30 to 50 cm/sec in the
case of Venus' Girdle, in which the great length aids the estimate of
velocity of the inhibitory wave. This inhibitory net acts on the whole
family of ciliated cells, which stretch from the balancers in the apical
organ, along the ciliated grooves and comb rows. The inhibition is easily
blocked by an excess of magnesium ions, which also blocks all contractions of muscles that are coordinated at a distance (that is, presumably
by nerve fibres). Therefore it seems reasonable to suppose that excess
magnesium ions block nervous activity as in most other animals.

Transmission of the ciliary waves, on the other hand, and the ability
of ciliated cells to act as pacemakers or give a beat after an electrical
shock are not prevented by excess magnesium ions, showing that the

pathway involved is not dependent on nerve fibres. We also observe that the comb-plate cells produce large potential changes and ionic currents when their cilia beat. These facts lead to the conclusion that transmission is nervous in the superficial inhibitory net but between the comb-plate cells it is electrical. However, waves in the abnormal reverse direction seem to be conducted by mechanical contact of the moving cilia.

DIFFERENTIAL CONTROL OF THE COMB PLATES

The apical organ is a cup of columnar epithelium, containing a statolith of calcareous grains that have been formed by endoplasmic reticulum within cells of the floor of the apical organ (Fig. 2.3). The statolith is supported on four groups of cilia called "balancers," and modifies the rate at which they beat. The balancer cilia are normally at rest in a stiff upright position, but they are the origin of the spontaneity. When each beats, towards the centre of the group of four, it initiates an antiplectic wave of ciliary beats that runs along the two ciliated grooves at the head of which the balancer stands. The system carrying the wave, including one balancer and a pair of adjacent comb rows, is one family of cells, all of which, except the balancers, have cilia characterized by compartmenting lamellae (Fig. 2.2, F).

Any damaged region or cut end in this family of ciliated cells can act as a pacemaker, setting off a wave that can run in both directions along the comb row and ciliated groove, but normally the balancer cilia at the head of the line drive the rest. Small pieces of isolated comb beat frantically, which is explained by assuming that some cells are depolarized and then act as rapid pacemakers. There is no need to introduce a release of lower centres or removal of inhibitory effects.

Swimming is effected by waves traveling down the eight rows from the apical organ, so that pairs of combs that are connected to a common balancer have waves in unison. A difference in the frequency differences between waves in the four pairs of comb rows keeps the animal swimming vertically up or down, as controlled by the mechanism at the statolith (Fig. 2.5).

Changes in geotactic sign are best seen in *Pleurobrachia*, which has a clear response to underwater vibrations (Fig. 2.6). When undamaged the animal generally swims upwards, with streaming tentacles. Rippling the surface as the animal approaches or vibrating a stylus through 1 mm at 10 c/s at a distance of 1 cm, or making any excitation in the superficial net that is revealed by ciliary inhibition, is adequate to make the animal turn over and swim downwards. The tentacles are the most sensitive area, but the response persists even after their removal. The receptors

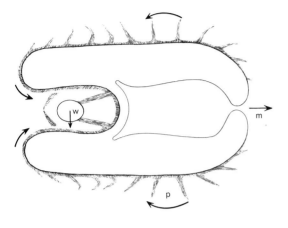

Figure 2.5

The mechanism of the reflex control of swimming direction in ctenophores. The diagram shows the statolith upon its balancer cilia, and the upper and lower comb plates in side view, connected around the aboral end by the ciliated grooves. The arrows show the directions of the power stroke of the cilia. The animal swims towards the right. As the statolith bears its weight on them, the balancer cilia change the rate of their beat. Depending on whether the animal shows a positive or negative geotactic sign, the effect is a decrease of the frequency of beating on one side and a decrease on the other side. The resultant change in direction is shown in Figure 2.6. *m*, direction of swimming; *p*, power stroke; *w*, weight of statolith. [Horridge, 1965.]

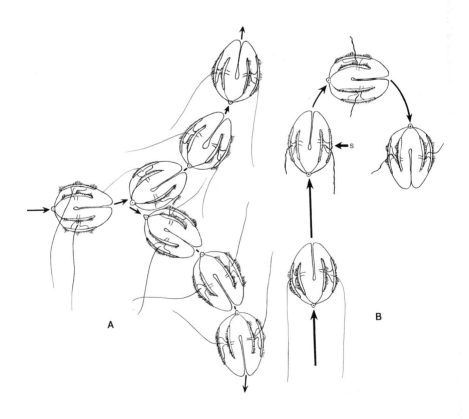

are probably stiff cilia similar to those on the fingers of *Leucothea* (see below). Underwater vibration from wind or waves causes ctenophores to sink away from the most dangerous situation for helpless pelagic animals, created by an onshore wind; they are carried down into the outgoing current safely away from the shore. However, a great sensitivity to hydrostatic pressure has been found in *Pleurobrachia*. Changes in pressure of as little as 50 cm of water cause these animals to rise or sink to maintain a constant position, but it is not known if they vary the frequency of their ciliary waves or actually turn over. But enough has been said to show that a simple pattern of nervous connexions, from a few sense organs to appropriately oriented effectors, provides an adequate set of reflexes. There must, however, be separate pathways of excitation for different responses, and even in this elementary organization we cannot account for long-term changes. Significantly, these last few sentences will apply throughout all the animal kingdom.

AN INDEPENDENT EFFECTOR; FINGERS OF *Leucothea*

A characteristic of many lower animals is the ability of their parts to perform essential functions when isolated from the rest of the animal. This is a by-product of the way in which the nervous system is decentralized; therefore independent effector organs, which are those that act in this way, are best known in the coelenterates. Isolated tentacles, mouths, parts of the jellyfish bell, all respond to stimuli as if still a part of the whole animal.

Leucothea multicornis is a large but delicate ctenophore of the Mediterranean, about 10 cm long, which has numerous finger-shaped protrusions scattered over its surface (Fig. 2.7). When retracted (at rest), these fingers are a few millimetres long, but at the slightest vibration in the water they suddenly shoot out to several times their original length. A passing copepod or similar planktonic animal within range creates enough disturbance in the water to set off this sudden extrusion of fingers. The tip is toxic, because copepods that are struck usually fall dead to the bottom

Figure 2.6

Responses of *Pleurobrachia* swimming forward (mouth foremost) in response to gravity.

A. When an animal that is swimming horizontally turns, it does so by more frequent waves along its comb plates on the side away from which it turns.

B. When an animal that is swimming upwards is excited by any vibration or touch stimulus (s), it contracts its tentacles, stops its cilia, then turns over and swims downwards as soon as the beats are resumed. See also Figure 2.5. [Horridge, 1965.]

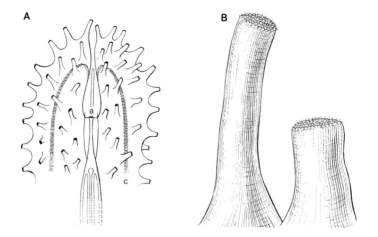

Figure 2.7

The fingers of the ctenophore *Leucothea multicornis*.

A. The aboral half of the intact animal (which is about 5 cm wide) with numerous fingers extended on all sides.

B. Two positions of a finger, extended and contracted, showing also the stiff cilia that project from sensory neurons between the gland cells on the flat tip. *a,* apical organ; *c,* comb plate. [Horridge, 1965.]

Figure 2.8

Movements of a single finger of *Leucothea* in response to vibration and electric shock. Muscles have been indicated by lines. Most of the transverse muscle fibres lie in the mesogloea, and most of the longitudinal fibres are ectodermal, but there is much overlap. No endodermal tissue is present.

A. A vibratory stimulus at 1 or 2 in A causes bending (as in B and C) towards the stimulus. A symmetrically placed vibration 3 causes extension, as in D. In each case the finger extends towards the object. Electrical stimulation of an extended finger as at 4 causes retraction to E. Stimulation of the ectodermal surface near to a finger causes it to bend over as at F. These responses are interpreted by different types of explanation in Figures 2.9, 2.10, and 2.11. [Horridge, 1965.]

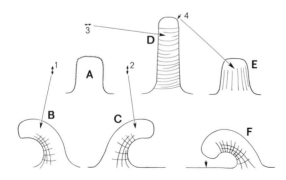

of the tank. This response, which occurs equally well in an isolated finger, depends on special vibration receptors that act indirectly on the circular and transverse muscles of the finger. But this is not the only response, for the fingers can also bend sideways and retract when appropriately stimulated (Fig. 2.8).

Sensitivity to vibration is very great, especially in specimens that have been left quiet for some minutes. A drop of water falling into the tank a metre away is an effective stimulus, as is also a thin glass fibre vibrating at an amplitude of $100\mu m$ at 10 c/s placed at 5 mm from the tip of the finger. The receptors are stiff, nonmotile cilia, each borne singly upon a sensory neuron (Fig. 2.1, C). Apart from being stationary, these sensory cilia have the appearance of normal cilia, but in section the shaft is commonly deficient in some of the details of structure that are typical of motile cilia.

The basal bodies of the vibration-sensitive cilia are remarkably specialized. Each consists of a spherical core surrounded by two concentric shells of dense protein, the inner of which is attached to the shaft, the outer to a fine network of tubules in the cytoplasm. The structure suggests that shearing forces between the shells excite the tubules and hence the cell membrane. The specialization of the basal body in these mechanoreceptive cilia suggests that it is the basal body rather than the shaft that is sensitive to shearing forces in the numerous examples throughout the animal kingdom in which cilia occur on mechanoreceptor cells.

The fingers of Leucothea also bend sideways in response to a lateral touch, and they retract when stimulated with an electric shock at their tip. Since these movements are carried out by longitudinal muscle fibres that are antagonistic to the transverse ones, there must be a distinction between pathways that carry excitation to two sets of muscles (Fig. 2.9). The underwater vibration receptors are connected to the transverse extensor muscles by a pathway that adapts rapidly, with the result that the animal is not perpetually dominated by its own high sensitivity. Lateral vibration receptors connect to longitudinal muscle fibres of their own side only, and so bend the finger. Contact receptors on the general body surface connect with the nearest longitudinal muscles, whereas contact receptors of the fingertip connect with longitudinal muscles all around and so bring about a symmetrical retraction.

The hodological pattern of the nerve fibres (that is, their pattern of connectivity to particular destinations) cannot be extracted from electron microscope sections and has not as yet been traced in material vitally stained with methylene blue. In this situation, which we find at the first sign of separation of pathways in a nerve-net animal, the pathways of excitation cannot be traced anatomically but are inferred to be distinct by their consequences. The same difficulty in discovering the exact

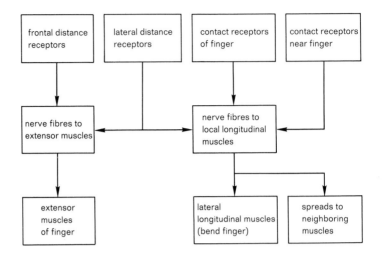

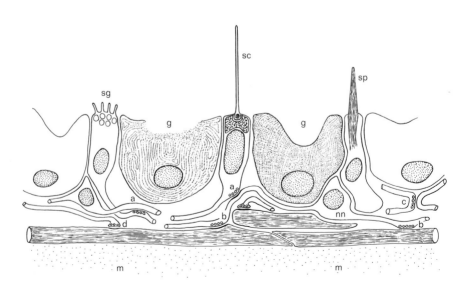

Figure 2.9

Representation of a series of interactions in the responses of a *Leucothea* finger by means of a block diagram, as inferred from the physiological observations of Figure 2.8 and consistent with the morphological picture of Figure 2.10. Retraction and bending are brought about by the longitudinal muscle fibres. There must be at least two types of sense organ, of which the vibration receptors set off the extension by the transverse muscle fibres. Vibration receptors at the side must connect with some longitudinal fibres that cause bending. A formal pattern of interactions as arranged here is sometimes of assistance if the further analysis is to be quantitative. [Horridge, 1965.]

"wiring diagram" recurs for all nervous tissue. The physiological pathways and the anatomical picture, corresponding to Figures 2.9 and 2.10, are each sets of abstractions separately derived from the animal, and can be combined by the human mind to make one diagram (Fig. 2.11). The quest of the neurophysiologist is to uncover structures and connectivity, as is further illustrated in Figures 12.7 or 13.12.

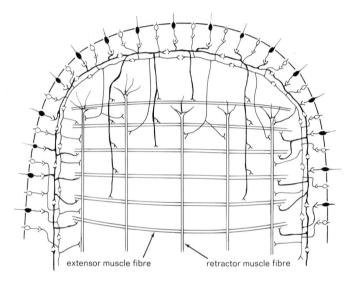

extensor muscle fibre   retractor muscle fibre

Figure 2.11

A largely hypothetical diagram of the pathways between sensory neurons, nerve net neurons, and muscle fibres in the finger of *Leucothea*. This describes a mechanism for the series of reactions in Figure 2.8. The anatomical background is restricted to that shown in Figure 2.10. In contrast to Figure 2.9, this method of drawing out a theoretical explanation leads to further qualitative questions of structure. The act of drawing it prompts such questions as the number and position of connections, the length of nerve and muscle fibres, the relative abundance of different cells, and the reality of the connections shown. The thicker nerve fibres show the system that is distinguished as that responding to vibration.

Figure 2.10

A formal anatomical diagram, which is a rationalization of electron microscope observations of the epithelium of the finger tip of *Leucothea*. There are three types of cells, which are clearly nervous because they gave rise to axons. Large secretory cells are shown between the neurons and unspecialized epithelial cells are omitted. Synapses are indicated by a row of vesicles.

a–d, types of synapse; *a*, sensory cell to internuncial; *b*, internuncial to muscle cell; *c*, unknown to unknown; *d*, unknown to muscle cell; *g*, gland cell; *m*, mesogloea; *nn*, nerve net neuron; *sc*, long sensory cilium; *sg*, group of short cilia on a sensory neuron of unknown function; *sp*, sensory peg, of unknown function. (From Horridge, 1965.)

CONCLUSION

The ctenophores have been granted a large share of attention for several reasons. They are quite different from the cnidaria and yet are proper nerve-net animals. They illustrate how a through-conducting swimming system is superimposed on a general nerve net and how the general net controls activities by exciting the muscles involved in feeding, but at the same time inhibiting the swimming system. Conduction that is clearly effected by nerve cells is sharply distinguished from conduction in the forward direction between ciliated cells (using the test with excess magnesium ions), and the latter appears to be electrical in nature. The structures are laid out over the surface, and the orienting reflex is a product of the anatomy and connexions of the sense organ with its oriented pacemakers. The ctenophores show the first signs of superimposed but distinct pathways of transmission in which nerve cells display contacts with other nerve cells of only a certain class. They also illustrate how a connectivity pattern is inferred by bringing together anatomical and physiological analysis, and the difficulty of discovering a wiring diagram in even the simplest examples of nervous systems.

REFERENCES FOR CHAPTER 2

1. Heider, K. 1927. Vom Nervensystem der Ctenophoren. *Z. Morph. Okol. Tiere.* **9:**638–678.
2. Horridge, G. A. 1965a. Non-motile sensory cilia and neuromuscular junctions in a ctenophore independent effector organ. *Proc. Roy. Soc. London B* **162:** 333–350.
3. Horridge, G. A. 1965b. Macrocilia with numerous shafts from the lips of the ctenophore *Beroë. Proc. Roy. Soc. London B* **162:**351–364.
4. Horridge, G. A. 1965c. Relations between nerves and cilia in ctenophores. *Amer. Zoologist* **5:**357–375.
5. Horridge, G. A. 1966. Pathways of co-ordination in ctenophores, in *The Cnidaria and Their Evolution.* W. J. Rees (Ed.). *Symp. Zool. Soc. London,* **16,** Academic Press.
6. Horridge, G. A., and Mackay, B. 1964. Neurociliary synapses in *Pleurobrachia* (Ctenophora). *Quart. J. Micr. Sci.* **105:**163–174.

3

Anemones and Medusae

For almost a century our concepts of coordination in polyps and medusae have been dominated by the idea of a diffuse but not necessarily random nerve net, any part of which can act in isolation. But despite the excitement of this discovery, the first good histological accounts of nerve nets only tentatively suggested that the scattered arrangement of nerve cells and their fibres could explain all the behaviour characteristic of these apparently simple animals. A single nerve net does explain well the independence of parts and the transmission in all directions. However, in any explanation of behaviour in the lowly and supposedly simple metazoans, the question to bear in mind is what fraction of the total known behaviour can be explained by the concepts derived from the analysis.

Some nerve nets are through-conducting. This is an inference based upon another inference—that a nerve impulse from any point spreads over the entire net. For the particular response concerned, such as the beat of a jellyfish bell or the protective closure of a sea anemone, the behaviour of the whole animal is then a consequence of the properties of single neurons, neuromuscular junctions, and rates of contraction, and an entire conducting and effector system in the animal acts as a single motor unit [12]. However, most of the behaviour of nerve net animals cannot be explained in this way: most nerve nets are not through-conducting or homogeneous, and in those few coelenterates for which we have adequate histological descriptions of the layout of the nerve cells, the properties of a single nerve net are not sufficient to explain even the more obvious rapid responses.

SEA ANEMONES AND CORALS

The concept of a nerve net as the basis of behaviour in the sea anemones dates from the early work of Parker in the period 1912–1919. He made

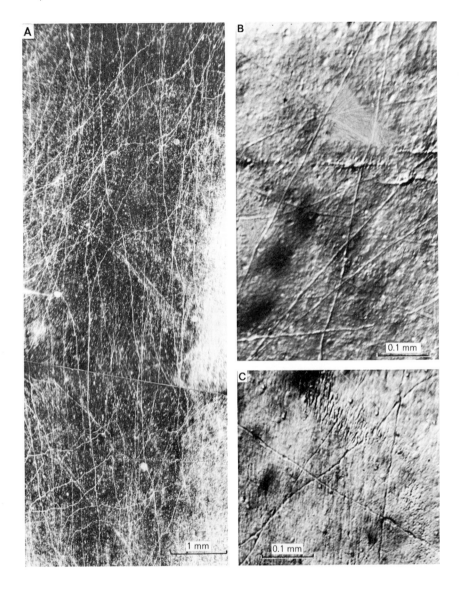

Figure 3.1

Nerve nets in a single sheet. Synapses are inferred at some of the points where axons cross each other.

A. Part of the mesentery of a sea anemone, *Metridium,* stained with silver and then photographed by dark-ground illumination. The direction of most of the large bipolar neurons is up and down the column, coinciding with the direction of maximum velocity of transmission of the symmetrical retraction of the column.

B and C. The subumbrellar surface of the living jellyfish *Aurelia,* unstained but viewed in oblique light. The long straight axons of the bipolar cells that run in all directions are essential for the transmission of the symmetrical contraction of the bell at each swimming beat. [A from Pantin, 1952; B and C from Horridge, 1954.]

cuts in different directions and demonstrated continuity in all directions, except that excitation was not conducted through the mesogloea.

In 1935 Pantin applied electrical stimuli and showed the existence of a refractory period for the symmetrical closure of the anemone *Calliactis*. Although a first shock has no effect, the second of two closely spaced shocks, applied to the column even at a distance from the first, does cause a symmetrical contraction. Therefore, the effect of the first shock spreads over the whole column without causing a contraction. By reducing the interval between the shocks we can measure the refractory period. Nowadays we may realize that cell-to-cell conduction without nerves could feasibly give the same results, but in the anemone column the velocities of transmission in different directions agree with the direction of the nerve fibres [12]. Histological studies revealed a net of nerves on the face of each mesentery where the longitudinal muscle fibres are situated, and the directionality of the fibres in this net agrees with the differences in longitudinal and transverse velocity of transmission (Fig. 3.1). The bipolar neurons of the muscle sheet of the jellyfish bell can be shown directly to be essential for transmission of a contraction wave.

Two shocks cause a much greater contraction of the anemone column when separated by a short interval than when separated by a long one (Fig. 3.2). The passage of an impulse is facilitated by the passage of previous impulses, with a decay of the effect over periods of 2–4 minutes. The concept of facilitation accounts for much of the behaviour of sea anemones [12]. First, considering the boundary (possibly the neuromuscular junction) between conducting and contracting elements, excitation at one per 10 seconds in the column nerve net excites only the circular muscle, but impulses at higher frequency cause contraction first in the sphincter and then in the longitudinal muscles of the mesenteries. One impulse triggered accidentally in the nerve net system would have no effect. Second, the progressively smaller response of tentacles further away from a stimulated tentacle can be explained as a consequence of the hypothetical facilitation of neuron-neuron junctions. It is supposed that for a short time each impulse from the stimulated tentacle clears a path that allows for progressively further spread of later impulses (Fig. 3.3). This idea of nerve-nerve facilitation in nets is again of value in explaining the coordination between coral polyps as well as many features of responses in higher animals. Basically, facilitation is the second commonest type of nonlinearity when response is plotted against interval between two stimuli: the commonest is its opposite, called adaptation or antifacilitation.

Spread of excitation, with various degrees of decrement in different species, is readily observable in coral colonies. The coral polyps contract when stimulated electrically or when damaged, as by coral-feeding fish. The conducting system between polyps may be negligible, or localized in its effect, or through-conducting [8]. When localized, it is possible in

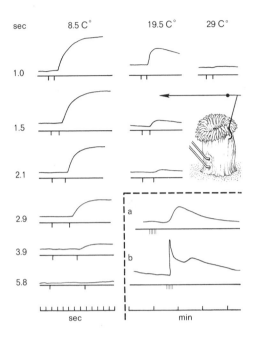

Figure 3.2

Whole-animal responses of an anemone. The shortening of the column in response to two shocks is all-or-none, and the animal acts as a single motor unit. The actual response, however, depends in size upon the facilitation by the first shock and upon other factors such as the temperature. Responses are to different intervals, as shown on the left, and at different temperatures as shown along the top of the figure. The inset, below, right, shows **(a)** the slow asymmetrical response of the lateral (parietal) muscle to a series of 5 shocks at 3 sec intervals, at first subthreshold for the mesenteric retractor system, and second **(b)** a quick retractor response at the second shock, followed by a slow parietal response. There must be two separate conducting systems—one to parietal and one to mesenteric muscles, because the slow response is typically asymmetrical. [Pantin and Vianna Dias, 1952.]

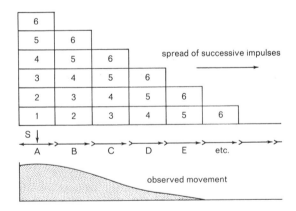

Figure 3.3

Simple explanation of decremental falloff in the strength of a response with distance from the point stimulated (s) in a homogeneous nerve net considered in one dimension only. A stimulus at s produces several impulses 1–6 in neuron A. The first impulse opens the path to neuron B and all subsequent impulses 2–6 get through. At each successive junction one less impulse gets across. The movement, shown at the bottom, is some function of the number of impulses reaching the muscle, but will diminish with distance from s. More complex theories of this type bring in values of the decay of the facilitation at junctions, proportions of branched fibres, and so on.

some species to increase the responding area progressively by successive shocks. However, in some instances further spread of retraction is limited no matter how often a stimulus is repeated at one place on the colony. The actual data are best represented pictorially (Fig. 3.4).

To explain these results by one family of relations, based upon a single nerve net, I first tried a model of a nerve net with a random fraction of the junctions initially conducting [8]. The representation of the model was a board in which holes represented synapses between neurons in a large array. By "stimulating" the model, the number of neurons reached by a stimulus could be counted. By hypothesis, an impulse that arrived at a synapse and did not pass made it possible for the next impulse to pass. This postulate took care of the progressive spread. An interesting conclusion was that a nerve net need not be ubiquitously conducting in order to show through-conduction, which could be achieved with as few as 15% of the synapses conducting, if each neuron connected to six others. However, a two-dimensional net with random connexions gives results that are too variable in comparison with responses of real corals, and fails to explain certain behaviour—for example, types B and C in Figure 3.4.

With the aid of a very large computer, Josephson was able to add such sophistications as distribution in the length of neurons, variation

Figure 3.4

Areas that are influenced by different numbers of shocks in certain species of corals. Each circle represents the outer boundary of spread of a visible contraction in response to the number of shocks shown, at a shock frequency of 1 per second. The scale shows the approximate diameter of the polyps. A, *Palythoa* and *Galaxea*; B, *Porites* (also in Fig. 3.6); C, *Sarcophyton*. Apart from through-conducting systems, these are the principal types of spread known in corals.

A simple explanation—that successive spreading nerve impulses open up progressively more synapses—is available for A, but B and C require an explanation in which single shocks set off a repetitive discharge from the stimulated point, adapting in B and facilitating in C. To work out even a simple model nerve net requires a very large computer that can remember the situation at each synapse [Horridge, 1957.]

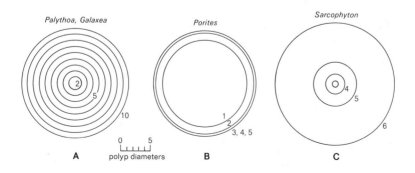

in synapse density, and different time constants in the decay of facilitation, but basically the model fails to explain all the relevant behaviour of corals [10].

As soon as we introduce the idea of repetitive firing as a result of a stimulus, however, it is possible to explain all observed types of spread in coral colonies. Spread of a response to a certain constant distance in all directions with little further spread at subsequent shocks presumably occurs because a rapid burst of impulses follows the first stimulus, and thereafter the net becomes less likely to fire repetitively. In *Sarcophyton*, which can grow to many feet in diameter, with millions of polyps, the wave of polyp retraction sets off from a point that is stimulated several times, and then runs over the whole colony. This, and all upward turning response curves from other corals, such as those in Figure 3.5, can be explained by a repetitive discharge from typical cells in the net; if neurons elsewhere in the animal also discharge repetitively, a wave will spread freely over thousands of neurons. Of course, even if the computer model gives an exact representation of the behaviour, we don't know that the animal really functions as we suppose. The only way to discover what neurons are doing is to observe them directly, even at this elementary level, but with its thousands of polyps a coral colony can be approached only by a statistical treatment (Fig. 3.6).

The recent discoveries of cell-to-cell transmission in hydroid polyps [11] and of potentials that appear to be propagated in sheets of non-nervous cells (as described in the next chapter) are bound to influence future work on anemones and corals, in which such possibilities have hardly been considered. However, one lesson to be learned from anemones and corals is that, usually having one nerve net and with no opportunity for spatial summation or occlusion, they utilize all the more the possibilities of temporal integration, such as facilitation and long latency. Another feature is that with only one net the neurons have no "labels" that indicate an individuality or define their synapses with other neurons.

COMPLEX ACTIVITIES OF SEA ANEMONES

Slow spontaneous movements and the special sensitivities of commensal animals confuse the simple picture of anemones as animals with conducting systems that are essentially *silent* except when stimulated. A few anemones are even more complicated in that they swim freely and have at least one conducting system that is set aside for swimming [18]. Fast through-conducting bipolar nets may in fact be normally silent, but it seems most unlikely that all the nervous system is quiet when no fast movement is visible. As will be seen, even in *Hydra* there are spontaneous potentials that are unaccompanied by any behaviour.

The slow cyclical activity associated with diurnal changes or the arrival of food is appreciated only when films taken with long intervals between shots are speeded up a hundredfold. Despite considerable effort we do not know how these slow responses are coordinated, whether nerves are involved or not, or how the slow time course may be explained. Similarly, in the disc and the foot of the anemones, with antagonistic muscle systems, we have no notion of how the separate muscles are coordinated. Certainly the apparent reciprocity of action in these muscles during creeping is hard to explain by one nerve net.

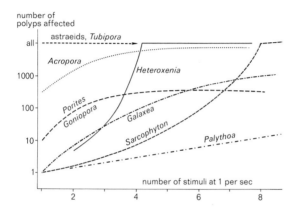

Figure 3.5

The relations between the number of stimuli (at 1 per sec) and the approximate number of polyps caused to contract for a variety of corals. The different slopes, some increasing, some decreasing, depend upon the different parameters of the nerve net in each case. Although the nerve cells of corals have rarely been seen, and their activity is certainly not known, all the above curves can be simulated by computations based upon the known properties of other coelenterate nerve cells, as investigated in solitary anemones and medusae. Whether coral nerve cells actually operate in the way the explanatory concepts suggest remains to be directly tested. [Horridge, 1957.]

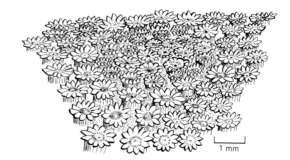

Figure 3.6

A group of expanded polyps showing the form of a colony of *Porites*. A single shock causes a small contraction of a large number of polyps, producing an effect such as that represented in the centre of this picture. [Horridge, 1957.]

A distinction in anemones between classes of nerve cells and perhaps of different nerve nets is beginning to emerge. In an analysis of the sphincter region of *Calliactis*, Robson shows how bipolar cells supply both the sphincter and the retractor muscles [17], and it is known that these muscles work together physiologically. In the same region, however, are

Figure 3.7

Neuron pathways adjoining the mesenteries of anemones.

A. Simplified innervation of portion of the anemone *Mimetridium*, showing individual bipolar neurons that run from body wall to mesenteries, from mesenteries to the ectoderm of the oral disc (via holes through the oral disc), and from oral disc to tentacle. The ectoderm of the tentacle is thus anatomically connected with the retraction system of the column, not only via the epithelium of the mouth. The presence of these bipolar cells sets a problem as to how the tentacles are coordinated without spread of excitation to the column, implying a second conduction system in the disc.

B. Bipolar neurons, similar to those in **A**, inside the column in the sphincter region of *Calliactis*. The vertical broken lines represent two mesenteries (*mes*) seen end on where they meet the outer wall. The bipolar axons pass around the body wall and through the mesenteries, as in **A**.

C. Another system of cells superimposed on those of **B**. The unipolar cells are probably sensory. The multipolar neurons make connections with sensory and bipolar neurons. [A from Batham, 1965; B and C from Robson, 1965.]

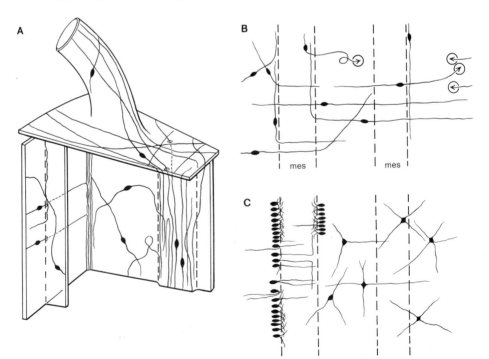

numerous multipolar cells that connect with sensory cells and with bipolar cells, but unlike the latter they remain superficial. The multipolar cells are located where we would expect to find a complex coordinating filter between sensory cells, which may be active all the time, and a through-conducting net, which is normally silent and active only at retraction (Fig. 3.7). Similar, but larger, multipolar neurons in the column of the swimming anemone *Stomphia* are thought to be the pacemakers for the side-to-side sway of the column during swimming. Recently Ross demonstrated by their different thresholds two separate systems in *Stomphia* [19]. The ordinary retraction of the column is caused by pairs of shocks with a short intervening interval. By contrast, swimming movements require 6 to 8 stronger stimuli, and the strength duration curve for these shocks is not the same as for retraction. Past work has shown that thresholds for fast and slow responses are the same in ordinary anemones, perhaps because the bipolar and multipolar cells have interconnections. But it would not be surprising if a similar net of multipolar cells turns out to act on the parietal muscle in the fast *sideways* bending which some anemones, including *Bunodactis*, make in response to a single shock [13].

Activity that involves a purposeful coordination of the whole anemone in a series of interrelated slow movements is best known from Ross's account of how *Calliactis* recognises and attaches itself to a shell of *Buccinum* that is occupied by a hermit crab. On contact with a suitable shell the tentacles adhere; it has been shown that a chemical originating from the original mollusc must be present on the shell. The anemone then relinquishes its hold with its foot, swings the column round by an asymmetrical slow bend, attaches the foot on to the shell at the side of the place where the tentacles adhere, and releases its hold with the tentacles [19]. If no hermit crab lives in the shell, the anemone will still climb on but will not stay for long. The anemone *Stomphia* moves similarly on to shells of *Modiolus* (Fig. 3.8), the whole process taking 20 to 30 minutes. The mechanisms are not known in detail but they clearly involve chemoreception by the tentacles, release of the foot as a result of a signal from the disc, release of the tentacles by a signal from the foot, and asymmetrical bending of the column. Specific line-labelled pathways between foot and tentacles must be present, but they are not necessarily nervous.

Associations with other animals, especially fish and crustaceans, are common among sea anemones and corals. Little is known of the sensory mechanisms involved in the anemone, but in some cases at least there is a specific recognition that prevents it from feeding on the commensal. For example, the small spider crab *Hyas*, when dropped onto the disc of the large anemone *Taelia*, walks calmly off, and will even climb out from between the tentacles of a contracting disc, whereas the crab *Carcinus*, of similar size and activity, is immediately enveloped by the tentacles and

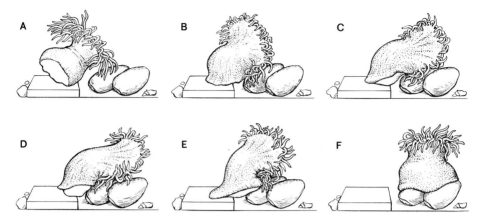

Figure 3.8

Very specific slow complex movements of an anemone. A large *Stomphia* anemone comes into contact with two shells of the clam *Modiolus* and climbs upon them.

A. The anemone has been swimming by oscillation of its column. The tentacles touch the *Modiolus* shells (stippled), stick to them, and become active.

B. More tentacles are drawn on the shells; the disc and then the column bend over.

C and **D.** The pedal disc swells out towards the shells, and eventually slides over them, **E**, displacing the tentacles. Finally, **F**, the pedal disc is firmly settled on both shells. There are 5-minute intervals between stages **A** through **E**; 25 minutes between **E** and **F**. [Ross, 1965.]

swallowed. Spider crabs that are soaked in *Carcinus* juice are still not taken by the anemone [5].

In the very simplest examples, in which an animal seems to have only one nerve net, with no centralization at all, a great deal of sophisticated behaviour emerges when the animals are carefully studied in relation to their own appropriate time scale. Even in this most elementary nervous system, behaviour cannot be explained by rapidly transmitted depolarizations of nerve cells alone. There must be long-term mechanisms—possibly secretions—that govern the sensitivity and slow behaviour.

TWO-NET SYSTEMS IN MEDUSAE

Two-net systems are characteristic of jellyfish and some anemones that swim, and one of the nets is set aside for coordination of symmetrical swimming movements. This is the only way that the necessary symmetry can be consistent with other simultaneous behaviour, such as feeding.

Eimer and Romanes, working independently on *Aurelia* in the years between 1870 and 1875, on opposite sides of the North Sea, observed that the spontaneous beats of the swimming rhythm arise from the 8 marginal ganglia and spread as a wave in all directions from whichever ganglion happens to be the pacemaker. So long as a bridge of tissue remains intact, the wave of contraction will spread around cuts that are made in any direction across the epithelium. Of these two pioneers Eimer was slightly earlier but Romanes' contributions were more numerous and more significant.

Romanes observed that contraction waves spread along a long narrow bridge without change in strength, and that when a blockage occurred it was always at a single definite point on the bridge. From this he inferred that the excitation causing the contraction wave always followed definite narrow "lines of discharge," which crisscrossed and connected in all directions. The concept of a single nerve net was defined as a system in which any line of discharge could act vicariously for any other. At about the same time, Schäfer found a net of bipolar neurons in the subumbrellar epithelium of *Aurelia*. However, it was not possible to identify the one nerve net as that conducting the wave of muscular contraction, because Romanes had already demonstrated two independent conducting systems. The system most likely to be nervous was that responsible for the tentacle movements and for the evocation of a contraction wave from a pacemaker, not for the contraction waves themselves.

Two overlying conducting systems in *Aurelia* were demonstrated physiologically as follows. A strip of the bell bearing a marginal ganglion at one end was cut into any complicated pattern, as shown in Figure 3.9. A touch to the relaxed tentacles at A sets off a wave that travels through the tissue at 25 cm/sec and is visible as a wave of contraction of marginal tentacles. When it arrives at the marginal ganglion at B, this wave initiates a wave of muscular contraction, which then runs back with a velocity of 50 cm/sec around all the cuts. Bipolar nerve fibres of the bell can be seen in life (Fig. 3.1 B), and it is possible to record a single nerve impulse from a single fibre at each beat of the bell. One such fibre is necessary and sufficient to carry a wave of contraction, for if the last fibre in a narrow bridge is cut the wave is no longer carried across. This is the only example of exact correlation between anatomically observed fibres and physiologically recorded waves in a nerve net [6].

Because a single impulse alone in the net of bipolar neurons causes a symmetrical beat of the bell, all other excitation must be transmitted by some other pathway.

Anatomical study of the ephyra larva leads to the conclusion that the second system is a net of small multipolar neurons, which spread over the whole surface. The ephyra larva of the jellyfish *Aurelia* is a dainty, transparent disc, 3 to 5 mm in diameter, which is split off from the sedentary scyphistoma stage. Unlike the adult, the larva feeds by catching planktonic animals with nematocysts of its long lappets. A successful

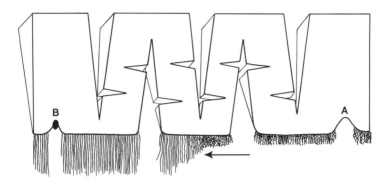

Figure 3.9

The arrangement of the classical experiment of Romanes, in which he showed the existence of two nerve nets in the jellyfish *Aurelia,* and at the same time demonstrated a kind of reflex action in the marginal ganglion. A part of the edge of the bell of the jellyfish is cut into a pattern such as that shown. The tentacles along the edge are allowed to relax. When tentacles at the right side in the region *A* are stimulated with a pinch, a wave of tentacle contraction spreads along the edge of the bell, although the excitation must obviously pass around the cuts. When this excitation reaches the ganglion shown at B, it initiates a wave of contraction of the muscle. This second wave travels in the opposite direction around all the cuts with a velocity of about 50 cm/sec, whereas the first wave travelled at only 25 cm/sec. Because the two waves have different velocities and cause different effects, there is strong circumstantial evidence for the existence of two nerve nets. In fact, two nets can be demonstrated by electrophysiological and by direct histological techniques. The wave of tentacle contraction can be compared with a sensory excitation and the wave of muscle contraction can be considered as a motor output of the ganglion. The interaction between these two kinds of excitation is always one-way in that the tentacle contraction excites the bell muscle excitation, so providing us with a primitive reflex arc.

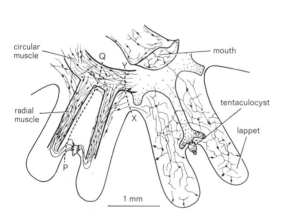

Figure 3.10

One of the most primitive examples of differentiation between types of neurons, such that a neuron makes synaptic connexions indiscriminately with its own class of neuron but not with the other of the two classes. Two arms of the bell of the ephyra larva of the jellyfish *Aurelia,* showing the two nerve nets, which can be stained with methylene blue. On the left are the muscle strips of the bell and the net of bipolar neurons, which coordinate them in the symmetrical swimming beat of the bell. The net of multipolar cells on the right connects with sensory cells and acts on the radial muscles in the local coordination of the feeding movements, in which one arm alone bends towards the mouth. [Horridge, 1956.]

lappet bends in towards the mouth, which leans out to meet it. This asymmetrical response is quite distinct from the beating of the bell, although the two may go on together. By staining with methylene blue it is possible to discern two different nerve nets, which differ in distribution and form of the cells [7].

A network of oriented bipolar cells overlies the radial and circular muscles, and does not spread elsewhere except where there is definite "tract" of 3 or 4 fibres from the marginal ganglia (Fig. 3.10). This "contraction" net has contact synapses of the type described for the longitudinal mesenteric net of anemones.

Other nerve cells and their axons form quite a different net, which spreads over the whole surface of the animal, including the aboral surface of the bell. This "feeding" net is made up of some bipolar cells—with one process to the surface of the epithelium, and therefore presumably sensory—and of multipolar and small bipolar cells that connect together. Some of these fibres stretch from the lappets across the disc and over the folds of the mouth. From their first appearance the rudiments of developing tentacles have nerve cells with fibres that belong to this net.

The argument for two separate physiological pathways, which applies to both whole animals and isolated parts, depends upon the independence of the feeding response and the beat. Short cuts through the circular muscle, along the line XY in Figure 3.10, cause each arm to beat at its own rate, but in response to a strong stimulus the animal still goes into a coordinated spasm, which is in effect a simultaneous feeding response of all arms. When the tract of fibres is cut on one side of the ganglion in an isolated arm (PQ in Fig. 3.10), the radical muscle still attached to the ganglion continues to beat as before, but the isolated muscle does not; however, both muscles contract in a spasm if the arm is induced to make a feeding response. The developing ephyrae stacked one above the other in the scyphistoma beat independently as soon as their marginal ganglia appear, but they go simultaneously into a spasm at a touch to any one of them. From all this it is clear that the pathway of the spasm can conduct over the whole animal but in the feeding movement is restricted to one arm. The beat is symmetrical and brief; the feeding response is local and maintained. With the known properties of nerve cells or nerve nets it is impossible to explain these observations by only one net, but we find two overlapping conducting systems ready-made in the two nerve nets. The conclusion then follows that the two nets meet and interact in the marginal ganglia, which therefore have three functions: (a) as the site of the pacemaker of the beat, (b) as a collection of sensory cells of unknown sensitivity but presumably connected with the multipolar net, as are all the peripheral sense cells, and (c) as the site of modulation of the frequency of the pacemaker of the beat by the afferent excitation in the net of multipolar cells (Fig. 3.11).

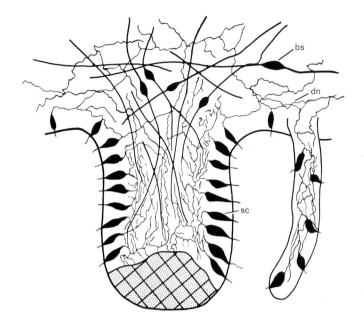

Figure 3.11

Hypothetical organization of a jellyfish ganglion, showing the three main nervous structures that have so far been distinguished: the sensory cells of the ganglion (*sc*), the bipolar cells of the motor nets (*bs*) with obvious contact synapses, and the diffuse nerve net of the bell (*dn*), which has connexions with the other two neuron types in the ganglion. The shaded area represents the region of calcareous particles of the statolith.

Figure 3.12

Excitation of one nerve net by another nerve net. An electrical recording from the epithelium near a marginal ganglion of the jellyfish *Cassiopea,* showing the temporal delay between the arrival of an impulse in the diffuse nerve net (first pulse) and the consequent initiation of an impulse in the giant fibre nerve net. The intraganglionic delay is here 890 msec. The two nerve nets are illustrated anatomically in a related species in Figure 3.10. [Passano, 1965.]

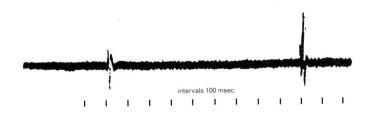

intervals 100 msec

With a suction electrode applied to the subumbrellar surface near the ganglion, Passano [16] was able to record directly two different action potentials of distinctive shapes in the jellyfish *Cassiopea* (Fig. 3.12). The slower of his two waves corresponds with the tentacle contraction wave found by Romanes, and on arrival at a marginal ganglion this wave initiates an efferent impulse that causes a contraction wave. A comparison of this input and output of a jellyfish ganglion with a simple reflex arc is possible, but it is not really valid because the multipolar net has other functions besides that whereby an impulse going into the ganglion initiates an outgoing impulse to the muscles of the bell via the other nerve net. Besides being the coordinating system for feeding and for tentacle movements in jellyfish, the net of multipolar neurons has the general property of modifying the frequency of the beat less directly; in some species it inhibits the beat, in others it acts also on the bell muscle.

The recent discoveries of cell-to-cell transmission in hydroid polyps and of potentials that appear to be from sheets of nonnervous cells, are certain to lead to advances in the study of medusae, and may help by providing more conducting pathways and an analysis of the pacemaker mechanisms in the marginal ganglia. However, the lesson to be learned from the medusae is that here, for the first time, a neuron cannot make synapses with any other it meets indiscriminately, but must keep only to neurons of its own net. We see here the beginnings of the rules of connectivity that make possible the growth of higher nervous systems.

REFERENCES FOR CHAPTER 3

1. Batham, E. J. 1965. The neural architecture of the sea anemone *Mimetridium crystum*. *Amer. Zoologist* **5**:395–402.
2. Batham, E. J., Pantin, C. F. A., and Robson, E. A. 1960. The nerve-net of the sea-anemone *Metridium senile:* the mesenteries and the column. *Quart. J. Micr. Sci.* **101**:487–510.
3. Bullock, T. H., and Horridge, G. A. 1965. Chapter 9. (See *loc. cit.*, p. 18.)
4. Cromwell, S. (Ed.). 1965. *Behavioral Physiology of Coelenterates. American Zoologist* **5**, No. 3. 335–589.
5. Davenport, D. 1966. Cnidarian symbioses and the experimental analysis of behaviour, in *The Cnidaria and Their Evolution*, W. J. Rees (Ed.). *Symp. Zoo. Soc. London* **16**, Academic Press.
6. Horridge, G. A. 1954. Observations on the nerve fibres of *Aurellia aurita*. *Quart. J. Micr. Sci.* **95**:85–92.
7. Horridge, G. A. 1956. The nervous system of the ephyra larva of *Aurellia aurita. Quart. J. Micr. Sci.* **97**:59–74.
8. Horridge, G. A. 1957. The coordination of the protective retraction of coral polyps. *Philos. Trans. B.* **240**:495–529.

9. Horridge, G. A. 1964. Non-specific systems and differences between neurons in lower animals. In *Comparative Neurochemistry*, D. Richter (Ed.). Pergamon Press.

10. Josephson, R. K. 1964. Coelenterate conducting systems, in *Neurol Theory and Modeling*, R. F. Reiss (Ed.). Stanford University Press.

11. Josephson, R. K., and Mackie, G. O. 1965. Multiple pacemakers and the behaviour of the hydroid *Tubularia. J. Exp. Biol.* **43**:293–332.

12. Pantin, C. F. A. 1952. The elementary nervous system. *Proc. Roy. Soc. London B* **140**:147–168.

13. Pantin, C. F. A., and Vianna Dias, M. 1952. Excitation phenomena in an actinian (*Bunodactis* sp.) from Guanabara Bay. *Ann. Acad. Brazil. Sci.* **24**: 335–349.

14. Parker, G. H. 1919. *The Elementary Nervous System*. Philadelphia and London, Lippincott.

15. Passano, L. M., and McCullough, C. B. 1963. Pacemaker hierarchies controlling the behaviour of Hydra. *Nature London* **199**:1174–1175.

16. Passano, L. M. 1965. Pacemakers and activity patterns in medusae. Homage to Romanes. *Amer. Zoologist* **5**:465–482.

17. Robson, E. A. 1965. Some aspects of the structure of the nervous system in the anemone *Calliactis. Amer. Zoologist* **5**:403–410.

18. Robson, E. A. 1966. Swimming in Actiniaria, in *The Cnidaria and Their Evolution*, W. J. Rees (Ed.). *Symp. Zool. Soc. London* **16**, Academic Press.

19. Ross, D. H. 1965. Complex and modifiable behaviour patterns in *Calliactis* and *Stomphia. Amer. Zoologist* **5**, 573–580.

4

Neuroid conduction

Neuroid, or cell-to-cell, transmission has long been considered a possible means of conduction of ciliary waves in ctenophores, but recent, experiments on hydrozoans have shown that the control of their movement depends on propagation that can be explained only in this way. This makes it necessary to reconsider the whole of the nervous physiology of the nerve-net animals, for some of the activities formerly thought to be due to nerves may in fact be coordinated without nerves. These results also lead to conclusions about the origin of the nervous system, and especially about the primitive nature of electrical transmission. Moreover, the demonstration of low resistance pathways between cells, in many diverse examples, now suggests that this is a major channel of communication in all animals.

SIPHONOPHORE EPITHELIUM

On the outer surface of the swimming bells of siphonophores there is an epithelium that is devoid of nerves—the cells are so transparent that any nerve fibres present would certainly be seen. In the group known as calycophores (Fig. 4.1), large areas of the exumbrella epithelium consist of one type of cell, which forms a pavement epithelium without nerve or muscle fibres; other large areas are syncitial. Stimulation of this epithelium causes a contraction of radially arranged muscle fibres some distance away, with a consequent inward rolling of the margin and velum of the bell. At the same time, all-or-none electrical potentials can be recorded by electrodes on the epithelium. The conduction velocity in the epithelium ranges from 24 to 35 cm/sec at 22°C (Fig. 4.2). A single wave caused by a single stimulating shock spreads in all directions with a refractory period of about 2 to 3 msec. Conduction is limited to the single layer of cells over the surface of the mesogloea but will travel around cuts, so evidently the edges of the epithelium can heal over. The mesogloea below the epithelium contains no cells or fibres and is clearly not involved [14].

This conducting epithelium can be likened to a continuous two-dimensional extended axon spread over the outside of the bell. When the bell comes in contact with any firm object (or even the water surface), this layer is stimulated and brings into operation the typical protective responses of stem contraction, swimming, and closure of the bell. That conduction occurs where the cells anastomose suggests that in other places where there are cell walls the transmission between them is electrical. Surely there is no simpler conducting system, but it is not nervous be-

Figure 4.1

A colony of zooids of the siphonophore *Nanomia cara*, with eleven swimming bells or nectophores (*n*) at rest, and the float (*f*) at the top. The nerve-free epithelium, which conducts excitation, lies superficially on the swimming bells. [Mackie, 1964.]

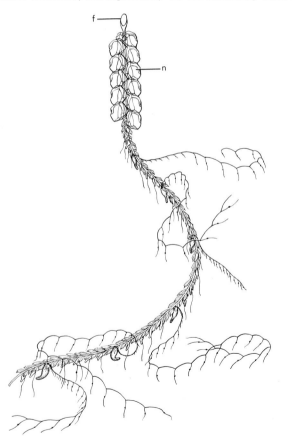

cause there are no neurons. The essential feature introduced with the neuron is the ability of the axon to bypass other cells. This would again imply that one cell type recognises only certain others as part of the conducting system.

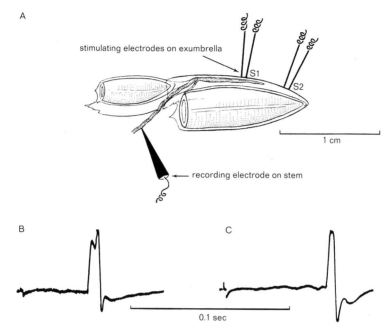

Figure 4.2

Conduction in the nerve-free exumbrellar epithelium of the bell of a siphonophore (*Chelophyes*). For convenience the response is measured in the stem, where it is large, and the bell is stimulated at two points, *S*1 and *S*2. The difference in the latency between B and C gives a velocity of 35 to 50 cm/sec in the bell. Detailed examination of the epithelium by a variety of methods shows that it consists only of adjacent epithelial cells without nerve fibres. [Mackie, 1965.]

CTENOPHORES

Elongated conducting cells occur in the ciliated groove of ctenophores (Fig. 2.4). Although they bear cilia that beat at each "impulse," they may have the appearance of neurons in being bipolar, and they will even stain with methylene blue. However, they have probably evolved by specialisation of a tract of ciliated cells; some of these have also given rise to the large comb plate cells (p. 23). Transmission of the normal forward wave of ciliary beats along the comb rows seems to occur by electrical transmission through the epithelium. Depolarisation causes a beat of the cilia, which are also mechanically sensitive and cause depolarization when moved [4]. The comb plates are isolated from each other, and therefore the transmission must involve nonciliated cells in the intervening spaces. Curiously, reverse waves are transmitted mechanically, but at a lower velocity [21].

Nervous cells are found in all ctenophores and cnidaria, and there is little difficulty in recognising them. It is significant, however, that many of them have definite neurosecretory activity in addition to their assumed role in rapid conduction. Moreover, where nerves first appear they seem to be definitely supplementary to the conducting, contracting, and pacemaker mechanisms that are already present in epithelial layers. This is illustrated in the hydrozoan polyps *Hydra* and *Tubularia*.

HYDROID POLYPS

An electrode on the surface of *Hydra* records potentials, and, conveniently for the investigator, the animal will live well in the insulating medium, distilled water. Two types of electrical record appear (Fig. 4.3). One is the contraction burst (CB) pulse of amplitude up to 30 mV, which occurs at intervals singly and in a high frequency burst when the body spontaneously contracts at regular intervals. These potentials arise near the base of the tentacles and are transmitted at 15 cm/sec, independently of the next type. Second, in contrast, the rhythmic potentials (RP) have no direct connection with behaviour; they arise from points over the column, which act like independent pacemakers. Local illumination of

Figure 4.3

Responses of a dark-adapted *Hydra littoralis* to localized illumination of the base. *Above*: electrical potentials showing a steady stream of rhythmical potentials (*RP*), ending in a contraction burst (*CB*); *below*: behavioural response with aborted locomotion. [Passano and McCullough, 1963.]

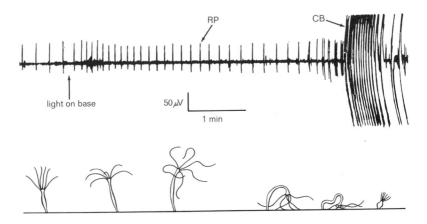

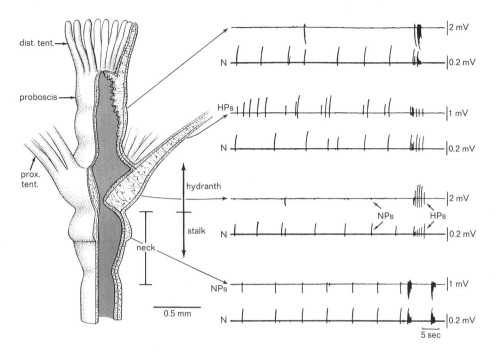

Figure 4.4

Spontaneous activity recorded with a small suction electrode on the surface of the marine hydroid *Tubularia*. The records were taken in pairs and the activity in different regions is compared with that in the neck, shown by traces marked *N*. Upward deflection is negative. Neck pulses (*nps*) are so called because they are attenuated in the hydranth and large in the neck; hydranth pulses (*hps*) are large in the proboscis but not so large at the neck. For interactions between the conducting pathways, see Figure 4.5. [Josephson and Mackie, 1965.]

the base of *Hydra* causes an abrupt change in RP frequency, and the CB pulses cease; the column then lengthens for a few minutes, and alternate periods of contractions or locomotion follow for the next half hour. When pinned down, animals may fail to show any electrical activity at all, although they clearly move. Apparently the RP system inhibits the CB system, but there is no clear-cut relationship between them as there is in *Tubularia*. The morphological basis for these potentials is not clear, but since they are so large and are recorded extracellularly at the surface of the animal, many cells must be involved. The potentials presumably represent waves of activity across a whole epithelium; of the two types of wave, one may be located in the ectoderm and the other in the endoderm [19].

Tubularia larynx is a marine polyp that occasionally has several hydranths on the same stolon. The polyp has two sets of tentacles (Fig. 4.4), which are spontaneously active twice a minute or so. In this action all the proximal tentacles flex synchronously towards the mouth; the distal tentacles may join in this simple activity, which is called a concert. A peristaltic contraction then sweeps down from the mouth and, as a result, the contents of the polyp cavities are moved between chambers. The concert is the polyp's principal activity, but an individual tentacle can also make spontaneous movements.

Two types of potential, recorded by small electrodes placed on the surface, are attributed to two distinct systems of pacemakers [8]. Neck potentials (NP) are large in the neck and small in the stalk; hydranth potentials (HP) are large in the proboscis and small in the stalk. NP's typically come in bursts, HP's singly. A burst of NP's usually fires the HP system, but even a single one of either sort can excite the other. NP activity usually has no behavioral correlate, but a burst of HP's always causes a concert.

There are at least three conducting systems in the stalk, two of which give distinct travelling potentials when the stalk is stimulated. The distal opener system (DOS) causes synchronous movement of the oral tentacles away from the mouth and conducts at about 15 cm/sec; the slow system (SS) conducts at 6 cm/sec and has no known behavioral output. The third system (TS) has no obvious electrical sign; its existence is inferred from the fact that NP's are triggered in the polyp even

Figure 4.5

Simultaneously recorded neck potentials (upper pair of traces) of a pair of polyps of *Tubularia* and of hydranth potentials of the same polyps, with the electrodes on the hydranths (lower pair of traces). The dots indicate single neck potentials, which were probably triggered by activity in the other polyp; this can be inferred from the constant time of transit. Bursts of hydranth potentials spread between polyps but single ones do not. [Josephson and Mackie, 1965.]

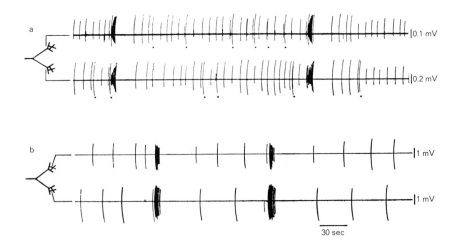

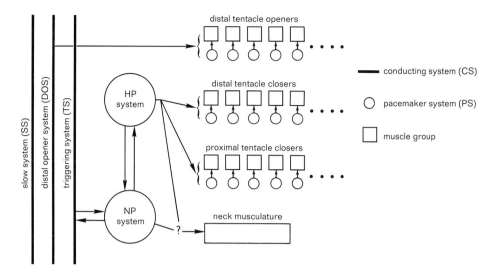

distal tentacle openers

conducting system (CS)

pacemaker system (PS)

muscle group

distal tentacle closers

HP system

proximal tentacle closers

slow system (SS)

distal opener system (DOS)

triggering system (TS)

NP system

neck musculature

?

Figure 4.6
The interaction between pacemakers, conducting systems, and contraction systems in *Tubularia* polyps. The thick lines on the left represent three distinct physiological pathways in the stalk, differing in velocity and effect. These pathways communicate with other polyps on the same stalk, inferred from observations as in Figure 4.5. The systems in circles are pacemakers, those in squares are muscle groups. Excitation of the triggering system normally causes a closure of both sets of tentacles. *HP*, hydranth potential; *NP*, neck potential. [Josephson and Mackie, 1965.]

when the stimulus is below threshold for the other waves, SS or DOS. The TS conducts at about 17 cm/sec. Polyps connected on a Y stalk usually have synchronous NP bursts, and a single NP in one is commonly correlated with one in the other, presumably via the TS (Fig. 4.5). Vigorous tentacle concerts are therefore synchronous but weak ones are not. The relations between all known systems are shown in Figure 4.6. As in *Hydra*, we have to accept regions of body layers as the conducting elements, because the potentials are recorded by relatively gross suction electrodes at the surface, and one simple nerve net is unlikely to be the cause of all these large potentials. No doubt an examination of other hydroid polyps will reveal other, perhaps even more complicated systems.

The spontaneous behaviour of *Tubularia* is therefore the product of a number of interacting pacemaker systems, which are recognized by constant features of their electrical waves. There is a major pacemaker in the neck region (NP) and another in the hydranth (HP). The electrical activity is conducted and it precedes the movements. The activity in these pacemaker systems appears to proceed without reference to minor external stimulation or possible proprioceptors, for both NP's and HP's continue to appear long after the movements have been anaesthetized with excess magnesium ions. This is also strong evidence that these potentials, which continue to be conducted in the presence of excess Mg^{++}, do not depend on the nerve net in any way. On the other hand, the distal opener system (DOS), with small fast potentials susceptible to Mg^{++}, presumably depends on the single nerve net of the stolon.

Although several pacemaker systems lie within the one small two-layered animal, they interact smoothly; but the whole system has not yet been elucidated. The control of the neck muscles, particularly those that cause the hydranth to sway on its stalk, is not yet clear. The identification of the factors that control the pacemakers is also problematical, and even their exact location is unknown. The potentials are recorded with suction electrodes on the surface of layers of cells. It is likely that these sheets of cells act as two-dimensional axons; this is the only explanation so far available, although it is possible that the sheets are demarcated into strips or even single conducting rows of cells. The polarity of the potential in different recording conditions is in agreement with the theory that it originates in activity of the surface membrane, and the unitary nature of the waves, which are equally large over wide areas, shows that they are due to one single widespread source, not many local ones. As an anatomical correlate, there are specialized contacts between the cells in the body layers of *Hydra*.

The idea of nonnervous conduction in coelenterates is not new, but it now seems to be established for the first time. Within the nonnervous conducting systems there are distinct pacemakers, with interaction between them rather like that between nerves, sometimes polarized and often showing facilitation. In the early evolution of multicellular animals, nerves were an addition to a more primitive system. We now think that that primitive system was in fact electrical conduction along sheets of cells. At any rate, many examples of the latter are found today.

TIGHT JUNCTIONS AND ELECTRICAL CONTINUITY

Cell membranes divide the animal (or plant) into a series of boxes, units that one nucleus can conveniently manage; they also constitute a fabric resisting tear by distribution of loads and are units of differentiation. But certain tissues, while retaining cell individuality, require transportation of solutes freely from one cell to another. Recently it has become apparent that cells of a wide variety of tissues have points of especially close contact, called tight junctions, or peculiar septate junctions (Fig. 4.7). The latter, in the epithelium of hydroids and between the salivary gland cells of *Drosophila*, seem to consist of a series of bridges every 10 nm or so, which may be solid in structure. Tight junctions are regions where opposed membranes of adjacent cells come together, so that the two outside layers of the unit membrane look like a single layer in section under the electron microscope, even with a variety of fixatives. Between cells of mammalian intestinal and tunicate heart muscle tight junctions are correlated with conduction of excitation by current flow between the cells [1]. Several examples of electrical synapses, in different phyla, have tight junctions between pre- and postsynaptic fibres. Tight junctions occur in central ganglia of insects [16], and once looked for they may prove to be quite common. In muscle there is a wide variety of mechanisms (including stretch, continuity of cytoplasm, and contacts with clefts) whereby excitation can spread [9, 22]. In theory, the tight junctions act as windows for the passage of ions and make possible an electrical transmission, resembling that along an axon.

A low resistance to ionic flow between adjoining cells is not necessarily accompanied by structural tight junctions, but the converse appears to be true, for wherever tight junctions occur there is low resistance in the examples measured. In the eye of *Limulus*, tight junctions exist between the numerous retinula cells and the single eccentric cell, all of which are normally electrically closely coupled (Fig. 5.11). However, instances of high permeability to ions in the absence of tight junctions will no doubt appear; we do not yet understand the nature of the high permeability between glial cells. Between the ganglion cells of the leech or between the salivary gland cells of *Drosophila* the pathway of high permeability is broken by removal of calcium ions, but when these are replaced the pathway does not return. In the epithelium of the urinary bladder of the toad there are lanes of high permeability from cell to cell in certain directions but not in others [15]. In salivary gland cells and in Malpighian tubule cells of *Drosophila* the membrane resistance of the permeable junctions between cells is at least four orders of magnitude lower than the outer membrane of the layer, where the cells are not in contact with others of the same kind [10]. Electrical measurements show that intracellular ions, at least the small ones, move freely between cells. Work with dyes shows that larger molecules, up to the size of serum albumin (mol. wt. 69,000), will pass between salivary gland cells of *Drosophila*. (Larger molecules of a synthetic polyamino acid of mol. wt. 127,000 would not pass, but it is difficult to know whether the substances tested were innocuous.) Sensory cells of the Lorenzinian ampulla of the dogfish [12], glial cells, and many groups of cells of epithelial origin are connected by low resistance pathways. During the cleavage of the egg of a sea urchin, the resistance between the cells develops at the same time as the wall. In the egg of the newt *Triturus*, however, there is electrical intercellular coupling even after completion of cell division and after all cells of the blastula are connected [6].

The capacity (explained as increase of junction resistance) of connected cell assemblies to seal themselves off from a damaged cell has long been

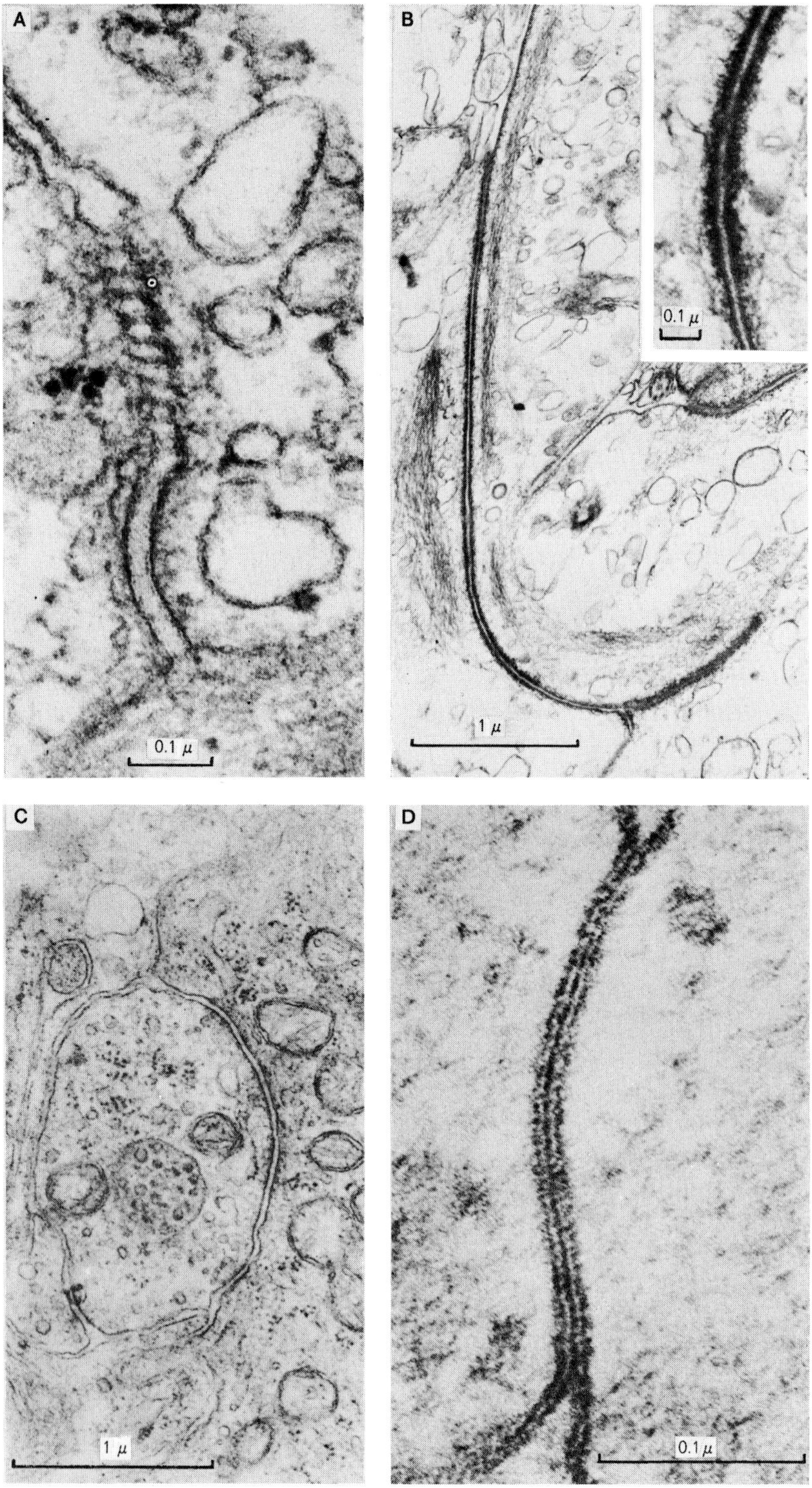

A

0.1 μ

B

0.1 μ

1 μ

C

1 μ

D

0.1 μ

recognized as an essential protective device. This must be of especial importance in superficial epithelial cells. In addition it has been known for many years that injured heart muscle can "heal" after a short time whereas skeletal muscle remains depolarized.

In the squid embryo [20] all cells are coupled to all others up to a time just before hatching, and they separate from each other in groups that are related to the formation of organs. A cell that is depolarized by damage is extruded from the embryo, and possibly the extrusion is triggered by the potential change. We are reminded of the question of why the pseudopod of an *Amoeba* fuses with another pseudopod of the same animal when they meet, but not with that of another *Amoeba*. May it be because the two animals are at a different potential? In the ommatidium of *Limulus* the low permeability pathways between retinula cells and eccentric cells (described on p. 80) suddenly increase in resistance when the potential between the two cells exceeds about 30mV. Apparently the near isopotential state can be a signal for close adhesion (or even fusion) of the membranes. This raises more questions—the importance of membrane potentials in driving nutrients from cell to cell, the self-isolation of layers of tissue in developing embryos, and the recognition of wounds by neighbouring cells—about which we have no answers. It even appears that cancer cells fail to communicate with each other because they lack tight junctions [11]. Low resistance bridges between paired motor neurons on the two sides of the nervous system have now been reported in arthropods; connexions between neighbouring muscle fibres in a block are also reported [18]. It may well be that interconnected muscle cells are the very ones that are connected to a particular axon, or that other effects, passed from cell to cell as suggested above, are instrumental in the recognition of postsynaptic cells by axon terminals in all higher animals (see p. 368).

Whether the connexions between similar cells in a tissue are a cause or a consequence of the similarity between the cells is not known. Genetic and hormonal controlling agents could move from cell to cell along re-

Figure 4.7

Examples of adhesions of presumed functional significance between cells.

A. Septate desmosome with a parallel adhesion, from epithelial cells of an echinoderm embryo. [Courtesy M. S. Laverack.]

B. Long adhesion between epithelial cells of a sea urchin with inset at high power. [Courtesy J. L. S. Cobb.]

C. Connection between a dendrite terminal and a neuron soma from a sympathetic ganglion of a guinea pig. There are 4 faint synaptic vesicles only, illustrating the difficulty of identifying a synapse.

D. Tight junction between two intestinal smooth muscle fibres of the mouse. These muscle fibres are thought to be electrically connected by low-resistance tight junctions, of which this may be one. [C and D from Taxi, 1965.]

stricted lines of flow, exerting a direct and mutual effect during development and in the maintenance of the adult form. The point is, however,
that excitable membranes and potential changes can be important in all
kinds of coordination apart from that with which we are familiar in
nerve cells. We will return to this important topic when we consider
how neurons recognize each other when they form connexions together.

Because of its wide occurrence, especially in embryos, we may suppose
that coordination between cells by tight junctions is a primitive feature.
Following this stage, certain cells (future neurons) evolved ways of
switching on and off their pumps and permeabilities to ions; perhaps the
siphonophores, hydrozoans, and ctenophores (and others?), before they

Figure 4.8

The origin of the nerve cell. Hypothetical evolution of nerve nets in epithelial systems of ctenophores and coelenterates.

A and **B.** Conducting epithelium leading to an epithelial muscle cell.

C. Muscle cells connected by their tails.

D. As in **C**, but with epithelial cells with processes that connect only with each
other and bridge over intervening cells. This is the critical stage of appearance of
axons, and there is no clue as to which type of cell gave rise to them.

E. Connections to muscle cells.

F. Origin of sensory cells, after the appearance of conducting systems.

G. The situation in medusae and some other coelenterates. There are two separate
conducting systems, with separate sensory inputs and motor outputs; one system
acts on the other at a definite place, as in the marginal ganglion in jellyfish.

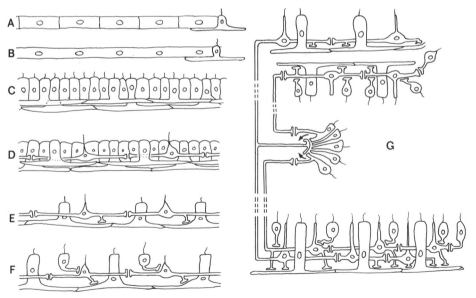

developed neurons, utilized propagation of action potentials through layers of cells.

Neurons first appear as insulated conducting lines within epithelia which themselves show pacemaker and conducting properties (Fig. 4.8). Presumably the nerves are not excited by the electrical activity of the surrounding epithelium because they do not project through its surface. Sensory neurons and nerve net neurons are distinct from their first appearance, and the former have so far never been found to connect directly with effectors. It seems certain that neurons evolved from cells that already conducted electrically, in sheets (as in the siphonophore bell) or in rows (as in the ctenophore comb plate). The later stages in the evolution of conducting systems reflect refinements in the mechanisms that define their connectivity. Little more can be said about the significance of tight junctions in nervous systems; even normal synapses may be places where substances are conveyed from cell to cell (see p. 361). It is possible that an even wider variety of coordinations will turn out to depend upon electrical transmission [16], but much more documentation is required before these questions can be usefully discussed.

REFERENCES FOR CHAPTER 4

1. Barr, L., Dewey, M. M., and Berger, W. 1965. Propagation of action potentials and the structure of the nexus in cardiac muscle. *J. Gen. Physiol.* **48:** 797–823.
2. Bennett, M. V. L., Alijure, E., Nakajima, Y., and Pappas, G. D. 1963. Electrotonic junctions between teleost spinal neurons: electrophysiology and ultrastructure. *Science* **141:**262–264.
3. Charlton, B. T., and Gray, E. G. 1965. Electron microscopy of axodendritic synaptic tight junctions in frog spinal cord thought responsible for electrical transmission. *J. Physiol.* **179:**2–4P.
4. Horridge, G. A. 1965. Relations between nerves and cilia in ctenophores. *Amer. Zoologist* **5:**357–375.
5. Irisawa, A., and Hama, K. 1965. Contact of adjacent nerve fibres in the cardiac nerve of mantis shrimp. *Jap. J. Phyisiol.* **15:**323–330.
6. Ito, S., Hori, N. 1966. Electrical characteristics of *Triturus* egg cells during cleavage. *J. Gen. Physiol.* **49:**1019–1027.
7. Josephson, R. K. 1965. Three parallel conducting systems in the stalk of a hydroid. *J. Exp. Biol.* **42:**139–152.
8. Josephson, R. K., and Mackie, G. O. 1965. Multiple pacemakers and the behaviour of the hydroid *Tubularia. J. Exp. Biol.* **43:**293–332.
9. Lane, B. P., and Rhodin, J. A. G. 1964. Cellular interrelationships and electrical activity in two types of smooth muscle. *J. Ultrastructure Res.* **10:** 470–488.
10. Loewenstein, W. R. 1966. Permeability of membrane junctions. *Ann. N.Y. Acad. Sci.* **137:**441–472.

11. Loewenstein, W. R., and Kanno, Y. 1966. Lack of intercellular communication in cancer cells. *Nature* **209**:1248–1249.
12. Loewenstein, W. R., Socolar, S. J., Higashino, S., Kanno, Y., and Davidson, N. 1965. Intercellular communication: renal, urinary bladder, sensory, and salivary gland cells. *Science* **149**:295–298.
13. Mackie, G. O. 1964. Analysis of locomotion in a siphonophore colony. *Proc. Roy. Soc. Lond. B* **159**:366–391.
14. Mackie, G. O. 1964. Conduction in the nerve-free epithelia of siphonophores. *Amer. Zoologist* **5**:439–453.
15. Nakas, M., Higashino, S., and Loewenstein, W. R. 1965. Uncoupling of an epithelial cell membrane junction by calcium ion removal. *Science* **151**:89–91.
16. Osborne, M. P. 1966. The fine structure of synapses and tight junctions in the central nervous system of the blowfly. *J. Insect. Physiol.* **12**:1503–1512.
17. Pappas, G. D., and Bennett, M. V. L. 1966. Specialized junctions involved in electrical transmission between neurons. *Ann. N.Y. Acad. Sci.* **137**:495–508.
18. Parnas, I., and Atwood, H. C. 1966. Phasic and tonic neuromuscular systems in the abdominal extensor muscles of the crayfish and rock lobster. *Comp. Biochem. Physiol.* **18**:701–723.
19. Passano, L. M., and McCullough, C. B. 1963. Pacemaker hierarchies controlling the behavior of Hydra. *Nature London* **199**:1174–1175.
20. Potter, D. D., Furshpan, E. J., and Lennox, E. S. 1966. Connections between cells of the developing squid as revealed by electrophysiological methods. *Proc. Nat. Acad. Sci.* **55**:328–335.
21. Sleigh, M. 1967. [Unpublished observations.]
22. Taxi, J. 1965. Contribution a l'étude des connexions des neurones moteurs du système nerveux autonome. *Ann. Sci. Nat. (Zool.)* **7**:413–674.

5

The responses of nerve cells and their processes

So far we have only said of neurons that they conduct, and in fact nothing more than this is known about them in most primitive animals. To proceed further requires an intimate knowledge of the factors that influence the initiation and frequency of impulses. Curiously, a thorough knowledge of the ionic nature of the membrane currents or of the biophysical features that make neuron membranes excitable is of little help in explaining how neurons coordinate behaviour. An understanding of the biophysical mechanisms of excitation of nerves is of no advantage in explaining what happens when a frog sees and leaps on a fly or why the song of an English thrush contains a rising note repeated three times. On the other hand, an appreciation of some of the observable *phenomena* in nerve cells is helpful because it is of explanatory value to see how graded electrical changes in nerve cells can interact and recombine over and over again in space and time, and in doing so lead to the abstraction of generalized features of the stimulus.

The discussion that immediately follows covers only the outstanding phenomena, which are the observable events as recorded electrically or directly inferred from recordings. Molecular and ionic mechanisms of a chemical nature underlie these events, but that level of analysis is not illustrated here.

PHENOMENA RECORDED AS POTENTIALS

All nerve cells and their fibres have a **resting potential** of about 80 mV, inside negative, across their bounding membrane; this can be measured by penetrating the cell with a microelectrode and measuring the potential difference directly between the two sides with a very high resistance voltmeter. All excitable membranes so far known are closed bounding membranes and the potential is maintained by the active metabolism of the contents. Excitation of nerve fibres is most readily observed as a change in this membrane potential and subsequent rapid recovery.

A large potential change is propagated along the membrane of a neuron because ionic currents that flow as a result of this potential change are sufficient to excite electrically the adjacent region of the membrane, which in turn becomes active for a few milliseconds and excites a further region. This series of events (called an *impulse* or *spike*) is followed by a refractory period of a few milleseconds, during which the membrane is not excitable; the passage of an impulse over a long distance is therefore necessarily an all-or-none event. All the energy in excitation, and in inhibition, is supplied by pre-existing ionic concentration differences. The ionic currents associated with an impulse are large enough to be recorded outside the membrane, either by gross electrodes that record from numbers of fibres, or by external microelectrodes that can approach close enough to single cells and fibres to isolate their activity from that of the surrounding neurons. This becomes of great practical value in the isolation of units in the central nervous system.

The all-or-none nerve impulse, however, is only the means of long-distance transmission in nervous systems. The impulse trains are initiated by graded potentials, and where they terminate their impulses cause other graded potentials. It is these graded potentials that are important at receptors, and they are the basis of interaction between neurons. The potentials have been distinguished as pacemaker, generator, local, excitatory synaptic, and inhibitory synaptic, but aspects of these different modes overlap to some extent. A region of membrane may be excitable by an ionic current, or excitable not electrically but only chemically, or may appear intermediate in its response to these stimuli.

When the membrane of an axon is stimulated by a small current (which is carried by ions, as are all currents in solution), the membrane is passively charged or discharged, depending on which way the current flows. A local potential change spreads because the membrane is a distributed capacitor. This **electrotonic spread** can be represented by a model circuit, as in Figure 5.1. At the sudden application of a maintained electrical stimulus the membrane potential *at that place* changes with a definite time constant; at an adjacent place the change is less and will reach a maximum somewhat later because it takes some time for the current from near by to change the potential across the membrane capacity. At a greater distance from the source the potential change across the membrane is smaller, and ultimately negligible. The time constant at each region is the time it takes the potential to decline to 37% of its original value when in isolation. This local feature contributes to the properties of the membrane whereby potential changes of different origins sum before they decay away. The space constant—the distance at which a steady potential declines to 37% of its original value—determines the extent of the summation of independent polarizations that have their

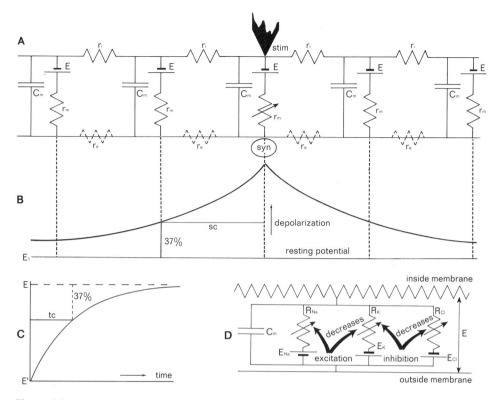

Figure 5.1

Space constant and time constant of a neuron membrane.

A. The distributed resistances, capacities, and potentials, which are in reality distributed uniformly along the membrane. The inside of the membrane is uppermost and the internal resistance (r_i) is large for a thin fibre but small for a cell. The external resistance r_e is small for cleaned isolated fibres but may be considerable for neurons, which are among other cells or within a sheath. The membrane resistance r_m is reduced under the influence of synaptic action or by depolarization of electrically excitable membrane. As drawn here the electromotive force is oversimplified in that it cannot reverse. r_m ranges from 10^6 to 10^{10} ohm-cm.

B. The membrane is depolarized at one point, either by a microelectrode (which can be external or internal, as at the point marked *stim*) or by a decrease in its own membrane resistance (as caused by synaptic action labelled *syn*). The depolarization spreads along the membrane, as determined by the distributed resistances and capacities. For equilibrium conditions with a constant maintained depolarization at one point, the distribution of potential will appear as in **B**. The actual value of the space constant $sc = r_m/r_i$, where r_m is membrane resistance and r_i is the resistance of 1 cm length of the internal solution. For a frog muscle fibre 100 μm in diameter, sc is about 2.5 mm.

C. If the potential of the whole membrane is displaced uniformly by a small amount to E' (so that r_m is not affected), it will return to its equilibrium value P by an exponential change with a time constant tc, which depends on the values of the capacities and resistances in **A**. All changes in potential and the velocity of conduction along a membrane are governed by this time constant at each point.

D. An element of the membrane shown in **A** with the potential F divided into components due to sodium, potassium, and chloride ions. Excitation decreases the resistance of the membrane to the first two ions, and synaptic inhibition acts by decreasing the resistance to the second two ions. So far as is known, this is the case for most nerve and muscle membrane, but there is a significant movement of calcium in the excitation of vertebrate heart and some arthropod muscle fibres.

origin at nearby points in the same neuron. Values of space constants in small dendrites are not known, but values from 0.3 mm to 1.0 mm have been proposed as reasonable for typical mammalian dendrites and thin axons. Therefore, all electrical events are readily summed within the length of a whole neuron or a typical branch of one. Because of this simple but crucial property, weighted sums and differences make possible the remarkable transformations at those interneurons upon which excitatory and inhibitory synapses converge.

Besides this passive or electrotonic effect, the membrane of a typical axon makes its own **active response** to a depolarizing, but not to a hyperpolarizing, current. Therefore, for small currents that are near the threshold to initiation of a spike—that is, about 10^{-11} to 10^{-10} amps/μ^2— there is a greater potential change to depolarization than to hyperpolarization. The active depolarization, or active response, adds to the effect of the stimulus. In fact the active response in Figure 5.1, E, is a decrease of the resistance to sodium ions. This decrease has a positive feedback action and causes a further conductance increase to Na^+. As described above, the depolarization spreads electrotonically to the adjacent region of the axon, and if it is large enough the depolarization is adequate to excite this region also. This point defines the spike threshold when the active response is large enough to invade and propagate. Propagation of the spike is therefore a consequence of the electrical excitability, together with the geometrical properties of the closed surface of capacitative membrane lying between two conducting solutions. The safety factor is the ratio of spike height to threshold, and is greater than 4 to 1 for most axons, so there is no likelihood of failure to propagate a spike in a fibre in which the diameter is constant or diminishes with distance.

In the nerves of vertebrates, leech, and cockroach, and in the somatic muscles of vertebrates, the spike is caused by the increase in sodium conductance, followed by the increase in potassium conductance. In contrast, in crustacean muscle, in some mollusc nerve cells, and in frog heart muscle, a substantial inflow of Ca^{++} causes the rising phase in spike activity.

A pacemaker potential can be considered as an active response that does not decay; it determines the frequency of a relatively conspicuous group of neurons or terminals that are spontaneously active at one point and fire repetitively with no apparent stimulus. In the best known example, cardiac muscle, the depolarization is due to increasing permeability to sodium ions, as in normal excitation. If interspike intervals are short it is impossible to distinguish a pacemaker potential from the natural recovery after an impulse is initiated. Sometimes pacemaker potentials are oscillatory—suggesting that yet undescribed factors stabilize the membrane potential—and only some of the peaks of depolarization may lead to impulses.

A **generator potential** in a region of membrane is any kind of graded potential that can reasonably be accepted as an active response of that specialised membrane, and it usually leads up to an impulse (Fig. 5.2, A). In the special case of receptors, the potential generated by the receptor ending is called a receptor potential, but the principles are the same (Fig. 5.2, B, C). Synaptic potentials are a similar class of postsynaptic generator potentials. As observed through a microelectrode, a graded potential is always necessarily the summed response of an area of membrane that may in fact consist of numerous distinct patches of membrane that cannot be distinguished by this technique. Frequently a generator potential spreads from a region that is chemically excitable (as at a postsynaptic membrane or at receptors) to an adjacent point, which then becomes a spike-initiating region by virtue of its electrical sensitivity (Fig. 5.3). When this interaction between regionally specialised parts is considered closely, the electrically excitable components are readily distinguishable from the nonexcitable only in special cases, as in electric organs, in which the two are extremely different and anatomically separate. The anatomical diversity is very great (Fig. 5.4), and every neuron has its own parameters, which define the code from stimulus to impulse train (Figs. 5.5 and 5.6).

An **excitatory postsynaptic potential** (e.p.s.p.), as recorded from the postsynaptic side of a synapse, is a depolarization, usually of a few millivolts, which is thought to arise from the permeability change caused by a chemical, the synaptic transmitter, acting on the membrane of the postsynaptic cell (Fig. 5.7, A). It is therefore analogous to the receptor potential in a chemoreceptor, except that in most synapses the chemical is not known, and in some synapses (electrical ones) the postsynaptic membrane is sensitive to the extracellular current caused by the impulse in the presynaptic membrane. Potentials that lead to excitation in postsynaptic elements may therefore have similar appearances but different origins.

An **inhibitory postsynaptic potential** (i.p.s.p.), may be a depolarization, a hyperpolarization, or one that evokes no change; but the potential still accompanies an inhibition of activity in the postsynaptic element. Excitatory and inhibitory actions at synapses differ: only in excitation is there a depolarization by increase in membrane permeability to sodium ions alone, just as there is in the electrical excitation of an axon. Sodium ions, normally pumped out of the nerve cell, flow back in when the permeability to them increases. Another way of saying this is that if the sodium ions were suddenly free to move through the membrane they would carry the membrane potential to a new equilibrium with the inside of the cell near zero potential or even positive (Fig. 5.1, E). In inhibition, in contrast, the effect at the synapse is to increase the permeability to all small ions—in natural circumstances, primarily chloride and potassium. The new equilibrium potential during the inhibition is then nearer to the resting potential. This change occurs in several preparations, such as mammalian nerve cells, crustacean stretch receptor and mollusc neurons, but in some there is an increased permeability to one ion (mainly to chloride in crustacean muscle and mainly to potassium ions in vertebrate heart muscle). This permeability change has two effects, both of which suppress depolarization. First, the postsynaptic potential is commonly, but not necessarily, a hyperpolarization, which takes the cell

Figure 5.2

Receptor and generator potentials and spike initiation.

A. An electrical stimulus, as shown in six increasing strengths, depolarizes the membrane to increasing extents. At a certain degree of depolarization, as indicated by the threshold, the membrane resistance to sodium ions is reduced and further current begins to flow, thus causing the spike. The upward phase of the spike is caused primarily by the increase in permeability to sodium ions, shown by Na⁺ curve below, allowing sodium ions to flow in. The recovery phase of the spike is caused primarily by the increase in permeability to potassium ions (curve K⁺ below), allowing potassium ions to flow out.

B. Typical graded receptor potentials in response to ramp stimuli of differing steepness. These curves are from an electrically inexcitable receptor membrane.

C. Typical graded potentials leading to a spike in an electrically excitable membrane, as in **A**. The latency to the initiation of a spike depends on the rate of increase of the prepotential. These are represented as caused by electrical stimuli, but changes at a nearby receptor or synaptic site has exactly the same effect.

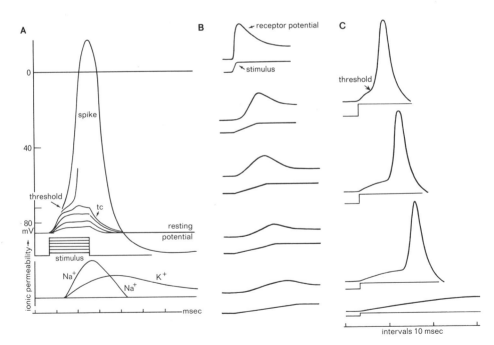

further away from its threshold for formation of spikes. Second, and more important, the increased permeability clamps the membrane of the postsynaptic cell at an inhibitory equilibrium potential that is near its resting potential, so that a much larger flow of sodium ions near by would be required to depolarize it by a given amount.

Whether an inhibitory postsynaptic potential is depolarizing or hyperpolarizing depends upon the position of the resting potential of the membrane at the time. The change in the membrane is felt mainly as an increased permeability to Cl' and/or K$^+$ ions, and the equilibrium potential for either of these ions is not far removed from normal resting potential; therefore, when the resting potential is artificially displaced,

Figure 5.3

The control of frequency of nerve impulses at a region where they are initiated.

A. The spikes show an increase in frequency because the depolarization of the membrane is more rapid after each impulse in this example, and threshold is reached correspondingly sooner.

B. The situation in which a record as in **A** can be made. Three regions of a neuron are shown in close proximity to each other. On the left the depolarisation is generated at a sensory transducer, a region beneath a synapse, or a naturally occurring pacemaker. The region penetrated by the microelectrode (commonly the cell body in invertebrates) is shown in the centre. The impulse is initiated on the right at a distance from the generator region. The impulse-initiating region is necessarily electrically excitable and of low threshold, but the generator region is usually not electrically excitable. The electrode between the two regions records an amount from each that depends on the space and time constants that determine the electrotonic spread of the generator potential and of the spike.

C. Successive thresholds, *a* to *f*, are preceeded by curves of differing shape as they lead up to a spike at decreasing frequency.

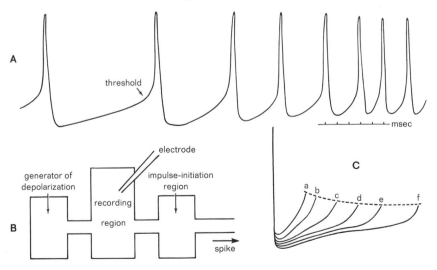

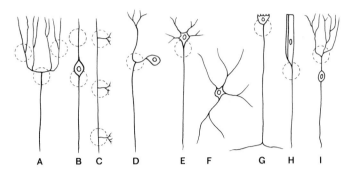

Figure 5.4

The anatomical situations in which impulses are initiated. The dashed circles indicate the probable region where neurons of these varied forms have electrically excitable regions of lowest threshold. Neurons with sheaths that have nodes of Ranvier can initiate impulses at the first or second node from the sensitive terminals.

A. Vertebrate sensory arborization.

B. Typical invertebrate sensory neuron.

C. Interneuron from a ladderlike cord with input and output in every segment.

D. Typical invertebrate motoneuron.

E. Typical vertebrate motoneuron.

F. Amacrine cell, or local interneuron, perhaps with no axon or spikes.

G. Stretch receptor cell of arthropod abdomen.

H. Arthropod primary visual cell, with rhabdom.

I. Invertebrate sensory cell as found in some annelid, mollusc, and other instances.

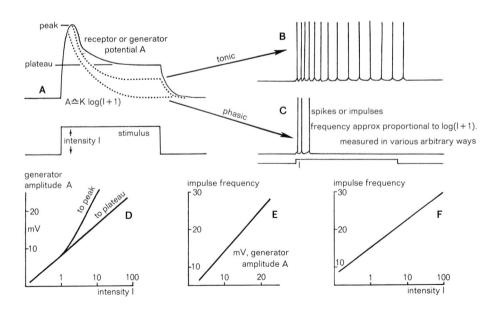

the inhibitory ionic current is still in a direction towards the inhibitory equilibrium potential, coming in with opposite sign from each side of this (Fig. 5.7, E). Inhibitory synapses are sometimes situated near a spike-initiating region of an axon hillock, where they have maximum effect in preventing the formation of impulses; however, they also occur upon the soma, as in hippocampus and cortex, or upon dendrites, as in the cerebellum.

All interactions between neurons take the form of excitation (which takes the postsynaptic membrane potential towards spike threshold) or of inhibition (which prevents it), or of the interaction between the two. No other process of functional importance is known, but within these two broad categories are a number of different mechanisms.

Electrical excitatory synapses are those in which the extracellular current generated by the presynaptic axon is adequate to excite the postsynaptic fibre directly where they meet, whether transmitter action is present in addition or not. In some cases—for example, the septate connexions between adjacent segmental regions of giant fibres of annelids (Fig. 6.6) and of crustaceans—they conduct either way. One synapse that is asymmetrical by virtue of the rectifying properties of the synaptic membrane is that between the lateral giant fibres of the crayfish and each of the giant motor fibres to the fast muscles that flex the abdomen (Fig. 5.8, A). These electrical excitatory synapses have little functional importance as integrating junctions, for every impulse jumps across. However, they show that electrical synapses may be common in the ladderlike nervous systems of annelids and arthropods, and that large axons owe their size to the effectiveness of the large currents thereby generated when they are electrically presynaptic.

Figure 5.5

Typical relations between stimulus, receptor potential, and spike activity in a receptor.

A. The magnitude of the receptor potential can be measured either to the peak or to the plateau.

B and C. Adaptation of impulses can depend on the decay of depolarisation in the generator region, as shown by the broken curves, or by change in sensitivity at the spike-initiating region. The resulting spike trains may be quite different.

D. Typical relation between receptor potential amplitude and stimulus.

E. Typical relation between receptor potential and spike frequency.

F. Typical relation between stimulus intensity and impulse frequency. One must take an arbitrary measure of frequency, either an instantaneous initial value, or an average over some arbitrary period in relation to the stimulus. Note where the plots are logarithmic. Statistical scatter has been ignored in these diagrams.

The difference between a phasic and a tonic receptor is due (at least for the crustacean MRO, Fig. 6.1) to the adaptation at the spike-initiating region, and not to mechanical slip or decay of the receptor potential.

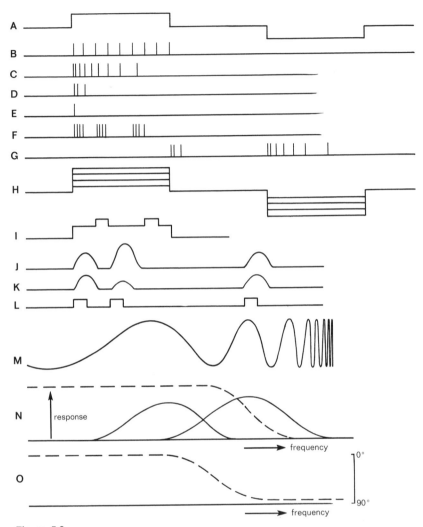

Figure 5.6

Controlled stimulation in the analysis of unit activity in sensory systems.

A–L. Maintained stimuli of sudden onset. This is the simplest to control and analyse.

A. Positive and negative stimulus. B–G. Various types of response with increasing adaptation in B–E, a temporally patterned response in F and an "off" response in G.

H. The control of intensity.

I. Test pulses superimposed on a stimulus as a test of the excitability while already active. This is important as a test of whether stimuli are linearly summed.

J–L. Facilitation in J and antifacilitation in K in response to the paired stimulation in L.

M–O. Oscillatory stimulation with small sine-wave changes over a wide range of frequencies. This is appropriate for analysis by control-system theory.

N. Responses over different frequency ranges. The dashed line shows the response of a unit that gives a maintained response to a maintained stimulus, as in A above.

O. The falling behind in the phase of the response of the unit shown dashed in N.

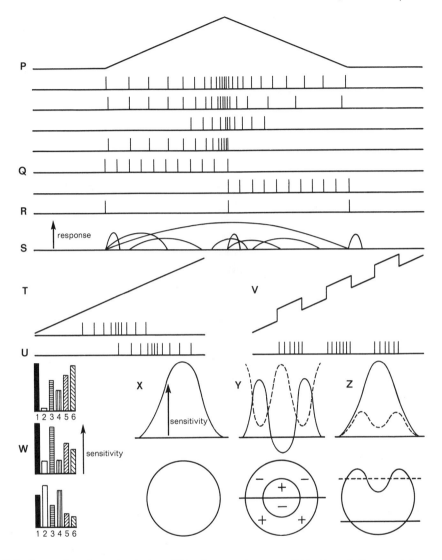

P–V. Ramp function stimulation. This draws out many distinctions between units in a way that is often related to natural function. Note the velocity detectors with constant response to a constant velocity as a special case at Q, with directional properties.

S. Responses of different types of units at different times during the stimulation with a rising and falling ramp.

T and U. Range fractionation whereby units come in at different parts of the range of the stimulus. This increases sensitivity over each part of the range and can reduce ambiguity in the stimulus-response relation.

V. Test pulses at different background intensities.

W. Response profiles to different types of stimulus 1–6, as in the analysis of chemoreceptors.

X–Z. Distribution of sensitivity in different parts of a receptive field; it is simple in X, with centre and surround in Y, and of irregular shape (note dotted traverse) in Z.

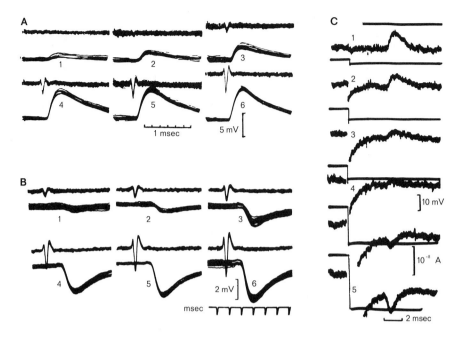

Figure 5.7

Typical e.p.s.p.'s and i.p.s.p.'s recorded intracellularly from motoneurons of the cat spinal cord.

A. Monosynaptic e.p.s.p.'s (depolarizations) from a medial gastrocnemius motoneuron, evoked by an afferent volley of the medial gastrocnemius nerve of progressively increasing size as indicated by the extracellular recordings 1–6 from the dorsal root (Group I_a responses).

B. Typical i.p.s.p.'s (hyperpolarizations) of progressively increasing size together with the extracellular dorsal root record, showing the increase in number of excited afferent fibres from the opposing muscle.

C. The upper and lower traces give the membrane potential and current for a cat motoneuron that was voltage clamped. C1, typical i.p.s.p. with normal membrane potential; C2–C5, increasing amplitude of rectangular hyperpolarization applied before the i.p.s.p. and continued beyond the end of the trace. Voltage clamping eliminates electrotonic spread and reveals the true time course of the inhibitory synaptic current. [A from Eccles, Eccles, and Lundberg, 1957; B from Curtis and Eccles, 1959; C from Araki and Terzuolo, 1962.]

Electrical synapses are recognized by a negligible delay in transmission across the synapse (Fig. 5.8, B), but measurements directly on the two sides are rarely possible. Chemical synapses of mammalian motoneurons have a delay of as little as 0.3 msec, though values longer than 1 msec are more typical of invertebrates (Fig. 5.8, E). Electrical synapses are recognized also by the large electrical change necessarily caused in the postsynaptic cell by the extracellular presynaptic current, but this effect is not necessarily revealed if potentials in small terminals have near-threshold effects on fine processes of a large cell.

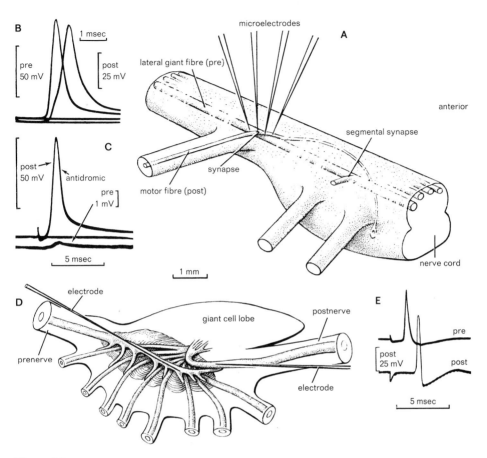

Figure 5.8

Electrical and chemical synaptic transmission.

A. The arrangement for recording from each side of the electrically transmitting synapse in a portion of a crayfish ventral cord. The synapse lies between the longitudinal giant fibre and the segmental motor (abdominal flexor) fibres.

B. Pre- and postsynaptic responses, showing negligible latency due to electrical transmission.

C. Almost no response in the prefibre to an antidromic spike in the postfibre, as a consequence of rectification in the synaptic membrane.

D. The stellate ganglion of the squid, showing one electrode in the internuncial giant fibre (left) and another in a motor giant fibre (right).

E. Pre- and postsynaptic spikes, showing the considerable latency, indicating chemical transmission. [A–C from Furshpan and Potter, 1959; D from Bullock and Horridge, 1965.]

For an electrical synapse to operate with maximum efficiency there should be a low resistance across the synaptic contact, but the remainder of the interstitial space represents a possible channel in which presynaptic

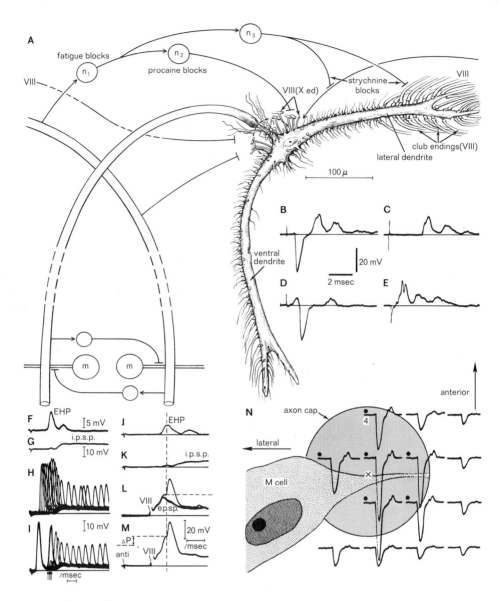

Figure 5.9

Pathways of interaction between Mauthner neurons of the medulla of the goldfish, as inferred from extra- and intracellular records.

A. The cell body of one side. The axon crosses its partner and runs down the spinal cord, where it forms synapses with motoneurons (m). The Mauthner cell is normally excited primarily by the club endings from nerve VIII. Each Mauthner neuron inhibits the other by several interneuron pathways, which are distinguished by the action of drugs. The excitation of n_1 is blocked by fatigue and n_2 by procaine. The presynaptic inhibition of n_3 upon the fibres of nerve VIII is peculiar in being blocked by strychnine. The remarkable early inhibition is caused by extracellular current in the region around the axon hillock (h). There is also an inhibitory pathway to the receptor.

B–E. Comparison of extracellular potentials at one point close to the axon hillock under different conditions.

B. Both M cells are stimulated antidromically in the spinal cord.

current would fail to pass through the postsynaptic cell. In a chemical synapse, on the other hand, the postsynaptic membrane must act as a current source, with the cleft necessary for current escape to the extracellular space. This agrees with the generalization that synapses in which the membranes are fused, or have clefts narrower than 20 nm, are electrical in the two or three cases that have been examined. The converse does not necessarily hold, but chemical synapses in general have synaptic clefts of 20 to 30 nm. If the presynaptic terminals are much smaller than the postsynaptic ones, the transmission cannot be electrical, for a small terminal does not generate sufficient current.

An **inhibitory synapse with electrical transmission** exists at the point at which a group of fine fibres form a spiral round the axon hillock of the giant Mauthner cells, which lie in the midbrain of most fish [13]. Each Mauthner cell has a decussating axon that runs down the spinal cord and synapses with axons of motor fibres on the side opposite the cell body. Excitation causes a flip of trunk and tail towards the side opposite the stimulated cell body and its input from the eighth nerve. Impulses in the spiral fibres around the axon hillock cause a hyperpolarizing potential in the Mauthner cell without change in membrane conductance. The presynaptic fibres are numerous, and may originate in the contralateral eighth nerve or from intercalated internuncials that are excited by either Mauthner cell (Fig. 5.9). Under optimal conditions this hyperpolarizing potential is sufficiently powerful to block impulses that arrive antidromically along the postsynaptic axon. This arrangement ensures that the cells of the two sides do not both fire at the same time. There are also chemically transmitting inhibitory endings near by

C. Only the contralateral M cell is fired antidromically.

D. The ipsilateral M cell is fired by VIII nerve stimulation.

E. Stimulation of the contralateral VIII nerve. The ipsi- and contralateral M cells and stimulation of the contralateral VIII nerve each produces its own characteristic hyperpolarizing current.

F and G. Simultaneous extra- and intracellular records, showing the extracellular hyperpolarizing potential (EHP) and the intracellular i.p.s.p., which is felt more strongly within the cell.

H and I. Antidromic impulses superimposed at different times on the i.p.s.p. are reduced in amplitude.

J and K. As in F and G, on a faster time scale.

L. e.p.s.p.'s generated by stimulation of the ipsilateral eighth nerve at different strengths (club ending pathways).

M. Raising the threshold to e.p.s.p.'s by ΔP as in L, by simultaneous arrival of an EHP This is the best indication of the inhibitory action of the extracellular hyperpolarizing potential.

N. Distribution of extracellular hyperpolarizing potential around the axon hillock of a Mauthner cell. The circle is 70 μm in diameter. Modifications to the pattern of interneurons have now been suggested by Furukawa [13] upon whose earlier work with Furshpan this figure is based.

on the postsynaptic cell body, so the electrical transmission merely saves some time. The input to the Mauthner cell can be inhibited by pre-synaptic inhibition of the eighth nerve terminals upon the Mauthner cell dendrite and by efferent axons to the otic receptor. The inhibition at each

Figure 5.10

Signs of pre- and postsynaptic inhibition. The figure shows an imaginary neuron bearing an inhibitory terminal (*I*), an excitatory one (*E*), and a presynaptic inhibitory one (*PI*). The records show typical responses as follows.

A1. Normal spike from excited cell.

A2. The same with presynaptic inhibition.

A3 and **A4.** The normal and reduced e.p.s.p. before and during presynaptic inhibition.

B1. Normal, and **B2** and **B3**, reduced reflex spike volleys in ventral roots before and during presynaptic inhibition.

C1 and **C2.** Intracellular (upper trace) and extracellular (lower trace) records from an excitatory synaptic terminal. The difference between these traces shows the *depolarisation* of the terminal itself as a result of presynaptic inhibition. This depolarization is thought to reduce the output of transmitter at each impulse.

D1. Typical hyperpolarizing i.p.s.p. **D2** and **D3**, interaction between this i.p.s.p. and an e.p.s.p. In each case one scan shows the e.p.s.p. alone.

E. The lowering of the threshold of excitatory presynaptic endings as a result of excitation of sensory terminals in the same region. Each vertical line represents the size of the antidromic response in the dorsal root in response to a stimulus of constant strength from a microelectrode in the cord. The break in the record shows the moment when an orthodromic sensory volley entered the cord, from the gastrocnemius (proprioceptive) nerve (**E1**), and with longer time constant from the sural (skin) nerve (**E2**). The change of excitability is attributed to the depolarization shown in C above. [A–D from Eccles, 1964; E from Wall, 1958.]

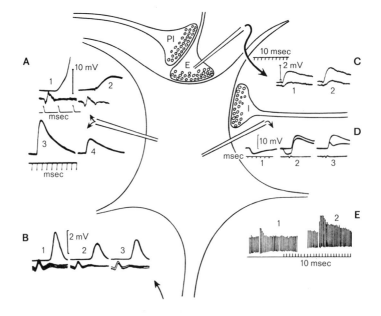

stage is illustrated in Figure 5.9. Even if both Mauthner cells fire simultaneously there is inhibition at the spinal level, which prevents the initiation of motor impulses simultaneously on the two sides.

Presynaptic inhibition is the inhibition of presynaptic excitatory endings. The mechanism can be a hyperpolarization of the terminals, causing spike blocking, or a depolarization or attentuation of them by increased permeability. In either case activity is blocked before the presynaptic spikes have an opportunity to reach their target. So far the best examples identified physiologically are (a) at the synapses of primary sensory endings in the mammalian spinal cord, especially in the cuneate nucleus, and (b) at the neuromuscular junction of the muscle that opens the claw (not other muscles) in the crayfish. Histological evidence suggests that presynaptic inhibition may be widespread, especially where amacrine cells occur, but a critical morphological check of the particular fibres that are anatomically presynaptic has, in general, not been made; a great deal of correlation of the physiological tracing of fibres remains to be done. Although accompanied by no change in the ionic permeability of the postsynaptic membrane, presynaptic inhibition can be made apparent in three ways: (a) by a reduction in the size of existing e.p.s.p.'s when a new pathway in the preparation is excited, if there is reason to suppose that other explanations are inadequate; (b) by an increase in sensitivity of the presynaptic (sensory) fibres to small extracellular electrical stimuli that can be applied just at the time when they are inhibited at their terminals [22]; (c) by direct recording of depolarizations with intracellular electrodes, which in a few favourable instances can be placed in the presynaptic sensory terminals (Fig. 5.10). Inhibition without change in the postsynaptic membrane may also be due to effects on dendrites far from the electrode, and there are strong indications that presynaptic inhibition on spinal motoneurons is not as typical as was formerly thought [14].

These techniques show that in presynaptic inhibition the inhibitory endings terminate sufficiently near the ends of the excitatory endings to be within inhibitory range of the synaptic transmission. The inhibitory terminal could, but need not, sit directly on the second axon ending, as in a serial synapse. The reduction in the height of the e.p.s.p., as recorded in the final cell, shows that, when inhibited, the sensory (intermediate) terminals release less than their normal total amount of transmitter. Further, it has been shown in vertebrate spinal cord that normal (postsynaptic) inhibition is usually but not always blocked by strychnine. Contrary to some accounts, picrotoxin is not a specific blocking agent for presynaptic inhibition [14].

Presynaptic excitation, defined as the enhancement of the effect of presynaptic terminals by the action of other terminals upon them, is not known with certainty in vertebrates. This is, however, the simplest explanation for one form of interaction in the sea hare *Aplysia*, but even there this explanation depends upon the assumption that the interaction is monosynaptic. Even so, it would be dangerous to assume that all morphologically described serial synapses have an inhibitory first component.

Electrotonic spread along pathways between one neuron and another has now turned up in several widely scattered places—for example, between giant fibres in earthworm, cells of crustacean heart ganglion, spinal neurons in fish, ganglion cells of leech, paired motoneurons of insects, and *Aplysia* neurons. The pathways are inferred from the observation that constant current passed through an electrode in either cell will cause an attenuated but maintained potential change in the other cell, and from the fact that slow oscillations of potential in the two cells tend to keep in phase. As known so far, these electrotonic bridges do not conduct rapid oscillations or nerve impulses, and they are therefore inferred to be long and narrow. They must necessarily have the effect of maintaining a similarity of resting potential in the connected cells. Other functions are not known, although follower neurons of the crab heart connect with pacemaker cells by an electrotonic pathway of this kind and so contribute by positive feedback to the avalanche of nerve impulses at each heart beat.

Where a group of nerve cells or their processes lie close against each other we may suspect that there is **interaction between neighbours** caused by flow of ionic currents and that normally the presence of glial cells and sheaths reduces this. But the situation is not fully understood and numerous different relations may well be found. As an example, the group of receptor cells for light in the ommatidium of *Limulus* contains about a dozen primary sensory cells together with one or two second-order (eccentric) cells on which the primary cells act. Simultaneous recordings from two cells show that potential changes caused by imposed current in any cell are closely followed by the potential of a neighbouring cell [5] except that a rectifier prevents the eccentric cell being indirectly hyperpolarized. Therefore resistive pathways connect all the cells in the cluster (Fig. 5.11, B, C, D). The ommatidial receptor cells are large, with broad mutual contacts where presumably there are tight junctions (see p. 56) and the group of cells is wrapped as a self-contained parcel in a glial sheath. This situation must not be considered as typical, but we have little knowledge of possible interactions, and many tight junctions may persist from the embryonic state. Motoneurons of the cat's spinal cord have some kind of electrical interaction of short latency, causing changes of threshold by 10 to 30% (ref. 30, p. 328).

Neurons with two or more axons are described here and there throughout the animal kingdom. Records from a few examples show that two or more all-or-none impulses can coexist in the same neuron [20]. The

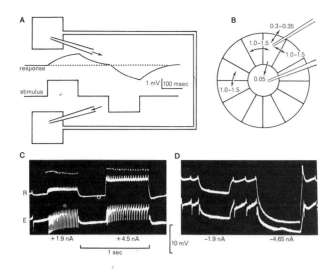

Figure 5.11

Electrical coupling between neurons.

A. Electrotonic spread between two diagrammatic neurons, as found in crustacean heart ganglion, leech ganglion cells, and neurons of the medulla of the puffer fish. Long pulses of current passed into one cell cause a maintained potential change in the other cell, and the effect is not necessarily symmetrical on reversal. Usually there is no means of telling whether anastomoses or membranes with tight junctions occur between the cells.

B. Diagrammatic cross section of an ommatidium of the compound eye of *Limulus,* showing the conductances between cells, with one electrode in a retinula cell and the other in the central dendrite of the eccentric cell (see also Figure 9.14). Tight junctions occur between all the cells in contacts. Approximate conductances are shown in nanoamps per millivolt of applied potential, and give rise to records as shown in **C** and **D**.

C and **D.** Responses from a retinula cell (*r*) and from an eccentric cell (*e*) in the same ommatidium, in **C** with depolarizing currents, causing impulses, and in **D** with hyperpolarizing current which suppresses impulses. In **C** and **D** the current pulse is applied first to the retinula and then to the eccentric cell. Note the spread of the spikes as well as of the polarisation. [**C** and **D** from Borsellino et al., 1965.]

prerequisite is that the separate all-or-none regions must be anatomically separated by a zone (usually the cell body) that does not carry an impulse. The recording electrode in this zone then picks up a reduced spike from each region (Fig. 5.12). By extension, all bipolar neurons could feasibly have a noncorrespondence of impulses on the two sides of their cell body; long dendrites could be spike-bearing and neurons with many branches could be broken up into regions.

In *Aplysia* neurons it has been observed that the region where an axon branches into two or more can have integrating properties or polarized transmission, because there the safety factor is low [15]. Where a fibre

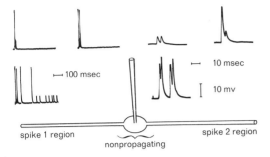

Figure 5.12
Two all-or-none spikes in one neuron. The intracellular recording electrode is within reception distance of two spike-initiating regions that must be separated by a nonpropagating region, as suggested in the diagram beneath. The records on the right are on a faster time scale. [Preston and Kennedy, 1960.]

Figure 5.13
A swelling or a branching of an axon may reduce the safety factor for propagation of a spike to such a point that an integrating or polarizing junction is formed.

A. A simple swelling (for example the cell body of a bipolar neuron) can theoretically act as a junction with through-conduction in only one direction.

B. The same at a side branch.

C. Stimulation of different branches of one neuron, as in *Aplysia*, can give rise to particular combinations of outputs as shown.

D. An interneuron with arborizations in three successive ganglia in a ladderlike nerve cord. Inputs as shown by letters could give rise to outputs as shown by numbers. Because these relationships could be labile, as in synapses, the possibilities for modulation of an apparently stable anatomical pattern are extensive and as yet unknown. [C and D after Hughes, 1965.]

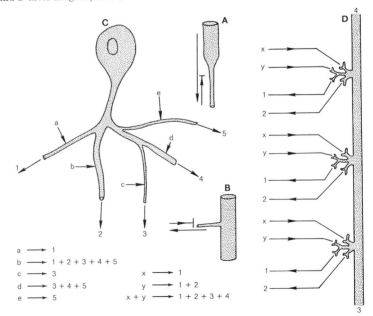

suddenly widens or acquires more membrane by any means, the action current must charge a greater capacity, so that several impulses may be required before one impulse gets through. The possibility of this type of integration in branched neurons means that one must speak of "units," not "neurons," when recording blindly. There are many degrees of freedom available (Fig. 5.13), but the actual abnormal occurrences are so far rather few.

GLIAL CELLS

In two situations, in which their large size has made it possible to study them in detail, the glial cells seem to play a passive part, although in each case the potassium released by the activity of nerve fibres has an effect in depolarizing the surrounding glial cell. In the central ganglia of the leech, the cell bodies of the neurons are grouped in packets in each of which one giant glial cell envelopes all the 60 or so cells of that packet. Each neuron is connected to the outside of the glial cell by a narrow channel (mesaxon or cleft). To reach the neuron from the outside, substances must pass either through the glial cytoplasm or through the cleft, or both. This situation is typical of vertebrates and invertebrates, but in the vertebrates the glial cells have end feet upon blood capillaries and in the invertebrates much of the space around glial cells is filled with a base-binding collagenous material of unknown ionic significance. The space immediately surrounding the neurons acts like a fluid that contains a concentration of Na^+ and K^+ similar to that in the bathing fluid of the coelomic cavity or experimental bath. This has been demonstrated by using the fact that the height of the spike of a neuron depends on the external Na^+ concentration and the value of the resting potential depends on the external K^+ concentration. Experiments show that removal of the glia and exposure of the neurons do not let in any additional bathing fluid, and therefore the glial cells do not maintain a special environment round the nerve cells. The channels around these neurons must therefore have an ionic composition similar to that of the bathing medium [17, 18, 19].

When the outside medium is changed, the ionic movements are completed in a few seconds. The rate of movement has been followed directly by the effect of the ions on the impulse height and resting potential of the nerve cell, while a simultaneous recording shows that the membrane potential of the glial cell does not change. Therefore **the ions move through the channels** between cells and not through the glial cytoplasm, and calculations show that diffusion is sufficiently rapid for this to happen in the observed time [19].

In the optic nerve of urodeles the glial cells are sufficiently large to yield records with microelectrodes. The amount of potassium ions released when a barrage of nerve impulses pass is sufficient to depolarize the membrane of the glial cells. This is caused by the delay in equilibration between the intercellular fluid and the bathing solution, agreeing with the theory that the glial cells play no special part in control of ionic movements. Nutritional metabolites, large molecules, and respiratory exchanges have not been studied by these micromethods, so that nothing can be said about the relative importance of the glial cells and the spaces between cells for substances other than the common ions.

From the evidence so far gathered, the glial cells do not seem to be important for the particularly nervous functions of the nervous system; the part they play in the determination of its growth has hardly been tackled experimentally, but it is probably slight according to the present evidence. It seems probable that new fundamental properties of quite a different kind will be discovered, if only because the present picture of glia is so dull.

SYNAPTIC TRANSMISSION

A synapse is recognizable on structural or functional criteria but not always on both together. Under the light microscope there is a wide range in types and shapes of endings of neurons where synapses are located. Under the electron microscope, on the other hand, there is a remarkable uniformity in the form of the actual contact, but some variety in number and position of associated organelles. There is no discernible receptor mechanism of the postsynaptic membrane. There are no anatomical or physiological features that are absolutely characteristic of chemical synapses, although many of these show something other than a one-to-one relation of nerve impulses. Historically, the suggestion has often been made that some synapses serve a trophic function, but so far there are no proved cases of purely trophic synapses. There may also be a physiological synapse where an anatomical one does not exist, as in Figure 5.13.

Chemical synapses are almost always one-way, but occasionally vertebrate muscle fibres generate electrical currents that are adequate to excite antidromically the terminals of their own motor nerves. Electrical synapses are commonly two-way; a few are one-way because one fibre is much smaller and cannot generate enough current to excite the larger one, or because the synaptic membrane has a greater resistance in one direction than in the other. At many chemical synapses the prolongation of the synaptic potential beyond that expected from the measured time constant of the membrane can be explained by supposing that some residual transmitter persists at the synapse. In all synapses, chemical or electrical, there is increased permeability of the membrane of the postsynaptic cell, the so-called active response, which is essential for the formation of the postsynaptic impulse. Artificial hyperpolarization of the postsynaptic membrane causes an increase in the size of the postsynaptic potentials in chemical synapses, and depolarization causes a decrease: this effect depends on the position of the equilibrium potential for the transmitter (Fig. 5.14). It is possible that all immediately postsynaptic membranes may be inexcitable to current flow (electrically inexcitable) because the synaptic membrane has merely to be an efficient channel for the depolarizing current while the neighbouring membrane creates the active response, but this is a difficult matter to test experimentally.

When a presumed transmitter substance is electrophoretically supplied in local doses, it should cause a change in membrane potential towards the same equilibrium potential as is produced by the natural transmitter. The equilibrium potential is found by artificially hyperpolarizing or depolarizing the membrane while the applications continue [16]. This provides one of the best tests for substances suspected to be transmitters, but the electrode is not necessarily equally accessible from the electrogenic and the chemosensitive regions of membrane.

A most important feature of a chemical synapse is the nature of the transmitter substance (Fig. 5.15). The best-established transmitter is

Figure 5.14

The equilibrium potential in the presence of a suspected inhibitory transmitter substance, compared with the reversal potential for normal inhibitory postsynaptic potentials in a snail neuron. The three records are superimposed but taken at different times.

A. Change of membrane potential towards the new equilibrium potential in the presence of acetylcholine, and suppression of spike activity.

B. Reversal of i.p.s.p.'s by hyperpolarization of the membrane, with the reversal potential at about 85 mV.

C. Change of membrane potential towards the acetylcholine equilibrium potential from a hyperpolarized position The i.p.s.p.'s could have the same equilibrium potential (same effect on the membrane) as the acetylcholine; the small discrepancy can be explained because in this experiment the two sites of action are not necessarily identical [Kerkut and Thomas, 1963.]

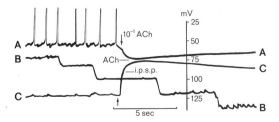

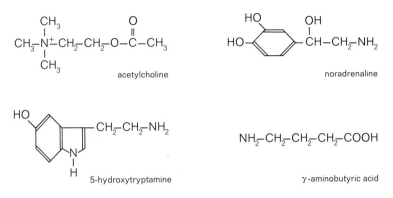

Figure 5.15
The chemical formulae of the commonest transmitter substances.

acetylcholine, which is excitatory at leech and vertebrate somatic muscle end plate, inhibitory on vertebrate cardiac muscle, excitatory on some mollusc neurons, and possibly a transmitter at some sensory junctions of arthropods, but other esters of choline may be involved also. Noradrenaline is the transmitter at some vertebrate visceral neuromuscular junctions. Gamma-amino-butyric acid is the inhibitory transmitter to crustacean muscle and also almost fulfils the requirements in the mammalian central nervous system. Substances with strong claims to be considered as transmitters are (a) 5-hydroxytryptamine, which accelerates mollusc hearts and has a wide variety of effects on molluscan preparations and some action in vertebrate central nervous systems, (b) catecholamines, which have a wide variety of effects in molluscs, crustaceans, and vertebrates, (c) the amino-acid ion glutamate almost mimics the excitatory transmitter at some vertebrate central synapses and especially at crustacean neuromuscular junctions. These substances all occur near their supposed site of action.

The function of an identifiable transmitter substance is difficult to analyse in situ, but in favourable cases, such as the vertebrate neuromuscular junction, which has been intensively studied, the following evidence is available. Sites that are specifically receptive to the appropriate concentration of the transmitter are located under and around the nerve terminal, where they are to be expected, and the specific enzyme that destroys the transmitter is found in the clefts beneath the synapse. Transmitter substance is presumed to be concentrated in the synaptic vesicles within the nerve ending. In one instance direct estimation showed that each synaptic vesicle of the cerebral cortex contained about 2000 molecules of acetylcholine, and that the concentration within vesicles was high (3M). However, in another case studied in detail, the rat sympathetic ganglion, only about 10% of the acetylcholine could be mobilized, the remainder being not available as a transmitter [3]. Pharmacological agents that block the receptor sites for acetylcholine quite specifically (curare), others that block its synthesis (hemicholinum), and others that inactivate the enzyme that destroys acetylcholine (eserine) are very useful in analysis, and are required for other transmitter substances. Some chemical synapses have randomly occurring miniature potentials, which are presumed to be caused by the random arrival of packets of transmitter even when the presynaptic fibre is not excited (Fig. 5.16). It is now accepted that in some instances the vesicles contain transmitter substance, but the diversity of synapses with a few vesicles, and the paucity of preparations showing miniature potentials, suggest that chemical transmission is not necessarily quantal in all. In frog neuromuscular junctions, and perhaps many others, there are tubular invaginations of the membrane among the vesicles, and the vesicles may feasibly be artifacts of fixation [2]. In several vertebrate and crustacean preparations there are strong indications that inhibitory synapses are sometimes distinguishable by their elongated vesicles, as normally fixed [21].

Usually, but not necessarily, a neuron has the same effect, excitatory or inhibitory, at each of its terminals (where there are more than one). In *Aplysia* there are neurons with opposite effects upon different post-synaptic cells, but the difference lies in the postsynaptic membrane. It seems to be a general truth that a neuron never produces more than one transmitter. Inhibitory axons and cell bodies in crustaceans can be recognized and mapped by their high content of GABA.

The increased complexity of pharmacological studies in the presence of multiple transmitters is already apparent, especially in the gastropod ganglia, in which the large cells have made possible numerous tests. The mammalian Renshaw cells in the spinal cord appear to have at least four different sites upon them, one inhibitory, and the others excitatory, of which one is noncholinergic. Some *Aplysia* cells have two types of excitatory junctions upon them, with different transmitters, and there is no saying what further complexity will be found.

Some electrical (and all chemical) synapses have synaptic vesicles arranged along the membrane on the presynaptic side, and even in chemical

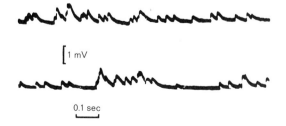

Figure 5.16

Typical miniature potentials from the neuromuscular junction of the frog, as recorded intracellularly. An upward deflexion is a depolarisation. [del Castillo and Katz, 1956.]

1 mV

0.1 sec

synapses there is no proof that to act the vesicles must burst through the membrane. There is some evidence that the vesicles can be formed during fixation by the breakdown of tubules from the outer membrane. Synaptic transmission cannot be assumed to occur if and only if vesicles, localized differentiations, or membrane thickenings are present. This point is even more important in the consideration of the actions of hormones and the possibility that substances may be slowly secreted upon neighbouring nerve cells. So far, the sharply defined examples of rapid chemical transmission have contributed most of our knowledge, but many slower chemical interactions surely remain to be found. We must probably soon modify the prevailing attitude that rapidly secreted transmitters are the chief chemical products of nerve cells. The chemical nature of connectivity (that is, how the neurons know where to form synapses) and of learning, and of secretory neurons without special neurosecretory end organs, assumes a greater importance as we try to understand the morphogenesis of the circuits that bring about discrimination and choice of action by line-labelling of numerous neurons in parallel.

REFERENCES FOR CHAPTER 5

1. Araki, T., and Terzuolo, C. A. 1962. Membrane currents in spinal motoneurons associated with the action potential and synaptic activity. *J. Neurophysiol.* **25**:772–789.
2. Birks, R. I. 1966. The fine structure of motor nerve endings at frog myoneural junctions. *Ann. N.Y. Acad. Sci.* **135**:8–19.
3. Birks, R., and MacIntosh, F. C. 1961. Acetylcholine metabolism of a sympathetic ganglion. *Canad. J. Biochem.* **39**:787–827.
4. Bodian, D. 1952. Introductory survey of neurons. *Cold Spring Harbor Symp. Quant. Biol.* **17**:1–13.
5. Borsellino, A., Fuortes, M. G. F., and Smith, T. G. 1966. Visual responses in *Limulus. Cold Spring Harbor Symp. Quant. Biol.* **30**:429–443.
6. Bullock, T. H., and Horridge, G. A. 1965. Chapters 4 and 5. (See *loc. cit.*, p. 18.)
7. Curtis, D. R. and Eccles, J. C. 1959. The time courses of excitatory and inhibitory synaptic actions. *J. Physiol. London* **145**:529–546.
8. DeBell, J. T. 1965. A long look at neuromuscular junctions in nematodes. *Quart. Rev. Biol.* **40**:233–251.
9. Del Castillo, J., and Katz, B. 1956. Localization of active spots within the neuromuscular junction of the frog. *J. Physiol.* **132**:630–649.
10. Eccles, J. C. 1964. *The Physiology of Synapses.* Heidelberg, Springer-Verlag.
11. Eccles, J. C., Eccles, R. M., and Lundberg, A. 1957. Synaptic actions on motoneurons in relation to the two components of the group I muscle afferent volley. *J. Physiol. London* **136**:527–546.

12. Furshpan, E. J., and Potter, D. D. 1959. Transmission at the giant synapses of the crayfish. *J. Physiol. London* **145**:289–325.
13. Furukawa, T. 1966. Synaptic interaction at the Mauthner cell of goldfish. *Progress in Brain Research* **21A**:44–70.
14. Green, D. G., and Kellerth, J. O. 1966. Postsynaptic versus presynaptic inhibitions in antagonistic stretch reflexes. *Science* **152**:1097–1099.
15. Hughes, G. M. 1965. Neuronal pathways in the insect central nervous system, in *The Physiology of the Insect Central Nervous System*, J. E. Treherne and J. W. L. Beament (Eds.). London, New York, Academic Press.
16. Kerkut, G. A., and Thomas, R. C. 1963. Acetylcholine and the spontaneous inhibitory post-synaptic potentials in the snail neurone. *Comp. Biochem. Physiol.* **8**:39–45.
17. Kuffler, S. W., and Nicholls, J. C. 1964. Glial cells in the central nervous system of the leech; their membrane potential and potassium content. *Arch. Exp. Path. Pharmak.* **248**:216–222.
18. Kuffler, S. W., and Potter, D. D. 1964. Glia in the leech central nervous system: physiological properties and neuroglia relationship. *J. Neurophysiol.* **27**:290–320.
19. Nicholls, J. C., and Kuffler, S. W. 1964. Extracellular space as a pathway for exchange between blood and neurons in the central nervous system of the leech: ionic composition of glial cells and neurons. *J. Neurophysiol.* **27**:645–671.
20. Preston, J. B., and Kennedy, D. 1960. Integrative synaptic mechanisms in the caudal ganglion of the crayfish. *J. Gen. Physiol.* **43**:671–681.
21. Uchizono, K. 1965. Characteristics of excitatory and inhibitory synapses in the central nervous system of the cat. *Nature. London* **207**:642–643.
22. Wall, P. D. 1958. Excitability changes in afferent fibre terminations and their relation to slow potentials. *J. Physiol.* **142**:1–21.

6

Ganglia with few neurons, crab heart, annelid cord

What constitutes a ganglion or a central nervous system? How many neurons must be brought together before patterns of interaction can evolve between them that confer on the group some recognizably new features, which are not those of single neurons? These questions suggest that an additional complexity exists in a central nervous system that justifies the use of such terms as "central properties." There are, however, several known small collections of neurons that are certainly ganglia but without purely neural feedback circuits, reciprocal inhibition, or choice of alternative outputs—features that are commonly considered as typical of central nervous systems. Examples of such collections of neurons are to be found among the peripheral ganglia in vertebrates and arthropods, usually in association with the viscera and heart.

The stretch receptor sensory neuron of a lobster, for example, is attached to a thin muscle between the plates on the back of the jointed abdomen. At a stretch to its dendrites, which are buried in its own special muscle fibre, this neuron is depolarized and produces impulses. Stretching is caused by passive bending of the abdomen or by active contraction of the muscle of the sense organ (Fig. 6.1). In addition, the cell is surrounded by ramifying terminals of an inhibitory axon, which makes synapses on it [8]. There are therefore three types of inputs to this system, one motor one to the special muscle, another motor one to larger body muscles, which act on the joint across which the receptor is stretched, and the inhibitory supply. (I omit the passive stretch caused by forces outside the animal.) From this system there is one output of impulses that represents an integration of the intrinsic spontaneity with the three types of input, yet a definition of a ganglion should exclude this example. It comes, instead, within a small class of receptor neurons that have efferent control.

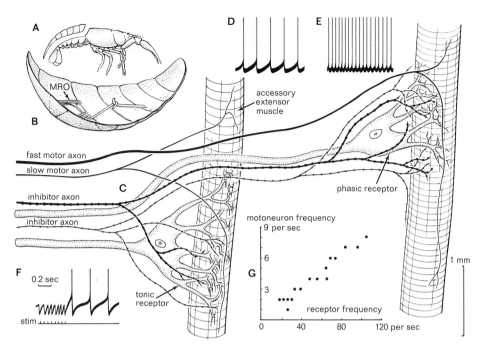

Figure 6.1

One of the pairs of muscle receptor organs (*MRO*) of the crayfish or lobster, with typical responses.

A. Removal of the dorsal side of the abdomen.

B. The boat-shaped preparation with one remaining accessory extensor muscle bearing a sensory neuron and other nerves.

C. The two modified slips of accessory extensor muscle from one side of one intersegmental joint as in B, showing the separate neurons.

D. Typical intracellular response of the slow (tonic) receptor neuron to a small degree of stretch.

E. The same, to a greater stretch.

F. Suppression of activity by stimulation of the thick inhibitor axon at 20 per sec.

G. The reflex relationship between the frequency of impulses in the tonic receptor and the impulses in a tonic extensor motoneuron of the same segment; that is, stretch of the sense organ causes a reflex contraction which relieves the stretch. [A and B from Florey, 1957; D, E, and F from Kuffler and Eyzaguirre, 1955; G from Fields and Kennedy, 1955.]

CRUSTACEAN HEART GANGLION

Consider next the group of nine neurons that lie on the inner side of the roof of the heart of higher crustaceans (Fig. 6.2). (The freshwater crayfish has 15 neurons here.) These are motor neurons to the heart muscle, but as a group they are spontaneously active and interact among themselves. The whole group participates in the initiation of bursts of impulses at intervals. Since the cells are motor neurons, each burst causes a brief tetanus of the heart muscle. The ganglion cells, their motor axons, and their other processes have a different arrangement in each species, as is characteristic of all nervous systems. In crabs and lobsters there are on each side always three axons that arise in the thoracic central nervous

Figure 6.2

The heart ganglion of a typical crustacean with elongated abdomen.

A. The location of the heart in the crayfish.

B. The lobster heart ganglion, which lies on the inside of the dorsal surface of the heart. Most of the intrinsic cardiac neurons have several axons, with branches to the cardiac muscle, and much of the ganglion is occupied by neuropile. The modulating axons, three of which are shown on each side, form basket arborizations and also end in neuropile.

C. A typical burst of impulses in which all neurons of the ganglion participate, in the upper trace, together with an intracellular record from a single follower cell in the lower trace. From these two records, the participation of the cell in the beat is clear. [From Hagiwara and Bullock, 1957.]

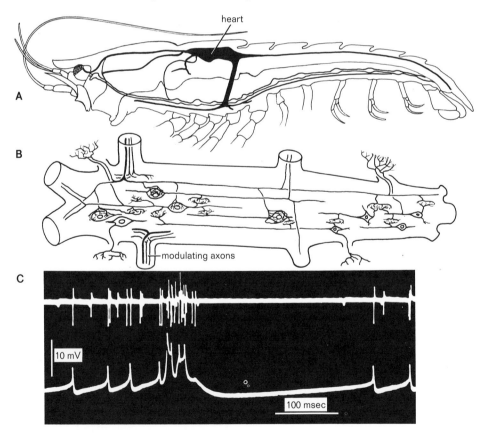

system and ramify among the side branches and over the neurons in the cardiac ganglion. Two of these fibres are excitatory at their terminals, produce e.p.s.p.'s, and accelerate the heart; the third one is inhibitory, produces i.p.s.p.'s, and slows the rhythm (Fig. 6.3).

Within the ganglion, the posterior group, usually of 4 smaller cells, initiates the first impulses of each burst, and therefore these cells are called pacemakers. The pacemaker excites the other cells in an avalanching fashion, so that together they produce a burst of 20–100 spikes. When they act on each other in this way, a single impulse in one cell causes a maximal large e.p.s.p. in other cells, and an impulse arriving later causes a smaller e.p.s.p., which is smaller for shorter intervening intervals (an-

Figure 6.3

Direct inhibition of a spontaneous pacemaker cell of a lobster heart ganglion.

A. Pacemaker potential interrupted by the onset of inhibition (90 per sec stimulation), which drives the internal potential negative towards an inhibitory equilibrium potential. The rebound at the "off" is prompt in respect to initiation of a new local potential but there is an apparent afterinhibition in respect to occurrence of the first spike, as revealed by the delay. (Calib., 200 msec.)

B. The same on an expanded time scale and with 60 per sec stimulation of the inhibitor. The first six stimuli produce only artifacts; beginning with the seventh, the response is a brief depolarizing and facilitating synaptic potential followed by a hyperpolarizing phase, which summates.

C. The same, showing the end of stimulation and the time course of the repolarization and subsequent five-step rebound. The first and the last steps may be synaptic potentials caused by presynaptic activity in other cells. The second step is interpreted as a local potential triggered by the rising pacemaker potential. The third and fourth events are two separate spikes in the same neuron. (Calibration 50 msec.) [Terzuolo and Bullock, 1958.]

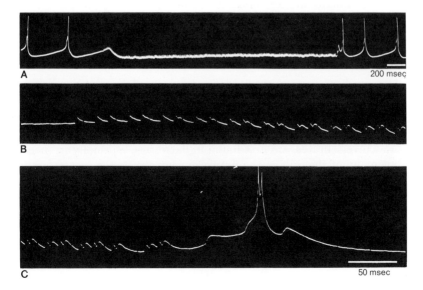

A   200 msec

B

C   50 msec

tifacilitation). This contrasts strongly with the excitatory effect of impulses that arrive in the acceleratory axon; these cause e.p.s.p.'s that are larger when they follow shortly after the one before (facilitation). Two accelerator axons from each side can influence the same ganglion cell; the acceleratory and inhibitory axons of the ventral cord run to every cardiac neuron, although their effects are caused mainly by their action on the pacemaker cells [5].

Another type of interaction between these cardiac neurons is the spread of graded potentials of low frequency between cells, such as would be caused by a long thin low-pass bridge between cells. This has two effects: first, in providing a long-term stabilization of the membrane potentials of two cells that are so joined, relative to each other; and second, in providing a positive feedback, which contributes to the avalanche at each burst of impulses.

There are other influences on the heart ganglion besides purely nervous ones. The nerves of central origin that supply the valves leading into the heart change the rate of filling, which in turn influences the stretching of the heart. The ganglion is sensitive to this, increasing its frequency with greater stretch. In addition, there are special release points, called pericardial organs, for hormones that are active on the heart ganglion. Precursors of these hormones are secreted in nerve cells of the ventral cord, transported down their axons from the central nervous system and released into the blood in the vicinity of the heart. As in much more complicated ganglia, we find an integration of diverse influences together with an intrinsic rhythm to produce a fairly consistent pattern that is not predictable in every detail of timing and sequence. Certainly this small group of cells justifies the name ganglion. It has features recalling those of much more complex nervous systems, although there is no ability to discriminate and no choice of output.

THE FIRST CENTRAL NERVOUS SYSTEMS

A central nervous system—defined as one having separate incoming sensory, outgoing motor, and intrinsic interneurons—first appears in the lower groups of worms. Before passing on to higher forms it is worth pointing out that centrally situated unipolar nerve cells, like those of most invertebrates, are first found in flatworms, especially in their brains, but many of the cells in the flatworm central nervous system are bipolar, like the typical coelenterate neuron. Some of these central cells have axons that reach outside the nerve cord, presumably to muscles, and peripheral motoneurons probably exist as well. As in all invertebrates, most sensory cells have peripheral cell bodies with a centrally directed axon. However, in flatworms the sensory axon does not necessarily run all the way to the central cord, but ends in branches, which presumably make synapses with interneurons along the course of the peripheral nerves. In fact the connectives and nerves have neuron cell bodies and neuropile distributed along them. On this point there is still doubt and uncertainty for the annelid worms. Among the different groups of flatworms the main pattern of the nerve trunks is very diverse but seems to be derived from 3 to 5 parallel trunks that are cross-connected rather irregularly at intervals along the body and joined anteriorly to a ring around the mouth. There is no functional network of connexions, however, even in the polyclad *Planocera*, which has an extremely netlike pattern of nerve trunks (Fig. 6.4). Here the sensory pathways run to the brain by the shortest direct route only. Similarly, when a nerve is cut close to the brain, the muscles served by it are paralysed and there is no evidence for alternative peripheral routes for either sensory or motor nerves [2]. This means that pathways of impulses are determined in a way that is different from any coelenterate preparation. Even in the highly developed ring nerve of hydromedusae, effective excitation travels either way round the bell (although perhaps in different axons).

A peripheral plexus of mixed sensory and motor fibres, with ganglion cells of unknown function distributed outside the central nervous system, is a common feature in many invertebrate groups. At least in the flatworms, molluscs, and echinoderms, where there has formerly been considerable doubt on the point, it is now conceded that the neurons are not all equivalent, and that conduction is not all-ways. A peripheral

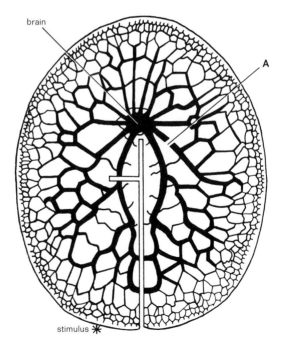

brain

A

stimulus ✳

Figure 6.4

The pattern of main nerve trunks in the flatworm *Planocera*, with experimental cuts. Despite the apparent network of nerve trunks, there is no suggestion of a nerve net in the true sense, and pathways are either afferent or efferent, involving the central ganglion. Stimulation at the asterisk will cause muscles over all the animal to contract, until the transverse cut is extended from the longitudinal cut. A section of the nerve at *A* results in a failure of only the correspondingly innervated section of the worm to participate in the waves of undulation in the swimming movements. [Ewer, 1965.]

plexus, if present, is complexly organized and cannot carry out all its functions without the central nervous system. The sole plexus of the foot of the gastropod *Limax* (but not that of the related *Helix*) is an example of one animal that can produce a reasonably normally coordinated loco-motory pattern when all central ganglia are removed. In all snails there are some local reflexes and others that act at a distance across the foot. Most of these animals having a so-called primitive nerve plexus, includ-ing the central nervous system of all the lower worms, are so poorly known, that, frankly, it is impossible to base any far-reaching arguments upon the existing fragmentary knowledge. In fact, to make comprehensible comparisons it is preferable to proceed at once to the annelids.

ANNELIDS

The annelid worms have a dorsal brain in the head, from which two longitudinal connectives run back along the ventral side of the body. In each segment, two ganglia, one on each connective, are sometimes fused; if separate, they are joined by two transverse commissures. This is the pattern also found in the arthropods, in which the arrangement of neu-rons is even more clear-cut and centralized.

Sensory axons run in from peripheral cell bodies in annelids and in the same nerves motor axons run out to the muscles from central cell bodies. Each ganglion consists of a central neuropile, which is surrounded by a rind of unipolar nerve cell bodies. Most of the cell bodies are of interneu-rons, which are of two main kinds: (a) with short processes restricted to the segment of origin; (b) with a long axon that runs far along the cord. This basic system is one that is reduplicated with astonishing constancy of pattern of branching and numbers of neurons in the successive ganglia, and is added in posterior segments as the worm grows. There is also a nerve supply to the gut and to the heart, both of which have motor cell bodies outside the central ganglia.

The basic system shown in Figure 6.5 will serve for an annelid or crustacean, but in the worms it has long been known that the incoming sensory axons divide where they enter the cord and send a branch in each direction along it for some distance. A general impression, from responses and from neuron connections, is that sense organs along the annelid body do not operate local or specific segmental reflexes. Surprisingly, perhaps, there are a very large number of nerve fibres in annelids. There could be one sensory axon from every peripheral cell body, as seems to be the case in the polychaete worm *Harmothoë* (see Fig. 6.11); although it is only an inch long, it has about 300,000 sensory axons. The common earth-worm *Pheretima* has about 500 motoneurons in a typical ganglion, sup-plying about 60,000 muscle fibres, and about another 500 interneuron cell bodies in each ganglion [1]. There is a comparable large number

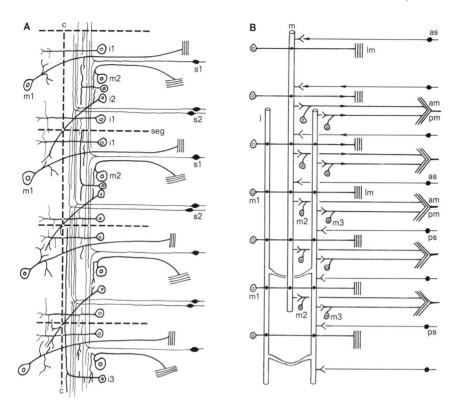

Figure 6.5

A. Actual neuron arrangement of a typical polychaete annelid nerve cord, with sensory, motor and internuncial neurons, some of which cross the mid-line (*cc*). Motoneurons of two types (*m1* and *m2*) run to different muscles. Interneurons are either local (*i1*) or to the adjacent segment (*i2*) or with long axon (*i3*). Sensory fibres of different peripheral origins have different central tracts, which cross the segmental boundaries (*seg*). In contrast to Figure 6.7, right, connections between cells are not indicated.

B. Connections of the giant fibres of earthworms and some polychaetes such as *Nereis* and *Harmothoë*. Anterior sensory fibres (*as*) connect with the median fibre (*m*), which directs all parapodia or setae forwards (*am*). Posterior sensory fibres connect with lateral or mediolateral fibres and direct them backwards (*pm*) all along the animal. All giant fibres connect with motoneurons (*m1*) to the longitudinal muscle but are selective in their connections to other motoneurons (*m2*, *m3*). Although consistent with the known anatomy, this type of diagram is derived from physiological results.

of motoneurons and somatic muscle groups in all the annulate elongate invertebrates with hydrostatic skeletons. A small number of neurons can never be claimed to be a primitive feature, but we can say that in all groups of animals so far studied we find some simple behavioural acts, coordinated by a few neurons.

Although there must be numerous types of interneurons in annelid cords, with diverse patterns of sensory input, the connections of only a few of the largest are so far known. Giant fibres, which have evolved by enlargement of the common types of interneuron, throw considerable light on the organization of the ladderlike nervous system. Some have a single cell body; others have many cell bodies, sometimes one or more in each segment, formed by fusion of corresponding interneurons in different segments along the worm. An illustration of giant fibre diversity in annelids (Fig. 6.6) is in fact an illustration of some types of interneurons. Some are ladderlike, as is inferred for many crustacean interneurons.

As an example of giant fibre action, the three giant fibres on the dorsal side of the nerve cord of the earthworm are syncytial products of many cells, each divided by transverse partitions or septa into segmental subunits (Fig. 6.5, B). The two lateral fibres, which are connected together in every segment by an electrotonic pathway of low resistance, are never active separately except when fatigued. The median giant fibre is excited by touch to the body surface of the anterior 40 segments (in *Lumbricus*) and the two lateral giant fibres are excited by touch behind this point, although all three may be stimulated electrically at any point, and all three carry impulses in both directions from the stimulated point. There is no interaction between the median and the other fibres. Impulses in all three giant fibres cause a rapid twitch of the muscles, which shorten the worm, but the median and lateral ones separately cause opposite effects on the direction of pointing of the setae, which project on either side along the worm. Median giant fibre impulses cause the setae to point towards the head end, so serving to anchor the tail; conversely, lateral fibre impulses (mediolateral in *Nereis*, Fig. 6.6, No. 10), make the setae point the other way and anchor the head. Therefore each giant fibre brings about a rapid retraction of the worm away from the region where this fibre alone receives a tactile input. When touched on the head, the worm pulls back, whereas it draws up its tail when that is touched. The synapse between the giant fibres and the segmental motor nerves is rapidly fatigued so that twitches are soon replaced by normal locomotion, even though the stimulus may continue. By this means the animal is not dominated too long by its giant fibre reflex (Fig. 6.7).

Giant fibre systems of other annelids operate similarly, but there is a wide variety of topological arrangement (Fig. 6.6). Most polychaetes that live in tubes have giant fibres that are internuncial between the sensory terminals at the crown of tentacles at one end and the segmental motor fibres going to the longitudinal retractor muscles along the worm. In *Myxicola* and perhaps a few other worms, the motor axons are continuations of the giant fibre; all other annelids examined have synapses between giant fibre and motor axons. The common ragworm *Nereis* has three sets of giant fibres (Fig. 6.6, Nos. 10 and 13): (a) the single median one is excited by mechanical stimulation at the front end of the worm;

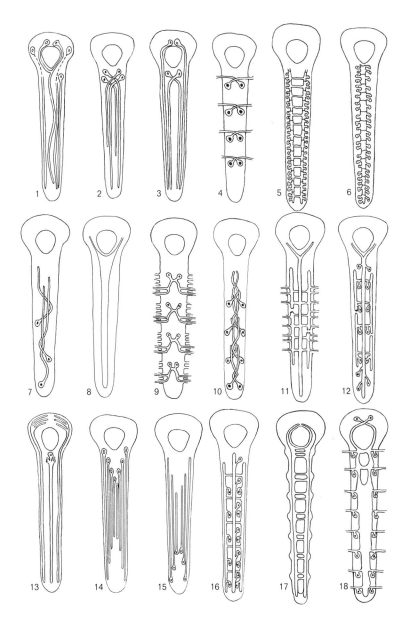

Figure 6.6

Interneurons have evolved as giant fibres in a wide range of worms, usually acting as the fast pathways in general shortening of the body. Only one limitation is placed on the structure—that it be adequate. Even at this level there is no one-to-one relation between structure and response. 1 and 2, *Euthalenessa*; 3, *Sigalion*; 4, *Lepidasthenia* and *Euthalenessa*; 5 and 6, *Lumbricus*; 7, *Euthalenessa*; 8, *Eunice*; 9 and 10, *Nereis* and *Neanthes*; 11 and 12, *Arenicola*; 13, *Nereis* and *Neanthes*; 14 and 15, *Halla* and *Aglaurides*; 16, *Mastobranchus*; 17 *Sabella* and *Spirographis*; 18, *Myxicola*. [After Nicol, 1948.]

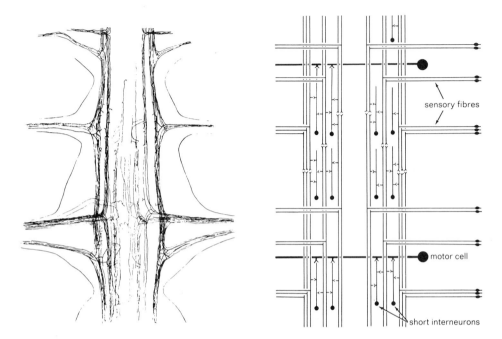

sensory fibres

motor cell

short interneurons

Figure 6.7

Left: sensory tracts in the ventral cord of one segment of the earthworm, stained by the Golgi method. Where it enters the cord in a bundle in the segmental nerve, each sensory fibre divides and sends a branch in each direction. These branches combine to form long central sensory tracts (Retzius, 1892). This anatomical picture, together with the existence of impulses that appear to be efferent in sensory nerves, suggests that the sensory axons stimulate each other in these central tracts, and that transmission along the tract occurs between terminals of primary sensory cells, as illustrated on the **right**. Motor cells (*large black circles*) are excited by interneurons (small unipolar cells) and possibly by the sensory tracts directly. Although the picture on the **right** shows an inferred plan so far as it is known in an annelid segmental ganglion, details must be extremely complex and different for each species.

(b) the paramedial pair (Fig. 6.6, No. 10), by posterior stimulation; (c) the larger lateral pair, by stronger stimuli at any point along the worm. As in the earthworm the different giant fibres are responsible for different responses—this time of the parapodia, which swing forward in response to impulses in the median fibre and backward to the paramedials. The large lateral giant fibres of *Nereis* seem to have no selective output but only reinforce the body shortening.

There are presumably numerous continuous longitudinal pathways that control creeping movements from either end. Some interneurons running down from the head cause the general inhibition of forward creeping when the head is tapped. The significance of the descending impulses in response to visual stimuli is not known. Altogether, we have a situation that is clearly the precursor of the better known system in the crustacean cord, with input-output relations typical of arthropods. The anatomy, especially of the giant fibres, suggests that the organisation of the annelid nerve cord is like that of crustaceans.

CONTROL OF MOVEMENTS IN ANNELID SEGMENTS

The relative importance of peripherally controlled reflexes and centrally controlled sequences in the locomotion of annelids is unfortunately still undecided. All the evidence suggests that reflexes play a minor role, especially at segmental level, and that the patterns of locomotion are inherent in the ventral cord. There is evidence that stretch of the body wall by the movements themselves reinforces the peristaltic wave and slows its velocity along the cord. In the earthworm the stretch in normal crawling is adequate to excite a neighbouring region of the worm across a gap at which the nerve cord is cut, but the initiation of peristalsis, its propagation along the cord, and the sequence of muscle movements are explicable as a product of central activity alone. Injection of oil into the coelom of oligochaetes and polychaetes, in amounts sufficient to prevent the normal activity of proprioceptors, causes only a physical impediment, which does not prevent the passage of a peristaltic wave. When the cord is isolated for a few segments by section of all segmental nerves, the nervous excitation still travels along this region, although its velocity is increased. In all three groups of annelids we can record impulses from stretch and touch receptors of the body wall, and although these receptors must be intensely active during crawling, there are no known effects of their impulses except to adjust an essentially central rhythm. This is reminiscent of jellyfish beats, caterpillar crawling, insect flight and ventilation (p. 139).

An annelid ganglion differs from the heart ganglion of a crustacean in that it can coordinate several different actions without confusing them: errant polychaetes and leeches can walk or swim; some worms show peristalsis in either direction; most worms make a rapid withdrawal when startled, as well as slower movements. According to the evidence all these responses are centrally controlled, and the primary stimulus determines only the choice of which action is made. The crustacean cardiac ganglion has only one output and so lacks the ability of choice that all central nervous systems show. In many lower animals two incompatible movements apparently do not exclude each other by operating through proprioceptive arcs. Instead, there seem to be mutually inhibitory central circuits where the sequences of motor impulses are generated. An illustration of this follows. When a *Nereis* is startled by a sudden touch or the giant fibres are excited electrically, the segmental motoneurons are excited (Fig. 6.5, B), and extracellular potentials are recorded from the longitudinal muscle (Fig. 6.7, A). If the worm then starts to crawl in the region where the electrode is attached to the muscle, the muscle action potentials are now sporadic, although still all-or-none. The only possible explanation is that for the duration of the crawling the central giant fibre-to-motor junction becomes depressed (Fig. 6.7, B). This is one way in which the animal is able to crawl away while still being stimulated, without twitching all the time. The movements recorded during crawling are slower and different from those at the twitch; their action potentials in crawling are graded and have a slower rate of rise, although the twitch is caused by a single motor impulse. The conclusion is that fast moto-neurons control the twitch, and a slow innervation to the same muscles controls locomotion. Certainly several motoneurons to one muscle block can be distinguished histologically, and, as for crustacea, different motor axons sometimes control different functions of a single muscle block.

An interesting question is whether there are any remnants of the nerve net in the annelid central nervous system. By a nerve net I mean a set of neurons that give no sign of being able to divide themselves into any subsets (see pp. 47, 60). Let us consider the individuality of neurons in relation to their repetition in every segment. The same motoneurons can be found in every similar segment along a worm, with axons to the same repeated muscle blocks; the only difference between segments is in small details of the dendritic trees. When a long interneuron has side branches in one ganglion, it is almost certain to have similar branches in exactly corresponding positions in all the other ganglia, as if it doesn't distinguish between them. On the sensory side the afferent fibres branch where they enter the cord and run up and down in tracts for a few segments [12]. Each tract is formed by sensory fibres of different peripheral origin (Fig. 6.8, A). Over large numbers of segments the behavioural responses don't depend on the segment stimulated, and there is no evidence that the sensory fibres of each tract do more than excite in a general way, without reference to the exact segment of their sensory ending. The crucial point is whether the sensory fibres of these tracts synapse with each other and form a sensory plexus along the cord, fed by sensory fibres of similar origin in each segment. Besides the anatomical picture (Fig. 6.8, A), there is physiological evidence that this is so, because when sense organs are stimulated, impulses emerge from the segmental nerves of nearby segments [7]. These impulses have the qualities of sensory bursts and are not necessarily accompanied by movement, distinguishing them from motor impulses. Present evidence suggests that the sensory fibres of similar origin in each segment do in fact form a kind of longitudinal nerve net in tracts along the cord (Fig. 6.8, B). It is supposed that interneurons are excited by this system (as the giant fibres certainly are) and that it arouses but does not determine the central sequences of motoneuron activity.

Other curious features of lower invertebrate nervous organisation will no doubt turn up as electrophysiological exploration is started in the lesser known groups. It is already becoming apparent that sensory neurons in the periphery can act as effector cells that secrete substances into the medium. Neurons containing obvious secretions are known in coelenterates and ctenophores, but it is in the worms that we first find secretions well-developed (Fig. 6.9) and recognisably constant in identifiable neurons of every individual examined. These neurons containing neurosecretion pass through cycles, with identifiable cells active in different parts of a cycle. As yet the significance of these slower activities can only be guessed as hormonal, but they may turn out to control behaviour by acting upon other nerve cells. This is clearly one of the crucial points for an attack upon the control of long-term behaviour.

DISTRIBUTED GANGLIA OF THE OCTOPUS ARM

The organisation of a peripheral sensory synaptic system is well illustrated by the tactile and proprioceptive interneurons of the arm of the octopus [4]. The sensory axons of the sucker run into a superficial plexus with lateral interaction, as in Figure 6.10. First- or second-order units recorded here have small receptive fields on the suckers. The peripheral axons run to the axial ganglia, which are masses of neuropile on the ven-

Figure 6.8

Central suppression of the twitch response by crawling movements in the polychaete worm *Nereis*. The positions of the electrodes are given in the inset. In each record the upper trace shows the lateral giant fibre spikes, monitored at the end of the worm, while the lower trace shows simultaneous action potentials from one point on the longitudinal muscle. In **A** the worm is not crawling and the giant fibre excites the motor axon at each shock, indicated by a spot. In **B** the worm is crawling when the stimulus starts and the giant fibre now fails to excite the motor fibre at every shock. Excitation of the muscle from another source during crawling appears as irregular potentials. Time scale, 1 second.

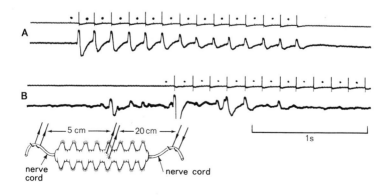

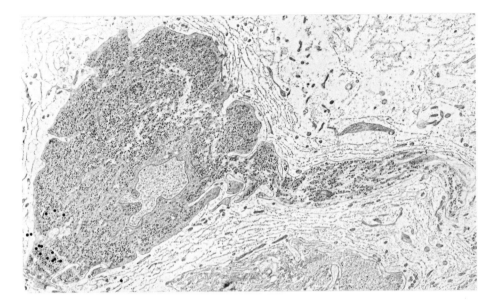

Figure 6.9

A nerve cell from a leech, showing a large number of secreted granules within the cytoplasm of the cell. These granules can be seen in the axon, which runs towards the foot of the picture. The nervous system of the leech contains a number of cells such as the ones shown. They fall into classes with differing appearance of the secretion in each class of cells. The function and the fate of the secretion is not known. Nerve cells filled with secretion are usually not so obvious among other invertebrates as in the leech but they are very widespread, and in general their function has yet to be discovered. [Bern and Hagadorn, in Bullock and Horridge, 1965.]

tral surface of the axial cord of the arm, one axon for each sucker. Here there are units of the following types: (a) the tactile for the ganglion's own sucker, (b) the tactile for adjoining distal suckers of the contralateral row, (c) the proprioceptive of the ganglion's own sucker. In the axial nerve of the arm there is a very detailed, though highly integrated, representation of tactile sensory input but no representation of movements of suckers or of the tip of the arm. Receptive fields of tactile interneurons are of numerous types—the rim of a single sucker, the rim of skin of two adjacent suckers, all suckers distal or central to the recording point, all ipsilateral suckers or all on both rows of the arm. All units are phasic and habituate locally to a repeated stimulus, but then they give a response when stimulated at another unhabituated place. Even though the suckers feel over the object for some time and then push it away, the afferent tactile interneuron that runs along the arm gives a burst of activity only at the first contact or if the object moves, and there is some evidence of some kind of peripheral "memory" of a stimulus pattern. The lack of long-distance postural information agrees with

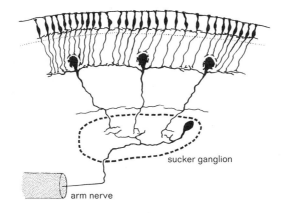

Figure 6.10

Sensory pathways in the sucker of the octopus. Primary sensory neurons in the epithelium converge upon the cell bodies and dendrites of second-order cells, which in turn converge upon monopolar third-order cells in the neuropile of the sucker ganglion, which is outlined by a dotted line. The third-order interneurons have axons that run along the arm. At each level in this system there are connections that suggest lateral interaction within each class of neurons. [Graziadei, 1965.]

the behavioural evidence of the inability of the octopus to make discriminations (by the brain), which would necessarily involve the proprioceptors of the muscles of the arm and suckers, but learning based upon tactile information is very acute. As in all animal groups, we find here a utilization of local sensory excitation at the purely local level, the rejection of much of it for transmission centrally, the abstraction of certain useful general features of the stimulus (such as newness), and an output of numerous units to other ganglia with a wide range of receptive fields (including some very wide ones).

CONCLUSION

The foregoing examples of ganglia with relatively few neurons illustrate the evolution of progressively more classes of neurons. A group of neurons may all look similar to each other, have similar connexions, and react similarly, showing that they have not differentiated away from each other during growth. They may even be still connected by anastomosing pathways. Pathways of excitation through successive stages of interneurons are able to form only insofar as the interneurons are differentiated into classes. If this differentiation has not occurred, we find a class of neurons between which there are indiscriminate connexions. On the motor side, where motoneurons are not differentiated from each other, they send axons indiscriminately to the same muscle (as in the crustacean heart)

Figure 6.11

A. A polychaete worm, *Harmothoë,* photographed from the underside, showing the segmental arrangement of the body and parapodia. Typical sensory neurons (5), with peripheral cell bodies, have axons that run into the central cord, as indicated in ink at the upper side. The motoneurons have central cell bodies and axons that run out to the neuromuscular junctions (*m*). Compare Figure 6.5 [Photograph by M. S. Laverack.]

B. The right eye of the crab *Carcinus* from the front. The eye pivots in all directions about a joint that lies approximately behind the broken line. The lines of facets of the compound eye, shown by white lines across the eye surface, are always held horizontal when the crab is near its normal posture. See also Figure 9.20. [Photograph by M. S. Laverack.]

or to corresponding muscles in different segments (in worms). Motoneurons that run to different muscles are also sharply distinguishable as individuals by other features, even with our limited means of discriminating between them.

REFERENCES FOR CHAPTER 6

1. Bullock, T. H., and Horridge, G. A. 1965. Chapters 14 and 17. (See *loc. cit.*, p. 18.)
2. Ewer, D. W. 1965. Networks and spontaneous activity in echinoderms and platyhelminthes. *Amer. Zoologist* **5**:563–572.
3. Florey, E. 1957. Chemical transmission and adaptation. *J. Gen. Physiol.* **40**:533–545.
4. Fraser Rowell, C. H. 1966. Activity of interneurones in the arm of *Octopus* in response to tactile stimulation. *J. Exp. Biol.* **44**:589–606.
5. Hagiwara, S., and Bullock, T. H. 1957. Intracellular potentials in pacemaker and integrative neurons of the lobster cardiac ganglion. *J. Cell. Comp. Physiol.* **50**:25–47.
6. Horridge, G. A. 1959. Analysis of the rapid response of *Nereis* and *Harmothoë* (Annelida). *Proc. Roy. Soc. London B* **150**:245–262.
7. Horridge, G. A. 1963. Proprioceptors, bristle receptors, efferent sensory impulses, neurofibrils and number of axons in the parapodial nerve of the polychaete *Harmothoë*. *Proc. Roy. Soc. London B* **157**:199–222.
8. Kuffler, S. W., and Eyzaguirre, C. 1955. Synaptic inhibition in an isolated nerve cell. *J. Gen. Physiol.* **39**:155–184.
9. Larimer, J. L. 1964. Sensory-induced modifications of ventilation and heart rate in crayfish. *Comp. Biochem. Physiol.* **12**:25–36.
10. Maynard, D. M. 1961. Cardiac inhibition in decapod Crustacea, in *Nervous Inhibition*, E. Florey (Ed.). Oxford, Pergamon Press.
11. Nicol, J. A. C. 1948. The giant axons of annelids. *Quart. Rev. Biol.* **23**:291–324.
12. Retzius, G. 1892. Das Nervensystem der Lumbricinen. *Biol. Untersuchungen* **3**:1–16.
13. Watanabe, A., and Bullock, T. H. 1960. Modulation of activity of one neuron by subthreshold slow potentials in another in lobster cardiac ganglion. *J. Gen. Physiol.* **43**:1031–1045.
14. Watanabe, A., and Takeda, K. 1963. The spread of excitation among neurons in the heart ganglion of the stomatopod. *J. Gen. Physiol.* **46**:773–801.

7

Arthropod ventral cord

A typical insect or crustacean is provided with a vast flow of sensory information, which arrives continually from all the body surface in the five or six modalities familiar to us. In addition, some arthropods have receptors for stimuli that elude us—those that might furnish the taste of water, the direction of the plane of polarized light, the humidity of the air, the "sight" of ultraviolet light or of movements in the visual field that are too slow for us to notice. The sensory neurons make connections with interneurons in a variety of patterns (Fig. 7.1), and many of these interneurons respond well to sensory stimulation. At first sight it is surprising how little of this activity appears in overt behaviour, and we are led to the conclusion that the interneurons are a stage in a filtering process that lets through only certain significant combinations of sensory excitation. Certainly arthropod interneurons reveal how every separate and identifiable neuron has its own peculiar constant receptive field, and the main features of interneurons are demonstrable in their simplest known form in these animals.

SENSORY NEURONS

Records from the sensory nerves of arthropods reveal that every joint and hair is innervated, usually by peripheral bipolar sensory neurons that have a wide range of thresholds, adaptation rates, and preferred directionality (Table 1). Receptive fields are almost always small and often restricted to a single hair or a part of the range of movement of a joint. Receptors with a maintained discharge for a maintained stimulus are much less common than ones that adapt.

Hairs have become specialized as touch receptors of all kinds, and they are ubiquitously distributed, singly or in lines, patches, tufts, and so forth. Specialized hairs at joints, often in insects in dense little groups called

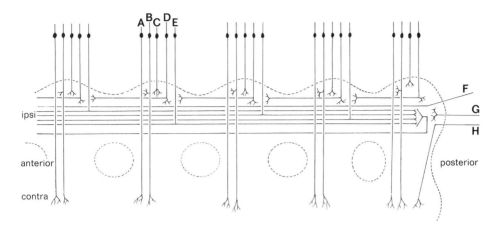

Figure 7.1

Types of distribution of the terminals of sensory axons of a typical primitive arthropod.

A. Axon to opposite side connecting with contralateral interneurons.

B. Axon with terminals in ipsilateral and contralateral ganglia.

C. Axon with terminals only ipsilateral.

D. Axon with ipsilateral terminals in its own ganglion and a branch running forward to the next anterior ganglion.

E. Axon dividing where it enters the nerve cord with one branch running to the posterior ganglion, there to be integrated with all other axons of the same type. This pattern is known for the terminals of the muscle receptor organs; see Figures 6.1 and 8.2.

F. Some sensory axons from the tail region pass apparently without synapses right up to the brain. They are presumably concerned with steering the animal when it is swimming backwards by repeated bending of the tail.

G. Some sensory axons from the tail region end in the last abdominal ganglion, either ipsilaterally as in **G** or contralaterally as in **H**.

The existence of all these types can be inferred from physiological recordings from interneurons. They have also been seen in histological preparations stained with methylene blue, which reveals the course of the ramifications of a single fibre. Most of the sensory terminations seem to be derived from the types shown here, but their numbers and properties must vary enormously between the different arthropods.

hair plates, are arranged so that they signal accurately the extent of joint movement. Even if the individual hairs adapt, a small vibration in any part of the range, as for all joint receptors, can ensure that an absolute measure of position is available centrally. This illustrates a general feature of groups of similar sensory cells and other neurons, called range fractionation.

Hair-peg organs of crustaceans are small bushy flaps, each lying in a pit and innervated by bipolar neurons that are excited when water currents deflect the flap. They are found on the legs, and especially on the

TABLE 1
Mechanoreceptors of decapod crustaceans

Mechanoreceptors: crab, crayfish, lobster

Cuticular
1. Most hairs individually innervated
2. Touch or pressure on many critical surfaces (e.g., claw edge)
3. Most flexible (joint membranes heavily innervated)
4. Underwater movement receptors (hair-peg organs)

Subcuticular
1. Multicellular ligament organs across joints, different units sensitive to
   (a) movement
   (b) position
   (c) vibration
2. Muscular sense organs at base of legs, central cell bodies
3. Muscle receptor organs between joints of dorsal abdomen

Statocyst receptors: lobster [Cohen, 1960]

1. 400 units (hairs) each excited by the weight of one common statolith, but each maximally excited only at one orientation of the animal with respect to the vertical. As a consequence, the units can be classified as forward, sideways, titling, etc.
2. 70 slender hairs excited by swirling of the fluid in the cavity in a common direction for all.

---

chela and carapace of crabs and lobsters. Anatomically distinct from them are the hair-fan organs; these are a fan of fine hairs that are directionally sensitive to minute rapid movements caused by pressure waves in the water and are therefore excellent receptors for any object that causes a disturbance from a distance. Besides the chemoreceptors on the mouth parts, there are numerous others buried in the cuticle at the tips of the legs, at least in higher crustaceans, but the olfactory (low-threshold chemosense) receptors are thought to be restricted to the enormous number of aesthetasc hairs of the antennule.

Joint receptor organs (proprioceptors) are noted, together with some of the reflexes with which they are associated (p. 130). Photoreceptors and their role in the integration of visual stimuli are also mentioned (p. 145). The above receptors are those which have been taken into account in the descriptions of the interneurons which follow. So far as other senses, some of which may be unknown at present, may contribute, all the descriptions are subject to revision.

INTEGRATION BY INTERNEURONS IN ARTHROPODS

The American crayfish *Procambarus* has been analysed in detail and can be accepted as representative of decapod Crustacea. Probably all arthropod and some of the annelid interneurons are closely comparable. Although only the larger fibres have been isolated, so many of them have been described that there is now a reasonable indication of the types and proportions that are present. The majority of the central interneurons seem to be unique in some feature such as receptive field or adaptation rate. Perhaps the only way to realise the range and complexity of their possible interactions is to study the lists of characterized interneurons of the crayfish (pp. 112 and 119). This immense task of analysis represents 10 years of work on one animal by Professor Wiersma and his associates (Table 2).

In general, interneurons of the abdomen are "simpler" (in that it takes less analysis to discover their properties) than those between thorax and brain. If detailed information is necessary at the front end, as from the unit that signals the spread of the tail fan on either side, it has its own private line to the brain. Apart from these exceptions, the integration of the "simpler" abdominal interneurons leads to a population of more "complex" thoracic interneurons, which run in the thoracic region and up to the brain.

We find that most of the abdominal units run for the whole length of the abdomen and are restricted to it. About 10 ipsilateral and 4 contralateral abdominal interneurons on each side, for example, respond to sensory fibres from hairs of the dorsal areas of only a single abdominal segment; 5 units, 4 of them ipsilateral, are stimulated from dorsal hairs of 2 abdominal segments. One contralateral and 5 ipsilateral units have inputs from dorsal hairs of 3 or more segments, and 2 similar ones have bilateral receptive fields. There are 4 units referring to ipsilateral uropod hairs and 1 contralateral one; corresponding to these, in each oesophageal connective there are 2 ipsilateral ones and 1 with a bilateral receptive field. Fewer interneurons have been found to refer to ventral areas of the abdomen. This is in keeping with the fact that only the dorsal hairs are effective distance receptors, whereas ventral hairs presumably operate mainly in local segmental reflexes.

The central representation of leg posture and movement is less extensive than might be expected; much of this information does not reach the long interganglionic fibres, and must therefore be handled locally in its own or the neighbouring segment. Proprioceptive fibres of the telson and uropod joints, however, have been traced all the way up the cord to the brain—appropriate if they have a function in steering during swimming. Several of them refer to the ipsilateral uropod joint and at least one is a primary sensory fibre, but these exceptions within the general framework have a special functional explanation. A few local abdominal interneurons have inputs from hairs of the pleural plate and also from proprioceptors of the swimmerets of individual segments. No intersegmental representation has been found that distinguishes between the various joints of the swimmerets, but the primary proprioceptive fibres of individual joints ascend about two segments from each ganglion and descend

TABLE 2

Fibres (mainly interneurons) between the 3rd and 4th abdominal ganglion of the crayfish

The location of the sensory fields to which the fibre responds is given after the number, followed by the type of stimulation to which it responds. Next is indicated whether the response is obtained from the same side of the animal as the prepared connective (Hom.), from the other side (Het.), from both sides (Bil.), or that the response is asymmetrical (As.). L. refers to location in cross section as presented in Figure 1. Id. C. indicates that the fibre is identical in reaction to the fibre with that number in Table 3.

Abbreviations used in table

App., appendages	Dors., dorsal
Abd., abdominal	Vent., ventral
Seg., segment	Prim., bundle of primary sensory fibres
SR_1, tonic stretch receptor	Med., medial location of the interneuron in the
SR_2, phasic stretch receptor	cord
Sw., swimmeret	Lat., lateral location of the interneuron in the
Tels., telson	cord
Urop., uropod	Pl. pl. I or II, pleural plate hairs innervated by
U. Seg., uropod segment (6th abdominal)	the first or second root

A1.	Abd. Seg. Joint. Tonic. Extension. Hom.? L78	
A2.	SR_1-Ab 5/6 Hom. L78–79	Id. C 100
A3.	Urop., Tels. Hair. Hom. L82	Id. C 19
A4.	SR_1-Ab 4/5. Hom. L78	Id. C 89
A5.	Sw. 2-Urop. Basal Joint. As. L82	Id. C 48
A6.	Urop., Tels. Hair Fringe. Prosser's. Hom. L85	
A7.	Abd. Seg. 4-U. Seg. Hair. Hom. L82	Id. C 91
A8.	SR_1-Ab 6/T. Hom. L78	
A9.	Abd. Seg. 5. Hair. Prim. L84	
A10.	Sw. 1-Urop. Basal Joint. Phasic. Hom. L84	
A11.	Sw., Pl. pl. I. Seg. 1–5 Hair. Bil. L84	
A12.	Abd. Seg. 3–5. Hair. Hom. L83	Id. C 65
A13.	Pl. pl. I. Seg. 2–5. Hair. Hom. L85	Id. C 38
A14.	Abd. Seg. 5. Hair. Med. Hom. L78	
A15.	U. Seg. Hair. Med. Hom. L78	
A16.	Abd. Seg. 3. Hair. Prim. Hom. L83	
A17.	Tels. Hair. Hom. L83	Id. C 15
A18.	Abd. Seg. 4 Hair. Prim. Hom. L84	
A19.	Sw., Pl. pl. I. Seg. 2–5. Hair. As. L80	
A20.	Urop. Joint. Tonic. Hom. L84	
A21.	SR_2-Ab 5/6. Hom. L79	
A22.	Abd. Seg. 4. Hair. Het. L79	
A23.	Abd. Seg. Joint. Phasic. Extension. Hom.? L79	
A24.	Sw. 1-Urop. Joint. Phasic. Bil. L81	
A25.	SR_1-Ab 3/4. Hom. L79	Id. C 93
A26.	Sw. 4,5. Joint. Prim. Hom. L83	
A27.	Sw. 2–5. Basal Joint. Hom. L83	
A28.	Sw., Pl. pl. I. Seg. 2-U. Seg. Hair. Hom. L84	

TABLE 2 (Continued)

A29. Abd. Seg. 2. Hair. Het. L82
A30. Abd. Seg. 3. Hair. Het. L82
A31. Sw. 4. Basal Joint. Tonic. Hom. L81
A32. Urop., U. Seg., Tels. Hair. Hom. L80   Id. C 3
A33. Sw., Pl. pl. I. Seg. 3 Hair. Joints? Hom. L81
A34. Abd. Seg. 2,3. Hair. Het. L84
A35. Sw. 5. Basal Joint. Tonic. Hom. L81
A36. U. Seg. Hair. Quack. Hom. L81
A37. Urop., Tels. Hair. Dors. Vent. Het. L81
A38. Abd. Seg. 3,4. Hair. Hom. L79
A39. Abd. Seg. 4. Hair. Med. Hom. L79
A40. Abd. Seg. 2,3. Hair. Hom. L83
A41. Abd. Seg. 2–5. Hair. Hom. L79   Id. C 71
A42. Abd. Seg. 3. Hair. Med. Hom. L79
A43. Anal Valve. Joint. Hom. L82
A44. Sw. 4. Joint. Prim. Hom. L78
A45. Sw. 5. Joint. Prim. Hom. L78
A46. Abd. Seg. 1–U. Seg. Hair. Dors. Vent. Hom. L83
A47. Sw. 3. Joint. Prim. Hom. L83
A48. Sw. 3. Basal Joint. Prim. Tonic. Hom. L76
A49. Abd. Seg. 5. Hair. Lat. Hom. L80
A50. Abd. Seg. 4. Hair. Lat. Hom. L80
A51. Pl. pl. I. Seg. 3. Hair. Hom. L84
A52. Abd. Seg. 2–5, U. Seg.? Hair. Dors. Vent. Bil. L78
A53. SR_1-Ab ⅔. Hom. L78   Id. C 51
A54. Abd. Seg. 2–5, U. Seg.? Hair. Het. L78
A55. Sw., Pl. pl. I. Seg. 2,3. Hair. Hom. L84
A56. U. Seg. Hair. Lat. Hom. L80
A57. Abd. Seg. 5, U. Seg. Hair. Hom. L80
A58. Abd. Seg. 4,5. Hair. Hom. L85
A59. Urop., Tels. Hair. Vent. Hom. L77
A60. U. Seg.-5th, Joint. Tonic. Extension. Hom.? L81
A61. SR_1. All Seg. Joint. Tonic. Hom. L77
A62. Abd. Seg. 3. Hair. Lat. Hom. L85
A63. Abd. Seg. 2–4. Hair. Hom. L84   Id. C 45
A64. Abd. Seg. 2-U. Seg., Tels.? Hair. Bil. L84
A65. Abd. Seg. 5. Hair. Het. L78
A66. Sw., Pl. pl. I. Seg. 3. Hair. Joint. Het. L76
A67. Sw. 3. Hair. Hom. L76
A68. Urop. Basal Joint. Hom. L77
A69. Urop. Basal Joint. Het. L77
A70. Urop. Joint. Bil. L78
A71. Abd. Seg. 3–5. Hair.-Bil. L80
A72. Anal Valve. Joint. Het. L76
A73. Abd. Seg. 4-U. Seg., Urop., Tels. Hair. Hom. L83   Id. C 56
A74. Sw., Pl. pl. I. Seg. 3. Hair. Prim. Hom. L83
A75. Sw., Pl. pl. I. Seg. 5. Hair. Joint. Hom. L84

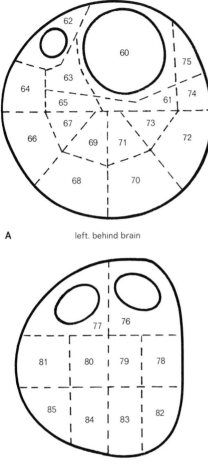

A   left. behind brain

B   right. abdominal segment 3–4

Figure 7.2

The interneurons of the crayfish cord can always be found in their own characteristic location in the transverse section. These diagrams show the key areas in Table 2 (page 112) and Table 3 (page 119) against the name of each interneuron.

A. Areas of the connective behind the brain.

B. Areas of the connective between 3rd and 4th abdominal ganglia.

at least one. Although details of the movements may be modifiable, the swimmeret sequence in the paddling movements is a centrally controlled pattern that emerges whether or not the appendages are actually moving or even still present. Therefore their individual joint receptors are not likely to be significant in the immediate control of the rhythmical movements.

Most of the interneurons of the cord run through several ganglia, and almost all have inputs from sensory fibres in a ganglion through which they pass. When an impulse is initiated, it travels both ways from the ganglion of origin. This may not have vital consequences if there is only one output, but if dendrites act as outputs as well as inputs the possibility of complex circuits with few neurons is greatly increased. Impulses originating simultaneously in different segments collide and eliminate each other. Although unique patterns of spikes are caused by collision, especially at high frequencies, no functional advantage is known. In fact, the fusion of ganglia that occurs in advanced groups of all phyla can be explained as an elimination of a separate impulse-initiating centre in each ganglion and consequently greater opportunities for summation of postsynaptic potentials of different segmental origins in one combined ganglionic mass.

An interesting feature, probably common to all animals with ladder-like cords, is that interneurons that have corresponding receptive fields in more than one segment often have a ladderlike arrangement, as shown in Figure 7.3, E or H. Some fibres with this ladderlike arrangement have a free circulation of impulses anywhere in the ladder, others have synapses between the two sides (Fig. 7.3, K). Experimentally the ladder-like plan is shown by the appearance of impulses at the anterior side of a severed connective when the stimulus is applied ipsilaterally at the posterior side of the cut. Other interneurons have bilateral representation without this free circulation up and down on both sides, implying that the sensory inputs divide to independent interneurons on each side.

Fibres that carry proprioceptive information about single joints of the walking legs have not been found in the connectives ascending to the brain, although there are a number of interneurons conveying to the brain information about the position of the claw and about pressure on its cutting edge. On the other hand, movements of the antennal joints are signaled back to the thoracic segments, perhaps to assist cleaning movements by the legs. A few proprioceptive interneurons of the thorax are multimodal, responding to strong visual stimuli and to hair and joint receptors on the ipsilateral or (in one case) both sides of the head. One notable fibre, ascending to the brain, is excited by extension of the second joint of the ipsilateral walking legs and by retraction of the corresponding joints on the other side, but inhibited by movements of the same joints in the opposite direction. Each muscle receptor organ (MRO) has one ipsilateral branch of its primary fibre ascending to the brain, making two from each segment all along the body. There is one interneuron that integrates all MRO's in the last abdominal ganglion and sends its fibre to the brain with the summed excitation from all.

The paucity of intersegmental proprioceptive traffic in arthropods—compared with a vertebrate that also makes complex coordinations of different joints—can only be explained by reference to the special organization of the ladderlike cord, in which premotor interneurons or "command" fibres cause the segmental ganglia to produce an orderly sequence of motor impulses unless "vetoed" at the local level (see next chapter). For this a detailed projection of proprioceptive data to the higher centres is not necessary. Simple conditioning of leg position, controlled by an isolated ventral ganglion in an insect, does not depend on proprioceptive feedback (see p. 343).

By taking the sums and differences of excitation in ascending units of different but overlapping wide receptive fields, the brain can feasibly refer a stimulus to an area smaller than any of the receptive fields taken singly. There is, however, no evidence that this occurs as a regular feature; moreover, there is no evidence that the brain is that important or interested. When one considers all the complex movements whereby the leg of one segment can clean parts of other segments, it is evident that the ganglion of the active leg always has adequate tactile information from the area that it cleans; orders are not necessarily given from the brain at all, and certainly detailed movements are not controlled by the brain, which can be removed with little effect on many arthropod responses.

The longitudinal connective between the brain and the anterior ventral ganglion contains interneurons that are more diverse and sophisticated than those in the abdominal cord. There are only a few ascending primary sensory fibres—notably one from each of the muscle receptor organs of the abdomen and a few from sensory pits of the carapace—a primary descending fibre from five hairs on the second joint of the ipsilateral antenna, and possibly a descending one from the ipsilateral cornea. A few large descending interneurons are excited by stimuli that influence the

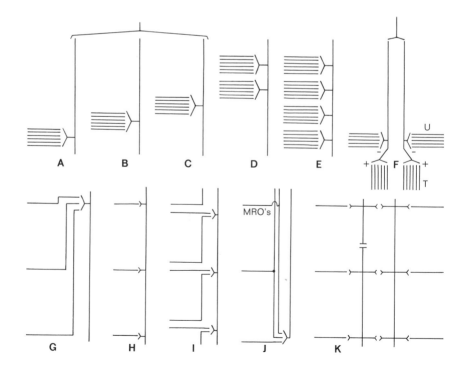

statocysts; presumably these are responsible for the compensatory postures of the legs. Numerous descending interneurons respond to particular patterns of hairs on the eyestalks, anterior carapace, antennae, and antennules. Judging from the behaviour of crabs and lobsters, some of these provide the longitudinal pathways by which the eye socket and head appendages are cleaned with the tips of several of the legs. As for the ascending thoracic interneurons responding to touch, these interneurons have a wide diversity of peripheral fields; some are quite local and perhaps subserve some specific reflex; others are larger and have a

Figure 7.3

Patterns of connexions between sensory axons and longitudinal interneurons of the ventral cord of the crayfish. Patterns such as these are probably typical of all arthropods, although the numbers and exact features must differ widely throughout that large group.

A, B, and C. Connexions of the sensory axons from groups of dorsal abdominal hairs to ipsilateral interneurons, which have inputs from sensory axons in only one segment. The input to the interneuron is in a different segment in each case.

D, and E. Dorsal abdominal hairs from several segments feed into ipsilateral abdominal interneurons.

F. A group of hairs on the uropods (inhibitory) and another group on the telson (excitatory) feed into an abdominal interneuron, and the two interneurons on the two sides together excite a bilaterally symmetrical pair of interneurons in the thorax.

G. Sensory axons within the abdominal cord form a common synapse with an interneuron an anterior segment. This allows summation upon the dendrites of the interneuron.

H. Sensory axons feed into a common interneuron, each in their own segment. This does not allow summation between postsynaptic potentials of the sensory impulses. In such a system impulses initiated in different ganglia are able to cancel each other where they accidentally meet.

I. Sensory axons feed into an interneuron in their own segment but other sensory axons from hair sensilla nearby run forward in the cord and make synapses that can sum with those of the other type. This special pattern causes the interneuron to be more readily excited by a pattern of stimulation that moves forward rather than backward along the animal.

J. The pattern of integration of the central terminations of the sensory axons of the muscle receptor organs. These axons divide where they enter the abdominal cord and the anterior branch from each runs directly to the brain. The posterior branch of each runs to the last abdominal ganglion, where they are summed all together by a single interneuron on each side.

K. Sensory axons that feed into a pair of interneurons having lateral connexions in each segment. This gives rise to a ladderlike arrangement in which an impulse initiated in one segment can run up and down the cord on its own side, and in cross connexions in every segment cross over to the corresponding interneuron on the other side. One result is that when a cut is made, as shown, across the longitudinal connective, it is possible to record impulses that originate in a distant segment when they arrive at both of the cut ends, because they have circulated around the closed loops of the ladder. Such patterns as this are relatively common among the abdominal interneurons of the crayfish. Where elongated segmental animals have evolved to shortened forms with condensed ganglia, this pattern of ladderlike interneurons has been replaced by one in which normal summation of postsynaptic potentials of sensory axons is possible.

variety of overlap with each other and with more local ones. Indeed, one fibre ascending to the brain has a receptive field covering the whole of the surface of the body on both sides; it is difficult to guess what could be its function, apart from a general arousal or reinforcement.

Of the descending interneurons from the crayfish brain to the ventral cord, more than 65 have been characterized: most are high-order ipsi-lateral interneurons responding to touch on the head or body or to visual stimuli. Types are listed in Table 3; notably there are only three bundles of primary mechanoreceptor fibres from the base and flagellum of the antenna and from the carapace edge. Because they are resistant to anoxia, about two-thirds of the interneurons, all having simple receptive fields, are thought to be first order; most but not all complex or multimodal ones are second or higher order, and the latter tend to have bilateral receptive fields. Movement of the basal joints of the head appendages is well represented. One fibre was found with a selectively directional input to visual stimuli, and definite optomotor responses of the legs of crayfish are known. A small selection of curious fibres respond to strong visual stimuli as well as to movements of joints of appendages along the whole length of the animal, some of them bilaterally. Of two ladderlike units (Fig. 7.3, K), one has a receptive field covering the whole body surface, the other covering the ipsilateral half. One interneuron has only descend-ing impulses from the brain in response to touch or movement anywhere on the body or appendages. Another unit (numbered C34), responds at the anterior side of a cut, to movement of basal joints of all appendages except eyestalks, but at the posterior side of the cut it responds to all basal joints except ipsilateral head appendages; an explanatory set of pathways is shown in Figure 7.4. Only two of the freely circulating ladderlike interneurons can be picked up just behind the brain, whereas such fibres make up 20% of the population at the thoracic-abdominal junction.

Numerous interneurons have a more or less constant background dis-charge, which cannot be modified by external stimulation; many of the impulses originate in the last abdominal ganglion. The only clue as to their function is that when a ganglion is progressively isolated from its neighbours, or when the ganglionic chain is progressively shortened, there is a change in the threshold of local reflexes or frequency of pace-makers. The inference is that each ganglion in the chain has a tonic, rather general action on the others; the only known continuous activity in the connectives is from the unmodifiable interneurons. It would be of interest to know whether the same identified fibre has different fre-quencies at different times according to the state of the ganglion in which its impulses are initiated. If so we could infer, rather than guess, that each ganglion keeps other parts of the nerve cord informed of some as-pects of its own long-term activity.

A detailed study of exactly where impulses are initiated in some of

TABLE 3

Fibres of the circumoesophageal connective of the Crayfish

The location of the sensory fields to which the fibre responds is given after the number, followed by the type of stimulation to which it responds. Next is indicated whether the response is obtained from the same side of the animal as the prepared connective (Hom.), from the other side (Het.), from both sides (Bil.), or that the response is asymmetrical (As.). L. refers to location in cross section as presented in Figure 7.2. ** in front of the number denotes that this is a "marker" fibre; * denotes that fibre was found many times; ± means that the features of the fibre are not known in detail. Id. indicates identity with a fibre found elsewhere.

---

1. Ascending interneurons and MRO fibres to the brain

**C1.	Mxpd. Joint. Hom. L70
**C2.	Claw. Distal Seg. Hair. Hom. L68
C3.	Urop., U-Seg., Tels. Hair. Hom. L73
*C5.	RM1 Abd. Seg. 1. L61
C7.	Mxpd-Urop. Basal Joint. Tonic. Hom. L72
C8.	Mthprts. Joint. Bil. L64
C12.	Th. L. 4-Urop. Basal Joint. Het. L64
C15.	Tels. Hair. Bil. L71
C16.	Sherrington's Joint. Tonic. As. L60
C17.	Th. L. 2-Th. L. 5 Hair. Hom. L67
**C18.	Claw-Th. L. 5 Hair. Hom. L67
*C19.	Urop., Tels. Hair. Hom. L67
C20.	Mthprts-Th. L. 5 Basal Joint. Bil. L67
C22.	Mthprts-mxpd. Joint. Hom. L66
C25.	Claw. Basal Joint. Bil. L66
C26.	Claw-Th. L. 3 Joint. Hom. L68
C27.	Claw-Th. L. 5 Basal Joint. Hom. L67
*C28.	Th. L. 2 Distal Seg. Hair. Hom. L68
*C29.	Th. L. 3 Distal Seg. Hair. Hom. L68
**C30.	Mxpd. Th. L. 4 Basal Joint. Hom. L70
±C31.	Mthprts. Joint. Hom. L70
±C33.	Carap, Abd. Seg. 1–5. Hair. Bil. L.
C34.	Antnl-Urop. Basal Joint. Bil L72.
C35.	Abd. Seg. 1. Hair. Hom. L68
C36.	Abd. Seg. 1-Tels. Joint. L63
C38.	Abd. Seg. 2–4. Pleural plates. Hair. Hom. L73
C40.	Abd. App., 1-Urop. Joint. As L68
C42.	Claw. 2nd Joint. Hom. L69.
C43.	Th. L. 2, Th. L. 3. 2nd Joint. Hom. L69
C45.	Abd. Seg. 2–4. Hair. Hom. L70
C46.	Mthpts-Urop. Joint. Bil. L62
C48.	Mthpts.-Urop. Basal Joint. As L70
C50.	Claw. Extensor Joint. Tonic. Hom. L69
*C51.	RM1 Abd. Seg. 3 L61
±C52.	Swimmeret. Abd. Seg. 2. Hair. Het. L61
C53.	Abd. Seg. 4–5. Extension. Hair. Hom. L61.
C54.	Urop. Joint. Hom. L67
C55.	Th. L. 4. Hair & Joint. Hom. L70
C56.	Abd. Seg. 4-Tels. Hair. Hom. L67
C57.	Mxpd.-Urop. Basal. Hair. Hom. L68
C58.	Th. L. 2–4. Mero-carpo Joint. Hom. L70

TABLE 3 (Continued)

Fibres of the circumoesophageal connective of the Crayfish

C59.	Claw-Th. L. 5. 2nd Joint. Tonic Bil. L66
C60.	Claw.-Th. L. 3. Hair. As. L69.
C61.	Claw. Mero-carpo. Joint. Hom. L68
C62.	Claw. Pro-dactyl. Joint. Hom. L70
C63.	Carap. Hair. Het. L68
C64.	Mxpd.-Urop., Dorsal Abd. Seg. 1-Tels. Hair. Hom. L68
C65.	Abd. Seg. 3–5. Hair. Hom. L71
C69.	Claw. 2nd Joint. Hom. L72
*C70.	RM1. Abd. Seg. 2. L61
C71.	Abd. Seg. 1–5. Hair. Hom. L72
±C72.	Mxpd.-Th. L. 5. Carap. Hair. Hom. L69
C73.	Body App. Hair. Bil. L69
*C75.	Th. L. 4. Distal Seg. Hair. Hom. L68
C76.	Claw-Urop. Basal Hair. Bil. L69
C77.	Th. L. 2-Urop. Basal Hair. Bil. L70
C79.	Claw-Th. L. 5. Mero-carpo Joint. Hom L66
C80.	Mxpd.-Th. L. 5. Hair. Hom. L68
C81.	Mxpd.-Th. L. 3. Hair. Bil. L66
C82.	Mxpd.-Th. L. 5. 2nd Joint. Tonic. Hom. L69
C89.	RM1. Abd. Seg. 5. L61–63.
C90.	Carap. Hair. Hom. L73
C91.	Abd.-Seg. 4-U. Seg. Hair. Hom. L72
C93.	RM1. Abd. Seg. 4. L61
C94.	Mxpd. Joint. Tonic. Bil. L66
C95.	Mxpd.-Urop. Basal Joint. Het. L65
C97.	Body Hair. Bil. L62
C98.	Body Hair. Het. L72
C100.	RM1. U. Seg. L63

2. Interneurons reacting to visual stimuli, either exclusively
   or in addition to other stimulus modalities

Light only

C114	L66	Bil. esp. med. and fast movement
C135	L72	Bil. esp. med. and fast movement
C136	L74	Bil. spont. inc. with illum.

Light and other modalities

C24	L65	Het. on/off. Eye and around Hair and Joint
C137	L74	Het. on? all appendages. Joint activity
C99	L75	Bil. esp. slow movement. Head and head apps. Hair and Joint Defense reflex fibre.
C120	L66	Bil. med./fast movement. Whole an. Hair (Joint?)
C125	L66	Bil. esp. on (V. slow movement?). Whole an. Hair and Joint Activity. All in a.l.
C128	L62	Bil. esp. med. movement Whole an. Hair and Joint Activity All in a.l.

3. Interneurons responding exclusively to head stimulation (excluding visual stimuli)

Eyes only

C78	L73	Hom. cornea. Hair
C109	L68	Hom. eyestalk. Joint phasic
C139	L74	Het. eye reflex. Joint

TABLE 3 (Continued)

Antennules only

C14	L71		Hom. flags., esp. outer Hair
C92	L66		Hom. flags., esp. inner Hair
C133	L72		Hom. outer flag. Joint phasic
C84	L62	(B119)	Hom. statocyst phasic
C87	L70	(B132)	Hom. statocyst phasic
C4	L75	(B138)	Het. statocyst phasic

Antennae only

C21	L70	Hom. flag. Hair
C86	L64	Hom. all parts Hair tonic. Inhib. by other head parts
C66	L71	Hom. basal segs. Hair
C83	L66	Hom. basal segs. Hair Inhib. by other head parts
C6	L70	Hom. gr. gl. Hair phasic
C122	L66	Hom. gr. gl. rather tonic
C140	L74	Het. gr. gl. (green gland area)
C104	L61	Bil. gr. gl.
C107	L70	Hom. flag. Joint phasic
C121	L65	Hom. flag. Joint phasic
C44	L64	Hom. flag. Joint backward tonic
C88	L66	Hom. basal and sq. Joint tonic
C23	L64	Hom. sq. Joint extens. tonic

Antennules and antennae

C9	L71	Hom. flags. Hair
C41	L74	Het. flags. Hair (and Joint?)
C111	L61	Bil. flags. Hair
C39	L68	Hom. flags. Joint phasic
C47	L71	Hom. flags. Joint inwards. phasic
C96	L69	Hom. flags. Joint inwards. tonic
C132	L68	Het. flags. Joint backwards phasic
C110	L66	Bil. flags. Joint phasic
C118	L74	Bil. flags. Joint tonic
C141	L70	Hom. basal (incl. sq.) Joint phasic
C116	L72	Hom. basal Joint backwards and downwards tonic

All head appendages

C126	L68	(B148)	Hom. all Joint phasic
C32	L70	(B149)	Hom. basal Joint backwards phasic
C127	L66		Hom. basal (incl. sq.) Joint tonic
C105	L64	(B135)	Het. all Hair and Joint activity
C103	L70		Bil. all Joint phasic
C112	L64	(B181)	Bil. basal Joint phasic

Head (excluding appendages)

C101	L72	Hom. top of A.C., rostrum and ridge. Hair
C113	L70	Hom. top and side of A.C. and ridge. Hair
C85	L66	Hom. whole Head. Hair
C37	L64	Hom. ridge. Hair
C106	L69	Hom. anterior tip of ridge. Hair
C67	L64	Het. side of A.C., ridge and rostrum. Hair
C117	L74	Bil. whole head. Hair

TABLE 3 (Continued)
Fibres of the circumoesophageal connective of the Crayfish

Head and head appendages

C74	L68		Hom. eye and around. Hair
C10	L61		Hom. flags., around eye. Hair
C123	L70		Hom. whole head incl. appendages. Hair
C131	L68		Bil. whole head incl. appendages. Hair

4. Interneurons reacting to stimuli on the body (thorax and abdomen) either alone or together with the head

Whole animal

C49	L66		Hom. everywhere Hair
C102	L72		Bil. everywhere. Hair Activity? All in a.l.
C124	L66	(B159)	Bil. everywhere (esp. apps.). Hair and Joint activity. All in a.l.

All appendages

| C34 | L72 | (B156) | Bil. all apps. except eyes basal Joint phasic |
| C108 | L66 | (B143) | Bil. all apps. Joint (basal) and Hair activity. All in a.l. |

Body appendages

C134	L70		Het. claw-th. L. 5 (mxpd?) Joint esp. mero-carpo. flex. All in a.l.
C130	L66	(B129)	Bil. mthpts-Urop. basal Joint All in a.l.
C129	L66		Bil. mthpts-Urop. Joint (esp.) and Hair activity. Inhib. by head stim. All in a.l.

Body and body appendages

| C119 | L72 | | Bil. everywhere. Hair Activity? phasic. All in a.l. |
| C138 | L74 | | Het. everywhere (Telson?). Hair and Joint activity. All in a.l. |

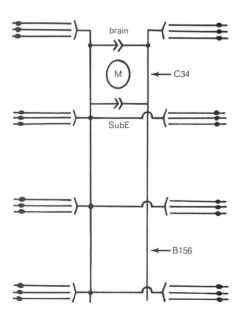

Figure 7.4

A particular pattern of connexions between mechanoreceptor hairs and a pair of interneurons of the crayfish. The sensory axons from the right and left sides make connexions with the left interneuron in the thoracic region. The interneuron on the left has a connexion with the interneuron on the right in the brain and again in the subeosophageal ganglion. It is only in the head that sensory axons feed directly into the interneuron on the right side. Such complex patterns as this are difficult to elucidate and their function is not known, but it is quite likely that such patterns are in fact quite common.

those abdominal interneurons that have sensory inputs of the same kind in more than one segment reveals the location of the synaptic terminals of the sensory fibres. Two possible modes of connexion have been found; either the primary fibres synapse with the interneuron in their ganglion of entry, or sensory fibres of different segments pass up or down the cord and connect elsewhere. Examples of these extremes occur (Fig. 7.3, H and J), but the commonest examples (Fig. 7.3, I) combine both situations. In these, some sensory fibres make synapses in the ganglion of their own segment, and others turn anteriorly (less commonly posteriorly as well). The anteriorly directed pathway is nearly as effective and populous as the intrasegmental one. The system is such that when a sensory volley is adequate to excite the interneuron intrasegmentally, the synaptic potential (which appears somewhat later in the more anterior ganglion) adds impulses to the bursts ascending the interneuron [4, 5]. For a stimulus that is below threshold at both segments, there is summation of postsynaptic potentials when the stimulus is moved *forwards* along the animal at a suitable rate, irrespective of its exact nature. The velocity of the stimulus on the examples known has to be about $1^m/_s$ for the mechanism to be effective, suggesting a directional reception of vibrations through the water, although this has not been tested. Whatever the function, the interneuron certainly discriminates in favour of stimuli that move across segmental boundaries with preference to a particular direction or velocity of movement. For this to happen there has to be a slowly evolved match between the geometry of the external stimulus pattern and the internal geometry of the synapses on dendrites, which in turn must have regularities in their spatial form. Whether or not this particular mechanism in the crayfish abdomen has a functional significance in the life of the animal (and presumably it must have *some* influence in an evolutionary sense), at least it illustrates how a linear arrangement of widely spaced synapses can be the instrument of a pattern discrimination of a special kind. On second thoughts, it is apparent that any regularity in the pattern of dendrites cannot help but be instrumental in selecting certain patterns of excitation. When tested, all interneurons in all nervous systems may reveal summations with a sophisticated dependence on the extended geometry of their dendrites. So far in invertebrates, however—even in the optic lobes where dendrites are wonderfully patterned in space—we cannot as yet illustrate a single real mechanism that is a consequence of a complex dendritic pattern.

Arthropod neurons are fundamentally constant in position in the central connectives and in properties from animal to animal. The sensory neurons have peripheral cell bodies, and when appendages regenerate the sensory fibres must at some stage grow in to the central nervous system and there establish appropriate contacts. Different and additional sensory fibres, in fact, are added at every moult; the compound eye, for example, adds facets at its edges. Developmental analysis reveals that the cuticular structures, in insects at least, can grow in their characteristic patterned perfection largely independently of the organs within; the sense organs of butterflies, for example, develop in the absence of the appropriate central ganglia. So the determination, in a developmental sense, which can be inferred from the consistency of the receptive fields of the adult interneurons, originates in the differentiation of the peripheral cell bodies. When they arrive at the central cord the sensory axons must be recognized by their "local accents," although we have no idea as to how these are expressed. The establishment of connexions with particular sets and subsets of interneurons implies that the interneurons are either predestined by their own differentiation to accept only certain subsets and

Figure 7.5

Discrimination and combination of receptive fields, illustrated by some interneurons that respond to stimulation of mechanoreceptors on the abdomen of the crayfish. The numbers refer to particular interneurons of Table 2 (p. 112) and the lines indicate the receptive fields on dorsal or ventral segments. In the diagram at top left the interneurons refer to discrete areas on single segments; other interneurons refer to two or more of the same areas. Ipsilateral fibres have numbers on the left of each figure and contralateral fibres on the right, except for **27** at bottom right. [Wiersma and Hughes, 1961.]

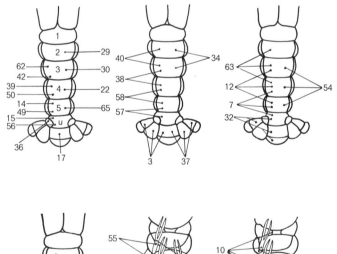

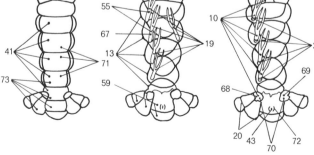

sets of sensory fibres, or perhaps as an alternative, that the differences between interneurons in the first place came about partly as a result of the settlement of primary sensory fibres on them. Implied in this last sentence is this question: Would a developing interneuron form synaptic connexions with an incorrect set of sensory fibres, if caught early enough, and would it thereafter and as a consequence tend to make other synaptic connections related to the abnormal set? The constancy shows that the whole system, down to every cell, is predetermined directly or indirectly from the earliest stage, without plasticity or possibility of subsequent modification. The pattern of interneuron receptive fields must be a result of the previous existence of overlapping and interrelated subclasses, classes, and superclasses of fibres—some of which would and some of which would not connect together during growth (see Fig. 7.5). For a reasonably simple nervous system there is probably enough genetic information that every neuron may be specified in much detail. The point, however, is that some neurons do grow first, and we have no idea of the extent to which they determine the connexions of others which develop subsequently.

GENERAL FEATURES OF INTERNEURONS IN LADDERLIKE CORDS

1. Interneurons are constant in function and position in the transverse section of the longitudinal bundles; fibres of one kind do not all occur together in tracts comparable to those of vertebrates. As for the axial interneurons of vertebrates, they have a specific definable receptive field, which usually overlaps with that of other units. For each tactile field in a crayfish there are about 20 interneurons.
2. At lower levels in the cord the units have simpler receptive fields, but at higher levels towards the brain there are more units of mixed modality, complex input, or large field, which behave as if they are excited by lower interneurons.
3. Interneurons that respond to several sensory neurons of like kind in one area are more abundant than those that respond to widely different sensory inputs.
4. Fibres that run through many segments cannot be defined as ascending or descending, for many of them have sensory inputs and impulse-initiating regions in several ganglia and impulse traffic both ways.
5. Even in the best-known example, the crayfish, only about 10% of the countable fibres have been identified, but many of the other 90% are primary sensory fibres turning up or down for a short distance.
6. Unlike the situation in vertebrates, ladderlike nerve cords contain ladderlike units from which it is possible to record impulses at the anterior stump of a section through one connective of the cord, from sensory stimuli that are all posterior to the cut (Fig. 7.3).

7. Even in the crayfish, a relatively highly organized invertebrate, central occlusion, inhibitory surrounds, and exclusion-type interactions are as yet uncommon, and certainly not as clear as in the comparable vertebrate interneurons.
8. Most of the variety of interneuron receptive fields cannot be sensibly explained in functional terms. There is too much summation and not enough discrimination for a reasonable agreement with known behaviour. Every stimulus excites a number of interesting interneurons but seems to have no other effect. Therefore we must infer that interneuron activity with a behavioural output is caused only by rather special stimulus combinations, which must act for relatively long periods of time upon ganglia that are in an appropriate state to be aroused to an adaptive response.

REFERENCES FOR CHAPTER 7

1. Hughes, G. M. 1965. Neuronal pathways in the insect central nervous system, in *The Physiology of the Insect Central Nervous System,* J. W. L. Beament and J. Treherne (Eds.). Oxford, Pergamon Press.
2. Hughes, G. M., and Wiersma, C. A. G. 1960. Neuronal pathways and synaptic connexions in the abdominal cord of the crayfish. *J. Exp. Biol.* **37:**291–307.
3. Kennedy, D., and Mellon, De. F. 1963. The organization of input to complex crayfish interneurons. *Amer. Zoologist* **3:**514–515.
4. Kennedy, D. and Mellon, De. F. 1964. Receptive field organization and response patterns in neurons with spatially distributed input, in *Neural Theory and Modeling,* R. F. Reiss (Ed.). Stanford University Press.
5. Kennedy, D., and Mellon, De. F. 1964. Synaptic activation and receptive fields in crayfish interneurons. *Comp. Biochem. Physiol.* **13:**275–300.
6. Kennedy, D., and Preston, J. B. 1960. Activity patterns of interneurons in the caudal ganglion of the crayfish. *J. Gen. Physiol.* **43:**655–670.
7. Laverack, M. S. 1962–1963. Responses of cuticular sense organs of the Lobster, *Homarus vulgaris* (Crustacea). *Comp. Biochem. Physiol.* **5:**319–325; **6:**137–145; **10:**261–272.
8. Wiersma, C. A. G. 1958. On the functional connections of single units in the central nervous system of the crayfish, *Procambarus clarkii* (Girard). *J. Comp. Neur.* **110:**421–471.
9. Wiersma, C. A. G., and Bush, B. M. H. 1963. Functional neuronal connections between the thoracic and abdominal cords of the crayfish, *Procambarus clarkii* (Girard). *J. Comp. Neur.* **121:**207–235.
10. Wiersma, C. A. G., and Hughes, G. M. 1961. On the functional anatomy of neuronal units in the abdominal cord of the crayfish, *Procambarus clarkii* (Girard). *J. Comp. Neur.* **116:**209–228.
11. Wiersma, C. A. G., and Mill, P. J. 1965. "Descending" neuronal units in the commissure of the crayfish central nervous system; and their integration of visual, tactile and proprioceptive stimuli. *J. Comp. Neur.* **125:**67–94.

8

Control of movement in arthropods

JOINT RECEPTORS

During the past decade the general pattern of receptors at joints of the larger decapod Crustacea has become clear: all important joints, except the eye cup (see p. 141), have internal specialized movement and position receptors upon ligaments.

There are various types of joint receptors. At each joint of the walking legs and claws there is a multicellular sense organ of many bipolar neurons, attached to an extensible elastic strand that spans the joint (Fig. 8.1). One of these sense organs is at the joint between the coxa (basal segment) and the endophragmal skeleton within the thorax, and there are two organs at the joint between carpopodite and propodite (5th and 6th segments from the base). In association with a receptor muscle there is another organ of this type—the myochordotonal organ—at the joint between carpopodite and meropodite (5th and 4th segments). There are examples of a different type across the coxal-thoracic articulation— muscular receptors—in which a specialized muscle bears arborizations, which are presumed to be of sensory neurons with central cell bodies. In addition to the multicellular organ at the coxopodite-basipodite joint (1st and 2nd segments) there is a pair of elastic strands, which are also innervated by fibres without peripheral cell bodies. For a full account, see reference [1], pp. 1012–1019.

The sense organs at the bases of the legs have not been analysed physiologically, but those at the more peripheral joints are known in some detail. The units of each receptor can be classed by the way in which they respond to the position, or change in position, of the joint. Some give different impulse frequencies when the joint is in different positions, others when the joint is moved at different velocities, and others at different accelerations. The classification of receptors is not, however, necessarily or simply based upon our conventional relation between posi-

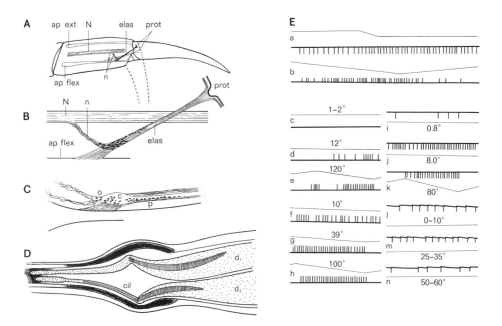

Figure 8.1

A typical multicellular proprioceptive organ of the joint of a crustacean appendage.

A. The terminal joint of the walking leg of a crab, showing the position of the elastic ligament (*elas*), which is attached to the apodeme of the flexor muscle (*ap flex*). The main sensory nerve (*N*) has a branch (*n*) to the multicellular organ.

B. Enlarged view in the extended position.

C. The flexed position, showing also the region of those cells that respond to the opening movement (*o*), closing movement (*c*), and to definite positions (*p*). Every cell has its own characteristic response pattern, which is unique but reasonably constant in different individuals.

D. Drawing from an electron/micrograph showing the terminals of two sensory dendrites (*d*) within a stiff cap (shaded), one dendrite with a modified ciliary segment (*cil*).

E. Responses of different units of the organ in A. The thin line indicates the movement of the joint, up closing and down opening. (*a*) Pure position fibre, whose frequency is dependent on position and not movement. (*b*) Position fibre, which is also sensitive to the direction of movement. (*c–h*) Six different movement fibres with different sensitivity profiles. The numbers show the rate of movement in degrees per second. (*i–k*) Records from one opening movement unit. (*l–n*) A closing fibre at three different angles with a constant stimulus of 1°/sec in each record. [A, and B from Burke, 1954; C and E from Wiersma and Boettiger, 1959; D from Whittear, 1960; for complete references and further details see Bullock and Horridge, 1965.]

tion and time; some, for example, respond best to movement at a particular velocity over only a small segment of the total possible range of movement. Like almost all receptors, the rates of adaptation are diverse. This diversity of responsiveness among units of a receptor organ, which is called range fractionation, has the effect of increasing the accuracy and

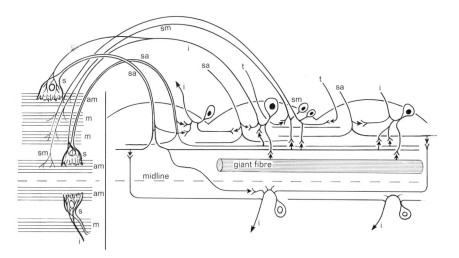

Figure 8.2

Connexions that would account for the reflexes shown by the muscle receptor organs, their efferent inhibitory supply, and accessory extensor muscles of the abdomen of the crayfish. Stretch of a receptor causes impulses that arouse inhibitory impulses in efferent neurons (i) on both sides in the same and adjacent segments. Impulses in slow motor axons (sm) to the stretch receptor accessory muscle (am) and other accessory extensor muscles (m) are also evoked by receptor activity, which sums with a local tactile input (t). The giant fibre excites the efferent inhibitors of the sensory cells and prevents their firing when the tail flicks. [Inferred from Fields and Kennedy, 1965.]

variety of total information to the central nervous system. However, in most cases we do not know whether the information is utilized, and another interesting question, to which we have no answer, is how the variety of receptor units arise in growth.

The muscle receptor organs of crustaceans with long abdomens consist of large sensory cells with numerous dendrites that spread over a specialized muscle (Fig. 8.2). In each segment there is a pair on each side, situated dorsally and so arranged that bending the abdomen, which opens the joints on the dorsal side, stretches the muscle and excites the sensory cell. Each pair of sensory cells is innervated by one or two inhibitory axons from the ventral cord; see Figure 6.1.

REFLEX MECHANISMS

The only reflexes studied in detail in crustaceans are some convenient ones that involve the postural receptors and the eyestalks. They are probably representative of arthropods but not of animals with softer skeletons.

When there is a tail flick, as in swimming or rapid escape, the inhibitory axon to the sensory cell of the muscle receptor organs is excited along with the flexor motor axons by the descending impulses in the abdominal giant fibres. The accompanying burst in the inhibitory axons all along the abdomen reduces activity of the sensory cells during the flick of the tail, although they respond briefly after a full flexion is achieved. This is a simple example of the cancelling of the proprioceptive effect of a central command.

Experimental stimulation of a single receptor cell causes a reflex excitation of the inhibitory axon to both fast and slow receptor cells; this occurs on both sides in the same segment and up to three segments away, the effect diminishing with greater distance. Even the simplest reflex pathway—from afferent receptor axon to the efferent inhibitory axons back to the same stretch receptor—involves two ganglia. The stretch receptor axons divide where they enter the cord: one branch ascends to the brain, the other descends to the last abdominal ganglion, where it is integrated with similar axons, which feed from all segments into one interneuron to the brain (Fig. 7.1, E). The latter branch is therefore nonspecific with reference to segment of origin of abdominal flexion.

To describe the action of the abdominal stretch receptors in controlling posture it is necessary to outline the pattern of motor innervation of the abdominal extensor muscles (Fig. 8.2). Each stretch receptor sensory neuron is situated upon a muscle; those of the slowly adapting receptors are slow muscle fibres (that is, they show a smooth summation in tetanus), and those of the rapidly adapting receptors are fast muscle fibres. The motor supply to the slow receptor muscle is a branch of one or two of the axons that supplies the slow extensor muscle fibres of the abdomen. This is comparable with the situation in amphibia, in which each spindle contains both fast and slow intrafusals; the fast are innervated by fibres that also run to the normal fast muscle fibres, and the slow intrafusals similarly by slow fibres.

Experimental stretching of the crustacean slow receptor alone, on one side, causes contraction of ipsilateral slow extensor motoneurons and curiously enough, summates dramatically with tactile input—that is, touch extends the abdomen in preparation for a flick. The deeper and larger extensor muscles are not involved in these reflexes. The fast receptor has so far shown no observable reflex effect when stretched.

Analysis suggests that at any position of rest the slow muscle takes up the slack in the receptor system. Passive bending then causes a sensory discharge and the extensors contract reflexly until the stretch receptor is unloaded. The point of equilibrium, with no reflex movement, is determined by the background discharge of the one or two out of five or six slow extensor motoneurons, which branch to the specialized stretch receptor muscles as well as to extensor muscles. The stretch receptor detects the difference between the set point, determined by central influences on these motoneurons, and the actual tail position. This explains

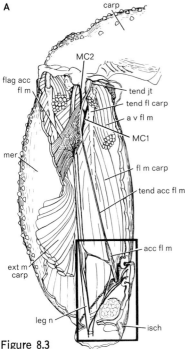

A

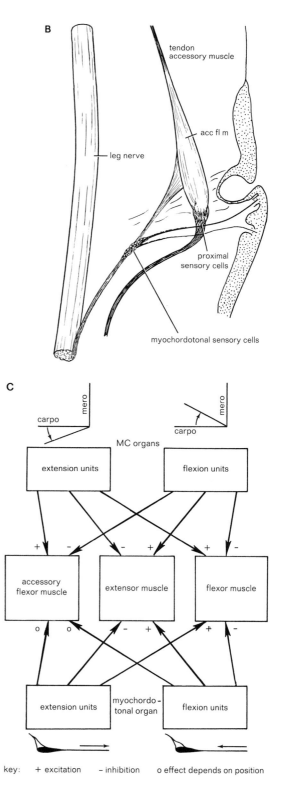

B

C

Figure 8.3

The myochordotonal organ of the crab *Cancer magister*.

A. Anterior view of a dissected meropodite of a left walking leg, dorsal to the left and lateral at the top, showing the positions of the joint organs MC1 and MC2 and the location of the myochordotonal organ which lies within the rectangle. The carpopodite is moved by its flexor and extensor muscles, (*fl m carp* and *ext m carp*). The accessory flexor muscle (*acc fl m*) has a tendon that reaches to the carpopodite and is innervated by two groups of myochordotonal sensory neurons.

B. Detail of **A**, within the rectangle.

C. Summary of the reflex responses at the meropodite-carpopodite joint. The relatively weaker responses, which are operated by the myochordotonal organ, are shown below and the relatively stronger one operated by the *MC* joint organs are shown above. The myochordotonal reflex back to its own muscle is such that the muscle is excited when the joint is moved away from its rest position. [Cohen, 1965.]

why, if one takes a crayfish and bends it by hand, the abdomen will, when released, slowly return to about the same position as before. The large flexor muscles of the abdomen are never excited tonically and so contribute nothing to the normal posture.

Detailed analysis of the superficial abdominal muscles has thrown considerable light on the way in which a muscle that is supplied by several motoneurons is controlled in crustaceans [6, 7, 11]. One particular group of forty or so muscle fibres is served by five motoneurons, with an overlapping pattern of branches, and by one inhibitor. All these efferent fibres show some spontaneous background activity. The innervation patterns of neighbouring muscle fibres are more similar than are the patterns of distant fibres. There is no distinction between relatively fast and slow axons, for one axon can cause a large postsynaptic potential in one muscle and a small one in another, and a second axon can have the reverse effect on the same muscle fibres. Some axons show facilitation in one muscle fibre and antifacilitation in another. Most muscle fibres receive only two or three excitatory axons, that appear to be distributed at random to the different muscle fibres. Interestingly, the different motoneurons may be separately excited by different reflex inputs, as by flexion or extension of the telson or by touch to different groups of hairs of the carapace, or by stimulation of different premotor interneurons. Since the muscle fibres receive a restricted sample of axons, it follows that the burden of tension shifts between different muscle fibres according to the source of reflex action. However, there is no evidence that particular motor axons have grown out to predetermined sets of muscle fibres; the counts of the actual connexions are random, as would be caused by haphazard growth, granted that some axons are more inclined to branch than others.

Reflex inhibition in the abdominal extensor muscle is mainly caused by central inhibition of the motoneurons, but these do not appear to influence each other directly [11]. Although the inhibitory axon is excited at this time, it runs to only about half of the muscle fibres, and inhibitory impulses are not timed well enough in relation to excitatory ones to be effective. The inhibitor axon in fact seems to serve as a device to bring about repolarization of the muscle fibres and thus to terminate contractions. It will be interesting to see whether this turns out to be a generally valid conclusion for the postsynaptic inhibition that is characteristic of almost all crustacean muscles.

In the meropodite of the walking legs (the largest, flat 4th segment), a receptor is also attached to its own special accessory muscle [4, 5]. This is the myochordotonal organ, which consists of a specialized receptor muscle attached to elastic strands upon which there are about 40 bipolar neurons. An elaborate mechanical suspension reduces the joint movement by a factor of about 20 (Fig. 8.3). Some of the sensory neurons are sensitive to position but relatively insensitive to movement; others have a selectively directional response to movement. The sense organ shows range fractionation by overlap of many sectors of the movement taken up by different sensory neurons. As in all the leg joints, there are also position and velocity receptors that are not under central control, so there is always a separate signal available to show the real position of the limb. A receptor that is attached to an accessory muscle has a special property: the frequency of motor impulses to the muscle can act as a zero setting for the receptor reflexes that operate the main muscles. Artificial bending or stretching of this joint causes reflex motor impulses in the antagonistic muscle (resistance reflexes), that are caused principally by the ordinary joint receptors upon ligaments without muscles. The accessory muscle can, however, take up the slack or set the system so that the myochordotonal organ elements come into their effective range at any point in the joint movement. However, it has proved impossible to demonstrate this on a single limb. The function of the accessory muscle in the freely moving animal apparently is to set the tone of the meropodite-carpopodite joint of the leg and thus fix the height at which the body is carried above the ground; however, the effect is summed over all walking legs, and a sagging posture is not noticeable until several myochordotonal organs are removed.

Control of the opening and closing of the crustacean claw (and of final joints of the walking legs) contrasts strongly with control of all other joints so far investigated. In the claw the excitatory and inhibitory axons are not reciprocally controlled by a central antagonism, but the tension is controlled by a delicate peripheral balance between the inhibitory and excitatory axons, dependent upon sense organs of the joint (Fig. 8.4). Touch to the inside of the claw, which prevents opening, may even increase the frequency of excitatory impulses to the opener muscle, but excites the inhibitor of that muscle much more. A stimulus that causes opening, such as touch to the hairs on the outside of the claw, excites the inhibitor axon less than the motor one [2, 3]. This dactylopodite opener muscle is the only one now known to have marked presynaptic inhibition; only a few, however, have been examined. In all the other joints of the limbs the "resistance reflexes"—by which the appropriate muscle resists an active or artificial passive bending of the joint—are not dependent on peripheral inhibition; instead, the cessation of a stream of motor impulses is brought about centrally when the joint is bent in the appropriate direction [3]. Clearly we cannot expect to find a consistent pattern of central or peripheral inhibition of antagonistic movements in crustaceans. In several instances in arthropods, any particular movement can be brought about by one of many alternative combinations of impulses to a variety of muscles. It is still not clear, however, whether these are alternative patterns, which are centrally predetermined on a very fine scale, or are the product of a flexible reflex control. The point is that a reflex can

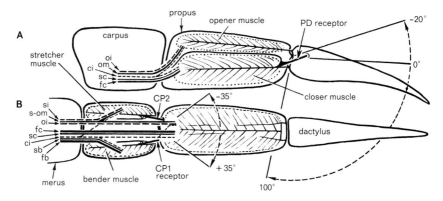

Figure 8.4

A diagram of the last three joints of the walking leg of the crab *Carcinus,* showing the arrangement of muscles and the position of the sense organs which are excited when the joints bend.

A. Lateral view; B, ventral view. Movement of the end joint excites the stretch receptive organ labelled *PD,* and movement of the next joint excites receptors *CP1* and *CP2.* Efferent axons are labelled as follows: *om = s-om,* stretcher-opener motor; *oi,* opener inhibitor; *si,* stretcher inhibitor; *ci,* common inhibitor; *sc,* slow closer (motor); *fb,* fast bender; *fc,* fast closer (motor); *sb,* slow bender. [Bush, 1962.]

be defined as a peripherally triggered central pattern of impulses or, more restrictedly, as a response that is dependent on feedback for the whole of its performance (p. 397).

CENTRALLY CONTROLLED SEQUENCES

In mammals, and possibly all vertebrates, feedback control of movement is in continuous dynamic operation during all movements, even before they begin. The situation is quite different in lower animals, especially arthropods.

As will be emphasized later, every movement that has been analysed in invertebrates is a result of a centrally determined sequence of motor impulses, and the control that is reflected from the periphery has (though only to a limited extent in invertebrates) an immediate or delayed effect that is distinguished as reflex. It is necessary to stress this widely applicable experimental finding because of the past history of the topic. The situation has been clarified only since 1959, when independent experiments were carried out on three different preparations to show that the normal pattern of a sequence of motor impulses need not depend on feedback from the periphery.

The central rhythm causing the oscillatory movements of the wings by direct flight muscles can very conveniently be analysed in the locust. Wind on the head, which imitates the normal air speed of flight, causes a flow of impulses down the neck connectives to the thoracic ganglia and bursts of impulses that run out along motor nerves to the wing muscles. Even when unable to produce any movement because the muscles have been removed, these bursts resemble those of normal flight, as can be demonstrated by gradual dissection of the wing muscles while the motoneurons are continually observed. With no sensory supply from the thorax, however, the frequency of the bursts in the motor output is considerably lower than in normal flight [21, 23]. If the rhythm is initiated by electrical stimulation in preparations that are only partially co-ordinated, we observe that the thoracic ganglia contain numerous independent oscillators, not one flight centre. When these oscillators, which are possibly the motoneurons themselves, are simultaneously active, they couple themselves and form a stable pattern. Tests with antidromic impulses would probably show that motoneurons have central collaterals that act on each other. In fact, in several flying insect preparations detailed measurements of the impulse patterns of several motoneurons recorded simultaneously reveal cross-correlation of interval length [21]. This is a very promising approach towards the building of models of interaction between motoneurons, which may be extended to identified interneurons.

The proprioceptive inflow from the wings, necessarily cyclic in flight, has a relatively small though important action in changing the position of single motor impulses which form part of the otherwise centrally determined sequence to the flight muscles. Wing proprioceptive impulses also increase the frequency of the wing beat. In normal flight, if the proprioceptors are intact, each of the several main flight muscles receives one or two motor impulses per cycle, with little flexibility in the timing of impulses. The only impulses which can be shifted in position are those in the two motoneurons to the subalar muscle of the forewing, which controls the twist of the forewing and lift in flight. By shifting these particular impulses, lift can be added just when it is most effective in the cycle of wing movement. Also, additional impulses may be added in some of the other motoneurons although a single motor impulse to each muscle at each stroke is the general rule; in this way graduated control is possible. If motoneurons fire a second time in the cycle, the interspike interval is 5 to 7 msec, and this evokes maximum additional work from the muscle. As a result of sensory input from the wing base when the animal is climbing, certain motoneurons fire earlier in the cycle; this has the effect of cutting short the excursion of the wing, and thus increasing the frequency above that set naturally by the elastic components. The main sensory element influencing the wing frequency seems to be a single stretch receptor cell at each wing hinge (22). This receptor fires once or several times at the top of each wing cycle, but has no immediate effect, and its impulse accelerates the central oscillator only when summed over the course of many cycles. The effect of this major proprioceptor is independent of just when, during the wingbeat cycle, its input arrives centrally. This is not unique, for many rhythms are controlled in this way. Such systems are intermediate between central and reflex control: they are central rhythms with peripheral modulation.

In the Diptera (flies), the wing muscles oscillate with a timing that does not depend on the timing of motor impulses. So long as the muscles receive a stream of impulses, the direct flight muscles oscillate at a frequency that is set by mechanical factors, such as the inertia of the wing. Impulses in different motor axons are not locked together, although they do interact, as shown by correlation of intervals in different ones. Even when of similar frequency, the phases of the motoneurons can drift smoothly past each other with no relation to the timing of the wing beat. Here the concept of movement control by a frequency or line-labelled code of nerve impulses breaks down. In addition, the effects of proprioceptive feedback are in no way related to the phase of the wing beat. Indeed, the asynchrony between different motoneurons to the same muscle appears to be of some importance in maintaining a steady mechanical oscillation, which would be irregular if the motor impulses were grouped in bursts. Fine control of wing movements, such as twist and bilateral asymmetry, is achieved by tonic accessory wing muscles, which are controlled by reflexes from the eyes and the halteres [19].

Song in grasshoppers produced by rasping of the elytra, is another clear example of a central command that descends from the brain; but some detail of the movement is determined within the brain (Fig. 8.5), as shown by the fact that electrical stimulation of the central body, a neuropile region of the brain, causes sound patterns that are never heard in the normal song. Electrical stimulation, having no subtlety, evidently excites the wrong cluster of premotor interneurons that descend from the brain. But the same muscles have other functions, and therefore the details of elytral movement are decided by the thoracic motoneurons. Electrical stimulation of the corpora pedunculata in the brain elicits a typical normal song pattern from the thoracic ganglion. This is almost independent of proprioceptive feedback, because the sequence of motor impulses is not changed by removal of the rasping muscles. This shows that the appropriate general command descends from the brain to the thoracic ganglion, which then initiates a centrally controlled sequence.

When a cicada makes its piping noise, the movement of the tymbal drum on each side is caused by single muscle twitches, timed so that they alternate on the two sides. A motor axon on each side of the animal fires at 100 per sec, exactly out of phase with the one on the other side, so that the two tympanic drums alternate. This impulse pattern continues irrespective of the presence of the muscle or tymbal, showing that we

Figure 8.5

The main interactions between ganglia that control singing outbursts in grasshoppers and crickets. Electrical stimulation of a nucleus called the corpora pedunculata in the brain causes a burst of normal song and simultaneously inhibits the motoneurons involved in jumping. The central body in the brain organizes the patterns of the song, and stimulation here produces abnormal noises. Stimulation in the 3rd thoracic ganglion excites motoneurons in a meaningless pattern. The alerting mechanism of the anal cerci, which are sensitive to sounds and air movements, is inhibited during song, thus preventing the animal's alarming itself by its own noise. [Based upon work by Huber.]

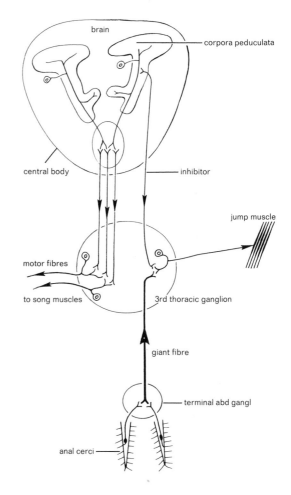

have here a rather simple central rhythm. The high basic motor frequency of cricket songs and of the maxilliped paddle of crustaceans, with sudden onset and cutoff, also suggests a central oscillator.

The regular opening and closure of the spiracles of insects is another activity that is operated by a centrally determined sequence (Fig. 8.6). A pacemaker that causes closure is distinguishable from a system that controls the degree of opening [15]. A pacemaker in the metathoracic ganglion of the locust has an endogenous rhythm in which inspiration and expiration are mutually inhibitory, with a pause between each. This controls the ventilatory movement of the abdomen, whose frequency is influenced by carbon dioxide in the tissues of all ganglia. Certain continually excited motoneurons in the prothoracic and mesothoracic ganglia are inhibited or excited by the centres for inspiration and expiration, but they have a continual background activity that normally keeps the spiracles shut. These motoneurons are influenced in their own segments by carbon dioxide, which always has an opening effect and exerts a fine control. Only the first thoracic spiracle has an opener muscle, and this is separately innervated on the two sides from the mesothoracic ganglion as well as by two median nerve axons, each of which divides to both sides. The whole of this system (Fig. 8.6) is a one-way flow without feedback from the periphery, and continues to act reasonably well in the isolated nerve cord. When guard hairs around a spiracle are touched, there is a reflex closure, effected by one of the two closer axons; the other axon continues the same rhythm as before. This illustrates how the reflex overcomes the central

Figure 8.6

A plan of the system that generates a centrally coordinated rhythm without feed-back in the control of the first and second thoracic spiracles of the locust. Carbon dioxide acts at a variety of points in thoracic ganglia and brain, causing the spiracles to open, admit oxygen, and let out CO_2. The spiracles are closed most of the time to retain water.

In ganglion III, inspiration (*INSP*) and expiration (*EXP*) are mutually inhibitory and are influenced in frequency by CO_2. These centres also directly control the motoneurons to the closer muscles (*MC*) of the spiracle, on left and right sides, and those to the opener (*MO*) of spiracle 2. Continuously excited interneurons (*E*), influenced by CO_2, keep the spiracles closed during pauses. There are also local effects of CO_2 on the motoneurons to the opener muscle of spiracle 2. [Modified from Miller, 1965.]

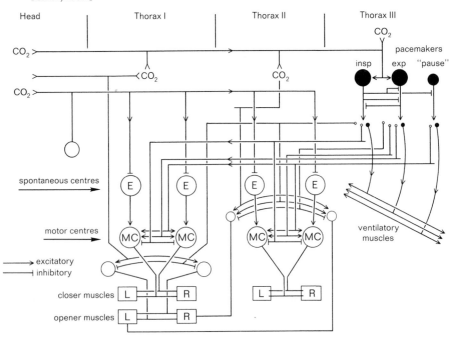

rhythm—not by central reflex modification of it but by sending a separate message down a different motor axon. Such a method of providing a separate fast pathway turns up again and again in annelids and arthropods, in which fast movements are superimposed upon slow ones.

The clearest examples of descending "commands" by premotor interneurons that drive a central rhythm are the interneurons that cause paddling of the abdominal swimmerets in the crayfish [18]. Five fibres on each side have been described; three of them are identical. Impulses in these (at about 30 per sec) cause the abdominal ganglia to produce the appropriate sequences of motor impulses, which in turn cause the swimmerets to oscillate back and forth. Below 20 per sec and above 100 per sec, impulses in the interneuron produce no oscillation of the limbs, but between these limits the swimmeret oscillation frequency depends quantitatively on the descending impulse frequency. The velocity at which the wave of pleopod movement sweeps anteriorly from segment to segment (starting at the posterior end) is, however, not modifiable. At least three different descending interneurons inhibit the pleopod rhythm.

Detailed examinations of complex movements in lower animals, especially in the arthropods, demonstrate that centrally controlled sequences of motor impulses and central inhibition of motoneurons to antagonistic muscles are the general rule; presumably they are genetically determined. Limited tests with antidromic impulses suggest that motoneurons do not inhibit each other directly. Reflex control also clearly exists, especially in those movements that are moulded in detail to the terrain, as in walking. The plastic modification, or conditioning, of a centrally controlled sequence does not necessarily take place by change in a classical reflex arc. In one example studied—the conditioning of leg position as controlled by an isolated insect ganglion—the reinforcement is effective if correlated in time with rises and falls in the motor output frequency, irrespective of whether the leg, with its proprioceptive apparatus, is intact (see p. 343). Another example of an adaptive modification of a central pattern is the control of the position of the onset of the fast flick-back when crab eyes follow the rotation of a striped drum, as described below. If this type of experiment is extended to numerous other preparations, we may discover some general mechanisms of how centrally coordinated sequences are perfected in detail.

As a final example of centrally initiated sequences, we recall the remarkable way in which the eye movement in crabs (Fig. 8.7) is controlled [8]. A movement of a contrasting object excites interneurons of one-way visual movement in the optic tract. In response to these excitations, a sequence of motor impulses runs out from the brain in the oculomotor nerve to each eye and causes the ten or so eyecup muscles to move the eyes in opposite directions in relation to the midline on the two sides. Therefore, when a muscle on one side shortens, the corresponding muscle

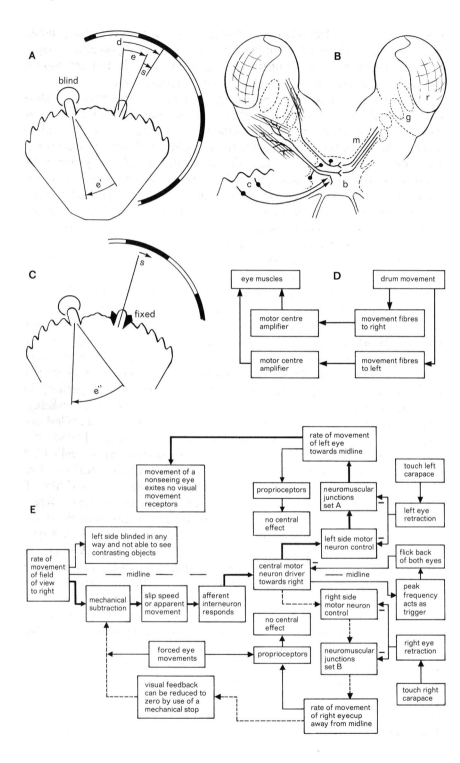

on the other eye lengthens. This motion continues until the eye has moved through about 15°, with increasing motor impulse frequencies to certain muscles causing greater deflections of the eye. After a time the eyes flick back almost simultaneously to their starting points, pulled by the appropriate muscles (which are antagonistic to those acting in the forward direction), and the motion starts all over again as before. Visual stimulation moving in the opposite direction causes the cycle to operate in the opposite way. The exact movement depends on the simultaneous excitation of all ten eye muscles. The nervous activity that controls the eye movement continues as before, even if both eyes are clamped and cannot move (see Fig. 8.7). Even when the oculomotor nerves are cut, an appropriate stream of motor impulses still issues from the brain, with its periodic "flick-back" and with a typical dependence of the rate of increase of motor impulse frequency on the relative speed of movement of the visual stimulus across the retina.

As there is no proprioceptive influence of the position or movement of the eyestalk, the only clue available to the brain as to the direction in which the eye points is the efferent motor frequency at the time. The onset of the fast flick-back of the eyes comes earlier in the traverse across the socket if there is any nonspecific stimulus to the edge of the socket. This indirect control seems to be the mechanism that keeps the traverse of the eye central in the socket. The generating mechanism of the flick-back is, in fact, a most sophisticated DC to AC converter upon which the opto-

Figure 8.7

General scheme of the control of the movement of the eye in the optokinetic response of the crab *Carcinus*.

A. The drum moves to right an angle d; the right seeing eye follows through an angle e; the stimulus to the eye is therefore the angle s. The freely moving blind left eye moves through an angle e', which is approximately equal to e.

B. The anatomical plan. Movement across the retina r is converted into nervous excitation in selectively directional movement interneurons m in the optic neuropiles g. Vision of one eye is sufficient to drive both eyes as in A. Motoneurons to the eye muscles have dendrites in the brain. Sensory neurons c on the carapace initiate a protective retraction of only the ipsilateral eye.

C. When the right seeing eye is no longer free to move, the left freely moving but blinded eye moves through an angle e'', which is much greater than the stimulus s because the feedback loop caused by the movement of the seeing eye is now broken.

D. Box diagram of relationships in C.

E. More complete box diagram of relationships between parts of the system. The retraction reflex is shown in the right column. The diagram is otherwise read from left to right; negative signs indicate an inhibitory effect. The directions of the responses are given with reference to A and B. The thick arrows show the system without feedback, as in C and D. When the seeing eye is free to move, as in A, the dashed lines take effect. [E from Horridge and Sandeman, 1964.]

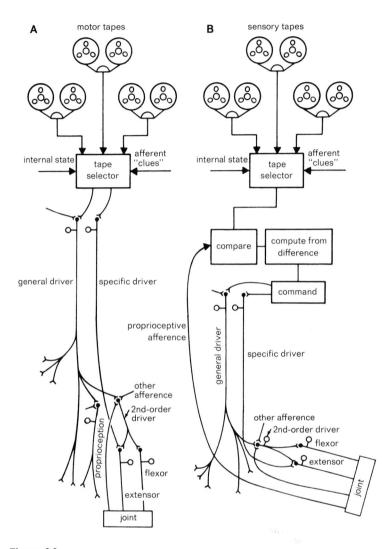

Figure 8.8

Two types of control by centrally determined sequences. On the left the system is driven by sequences that determine motor output directly. Driving commands can be general or specific to any degree of detail, and at a lower level they can be modified by proprioceptors. On the right the system is driven by tapes of the sensory feedback that must be expected. A comparator makes the actual commands on the basis of the differences between the proprioceptive afference and the instruction from the tape. There can also be proprioceptive control lower down, as before. This system is more adaptable, but requires much more circuitry in addition to a comparator and a command centre, which themselves must produce highly complex adaptive sequences of impulses. Most invertebrate responses investigated use an "in-line" system, as on the left. [Hoyle, 1964.]

motor response of crustaceans (and perhaps of vertebrates) depends. The whole optokinetic response illustrates very beautifully the interaction between a patterned stimulus, a complex sense organ, coding of excitation to the brain, and the central control of a movement in response.

An abundance of centrally initiated sequences of motor impulses is almost certainly not a feature unique to arthropods, which merely happen to be convenient for these experiments. Mechanisms of this type are likely to be abundant because they require less circuitry than those involving continual reflex monitoring of each aspect of a movement (Fig. 8.8). In the production of a centrally controlled sequence the motoneurons act like any interneurons, and, studied by this method, they provide points of access and illustrate the importance of identifying the neurons individually when interaction of any kind is analysed.

REFERENCES FOR CHAPTER 8

1. Bullock, T. H., and Horridge, G. A. 1965. Chapter 20. (See *loc. cit.*, p. 18.)
2. Bush, B. M. H. 1962. Proprioceptive reflexes in the legs of *Carcinus maenas* (L). *J. Exp. Biol.* **39**:89–105.
3. Bush, B. M. H. 1965. Leg reflexes from chordotonal organs in the crab, *Carcinus maenas. Comp. Biochem. Physiol.* **15**:567–587.
4. Cohen, M. J. 1964. The peripheral organisation of sensory systems, in *Neural Theory and Modeling*, R. F. Reiss (Ed.). Stanford University Press.
5. Cohen, M. J. 1966. The dual role of sensory systems: detection and setting central sensitivity. *Cold Spring Harbor Symp. Quant. Biol.* **30**:587–600.
6. Fields, H. L. 1966. Proprioceptive control of posture in the crayfish abdomen, *J. Exp. Biol.* **44**:455–468.
7. Fields, H. L., and Kennedy, D. 1965. Functional role of muscle receptor organs in crayfish. *Nature. London* **206**:1232–1237.
8. Horridge, G. A. 1966. The optokinetic response; a study of a system. *Symp. Soc. Exp. Biol.* **20**:179–198.
9. Hoyle, G. 1964. Exploration of neuronal mechanisms underlying behaviour in insects, in *Neural Theory and Modeling*, R. F. Reiss (Ed.). Stanford University Press.
10. Hoyle, G. 1966. An isolated insect ganglion-nerve-muscle preparation. *J. Exp. Biol.* **44**:413–428.
11. Kennedy, D., Evoy, W. H., and Fields, H. L. 1966. The unit basis of some crustacean reflexes. *Symp. Soc. Exp. Biol.* **20**:75–110.
12. Kennedy, D., Evoy, W. H., and Hanawalt, J. T. 1966. Release of coordinated behavior in crayfish by single central neurons. *Science* **154**:917–919.
13. Kennedy, D., and Takeda, K. 1965. Reflex control of abdominal flexor muscles in the crayfish. II. The tonic system. *J. Exp. Biol.* **43**:229–246.
14. Maynard, D. M. 1966. Integration in crustacean ganglia. *Symp. Soc. Exp. Biol.* **20**:111–150.

15. Miller, P. L. 1965. The nervous control of respiratory movements, in *The Physiology of the Insect Central Nervous System,* J. E. Treherne and J. W. L. Beament (Eds.). New York, Academic Press.
16. Parnas, I., and Atwood, H. L. 1966. Phasic and tonic neuromuscular systems in the abdominal extensor muscles of the crayfish and rock lobster. *Comp. Biochem. Physiol.* **18:**701–723.
17. Székely, G. 1965. Logical networks for controlling limb movements in Urodela. *Acta Physiol. Acad. Sci. Hung.* **27:**237–246.
18. Wiersma, C. A. G., and Ikeda, K. 1964. Interneurons commanding swimmeret movements in the crayfish *Procambarus clarkii* (Girard). *Comp. Biochem. Physiol.* **12:**509–525.
19. Wilson, D. M. 1965. The nervous control of insect locomotion, in *The Physiology of the Insect Central Nervous System,* J. E. Treherne and J. W. L. Beament (Eds.). New York, Academic Press.
20. Wilson, D. M. 1966. Insect walking. *Ann. Rev. Entomol.* **11:**103–122.
21. Wilson, D. M. 1966. Central nervous mechanisms for the generation of rhythmic behaviour in arthropods. *Symp. Soc. Exp. Biol.* **20:**199–228.
22. Wilson, D. M., and Gettrup, E. 1963. A stretch reflex controlling wingbeat frequency in grasshoppers. *J. Exp. Biol.* **40:**171–185.
23. Wilson, D. M., and Weis-fogh, T. 1962. Patterned activity of coordinated motor units, studied in flying locusts. *J. Exp. Biol.* **39:**643–667.

9

Reception and integration in the compound eye

Understanding the operation of the compound eye depends upon knowing a combination of facts—the details of the structure, the optical properties of the light path, the responses of the sensory cells and the interneuron paths behind them as recorded electrophysiologically, and the ability of the whole animal to see, as revealed by its response to movement and to objects that are stationary relative to the eye. The compound eye provides an excellent example of the problems encountered when we try to understand the perception of pattern by many neuron pathways in parallel. The past three or four years have witnessed a surprising interest in this beautifully adapted structure, but the results are still incomplete and difficult to interpret.

THE RETINAL RECEPTOR CELLS

The surface of the compound eye is composed of an array of facets (Fig. 9.1), each of which may be flat or curved, sculptured or smooth. Each facet covers a highly differentiated group of cells called an ommatidium, which is the obvious anatomical unit of the retina. The ommatidium commonly has a cuticular lens of optically homogeneous laminated cuticle, beneath which is a transparent homogeneous solid (or sometimes almost fluid) cone that leads down to the highly refractile rhabdomeres. These are arrays of tubules formed by the individual retinula cells and are loaded with visual pigment. Many experimental facts show that the rhabdomeres are the specialized regions where light is absorbed in the reception process [28, 39]. In some eyes (as in the firefly, typical flies, and in *Limulus*), the cone is formed from the cuticle but—however it arises—the cone is the most obvious and puzzling feature of the optical pathway. The anatomical diversity of eyes in different groups of arthro-

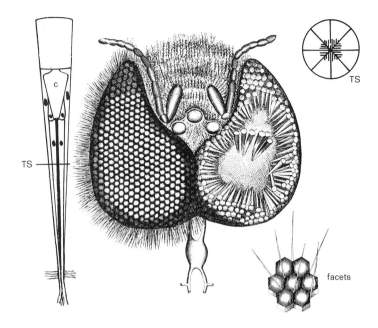

Figure 9.1

Eyes of the worker honeybee. The central picture (showing the ommatidia and their facets) and the facets at lower right are from Swammerdam, **1737**. The other two (showing the structure of an ommatidium) are based upon electron microscopy by Goldsmith, 1962. Below the cone (*c*) is a group of eight similar retinula cells, which are shown at upper right in section along the line indicated (*TS*). Rhabdomeres lie in pairs so that there are two main orientations of the tubules, upon which depends the sensitivity to the plane of polarization of light.

pods lies in the arrangement of the tubules of the rhabdomeres, in the pattern of the sensory cells bearing the tubules, in whether the rhabdomeres of different sensory cells are separated or fused to form a common rhabdom, and in the distance between the cone and the rhabdomeres. Apposition eyes are those in which the rhabdomeres stretch from the point of the cone to the basement membrane, as in the bee (Fig. 9.1) [14]. In the fly there are eight in a peculiar geometrical pattern of great functional significance; arthropods as a whole show a wide diversity of retinula cell patterns [8].

Arthropods are the group, par excellence, among which the ability to discriminate the intensity, direction, colour, and plane of polarization of light is clearly made possible by the specialized structure and physiological diversity of the first-order sensory neurons. Discrimination of the plane of polarized light (on the optical axis) by individual retinula cells depends on the orientation of the visual pigment molecules along the long

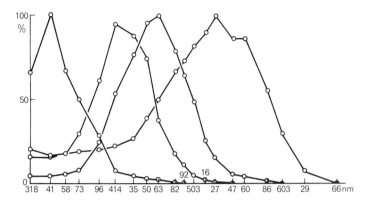

Figure 9.2

Line labelling according to a physical attribute of the stimulus. Sensitivity of four types of retinula cell of the eye of the worker bee, plotted from measurements of the intensity of light of different wavelengths required to cause a constant depolarisation. Note the large overlap between the curves. The range of these curves corresponds well with the range over which the worker bee can discriminate colours, as shown by behavioural tests. [Autrum and von Zwehl, 1964.]

axis of the tubules of the rhabdomeres, as shown by stimulating *from the side* in cut eyes [13]. Direct observation of light transmitted on the visual axis through rhabdomeres shows them to be dichroic [27]. Different eyes show different ratios of sensitivity of single cells to light that is shone down the optical pathway of the ommatidium (10:1 in the crab) in the maximum and minimum directions; in the locust, even different cells in the same eye are very diverse in this respect [38, 39]. The ability of some arthropods to distinguish colours is based on the known differences in spectral sensitivity of different classes of receptor cells (Fig. 9.2). Apart from flies (see below), there is no unequivocal evidence that cells of different colour types occur together in one ommatidium, although in some insects there are large differences in colour sensitivity between different areas of the eye [1].

Just what the functional element is must be considered separately for the different features of the stimulus, because colour, polarized light, movement, and direction are coded by different systems, in which retinula cells, whole ommatidia, or pairs of ommatidia may be the essential units.

The retinula cells of one ommatidium have identical visual axes in the locust (Figs. 9.3, 9.4, and 9.5), and presumably in the bee, dragonfly, and in crabs, which are all examples with fused rhabdomeres. In flies, however, the rhabdomeres are far apart from each other, optically separate, and certainly they look in different directions from one ommatidium (Fig. 9.6) [6]. In the locust the angles of acceptance and the fields of

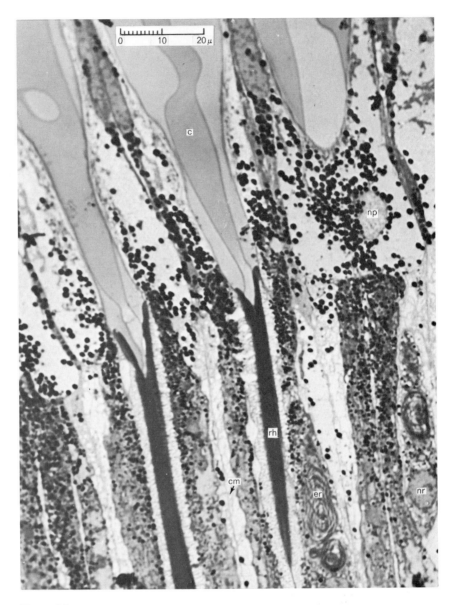

Figure 9.3

The separation of line-labelled sensory neurons in different ommatidia by pigment in an apposition compound eye. This is a longitudinal section through the peripheral part of the compound eye of the locust, photographed with a light microscope. The high resolution is achieved by utilising a 1 μm section cut in araldite and stained in toluidine blue. Pigment grains are extremely abundant even in a section so thin. c, cones; cm, outer membrane of retinula cell; er, endoplasmic reticulum; np and nr, nucleus of pigment and retinula cell; rh, rhabdom.

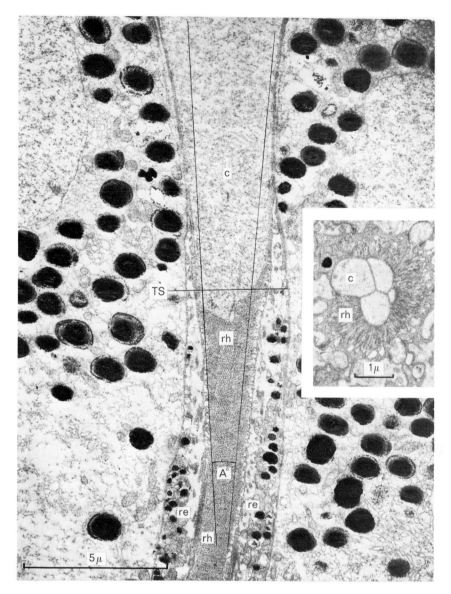

Figure 9.4

The region where light on the optical pathway first encounters the absorption system of the primary sensory cells in the retina of the locust (see Fig. 9.3). The section is along the axis of an ommatidium and the tip of the cone meets the rhabdom at the centre of the picture. The cone is clearly on the optical pathway; the rhabdom is the region of visual pigment, and presumably a part of the optical pathway. The inset shows a transverse section at the region marked *TS* on the main figure. Note the large pigment grains in the cells on each side of the cone and the smaller grains in the cytoplasm of the retinula cells around the rhabdom. An outstanding problem of the optics of the compound eye is whether the acceptance angle of individual facets depends mainly on the direct view of the outside world by the rhabdom, as shown by the angle A°, or whether there is internal reflection at the sides of the cone. *c*, cone; *re*, retinula cells; *rh*, rhabdom.

view of different retinula cells in the same ommatidium are identical, as can occasionally be demonstrated directly by recording from two cells, but the preferred planes of polarization of the same two cells can be different [39].

Typical decapod crustacean eyes have a central rod-shaped rhabdom composed of a stack of plates, which consist of tubules lying in directions at right angles to each other in alternate layers [36], with the interlocking processes of the retinula cells arranged as in Figure 9.7. Therefore, once more, the retinula cells of one ommatidium must all have the same axis. Crabs have an apposition eye with the layered rhabdom stretching from an elongated cone to the basement membrane,

Figure 9.5

A summary of the anatomy and optics of the retina of the locust. **Top:** structure of an ommatidium, showing how the roots of the cone spread between the retinula cells. The two basal retinula cells have no rhabdomere. **Bottom:** a diagram of the cornea, cones, and retinula cells, showing the presumed pathways of light in the dark- and light-adapted states. The curves at the right, lower figure, show the acceptance angle curves as shown by recording the sensitivity to illumination from different directions. Note the palisade around the rhabdom and its presumed affect in promoting internal reflection. There is evidence that the retinula cells of one ommatidium all share the same receptive field because the rhabdomers are fused, and that the shape of the peak of sensitivity of the receptive field is governed by the total internal reflection in the rhabdom.

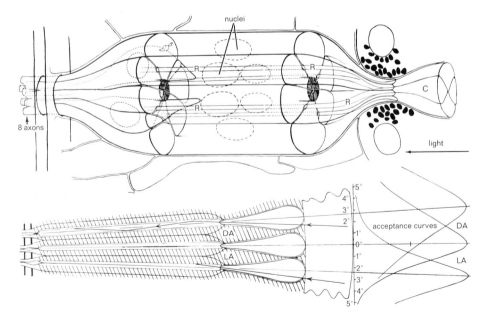

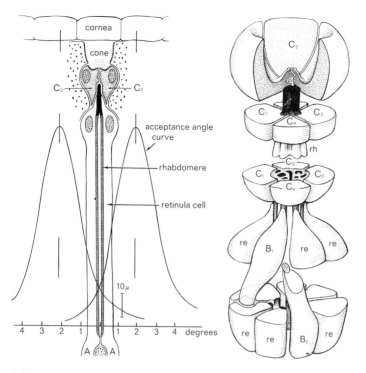

Figure 9.6

Two diagrams of an ommatidium of the fly, which has an open type of rhabdom. Beneath the corneal facet is a cone and a group of four cells (C_{1-4}) which secrete the cone. Between the elongated retinula cells (re) except at their peripheral end, is a space, but a dense amorphous substance (*shaded black*) binds together the ends of the otherwise separate rhabdomeres. Each retinula cell forms its own discrete rhabdomere (rh) and six of them with spectral peak in the green each have an axon (A) that runs to the lamina. Two retinula cells (B_{1-2}), with tubules at right angles and sensitivity more towards the blue, have axons which run to both 1st and 2nd optic neuropiles. The acceptance angle curves for two retinula cells of one ommatidium and the interommatidial angle are shown on a scale of degrees. The axes of the seven retinula cells are inclined to each other with an angle of about 2°, which is about equal to the angle between ommatidia at the front of the eye, as illustrated in Figures 9.9 to 9.12. This figure should be compared with that for an eye with a fused rhabdome (Fig. 9.5).

but most crustaceans have eyes with crystalline threads leading from the tips of the cones down the corresponding rhabdoms below. In the crab the tubules of the rhabdomeres and the plane of polarization for maximum sensitivity are horizontal and vertical with reference to normal posture. Therefore, in the crab, cells of one ommatidium act as one unit in regard to light direction, but they act as two contrasting groups when polarized light is analysed (see p. 169).

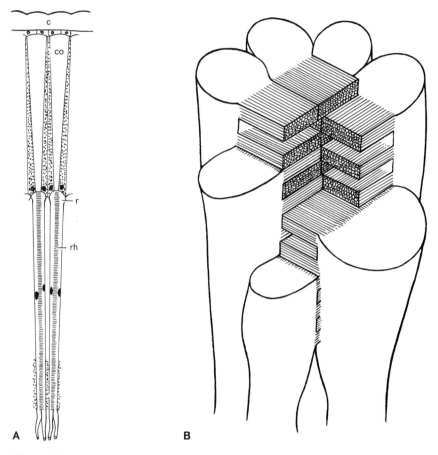

Figure 9.7

Retina of typical decapod crustacean.

A. General view of two ommatidia of the retina in longitudinal section, showing the optic axis passing successively through cornea (*c*), cone (*co*) and retinula cells (*r*). The orientation of the rhabdom (*rh*) remains constant along its whole length.

B. The organization of the rhabdomeres into a rhabdom. The layers alternate in tubule direction. Four retinula cells participate in the vertical direction, three in the horizontal, while all cells have the same optical axis.

THE OPTICAL SYSTEM AS A LIGHT GUIDE

Exner suggested about 80 years ago that light which strikes the end of the rhabdom is internally reflected from its inside surface (Fig. 9.5). In slices of arthropod eyes, illuminated in front and viewed from behind, the rhabdoms are certainly seen as bright spots of light, in agreement with this view. The palisade of vacuoles formed by the endoplasmic reticulum around the rhabdom (Fig. 9.8), which is obvious in some apposition eyes with fused rhabdoms (as in crabs, locusts, and butterflies), is thus explained as a device that increases the difference in refractive index between the rhabdom and the surrounding cytoplasm. In the locust the palisade in the dark-adapted eye is replaced in the light-adapted eye by a layer of mitochondria that have a high refractive index, similar to that of the rhabdom [22]. Therefore the mitochondria must prevent internal reflection in the rhabdom. This has three consequences: (a) a reduction in sensitivity, which is hidden by the much greater dark-light adaptation change over 3 or 4 orders of magnitude, (b) an increase in acuity, which results from narrowing the angle of acceptance (Fig. 9.4), thus proving that the reflection at the rhabdom/cytoplasm interface controls the width of the acceptance angle [43], (c) an improvement in the discrimination of the plane of polarization in the stimulating light, because internal reflection influences polarization.

By extension of the above theory for the rhabdom of apposition eyes, an action as a light guide has been attributed to the crystalline thread and so to the cone, from which the crystalline thread extends for a considerable distance to the rhabdom in superposition eyes. Many years ago Exner suggested the same mechanism for the eye of the amphipod *Phronima*.

The retinula cells of apposition eyes are each excited by only a narrow pencil of light from the external world, as shown by direct recording, but single cells of superposition eyes have not yet been investigated. The width of this pencil is a compromise between sensitivity and acuity, because less than the maximum light is admitted for vision if the angle is too narrow, whereas if it is too wide there is loss of acuity and unnecessary overlap in visual fields of retinula cells or whole ommatidia [15]. The beam of light reaching the rhabdom corresponds approximately to that calculated from the curvature of the cornea and the size of the aperture (Kuiper in [3]). In light-adapted locust eyes, however, this beam in the optical system is wider than the acceptance angle of the retinula cells below, and they seem to be governed by the ability of the rhabdom to accept light and contain it by internal reflection. Although the mechanism varies in different compound eyes, both the optical path and the elongated rhabdom are each adapted to select only a narrow beam of light at each facet.

To measure the optical constants in such a small system is difficult, because the width of the narrowest parts is not much larger than the wavelength of light. However, the angular sensitivity of the retinula cells to light is the most relevant measurement to make, because the succeeding neurons in the pathway of visual stimuli are concerned only in what

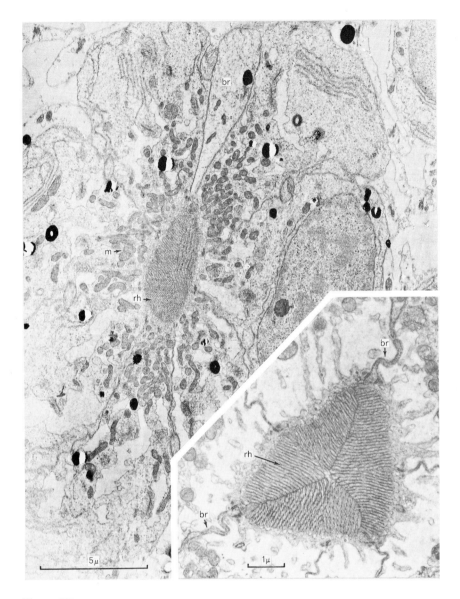

Figure 9.8

Transverse sections through an ommatidium of a locust. The ommatidium consists of eight cells arranged like segments of a grapefruit, with their fused rhabdomeres at the centre; one of the cells (*br*) is called a basal retinula cell because of the position of its nucleus, and in the locust it has almost no rhabdomere (see Fig. 9.5). Some ommatidia have two basal retinula cells, as shown in the inset. The eye in the main picture was light-adapted and the mitochondria (*m*) are crowded round the rhabdom. The eye shown in the inset was dark-adapted when fixed, and the rhabdom is surrounded by endoplasmic vacuoles called palisades. The fact that the angle of acceptance is narrower in light-adapted eyes, without a palisade, is evidence that this angle is limited by the internal reflection at the surface of the rhabdom.

the retinula cells accept. This is illustrated by the fly (Burkhardt in [2], p. 419) and in light-adapted locust eyes, in which some of the light that is let in by the cornea and cone is not internally reflected by the rhabdom but is lost, presumably in the dense cytoplasmic pigment of the retinula cells.

The acceptance angle curve is measured by using a distant point source rather than a collimated beam, which may cause errors because of difficulties of centering. The sensitivity (derived from the receptor potential of single cells) is plotted at different angles of the light. All single retinula cells so tested yield a similar type of curve, with the sensitivity falling off very steeply on either side of a peak. The white-eyed mutant of the blowfly (without eye pigment) yields a curve like that of pigmented flies in the middle region but with lateral extensions [45], suggesting that the pigment in normal eyes does not control the acceptance angle but rather, controls the spread of scattered light from adjacent ommatidia. The effect of a more complicated pattern of light cannot be theoretically predicted from the effect of a single source at different angles until interaction between retinula cells has been ruled out, as in the locust [39]. Typical values are 2° (fly and bee) to 6° (crab and locust) for the acceptance angle, which is defined as the width of the acceptance angle curve at half sensitivity [15, 16]. The repeat angle projected at the eye by the finest perceived stripes is about the same as the acceptance angle (see p. 172).

THE OPEN-RHABDOM EYE OF *Diptera*

Recently a remarkable correspondence has been demonstrated between the directions in which the six separated green-sensitive rhabdomeres of the fly are orientated within each ommatidium and the anatomical connexions of the corresponding axons with the second-order interneurons of the lamina [6]. A difference in transmission by individual rhabdomeres can be seen in section from behind a sliced retina illuminated by one light (Fig. 9.9). The corresponding pattern can be seen by reflection from the front of the eye. Direct measurement shows that the angle between the axes of different retinula cells of one ommatidium is equal to the interommatidial angle (Fig. 9.10). Where the cone meets the rhabdomeres, the anatomical arrangement is such that an inverted image of the visual field projects upon the ends of the seven rhabdomeres at the point of the cone (Burkhardt et al. in [3]). The pattern of directions of the rhabdomeres is asymmetrical because it is a consequence of the positions of the tips of the rhabdomeres in cross section (Fig. 9.11, A). When the axons of the six green-sensitive retinula cells are traced to their terminals,

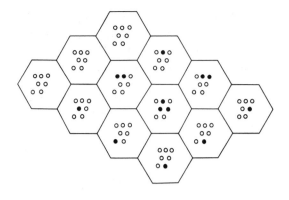

Figure 9.9.
A view of a dozen facets of a fly's eye from behind when a small light is placed in the field of view. The pattern of rhabdomeres of the seven individual retinula cells is visible in each facet. The light source is seen in a different rhabdomere of each facet (solid circles), showing that those in each facet look in different directions. Actually, in this example the retina was abnormally flattened and the pattern is distorted. The rhabdomeres that point in the same direction from different facets are of cells with axons that converge on one second-order cell, as in Figure 9.10. [Wiedmann, 1965.]

the astonishing result is that, at least in some parts of the eye, the sensory cells that face in the same direction from different ommatidia have terminals upon the same second-order neuron in the lamina. Therefore, for these regions, retinula axon terminals are grouped in optic cartridges, each one of which corresponds to one direction (Figs. 9.11, B and C, and 9.12).

There are two other blue-sensitive retinula cells in each ommatidium, with rhabdomeres one above the other and at right angles to each other. The axon of one bypasses the lamina and runs directly to the next neuropile.

The significance of this fibre projection cannot be explained until we know what pattern of excitation and inhibition exists or whether acceptance angle curves of the six green-sensitive retinula cells have equal areas and sensitivity to polarization plane. The following is therefore hypothetical, and similar studies are required on the retina-lamina connexions in eyes with fused rhabdomeres in which the 6–8 retinula cells of an ommatidium face in the same direction.

Critical evidence is lacking as to whether insects and crustaceans with fused rhabdomeres have interweaving axons between retina and lamina, as in dipterans. Preliminary unpublished work by Shaw suggests that in bees, moths, and locusts, which are typical insects with fused rhabdomeres, there is not a highly organized plexus as there is between the retina and the lamina of the fly. Instead, there appears to be a direct projection of the 6 or 8 fibres of one ommatidium to the corresponding cartridge of the lamina below. In the locust, recordings from units of the lamina presumed to be second-order confirm that angles of acceptance are similar to those in the retina. The action of the retinula terminals upon the second-order units in the locust is curious in that presynaptic depolarization causes postsynaptic hyperpolarization. At very low light intensities the hyperpolarization miniature potentials are about as numerous as the depolarization potentials of the retina that are believed to represent captures of individual photons. Therefore it seems that the retinula cells of one ommatidium, all having the same axis and receptive

Figure 9.10

The relation between the optical axes of retinula cells and the connexions of their terminals to second-order neurons of the optic lamina of the fly. Three ommatidia are inclined at an angle of about 2.5° to each other, with acceptance angle curves of sensitivity to light of a typical retinula cell on the axis as shown. The axes of retinula cells, along the lines a, b, c, d, e, are inclined to the axes of the ommatidia. The important experimental finding is that the connexions of the ommatidia with the optic cartridges of the lamina, as effected by the axons of the retinula cells, bring together the axons of retinula cells that are pointing in the same directions. Note the inversion in the optical path, and subsequent erection by the crossings of the axons. [After Braitenberg, 1966.]

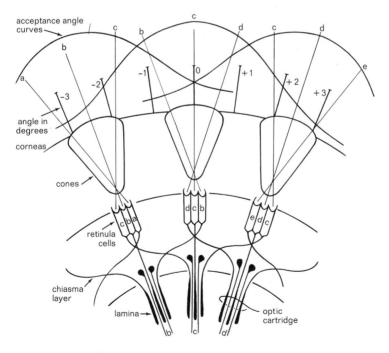

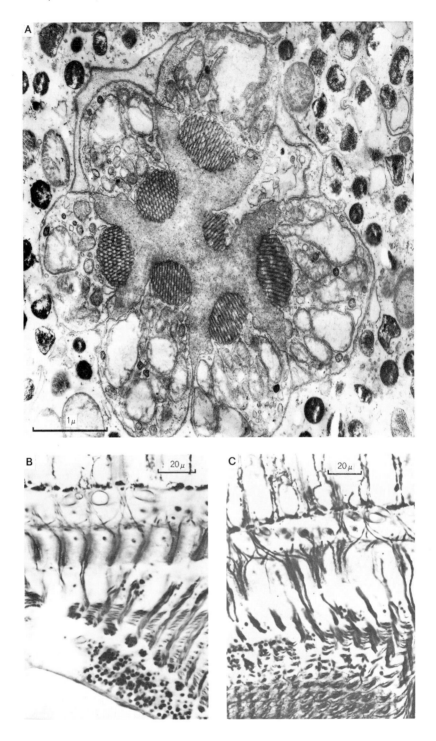

field, sum with an inhibitory effect on second-order units of the lamina. The special interweaving plexus of the fly is appropriate to achieve a similar summation of the retinula cells with a common axis, although these are in different ommatidia.

This arrangement favours the perception of very faint lights and provides optimum perception of intensity and direction. On the other hand, it is not so efficient for perception of the plane of polarization, or for colour vision, by making use of possible differences in spectral sensitivity of retinula cells of one ommatidium. The retina of the fly has two eccentrically placed retinula cells in each ommatidium. These cells have the same axis but tubules oriented at right angles to each other and at least one runs past the lamina to the next neuropile, the medulla. Other insects have other patterns of eccentric or basal retinula cells and one of the eight similar retinula cells of the bee has a long axon, thereby introducing an asymmetry that would allow analysis of the plane of polarization or colour.

As an additional complexity, it must be remembered that the interommatidial angle is not constant over the eye of the fly but varies from 2.0° to at least 4.0° (Burkhardt et al. in [3]). The regional differences in all the parameters of the retinula cells are not yet explored and are likely to be diverse. Other parts of the eye with different interommatidial angles might well have other differences between the receptive fields of the retinula axons that converge.

EYES WITH CRYSTALLINE THREADS

Many arthropods have eyes in which the rhabdoms lie relatively far from the proximal tips of the cones, and in each ommatidium the two are connected by a long transparent thread of high refractive index (Fig. 9.13, B). This is characteristic of the crustaceans related to lobsters (Astacura) and insects related to moths, as well as to many other forms, mainly nocturnal.

Figure 9.11

The relevant details of the integration of excitation from retinula cells pointing in different directions in the eye of the fly.

A. The pattern of rhabdomeres immediately at the base of the cone. This plan as seen from above corresponds with that in Figure 9.12.

B and C. Silver-stained sections at right angles to the corneal surface, showing the interweaving of axons between the ommatidia and the optic cartridges. B is a sagittal section of the front of the eye; C is a horizontal section of *Musca domestica*. These preparations were the basis of the inferences shown in Figures 9.10 and 9.12. [A from Pedler, 1965; B and C from V. Braitenburg.]

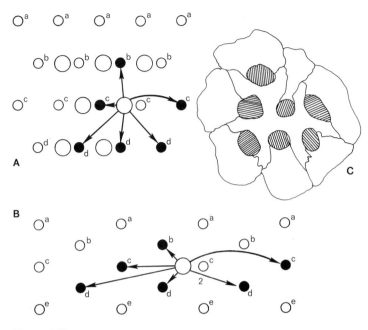

Figure 9.12

Plan of the destinations of the axons of one ommatidium at six of the optic cartridges in the lamina. A side view of the plan is shown in Figure 9.10. The larger open circles represent ommatidia, one of which is shown sending each of its six axons to different optic cartridges (*shaded black*) in the lamina below. Because the pattern is repeated for all cells, each cartridge receives six axons.

A. The pattern undistorted.

B. The pattern distorted, as at the front of the eye.

C. The pattern of rhabdom arrangement, which causes each retinula cell to have its axis of sensitivity in a different direction. This pattern corresponds with that of the axons in A, so that retinula cells that point in the same direction come together in the lamina (see Fig. 9.10). [After Braitenberg, 1966.]

In 1891 Exner published his theory that a combined image is produced by superposition of an erect image from each ommatidium, and illustrated this image in the eye of a firefly. The theory has been extended uncritically to all eyes in which the rhabdom layer is far from the crystalline cones. In fact, no examples of superposition images can be found in Crustacea and direct optical measurements rule them out [11]. In the firefly a first image *within* the optically homogeneous cone can form a second erect image behind the cone, as in Figure 9.13, but both calculation [5] and direct observation [32] strongly suggest that this second image from each facet is not in the plane of the rhabdom layer. Superposition of the separate images would be extremely sensitive to the exact

curvature of the cornea. For all so-called superposition eyes a more satisfactory suggestion is that light from the cone enters the crystalline thread
and passes down it by internal reflection to the rhabdom below. This
would explain why pigment migration in decapod crustacean eyes changes
the sensitivity greatly, but has little effect upon the acuity of the retina

Figure 9.13

Theories of image formation in compound eyes in which the receptor layer (*cross-hatched*) is far from the crystalline cones.

A. Modern form of the superposition theory. All cones examined have proved to be
optically homogeneous, and therefore the first image must be within the cone if an
erect image is to be formed below. Superposition of the erect images from several
cones is possible but demands perfect refracting surfaces and curvature of the eye.
The only likely occurrence is in the firefly, but direct observation of the erect image
there suggests that it lies behind the receptor layer.

B. A crystalline thread carries light by internal reflection to the receptor belonging
to that cone. Only light near the axis is accepted so long as the scattered light is
absorbed by pigment outside the light-pipe of high refractive index. The acceptance
angle will be similar to that for an apposition eye, or for any rod-shaped structure
when light strikes it end-on, for the cone has the same relation to the rhabdom in
an apposition eye as it has here to the crystalline thread. Arguments based upon
anatomy suggest that this is the true situation in superposition eyes; the chief experimental evidence is that the movements of the pigment grains, caused by changes in
background intensity, have little effect on the acuity.

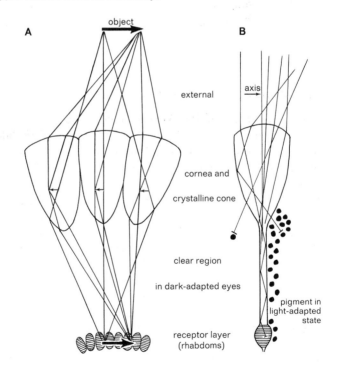

[7]. Each ommatidium of the firefly *Photuris* has a crystalline thread down which light is guided in both dark and light-adapted states. This was not noticed by Exner, and was presumably displaced in his photography of superposition images. The dark-adapted firefly eye, with little pigment between retina and rhabdom, must have enhanced sensitivity but reduced acuity that is achieved by the capture of nonaxial light upon the enormously developed rhabdom layer.

The most reasonable conclusion, but based upon few experiments, is that the only difference between an apposition eye and a superposition eye lies in the extended pathway of internal reflection along the crystalline thread of the latter [26]. A number of insects with an intermediate arrangement do not then have to be placed between two sharply contrasting models. The only apparent advantage of having a long crystalline thread is to increase the light-catching area, because with it larger cones can be placed at a greater radius from the rhabdoms. A disadvantage is that the plane of polarized light is not so readily discriminated, insofar as polarization must be reduced by numerous internal reflections in the crystalline thread. In crustacean eyes there is considerable pigment migration away from the rhabdoms and crystalline threads in the dark-adapted eyes. The hypothesis that the light reaches the rhabdom by internal reflection in both light and dark-adapted states removes the problem of how the optic ganglia could otherwise analyse two different types of image. With internal reflection in all cases, only the intensity of the image pattern changes.

ELECTROPHYSIOLOGY OF RETINULA CELLS

The ommatidium of the American horseshoe crab *Limulus* consists of about a dozen retinula cells, each with a flattened rhabdomere of tubules that lies closely against the adjacent cells. At the base of this group of receptor cells are one or two eccentric cells with no rhabdomere, but each eccentric cell has a process comparable to a dendrite, which penetrates up the central core between the retinula cells (Fig. 9.14). After a great deal of research on this tight cluster, the following conclusions emerge. Light excites the retinula cells, probably at the rhabdomeres, and the ultimate effect is a change in the voltage/current relations which can be seen as a change in resistance of the membrane and a depolarization of the retinula cell. The eccentric cell is not sensitive to light but is depolarized by depolarization of the retinula cells. Tight junctions, with low resistance at low currents, lie between the retinula cells. Tight junctions between retinula cells and eccentric cells act as rectifiers which allow depolarization of the eccentric cell. All electrical responses of one cell are seen to a lesser extent in the other cells, unless the potentials

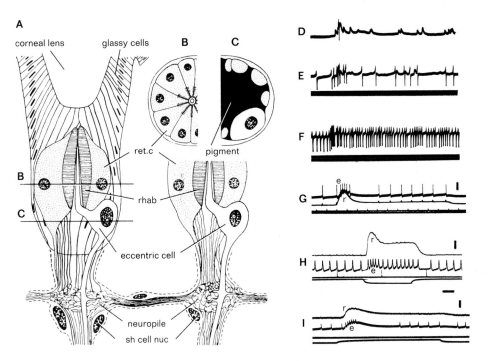

Figure 9.14

The sensory neurons of an ommatidium of the compound eye of the primitive arachnid *Limulus* and their electrical responses to illumination.

A. Vertical section through two adjacent ommatidia, showing the relationships between the retinula cells (*re*), which have rhabdomeres (*rhab*), and the eccentric cell (*e*), which has a terminal dendrite that runs up between the rhabdomeres. The lateral branches of both types of neurons form a plexus together beneath the basement membrane.

B and C. Transverse sections at the levels indicated.

D. Miniature potentials, which are thought to arise from the capture of single photons at low light intensities (see also Fig. 9.15).

E and F. Spikes at higher light intensities.

G, H, and I. Simultaneous pairs of records from a retinula cell (*r*) and an eccentric cell (*e*), showing the greater depolarisation in the former and the greater amplitude of spikes in the latter. Note the inhibition of spikes after the first initial burst in G and I, probably due to inhibition originating in the neuropile plexus. Activity in each ommatidium inhibits other ommatidia around it via synapses in this neuropile layer. [A–C from Bullock and Horridge, 1965; D–F from Fuortes, 1959; G–I from Behrens and Wulff, 1965.]

of the cells are forced far apart. The latency of the electrical changes is long, so that unobserved chemical processes must precede them. The relation between light intensity, latency, and the form of the response is compatible with a series of about 10 RC filters, which could represent a series of chemical reactions [19]. The ratio of electrical energy in the minimal membrane response to the energy of light in the stimulus is about a million in the dark-adapted retinula cells, and the active electrical response requires ATP. The amplifying process is evidently chemical, and a series of chemical reactions have been proposed between the initial absorption of a quantum and the appearance of the electrical effect, each stage in the series with an energy gain greater than unity. The light-adapted ommatidium, however, has a much lower energy gain, nearer to unity. The fall in sensitivity and the shortening of the electrical effect during light adaptation have been explained tentatively as due to the inhibitory action of intermediate products (Fuortes in [33]).

MINIATURE POTENTIALS

Some retinula cells of *Limulus, Locusta,* and *Calliphora* respond to very weak light by a series of miniature potentials, 1 to 2 mV in amplitude (Fig. 9.15). For any constant low illumination these potentials appear

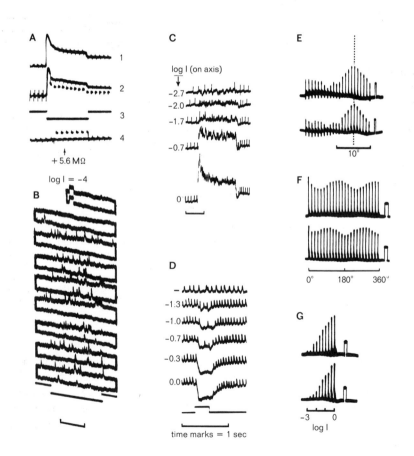

to have no dependence of one interval on the next. The average frequency of miniature potentials is proportional to the light intensity over a fifty-fold range, up to about 10 miniature potentials per second, above which it is no longer possible to distinguish them from each other. If a total amount of light energy has a 50% chance of producing a miniature potential, it makes no difference whether the light is presented within 10 msec or over a period of 10 sec, in any period between, or in a series of pulses. Similarly, with pairs of light flashes, the total expectation of seeing a miniature potential depends on the number of photons and reveals no neural phenomena such as facilitation [34]. However, the best evidence that miniature potentials owe their individuality to single photons is that the light flux in the retinula cell is so low that there must be long intervals between the randomly arriving photons. The efficiency of capture and registration of photons has been estimated to be as high as 8% in the retina of the fly and 50% in the lamina after summation (papers by Kirschfelt and Reichardt in [3]).

Including the eye of the blowfly and locusts, all arthropod eyes that have so far yielded miniature potentials have basal retinula cells with

Figure 9.15

Recordings from the retina of the locust, showing that retinula cells with fused rhabdomeres are electrophysiologically distinct, but share one optical path. Records A, B, E, F, and G are from the same pair of cells in one ommatidium.

A. Relative electrical independence of cells of one ommatidium (tested as in E). Current pulses through one cell are hardly measurable in the neighbouring cell whether light is shining or not. Traces 1 and 2 show responses in the two cells to a light, as shown in 3. Superimposed on trace 4 is the effect of a calibrating resistance change of 5.6 MΩ. In fact a voltage in one cell shows about one-fifth of its magnitude in the other cell.

B. Miniature potentials (photon captures) in the same pair of cells (shown by connected traces) are independent at low light intensity.

C. Responses of a retinula cell that yielded all-or-none spikes and a typical depolarization. Light intensities are shown on the left: the spikes are inhibited by the natural stimulus. Note the postinhibitory increase in frequency. In contrast, electrical depolarization *increases* spike frequency.

D. Spikes, again inhibited by light, but in this relatively rare case the slow potential is a hyperpolarization, which possibly spreads from inhibition at the first synapse in the lamina. Even the spikes may spread from second-order cells; the part played by the eccentric cell is unknown.

E. Simultaneous records from the two cells, as in A and B. The stimulus is moved horizontally across the axis of the cell in steps of 1°. The two cells have the same optical path as was shown also in the vertical plane for this pair of cells.

F. The same two cells tested with flashes of polarized light, the plane of which was rotated 15° between each flash. Note that the optimal planes are about 60° apart.

G. The same pair of cells stimulated by flashes of graded intensity. This calibration serves to convert the responses of E and F to equivalent light intensities. [Records by S. R. Shaw.]

long axons or eccentric cells. According to one school of thought, the miniature potentials are postsynaptic potentials produced by packets of transmitter from retinula to eccentric cell (Adolph in [3]). (The miniature potentials may still be referable to individual light quanta at the low light intensities referred to above.) Another school considers that the miniature potentials are caused by a local breakdown in the cell membrane, a rupture or a closure of a tubule of the rhabdom, and are only secondarily induced by a single quantum. Both theories agree that the long latency before the miniature potential reveals that many chemical (not only diffusion) stages intervene between light adsorption and the first electrical effect. Calculation shows that many thousands of electronic charges flow when a single quantum is effectively absorbed. The temperature coefficient (Q_{10}) of the rate of production of miniature potentials in *Limulus* is 3 to 4. This is the same as at the neuromuscular junction of the frog, in which packets of acetylcholine are thought to cause each miniature potential. A breakdown of membrane resistance by the indirect influence of light is postulated by both of the above theories; the question is settled by the observation that in the locust (always) and in *Limulus* (when the retinula cells are separable by polarization) the miniature potentials recorded in two different retinula cells are distinct and asynchronous. Therefore the miniature potentials must arise presynaptically in the primary photoreceptor neurons. All this complexity points up the necessity for detailed studies on eyes known to have only one type of cell and no lateral interaction. Such an eye has now been found in the olfactory organ or ventral eye of *Limulus*.

At higher intensities the miniature potentials, if present, fuse to a smooth depolarization with an initial peak (Figs. 5.16 and 9.14, D). This depolarization spreads to the axon, which passes through the basement membrane. In retinula cells of the locust and drone bee and in *Limulus* retinula and eccentric cells, impulses in the axon can be recorded in the cell body, which does not itself fire (Fig. 9.15). Spikes recorded in the locust retinula cells are only 1 mV in size and therefore must be conducted electrotonically from far down the axon or from another cell. The increase in permeability that is caused by stronger light reduces the spike height even more in the locust retinula cell, and at best spikes are seen only at low levels of illumination. Electrical depolarization certainly increases spike frequency but, contrary to earlier statements (Horridge in [3]), spikes are inhibited by light falling on the axis (Fig. 9.15). A few rare cells are hyperpolarized by light but spikes are still inhibited. Probably an inhibitory effect spreads from the lamina. Transmission between retina and lamina is not as yet understood but could be electrotonic, and the spikes do not necessarily originate in the retinula cell. Ideally, two photons captured in adjacent ommatidia could be sufficient for perception of motion. Analysis of the optomotor response of the fly shows that no coincidence of photon arrivals is required in the receptor element and that there is no nervous threshold. A single photon, if absorbed, sets a finite probability for the elicitation of a physiological event, which in turn sets a probability for motion perception, but it remains a problem as to how the motion perception system can operate with a low-frequency random input.

INTERACTION BETWEEN RETINULA CELLS

Low-resistance pathways allow a flow of ionic current between the retinula cells and, in *Limulus*, between retinula cells and eccentric cells (Fig. 5.11). When electrodes depolarize retinula cells in *Limulus*, they influence each other, but there are theoretical and experimental reasons for thinking that this effect is smaller when light is the stimulus. The eccentric cell sums the depolarization for the whole ommatidium. Depolarization of the eccentric cell generates trains of spikes that can be recorded, at lower amplitude, by an electrode in any of the retinula cells. Retinula cells of *Limulus* also generate spikes, at least when stimulated electrically. The eccentric cell thus speaks for the whole ommatidium but loses possible information of the colour and plane of polarization. The function of the eye of *Limulus* remains a puzzle because the cuticle is rather opaque (except to red) and visual responses are poor.

Interaction is negligible between the retinula cells of the locust [39], and it must be remembered that interaction between retinula cells with one ommatidium would tend to throw away information about the plane of polarized light and about the colour of a stimulus (Fig. 9.15). In the locust there are two types of cell, with peaks in the blue and in the green parts of the spectrum; some cells show double peaks. Locust retinula cells of a single ommatidium fall into three or four groups with reference to the plane of polarized light that stimulates most effectively. The bee, with the best known abilities in analysing polarization and colour, has four pairs of retinula cells in each ommatidium, with two principal directions of tubules [14], but these cells are not necessarily equivalent in spectral sensitivity; at least one of the eight is distinct in having a long axon to the second optic neuropile [11]. The whole subject requires a great deal of detailed critical work before the mechanism of the separate discrimination of polarized light, colour, horizontal movement, vertical movement, and direction in any arthropod is understood in electrophysiological terms.

In crustaceans each ommatidium contains two types of retinula cells, with tubules that are either horizontal or vertical in normal posture. This has been directly demonstrated to be the basis of the discrimination of axial polarized light by single cells in the crab [38]. In such a system an electronic interaction between retinula cells is ruled out because it would reduce the sensitivity to the plane of polarization.

ACUITY OF THE COMPOUND EYE

Acuity can be defined only arbitrarily for any whole optical system, and further, the existence of noise always means that the threshold must be defined statistically. The 50% point on an **S**-shaped curve of the stimulus variable plotted against the frequency of seeing is only one definite value; it is preferable to have the whole curve (Fig. 9.18). Optical acuity is commonly defined by the ability to resolve the images of two point sources at a minimum angle of separation, but this test cannot be used for animals with compound eyes because it produces no measurable output. The acuity depends on the aperture of the system if the optics and the design of the receptors are perfect, but these conditions are not necessarily met. If a receptor system has sufficient information about the exact light intensity in each part of the diffraction pattern, it is theoretically possible to achieve slightly but not indefinitely more resolution than the limit set by aperture, but there is no evidence of a complex mechanism within the retina to recover visual information from a diffraction pattern across an array of receptors. The determination of acuity depends on the type of stimulus employed and gives an over-all measure for the whole system down to the level where the measurable output is drawn off.

In all compound eyes that have been investigated, the acuity of individual receptors and therefore of the whole eye is limited by the imperfections and breadth of the acceptance angle curves. In the locust, at least, the optical system, composed of cornea and cone, accepts a wider angle than can be absorbed by the rhabdom. In the light-adapted eye it is internal reflection in the rhabdom which physically determines the angle of acceptance, as shown by the increase in angle of acceptance upon dark adaptation. We assume that selection pressure has led to a situation in which facets are as close and numerous as is compatible with retaining a large aperture, and that the acceptance angle curves are on the average of optimum width—a compromise between letting in as much light as possible while being as narrow as possible. But there are imperfections of all kinds, and being unpredictable, they cannot be taken into account by a genetically fixed neural integrating mechanism. For example, some retinula cells show acceptance angle curves with double peaks; the axes of the retinula cells and the ommatidia are inclined at slightly irregular angles, and acceptance angle curves are not sym-

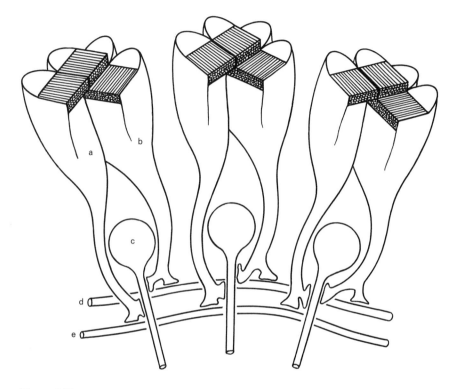

Figure 9.16

Model of probable retina lamina connexions of arthropods, e.g. decapod crustacea, bee and locust, with fused rhabdomeres. Retinula cells a and b of one ommatidium are optimally stimulated by light in the same direction, which is conserved by their convergence upon the lamina neuron c. The known synapses with horizontal fibres of the retina could be specific with reference to polarization plane as shown by fibres d and e. We do not know whether colour is coded within ommatidia or by different ommatidia.

metrical or identical in shape. These imperfections are caused by irregularities in growth, and in eyes of all different stages of complexity it is the structural errors in the eye rather than the aperture which probably limit the development of more perfect vision in each species.

The movement of a striped pattern has been the commonest stimulus used, because arthropods respond well to it, and the acuity has been defined as the angle subtended by the repeat distance of the narrowest stripes to which the insect as a whole gives an optomotor response, or to which interneurons respond by firing. There are a number of experimental pitfalls, the most serious of which is an irregularity in the stripes, which still causes responses when the individual stripes are no longer resolved. Moreover, the response is made by the whole animal, and each aspect of the response could be limited by unknown mechanisms between the stimulus and the final output. The information contained in such a simple output is insufficient to exclude many possible models of the mechanism (Fig. 12.14). Because of the numerous mechanisms and the unknown extent of correlations between facets and over the whole

Figure 9.17

Contrasting stripes that pass through the field of view of single retinula cells, with the resulting oscillations in membrane potential. The peaked curves show the sensitivity of the cell to light at different angles of incidence to the eye. Each vertical column represents the movement of stripes across the visual field of a cell. The different columns represent different values of angle of acceptance $\Delta\rho$ and stripe period λ. The resulting contrast transfer (ct), calculated from the equation $ct = \exp - (\pi^2/4 \ln 2)(\Delta\rho/\lambda)^2$, as in Figure 9.18, is equal to the contrast in illumination within the retinula cell. This can be found independently as $(I_{max} - I_{min})/(I_{max} + I_{min})$, where I_{max} and I_{min} are the illuminations that produce receptor potentials of P_{max} and P_{min}. The relation between P and I is found separately by varying the intensity of axial illumination. The correspondence of this theory with experimental values of contrast transfer is shown in Figure 9.18.

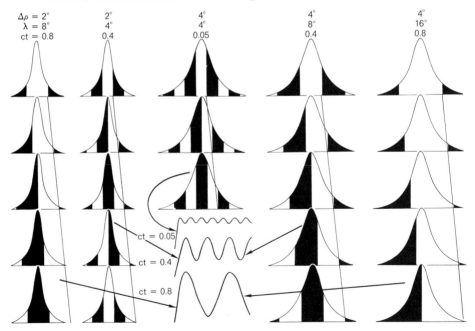

$\Delta\rho = 2°$	2°	4°	4°	4°
$\lambda = 8°$	4°	4°	8°	16°
$ct = 0.8$	0.4	0.05	0.4	0.8

eye, the acuity of single retinula cells can best be found by direct measurements on them, and this is possible in the following way.

A single receptor cell has a sensitivity to light at different angles to its axis, as defined by its acceptance angle curve in a particular plane (Figs. 9.5 and 9.6). When a series of vertical stripes of regular repeat period is put before the receptor cell, the total stimulus at the cell is obtained by summing the black and the white areas separately, as they are distributed over the acceptance angle curve in the horizontal plane (Fig. 9.17). As the stripes move along in front of the receptor cell there will be an oscillation in the light intensity in the receptor as a function of time. Assuming that the acceptance angle curve (Fig. 9.17) is a Gaussian curve, this oscillation can be calculated as a function of the acceptance angle $\Delta\rho$ and stripe width λ. The contrast transfer, h, is defined as

$$h = \frac{I_{max} - I_{min}}{I_{max} + I_{min}} = \exp - \left(\frac{\pi^2}{4 \ln 2}\right)\left(\frac{\Delta\rho}{\lambda}\right)^2$$

where ρ = width of acceptance angle curve at half height,
λ = angular stripe repeat period,
I = light intensity at the receptor (see Fig. 9.17).

We must assume that (a) the acceptance angle curve is a symmetrical Gaussian curve, and (b) the stripes form an infinite field.

The formula means that as the stripe width is reduced the maximum intensity change, caused by movement from a black to a white stripe on the axis, falls in a well-defined way (Fig. 9.18). With an infinite field of stripes and a Gaussian acceptance angle curve, the contrast falls to zero at a point that is not easily defined on account of the noise in the system, but at which λ is approximately equal to $\Delta\rho$.

For an insect primary receptor cell, where intracellular records from the cell itself are feasible, the transfer of contrast from the moving spatial pattern to the temporal oscillation of the membrane potential is directly measurable, and the observed oscillatory electrical changes, as the stripes move past, can be converted into relative light intensities at the receptor. For the locust, experimental and theoretical values of contrast are plotted for various values of $\Delta\rho$ and λ in Figure 9.17. The experimental results show a reasonable agreement with the values of acceptance angle of retinula cells as measured directly with a single movable light. Thus other factors, such as lateral interaction and flicker fusion frequency, can be reasonably ignored. The light-adapted locust eye performs rather better than expected from its value of $\Delta\rho$, because the acceptance angle curve is actually more pointed than a Gaussian curve, and this shows up in high values of contrast transfer for the narrowest stripes.

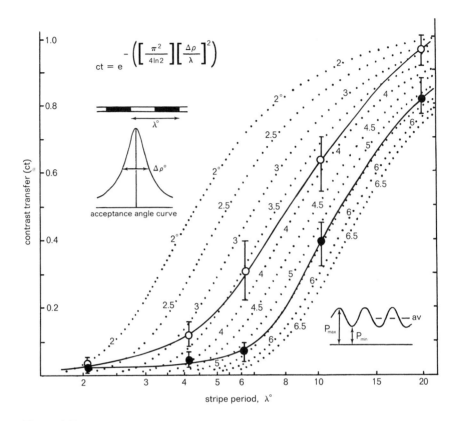

Figure 9.18

Theoretical (*dotted line*) and experimental (*solid line*) contrasts between peaks and troughs when stripes of various repeat periods ($\lambda°$) are moved in front of a window with a Gaussian acceptance angle curve as in the inset at upper left. The contrast transfer is defined as $ct = (I_{max} - I_{min})/(I_{max} + I_{min})$, where I_{max} and I_{min} correspond to the light intensities that would produce the retinula cell membrane depolarisations at the peaks P_{max} and troughs P_{min}, as shown in the inset at lower right. These curves show how the contrast of illumination produced by the stripes increases with increasing $\lambda°$, and that retinula cells with narrower acceptance angle curves give equivalent contrasts with finer patterns. *Solid circles* show experimental points for the dark-adapted locust eye; *open circles,* for the same eye when light-adapted. The position of the experimental curves agrees reasonably well with the angles of acceptance of locust retinula cells, as measured directly with a narrow pencil of light. The small disagreement between theory and experiment (shown by crossing of dotted and solid curves) is presumed to originate in the non-Gaussian form of the experimental acceptance angle curve.

In reality the receptor cell accepts a cone of light (with the angle of acceptance in the vertical plane differing from the angle in the horizontal plane), but the main point is that the acuity of the single receptor depends entirely on the width of its acceptance angle curve. The eye as a whole is limited by the acuity of its elements.

When an artificial window is put before the receptor cell, the apparent acuity is increased if the response depends on intensity changes. In the most extreme case, if the window has a width of half a stripe period, the movement of the pattern behind it will always produce a large change even if the stripe period is well below the normal lower limit for the eye. For example, the movement of a hair that covers an illuminated slit of its own width is very effective in causing an intensity change. Windows of this kind, however, are unimportant in nature. One of the problems encountered in the laboratory is the difficulty of providing rotating striped patterns that have no irregularity. For example, a finger mark on a striped drum is sufficient as an irregularity to affect the response. This kind of artifact can sometimes be reduced by use of to-and-fro oscillations instead of rotations, or by looking only at changes having the appropriate repetition rate in electrical records from single receptor cells that are stimulated by striped patterns [41].

The smallest movement that will elicit a response is no measure of acuity. Arthropods are incredibly sensitive to movement of lights or contrasting edges. They may see them with fuzzy edges but the response to the least movement merges into the mechanical lower limit of the recording system. Movements as small as $0.01°$ or as slow as one revolution a day easily evoke a response in several arthropods (for example, locusts and crabs), so long as the moving objects are large enough to be resolved. It is interesting to speculate on the possible functions of these high sensitivities, which must assist in stabilizing the eye over long periods. Small eye movements assist in the perception of stationary objects [21].

MOVEMENT PERCEPTION

Movement in the visual field involves a shift of a pattern from one set of receptors to another and therefore is inseparable from the resulting intensity changes upon single receptor cells. To infer the movement from the visual stimulus, the animal must make a correlation between the pattern of a visual field as seen initially on one set of receptors and as seen a short time later at another point along the retina by another set of receptors (including some of the first set) [35].

In the direction of average movement, the optomotor responses of the eyes or head in freely moving animals serve to stabilize the visual field. Besides showing that the movement is seen, they are convenient for further analysis of the mechanism. Efferent motor fibres in the oculomotor nerve from the brain of the crab control the movements of the stalked eyes. In the locust comparable motoneurons of the ventral cord control the muscles of the neck, and in the fly the optomotor response is observable as a turning during flight. The lower limit of velocity detection seems to be governed by adaptation in the photoreceptors, and the upper limit of the optomotor response is determined by the maximum speed at which the muscles contract. Therefore, bell-shaped curves of the strength of an optomotor response plotted against velocity do not measure the parameters of the mechanism of movement perception [41]. This means that the original Reichardt model [35] cannot be distinguished from alternatives such as those in Figure 12.16.

Experiments with crabs show that several correlating pathways for movement run in parallel, and pathways that correlate over short time periods can be adapted out by regular rapid oscillations, while at the same time the correlation for slow movements remains unchanged (Fig. 9.19). In the optic tract a variety of afferent interneurons run from the optic ganglia to the brain, and different classes respond best over different velocity ranges [46, 48]. It is accepted, but not proved, that afferent interneurons directionally selective to movement in the visual field are those which provide the input to the brain for the optomotor response.

Two principal mechanisms have been suggested for the abstraction of movement from intensity changes in the receptors: (a) multiplication of the outputs of neighbouring receptors [35]; (b) inhibition by horizontal pathways [18]. Many other systems, however, are possible (see p. 372). One of the central problems is to find a single simple system that is independent of contrast reversal. At present there is no direct electrophysiological evidence to decide between theories or to identify intermediates and combinations of them, and we await recordings from cells that are components rather than outputs of the mechanism. The movement perception system of arthropods has not yet been located, but the obvious

Figure 9.19

The influence of repeated small oscillations on the optokinetic response of the eye of the crab. A sudden movement of all contrasting objects in the visual field as at A, causes a response that is initially rapid, with a slower conclusion. The same stimulus, when superimposed upon oscillations at 2 per second (B), gives rise to a response with no rapid component. The inference is that there are normally at least two systems, of different time constant, in parallel.

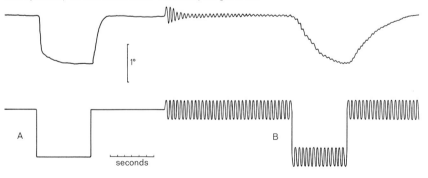

seconds

place to look for its inputs and first components is in the 2nd optic ganglion, the medulla.

The question as to whether arthropods see only moving stimuli can be resolved in the following way. The eye continually makes small eye movements, which are nevertheless large enough to excite the very sensitive movement perception system [23]. These movements sharpen up vision, but when the eye is clamped we can still find evidence (given on p. 339) that strongly contrasting objects are seen, even though we cannot exclude small residual movements of the retina behind the clamped cornea.

The function of the optomotor response is to stabilize the eye, head, and whole body by the whole visual field, and optomotor responses are made towards the average movement of all contrasting objects in the visual field. In this stabilization, the effect of small eye movements is averaged out by movement perception systems of very long time constant (see p. 338).

PERCEPTION, WITH REFERENCE TO THE FIRST SYNAPSES

Considerable information is available about the line labelling by the individual retinula cells, and attention is now turning towards the connexions of their axon terminals with second-order neurons. Relatively little is known, but it is certain that any behavioural discrimination of colour, movement, direction, and plane of polarisation must depend upon preservation of information at these synapses.

In *Limulus* the dozen or so retinula cells of each ommatidium have axons in the optic nerve, but their activity is undescribed. Where they come through the basement lamella the axons have lateral branches, and the eccentric cell axon also has side branches in the same region (Fig. 9.14). These side branches form a plexus, in which apparently there are indiscriminate synapses between any one fibre and any other, and all are mutually inhibitory. The effect is for any strongly stimulated cell to inhibit its neighbours more than they inhibit it. Therefore a gradient of excitation caused by a black-white edge is steepened, and the response to a moving edge is strengthened by rebound from inhibition. The significance is unknown, for *Limulus* has a poor eye; the eccentric cells have an acceptance angle ($\Delta\rho$) of about 14°. Although directional responses to lights are known in young *Limulus*, the adult eye seems to be functionless and is often covered with algae or barnacles.

Crustacean and insect eyes are quite different, although evidence is accumulating that the terminals of the retinula cells are inhibitory [18]. Transmission from retina to lamina is not understood. Curiously, in the locust, electrical depolarisation of retinula cells increases the frequency of spikes of unknown origin, but light always inhibits the spikes (Fig.

9.15 and p. 166). There is no peripheral, synaptic plexus in the insect retina and the retinula axons do not branch. In the fly, six of these axons end with a remarkably regular but asymmetrical connectivity pattern in the first synaptic layer in the lamina ganglionaris (Figs. 9.10 and 9.12). At the lamina, the summation of depolarizations of endings of the six retinula cells that look in one direction increases the equivalent aperture and efficiency of the process of converting photons to neural excitation in the fly. The other two axons have not been followed with perfect clarity, although in the fly, moth, and bee at least one goes directly to the second neuropile layer. In the fly, the retinula cells with the long axon are the two with the central rhabdoms one above the other. They have a peak sensitivity towards the blue, but the six others have a maximum in the green end of the spectrum [28]. The groups of terminals—the optic cartridges—are equal in number to the ommatidia; the pattern of connexions ensures that the six incoming fibres to a cartridge of the lamina converge from six different ommatidia [6]. In the fly, at least, there is a lateral synaptic plexus between processes of the second-order ganglion cells [42]. The special case of the fly has already been considered (see p. 155 and Figs. 9.10 to 9.12).

Almost all observations of arthropod visual behaviour can be interpreted as demonstrating that only moving stimuli are seen; that is, all excitation passes through a filter that passes only differentiated excitation, although time constants can be long, as in optokinetic memory [21]. When movement is abstracted, the excitation of an ommatidium is thought to be correlated only with that in the next ommatidium, or the next-but-one. This movement-abstracting mechanism may be expected to lie as close behind the receptors as possible for maximum sensitivity, because the retinal location and time of arrival of the signal must be as sensitive and accurate as possible, and the relation between illumination and nervous excitation must be as unmodified as possible by neural events. For maximum effectiveness a movement perception system should also have inputs with fields as small as possible and of similar spectral sensitivity; see p. 271 for vertebrates and p. 338 for crabs. Unfortunately, direct recording with microelectrodes suggests that the movement perception system lies deeper (see below).

The mechanism of the cartridges cannot code for colour in the fly because they apparently operate entirely with green-sensitive retinula cells. The anatomical correspondence in Figure 9.10 between the retina and the lamina in the fly is not suitable for the integration of polarized light analysers, which is presumably done by the two cells (with tubules at right angles) with axons to the medulla. Apparently colour analysis in the fly depends on the excitation going to the second neuropile from the two bluish receptor cells, relative to all the other green cells, which go to the lamina. Even in the bee a primary axon from each ommatidium runs direct to the second optic neuropile (10). Many arthropods can distinguish the plane of polarization, as distinct from mere intensity effects. Therefore, as in the crab (Fig. 9.16), there must be a regularity of connexions that preserve polarization, colour, and movement in two dimensions. Colour is necessarily differently projected by the long and short retinula cell terminals, and the general position on the retina by a discrimination between the optic cartridges or long axons. Microelectrode recording in the lamina of the locust reveals that presynaptic depolarization of the retinula cell terminals causes a hyperpolarization (and presumably inhibition) of second-order units. The narrow fields of view of these summed hyperpolarizations in the locust, and the anatomical plexus of the retinula cell terminals of the fly, suggest that the principal function of a cartridge of the lamina is the summation of the inhibitory terminals of retinula cells that point in a particular direction. Considering what happens subsequently to the pattern of excitation from the retinal cells, it is meaningless to conjecture whether the functional unit is the ommatidium.

ORDER IN THE RETINAL CONNEXIONS OF THE CRAB

The first optic neuropile of the higher crustaceans is also organized in cartridges, but these are more complex than in the insects, with two types of horizontal fibres running through numbers of cartridges, and with a different type of synapse between each combination of fibres [17, 18]. The structure suggests that several sorts of information are extracted simultaneously from the terminals of the visual cells, but none of the arthropods shows the diversity of connexions of primary visual cells that is found in the retina of vertebrates (see p. 248).

A very definite inference of the separate discrimination of movement and polarized light by different lamina fibres comes from behavioural responses of the crab. Each ommatidium contains seven retinula cells, as illustrated in Figure 9.7. When there is nothing else for it to stabilize upon, the crab's eye follows the movement of a single light, which can be varied in colour and plane of polarization. By direct recording from retinula cells it is known that turning the plane of polarization through 90° is equivalent to changing the intensity by a factor of 10. Therefore, near threshold, polarized light selectively stimulates one class of cell. Rotating the polarization plane, however, does not affect the white light movement sensitivity, or the peak colour sensitivity of movement perception in either vertical or horizontal planes.

Convergence of retinula cell pathways means that some discrimination properties must be lost. In the search for a possible model, the important point is to find which attributes of the stimulus survive together. Angle

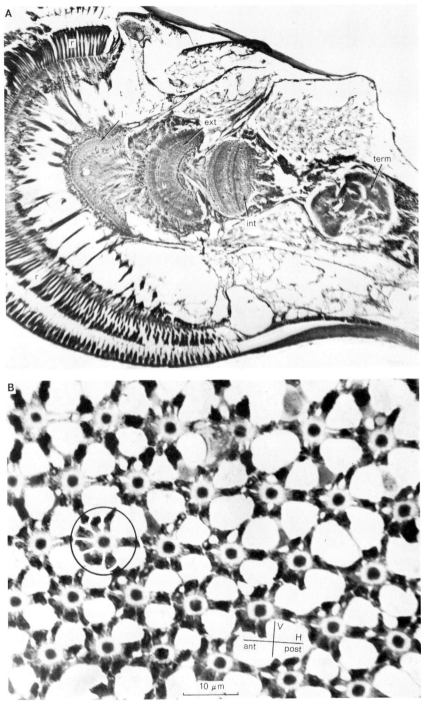

subtended at the eye together with intensity is conserved very well, as shown by responses to small movements of a point source in any direction. However, there is no evidence that colour or polarization plane is discriminated at each angle; instead a general integration over large parts of the eye would suffice for these parameters, so far as behavioural responses indicate. Second-order neurons of the optic cartridges of the lamina apparently conserve angle at the expense of polarization plane by having inputs from all seven cells of one ommatidium. But the retinula cell endings also make synapses with horizontal lamina fibres, which could be abstracting polarization plane from either horizontally or vertically oriented cells of many ommatidia (Fig. 9.16). With this model, which also applies to insects, movement perception and form vision would necessarily be little influenced by polarization plane although the receptors are excellent analysers of polarized light.

THE OPTIC GANGLIA

Immediately behind the compound eye of crustaceans and insects we find a series of regions of laminated neuropile. To Cajal, accustomed as he was to intricate anatomical systems, the optic lobes of the insect brain were unsurpassed in fineness, complexity, and regularity. "Ciertamente, la substancia gris ha crecido considerablemente en masa; pero cuando se compara su estructura con la del cerebro de los apidos o libelulidos, se nos aparece como algo excesivamente grosero, basto y rudimentario. Es como si pretendieramos igualar el mérito de tosco reloj de pared con el de una saboneta, maravilla de finura, delicadeza y precisión. Como siempre, el genio de la vida, al construir sus obras portentosas, brilla en lo pequeño mucho mas aun que en lo grande" [10].

Cajal says that when we compare vertebrate grey matter with the structure of the brain of the bee or dragonfly, the former seems gross and rudimentary. It is like comparing the merits of a great clock with the finest watch, which is a marvel of delicacy.

Figure 9.20
The retina and optic neuropiles of the crab *Carcinus*.

A. Optic neuropiles of *Carcinus*, showing the laminated neuropiles and the chiasmata between them. *r*, retina; *l*, lamina; *ext*, external medulla; *int*, internal medulla; *term*, medulla terminalis. See also Figures 6.11, B, 9.7, and 16.2.

B. Transverse section through numerous ommatidia, showing the regularity of the pattern of seven retinula cells in each. In the circle the cells are outlined in white: their orientation is constant across the whole eye, with reference to the axes shown. The palisade around the central rhabdom stands out as a clear ring.

TABLE 4

Efferent fibres in the optic tract that respond to mechanoreceptive stimulation

Fibre number	Location	Sensory field and response features
A. Fields restricted to head (14 + 3)		
Homolateral (8)		
41	5b/6	Eyestalk and socket: hairs: small
42	1a	Eyestalk, socket, antennule: hairs: tonic: large
43	7b	Eyestalk, socket, antennule: hairs: phasic: large
44	7b	Eyestalk, socket, antenna (not antennule): hairs: large
45	5a/6	Eyestalk, antennule, antenna: hairs and joints
46	3a/4	Socket, carapace-spine, cheliped elbow: hairs
47	4	Antennule—statocyst: phasic: large (found 7+ times)
48	2	Antenna: basal joint: large
Heterolateral (7)		
49a	?	Eyestalk and socket: hairs
49	7a	Eyestalk—distal joint: tonic: small (found 2 times)
50	6	Eyestalk—distal joint: phasic: large
51	6	Eyestalk—both joints, antennule: joints: phasic: large
52	5b	Eyestalk—basal joint depression: tonic: small
52a	?	Eyestalk—basal joint depression: antennule, antenna: tonic
53	5a/6	Antennule—statocyst: phasic: large
Bilateral (2)		
54	1a	Eyestalks, antennules, antennae: hairs and joints
54a	?	Antennules and antennae, inhibited by eyestalks: tonic: joints (?)
B. Limited fields involving thorax (16 + 1)		
Homolateral head and mouthparts (3)		
55	1a	Anterior carapace, spine, socket, eyestalk, head, mouthparts: hairs: large
56	2/4	Eyestalk, antennule, antenna, mouthparts: hairs and joints
57	3b	Antennule, antenna, mouthparts: joints and hairs
Heterolateral head and mouthparts (1)		
58	3a	Eyestalk—both joints, antennule, third maxilliped: joints: large
Asymmetric head and mouthparts (2)		
59	4	Ipsilateral anterior carapace, socket, eyestalk: bil. head and mouthparts: hairs: tonic: large
60	3a	Contralateral eyestalk—both joints: bil. spines, sockets, head and mouthparts: hairs and joints: phasic
Bilateral head and mouthparts (1)		
61	3b/5a	Eyestalks, antennules, antennae, mouthparts: hairs and joints
Homolateral mouthparts (1)		
62	1b	Mandible to third maxilliped: joints
Bilateral mouthparts, thorax, and abdomen (1)		
63	5a	Mouthparts, pereiopods, ventral body surface: hairs (and joints)

TABLE 4 (Continued)

Fibre number	Location	Sensory field and response features
Homolateral pereiopods (6)		
64	3b	Cheliped and legs, inhibited by mouthparts (spontaneous)
65	6	Cheliped and legs: hairs and joints
66	7b	Cheliped and legs: hairs and joints
67	4	Cheliped and legs: joints, especially MC flexion and CB depression
68	5a	Legs, especially 4th and 5th: joints, especially MC movement
68a	?	Legs, especially 4th and 5th: hairs
Heterolateral pereiopods (1)		
69	1a	Cheliped and legs: joints (especially active CB movement?)
Bilateral pereiopods (1)		
70	8	Chelipeds and legs: joints, especially active movements (and hairs?)

C. Large mechanoreceptive fields (29)

Homolateral (9)		
71	1b	Whole ventral surface, especially eyestalk and socket, diminishing progressively posteriorly: hairs and joints: tonic: large
72	5a/6	Whole dorsal and ventral surfaces, especially socket: hairs and joints: large (spontaneous)
73	7b	Similar, but especially eyestalk and antennule: large (not spontaneous)
74	1b	Similar, but especially anywhere anteriorly: small
75	1b	Uniform over whole dorsal and ventral surfaces: tonic: large
76	5a	Similar field, but especially mouthparts and cheliped
77	2/4	Whole dorsal and especially ventral surfaces, especially legs and cheliped, diminishing anteriorly
78	3a/b	Similar, but higher threshold and weaker responses
79	6	Whole ventral surface, especially abdomen and legs: hairs and joints
Heterolateral (4)		
80	5a	Anterior carapace and especially socket, head, mouthparts, chelipeds: hairs and joints: large
81	5b	Whole dorsal and ventral surfaces
82	1b	Similar
83	3a	All appendages (and ipsi. third maxilliped and pereiopods?): joints: large
Bilateral (16)		
84	5a	Whole body, especially eyestalks and sockets, head: phasic: large
85	5b	All appendages, but especially eyestalks: hairs and joints: large
86	3a/b	Similar, but especially antennules and antennae: large
87	8	Whole body, especially head and mouthparts: hairs and joints
88	1b/2	Whole body, especially ventral sterna and abdomen
89	1b	Whole body, especially head, mouthparts and distal chelipeds: large

TABLE 4 (Continued)

Efferent fibres in the optic tract that respond to mechanoreceptive stimulation

Fibre number	Location	Sensory field and response features
90	2	Whole body, especially mouthparts: hairs (and joints?)
91	2	Whole body, but inhibited by mouthparts: hairs (and joints?)
92	1a/2	Whole body uniformly, but weakly on dorsal surface
93	3a	Whole body uniformly, tonic
94	5a/6	Similar
95	1a	Similar
96	7b	All appendages: joints
97	3b	Similar, especially pereiopods: joints: large
98	5b	Similar, especially legs: joints: large
99	5a	Whole body, especially legs, ventral thorax abdomen: hairs: large

D. Limited mechanoreceptive and visual fields (4)

Heterolateral (4)

101	1a/2	Eyestalk, socket, head, and cheliped elbow: large
102	1b/2	Similar, but not cheliped
103	1b/3a	Similar to 65
104	1b/2/3a	Similar, and also pereiopods weakly

E. Large mechanoreceptive and visual fields (13)

Homolateral (2)

| 105 | 3a | Ventral surface of whole ipsilateral side; light, especially on tip of eye |
| 106 | 1b/2 | Whole ipsilateral side, especially pereiopods |

Heterolateral (2)

| 107 | 1b/2 | Whole contralateral side, especially legs |
| 108 | 3a | Similar, but especially eyestalk (possibly should be in Group D?) |

Bilateral (9)

109	5a	Whole ventral surface, especially eyestalk and head: tonic (spontaneous)
110	3a	Similar, but especially also statocyst: phasic (not spontaneous)
111	1b	Whole ventral surface, uniformly: light, especially on tip of eye
112	5b	Whole body, uniformly: large: low threshold
113	8	Similar, but less sensitive
114	4	Similar, but including statocysts
115	4	Whole ventral surface, uniformly
116	4	Similar, but probably also dorsally (different visual response)
117	4	Whole body—modulation of spontaneous discharge

The optic lobes consist almost invariably of three or four neuropile regions, separated by chiasmata where interneuron axons cross (Fig. 9.20). Whether or not the eyes are on movable stalks, the optic lobe is joined to the other protocerebral lobes of the brain by a large optic tract.

TABLE 5
Visual interneurons of the optic tract of the crab Podophthalmus

I. Purely visual; no very small field units were isolated.
　　A. Simple movement
　　　　1. Movement　2. On-off　3. Sustaining
　　B. Compound type
　　　　1. Nonspontaneous　2. Background discharge
II. Visual mechanoreceptor (mixed modality)
III. Fibres responding to contralateral visual stimulation, with approximate orientations and sizes of the receptive field, and location in nerve

Location in nerve	AM	A	AL	L	PL	P	PM	M	T	Visual field size
1a/b	←1→		←2→		←3→		←(4)→			
1b	←5→		←6→		←7→					
1a/b/2			←8→	←9→		←10→				
1a/2		←11→		←(12)→		←13→				Small field fibres
1a/2		←14→	←15→							(30–45°)
1b			←16→		←17→		←18→			"First group"
1a			←19→		←20→			←21→		
1a/7b				←22→						
1a/2							←23→			
1a/2								←24→		Small field fibres
4					←25→					(30–45°)
3a/4					←26→					"Second group"
4					←27→					
1b/2	Refer the horizontal line to the headings at the top								←28→	Small field fibres (30–45°)
5a	to obtain the size of the visual field.								←29→	"Third group"
4	←30→									
2			←31→	←32→						
1a/b			←33→							
1b			←34→							
1b/2			←35→							Intermediate
1b				←36→						field fibres
2/8				←37→						(60–90°)
8				←38→						
1b/2/3a/4					←39→					
1a/b				←40→						
6	←————————100————————→									Very large field fibre (whole eye) Visual only
1a/2			←———101———→							Large field fibres
1b/2			←———102———→							(120–180°)
1b/3a			←———103———→							Heterolateral
1b/3a			←———104———→							anterior touch
3a	←————————105————————→									Very large field fibres (whole eye) Homolateral touch
1b/2	←————————106————————→									
1b/2	←————————107————————→									Very large field fibres (whole eye) Heterolateral touch
3a	←————————108————————→									
5a	←————————109————————→									
3a	←————————110————————→									Very large
1b	←————————111————————→									field fibres
5b	←————————112————————→									(whole eye)
8	←————————113————————→									Bilateral touch
4	←————114, 115, 116, 117————→									

* A, anterior; L, lateral; P, posterior; M, medial; T, tip

The optic tract of crustaceans and insects carries a large proportion of axons of mechanoreceptor interneurons with receptive fields over various parts of the body, as well as visually excited interneurons from the contralateral eye (see Tables 4 and 5). Some, probably, are second-order neurons, such as those in crustaceans referring to the statocysts; others, especially those responding to visual and mechanoreceptors bilaterally, must be much more complex; and some of them may turn out to be command fibres on the motor side of the watershed. Although at first sight remarkable, the large number of channels carrying impulses to the optic ganglia is no more than another example of the decentralized nature of a multiganglionic central nervous system. There are even a few units that carry excitation from optic lobe to brain and have mechanoreceptor fields on the body. Conversely, optic interneurons run right down the ventral cord in both crustaceans and insects.

The significance of these interganglionic fibres must be very great in an animal in which the brain is not responsible for details of execution of movements at the segmental level, even though few explicit examples are known. In the locust an auditory stimulus can cause arousal of a visual unit that has habituated to a repeated flash of light. The optokinetic response of crabs increases in gain when the legs move, and the response of crabs to visual stimuli is changed by tickling their legs. The properties of the movement-sensitive visual fibres can also be changed by widespread stimuli, and one explanation offered for the numerous interneurons with broad (including multimodal) receptive fields is that they cause a predisposition for other interneurons to respond in a certain way, or that they exclude a class of possible responses. If so, we might be justified in saying that impulses in the broad field interneurons constitute the predisposition.

The optic neuropiles have, unexpectedly, been found to be essential in another way. After removal of one eyecup in the spiny lobster, the animal no longer takes in its chela a piece of food presented to the chemoreceptors of the ipsilateral antennule [30], showing that the optic ganglion is an essential link in a feeding reflex in which vision plays no part. There is also evidence that the contralateral optic ganglion plays some part in learning to respond to a visual stimulus.

One of the most intriguing examples of neural interaction in the animal kingdom is the effect of statocyst interneurons upon the responses of two visual fibres in the crayfish optic tract, one of which responds to shaky movements and the other to steady movements. Both have visual fields on the dorsal side of the eye when the animal is in its normal position. When the animal is rotated on its long axis, the edge of the visual field of these units stays in the same absolute direction in space [51, 52]. Rotation of the animal has the effect, via statocyst interneurons, of tailoring the visual field of that unit (Fig. 9.21). In this unit the brain (or

Figure 9.21

The effect of tilting on the receptive field (*shaded black*) of a visual unit of the crayfish, as recorded in the optic tract. There are at least two units of this type, one phasic and the other giving a maintained response to light. With the animal in its normal position (left), the visual field looks upwards. As the animal is tilted, progressively more of the field is removed by interaction in the optic lobe with an input from the statocysts.

maybe the other optic lobe) only sees movement that is directly above the eye. An imaginative but careful cataloguing of units in any nervous system may be expected to yield many such curious interactions.

Recordings are available from units of the optic tract between medulla terminalis and brain in a few decapod crustaceans [46] and from indeterminate depths in the optic lobe of the locust and a few other insects [24]. Few of these units have so far been identified as meaningful in a behavioural sense, and comparison with the frog and cat suggests that much imaginative analysis remains to be done. In fact there are many indications that in arthropods we do not understand at all the principles of transforming the visual stimulus into a pattern of responses of neurons. An exception is the one-way movement units (Fig. 9.22), which we trust are essential for the optokinetic responses. These units fall into different classes, which respond over different ranges of rate of movement of a contrasting stimulus; this confirms the behavioural experiments. These experiments indicate at least two pathways, one for slow and one for fast movement perception, which can be separated by fatigue [21].

In the crab *Podophthalmus* the unidirectional movement fibres fall into classes; some respond well to velocities of 1°/min to 60°/min, but optimally at 12°/min, and the fastest types have optima at 7 to 8°/sec. Presumably others sensitive to very slow movement have been missed because the appropriate stimuli were not applied. There is certainly not one class corresponding to the optimum of the optokinetic response. Our present ideas suggest that the forward gain in the optomotor response depends on which movement interneurons are active. Unidirectional movement receptors also fall into classes referring to the direction of preferred movement across the eye; both vertical and horizontal have been found. There are also classes of movement detectors that are distinguishable by rates of adaptation to a steady movement. In *Podophthalmus* the "novelty" units that respond to any movement introduced

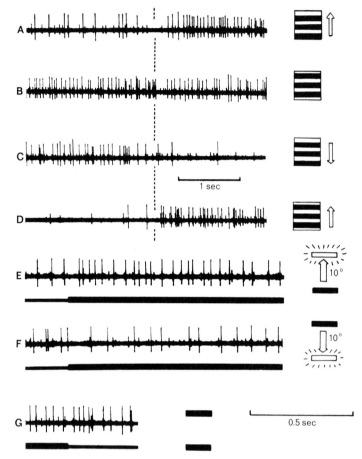

Figure 9.22

Undirectional movement discrimination in a visual unit of the optic lobe of the locust.

A–D. The unit, with a receptive field of 50°, is presented with vertically moving stripes behind a window. The dotted line shows the onset of movement in the direction indicated except in B, where it shows the halt. There is excitation by movement in one direction and inhibition of ongoing activity in the other direction. Background discharge and response to movement are little influenced by general illumination.

E–G. A selectively directional detector of movement responds also to virtual movement, which is caused by switching a light to a new position. The change, which is effective anywhere in the visual field (at the thickening of the lower trace), has no detectable latency but the response persists for a few seconds.

G. In agreement with the insensitivity to general illumination, there is a negligible response when both lights are switched on and off together. [Horridge, Scholes, Shaw, and Tunstall, 1965.]

into a new part of the visual field are classed as movement detectors, but in the locust a careful analysis shows that they respond to incidental local brightness changes. True movement detectors are defined as those which respond to movement but not to brightness changes, and the test is that they respond to the switching of a light only when it moves to a new position (Fig. 9.22). The very great sensitivity of some fibres to small movements means that tremble of the preparation must be ruled out. A locust will easily see a movement of 0.01° of its whole surroundings and make an optokinetic response to it. Calculation shows that to achieve this the locust must be sensitive to an intensity change of 0.3%, and therefore stimulus intensities must be equally carefully controlled. Besides movement fibres, crabs have a variety of "on," "on-off," and "off" afferent fibres as well as sustaining fibres, but these classes are not clearly distinguishable, either in type of effective stimulus or in visual field; possibly every unit is unique. All optic tract units so far isolated in crustaceans and most in insects have wide (30°) visual fields, although some have elliptical fields with a minor axis down to 10°. The diversity of movement fibres of the optic tract, together with their wide visual fields, suggests that they do not originate in the uniformly repeated optic cartridges of the lamina (Fig. 9.7) but in deeper neuropile. If these movement fibres are the signal that excites the motoneurons of the brain in the optomotor response, there is no difficulty in rationalizing their broad receptive fields with their incredible sensitivity to movement of objects which are clearly resolved. The broad fields could arise in two ways: very small intensity changes, caused by small movements of large objects, might be summed over large visual fields; or, more likely, many inferences of movement in separate small visual fields might be summed, thus increasing the sensitivity. Units specially sensitive to particular patterns or to the plane of polarized light have not appeared. One interesting unit in the crab responded to a 5° circular black object against a white background, but the distinction from a nonspecific brightness detector was not clear. In these animals it is very difficult to understand how the responses of visual interneurons *as we see them* are of use to the animal or explain its behaviour.

For the technical reason that the vital blood supply to the functioning optic neuropile is not touched during dissection, the visual interneurons that project into the optic tract from the eye of the opposite side are known better than the truly afferent ones. In Table 5 the horizontal lines show the visual fields of units in relation to nine areas of the eye. It is not known whether these units are continuous axons from the opposite optic tract or whether they originate in the brain. The first group, all with fields of 30–45°, respond to movement of any contrasting object in the range 1 to 3°/sec, with little effect of "on" or "off" and with a preferred direction of movement with little habituation on repetition. The second group look backwards and respond to illumination as well as to movement. The third are similar but have restricted fields at the tip of the eye. Intermediate field fibers are more heterogeneous, being mostly movement detectors with varied additional sensitivity to contrast, target size, novelty, and shape of visual field. One, No. 33, shows a marked difference in responses to stationary and moving lights, besides a change in its response when a moving stimulus is repeated several times, when the background is changed, and as a result of dark adaptation. There are similar fibres in the locust's optic lobe. About a third of the efferent fibres of the crab eyestalk respond to touch of the body or bending of joints as well as to visual stimuli of the other eye, usually with complex properties and with very large visual and mechanoreceptor fields.

Why the interneurons of one optic tract should be so fully represented (at least the large diameter axons) in the contralateral optic tract is not at all clear. Binocular vision is not known to be important. The optic lobes certainly receive a deal of information that appears superfluous to their immediate function, and most activity seems useless for seeing things. The efferent impulses may turn out to be a nonfunctional by-product of connexions of T-shaped axons, in which only the afferent impulses have any significance because the terminals lie in the brain. However, it is possible that movement receptors, as indicated by the opto-kinetic response, are integrated not only in the brain. Motoneurons of the oculomotor nerve move the two eyes of the crab in the appropriate direction through an angle of about 15° when either eye is stimulated. Different motoneurons control movement in the vertical plane, protective retraction of the eye, and movements of the eye when the crab is tilted. These different actions are caused by different combinations of the eye muscles and possibly there is a distinct motoneuron for each major function. Recently we have found that the velocity gain is not the same for the two eyes, and stimuli in opposite directions across the two eyes can cause a small squint. This partial independence reveals that there cannot be a single motoneuron mechanism serving the two eyes, but that the eyes are loosely linked. This linkage, if between the optic lobes, suggests a function for the contralateral movement fibres of the optic tract.

In the locust—perhaps typical of insects—about twenty types of unit have been distinguished in the optic lobe. Most of them are the usual "on" and/or "off" sustaining units, so far distinguished only by difference of time constants and similar quantitative features (Table 6). Lateral inhibition is negligible. The most interesting units, besides some that are selectively sensitive to direction of movement, are those with excitatory centre and inhibitory surround, or vice versa, and the "novelty" units. For these a movement soon fails to excite when repeated but immediately becomes effective again when shifted to a different part of the

TABLE 6
Units of the optic lobe of the locust

Some units—particularly the narrow field units of type BC and BD—have been found only on particular occasions under favourable recording conditions. Some units are easily found and others with great difficulty, so it is impossible to give realistic figures of the relative abundances.

Class A:
Simple total monocular fields, responses of low sensitivity to net luminosity, invariant of factors such as contrast, state of adaptation, size of stimulus source, or pattern. Responses to repeated presentations are stable so long as the repetitions are not repeated more often than one per second. Similar types, with monocular or more commonly binocular fields, are common in the brain.

AB: "On-off" transient response, ratios variable. Weak maintained discharge. Sometimes reverberatory (with an oscillatory response to a maintained stimulus). Low sensitivity.

AC: Pure "on," transient response, very low sensitivity, maintained discharge weak or absent. Sometimes reverberatory.

AD: Sustained net luminosity response, slow adaptation, marked rebound. The maintained discharge frequency indicates the level of illumination and is weak or absent in the dark. Moderate sensitivity.

AE: Sustained net luminosity response; a variant of AD that is transiently inhibited or accelerates only slowly at "on."

AF: Sustained net dimming response. Mirrors AD.

Class B:
Monocular fields limited in extent or different in different areas. The response may be complex or vary with dark adaptation, stimulus position, or stimulus figural qualities. There is a high sensitivity, and responses to repeated presentations are stable. This class has not so far been found in the brain, except in the optic commissures.

BC: Small receptive fields down to 7°, pure "on" transient response of relatively low sensitivity, no maintained discharge. There is sometimes a widely spread weak peripheral inhibition that does not override the centre "on" response.

BD: Narrow field (15–25°) net dimming response, of high sensitivity without lateral interaction, with slow adaptation and strong rebound. On histological grounds these could be some of the ganglion cells of the lamina. Subtypes are as follows.

BDE: No changes in properties on dark adaptation of the eye.

BDF: Acquire postflash depression in the dark (Fig. 9.23).

BDG: Response weighted by contrast, and sometimes showing erasability by large changes in background illumination.

BE: Wide (60°) graded field, net dimming response with a complex rebound. Subtypes are as follows.

BEF: Pure "on" response in the periphery of the field after dark adaptation.

BEG: Postflash depression in the dark.

BEH: Neither BEF nor BEG.

BEI: Both BEF and BEG.

BF: Twenty-degree fields, inhibitory centre, excitatory surround, optimally sensitive to centrifugal movement, maintained background discharge.

BG: Sensitive to the direction of movement, by increase and decrease of maintained discharge with movement in opposite directions (Fig. 9.22).

TABLE 6 (Continued)

Units of the optic lobe of the locust

Class C:

Total monocular or binocular fields, sometimes converging with auditory and tactile modes, varied sensitivity to illumination changes, sometimes enhanced sensitivity to movement of a contrasting object. Transient responses, adaptation curves sometimes enhanced by inhibition, responses to successive presentations unstable and fatigue away. The rate of habituation depends on the response magnitude and is independent of the stimulus form but specific to a visual locus. There is a maintained background discharge, often spontaneously variable. This group is commonly found also in the protocerebrum.

> CD: Responses of low sensitivity to general illumination steps, contrast not a factor. Movement sensitivity low. Habituation memory short.
>
> CE: Intermediate sensitivity to movement which causes brightness changes. Typical audiovisual units, not responding to movement per se.
>
> CF: Gated against changes of light intensity; highly sensitive to movement, never convergent with other modalities. The form of response is influenced by dark adaptation and by source size. The recovery from habituation to light can extend up to fifteen minutes.

In some audiovisual members of class CD and CE, full recovery from habituation to sound can take many hours.

Class D:

Pure auditory, responding as ventral cord auditory units. In the locust there is a diversity of units, see Table 8.

Class M:

These are units mainly found in the protocerebrum, with an intermittent series of bursts of impulses up to 150 sec, not modifiable by any of the stimuli tried.

---

visual field. Within each small area the type of movement is of no consequence; for example, a response that is fatigued with reference to oscillatory movement does not return when a rotary movement is substituted at the same spot. A neuron that became adapted in only a small region of extensive dendrites would have this behaviour. Times of recovery can be long, up to several minutes. Some units respond to sound impulses with a shorter latency than they do to light. Such a multimodal unit does not itself "coordinate" light and sound because it responds to both and confuses them; such a result only emphasizes our lack of understanding. In the locust we fail to find any units that discriminate particular patterns such as those mentioned for the bee [44]. As in all interneuron systems, the activity of units shows that stimuli are combined and converge, whereas behaviour shows that generalized features of the environment are discriminated.

Three conclusions may be made apart from those true for all interneurons. First, visual fields are so wide in the larger optic tract units as to be of little use to the brain if the excitation is not already heavily

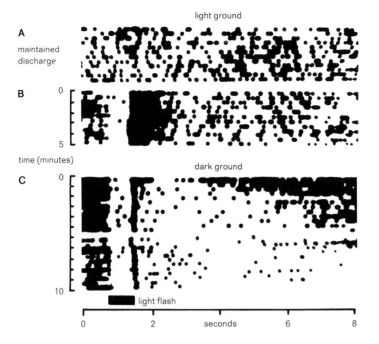

Figure 9.23

Changes in the responses of a unit in the optic lobe of the locust as a result of dark adaptation when the surround of the stimulus is changed from light to dark. Each spot represents a nerve impulse. The most obvious response is an inhibition by light, with a receptive field of about 15°, but more subtle changes are seen when the responses are plotted as above.

A. The maintained discharge with a uniform grey background and no stimulus.

B. The response to a light flash on the grey background repeated every 30 sec.

C. The background is now changed to black, and as dark adaptation proceeds the response at "off" is reduced but a long period of inhibition follows the "off" response. The background discharge, however, as seen at the beginning of each trace, is much increased. Changes of this nature are likely to occur with many of the visual units of the locust, and a characterization in one state may be considered inadequate once the above phenomenon has been demonstrated. [Horridge, Scholes, Shaw, and Tunstall, 1965.]

predigested and runs in specifically labelled axons for which we have yet to discover the code. The brain can receive the information "horizontal waving of object of chela size and frequency directly ahead," but apparently it doesn't have the necessary visual information to make out the shape of the chela itself. Of course, a majority of the fibres are too fine to record from, and their receptive fields are unknown. Second, the crustacean optic ganglia have been described in detail as major centres of neurosecretion with influence upon moulting, colour change, and homeostasis, and yet the impulses in the neighbouring neurons are as yet unrelated to these functions. Third, the deepest optic neuropiles serve functions other than vision and are well developed in eyeless forms.

In conclusion, the arthropod visual system is a pattern-abstracting complex. Microelectrode analysis shows that the mechanisms that separate the attributes of the stimulus are unexpected and as yet too subtle for comprehension at any part of the visual pathway, although there has already been a great expenditure of effort that has led to partial descriptions of many of the components and their activity and to many new principles of relevance to pattern abstraction in general.

REFERENCES FOR CHAPTER 9

1. Autrum, H., and von Zwehl, V. 1964. Die spektrale Empfindlichkeit einzelner Sehzellen des Biennenauges. *Zeit. vergl. Physiol.* **48:**357–384.
2. Behrens, M. E., and Wulff, V. J. 1965. Light-initiated responses of retinula and eccentric cells in the *Limulus* lateral eye. *J. Gen. Physiol.* **48:**1081–1093.
3. Bernhard, C. G. (Ed.). 1966. *The Functional Organization of the Compound Eye.* Oxford, Pergamon Press.
4. Borsellino, A., Fuortes, M. G. F., and Smith, T. G. 1966. Visual responses in *Limulus. Cold Spring Harbor Symp. Quant. Biol.* **30:**429–443.
5. Braitenberg, V. 1966. Unsymmetrische projection der Retinulazellen auf die Lamina ganglionaris bei die Fliege *Musca domestica. Z. vergl. Physiol.* **52:** 212–214.
6. Braitenberg, V. 1967. Patterns of projection in the visual system of the fly. I. Retina-lamina projections. *Exp. Brain Res.* **3:**271–298.
7. de Bruin, G. H. P., and Crisp, D. J. 1957. The influence of pigment migration on vision of higher crustacea. *J. Exp. Biol.* **34:**447–463.
8. Bullock, T. H., and Horridge, G. A. 1965. Chapter 19. (See *loc. cit.,* p. 18.)
9. Bush, B. M. H., Wiersma, C. A. G., and Waterman, T. H. 1964. Efferent mechanoreceptive responses in the optic nerve of the crab *Podophthalmus. J. Cell. Comp. Physiol.* **64:**327–346.
10. Cajal, S., Ramon y, and Sánchez, D. 1915. Contribución al conocimiento de los centros nerviosos de los insectos. *Trab. Lab. Invest. Biol. Univ. Madrid.* **13:**1–164.
11. Carricaburu, P. 1966. Etude interférométrique des cônes crystallins du crabe *Callinectes sapidus. C. R. Acad. Sci. Paris* **263:**1408–1410.
12. Fuortes, M. G. F. 1959. Discontinuous potentials evoked by sustained illumination in the eye of *Limulus. Arch. Ital. Biol.* **97:**243–250.
13. Giulio, L. 1963. Electroretinographische Beweisfuhrung dichroitischer Eigenschaften des Komplexauges bei Zweifluglern. *Zeit. vergl. Physiol.* **46:**491–495.
14. Goldsmith, T. H. 1962. Fine structure of the retinulae in the compound eye of the honey-bee. *J. Cell. Biol.* **14:**489–494.
15. Götz, K. G. 1964. Optomotorische Untersuchung des visuellen Systems einiger Augenmutanten der Fruchtfliege *Drosophila. Kybernetik* **2:**77–92.
16. Götz, K. G. 1965. Die optischen Ubertragungseigenschaften der Komplexaugen von *Drosophila. Kybernetik* **2:**215–221.

17. Hámori, J., and Horridge, G. A. 1966. The lobster optic lamina. I. General organization. *J. Cell. Sci.* **1**:249–256.

18. Hámori, J., and Horridge, G. A. 1966. The lobster optic lamina. II. Types of synapses. *J. Cell. Sci.* **1**:257–270.

19. Hodgkin, A. L., and Fuortes, M. G. F. 1964. Changes in time scale and sensitivity in the ommatidia of *Limulus. J. Physiol.* **172**:239–263.

20. Horridge, G. A. 1966. Study of a system as illustrated by the optokinetic response. *Symp. Soc. Exp. Biol.* **20**:179–198.

21. Horridge, G. A. 1966. Optokinetic responses of the crab *Carcinus,* and of the locust. (6 papers.) *J. Exp. Biol.* **44**:233–246, 247–254, 255–262, 263–274, 275–284, 285–295.

22. Horridge, G. A., and Barnard, P. B. T. 1965. Movement of palisade in locust retinula cells when illuminated. *Quart. J. Micr. Sci.* **106**:131–135.

23. Horridge, G. A., and Sandeman, D. C. 1964. Nervous control of optomotor responses in the crab *Carcinus. Proc. Roy. Soc. London B* **161**:216–246.

24. Horridge, G. A., Scholes, J. H., Shaw, S. R., and Tunstall, J. 1965. Extracellular recordings from single neurones in the optic lobe and brain of the locust, in *Physiology of Insect Central Nervous System,* J. E. Treherne and J. W. L. Beament (Eds.). New York, Academic Press.

25. Kirschfeld, K. 1965. Das anatomische und das physiologische Sehfeld der Ommatidien im Komplexauge von *Musca. Kybernetik* **2**:249–257.

26. Kuiper, J. W. 1962. The optics of the compound eye. *Symp. Soc. Exp. Biol.* **16**:58–71.

27. Langer, H. 1965. Nachweis dichroitischer Absorption des Sehfarbstoffes in den Rhabdomeren des Insektenauges. *Z. vergl. Physiol.* **51**:258–263.

28. Langer, H., and Thorell, B. 1966. Microspectrophotometry of single rhabdomeres in the insect eye. *Exp. Cell. Research* **41**:673–677.

29. Maynard, D. M., and Cohen, M. J. 1965. The function of a heteromorph antennule in a spiny lobster, *Panulirus argus. J. Exp. Biol.* **43**:55–78.

30. Maynard, D. M., and Dingle, H. 1963. An effect of eye stalk ablation on antennular function in the spiny lobster, *Panulirus argus. Z. vergl. Physiol.* **46**:515–540.

31. McCann, G. D., and MacGinitie, G. F. 1965. Optomotor response studies of insect vision. *Proc. Roy. Soc. London B* **163**:369–401.

32. Nunnemacher, R. F. 1959. The retinal image of arthropod eyes. *Anat. Rec.* **134**:618–619.

33. Nye, P. W. (Ed.). 1966. Information processing in sight sensory systems. Symposium at Pasadena. Publ. Calif. Inst. of Technol.

34. Pedler, C., and Goodland, H. 1965. The compound eye and the first optic ganglion of the fly. *J. Roy. Microscop. Soc.* **84**:161–179.

35. Reichardt, W. 1962. Nervous integration in the facet eye. *Biophysics. J.* **2**:121–143.

36. Rutherford, D. J., and Horridge, G. A. 1965. The rhabdom of the lobster eye. *Quart. J. Micr. Sci.* **106**:119–130.

37. Scholes, J. H. 1966. Discontinuity of the excitation process in locust visual cells. *Cold Spring Harbor Symp. Quant. Biol.* **30**:517–527.

38. Shaw, S. R. 1966. Polarized light responses from crab retinula cells. *Nature* **211**:92–93.

39. Shaw, S. R. 1967. Simultaneous recording from two cells in the locust eye. *Z. vergl. Physiol.* **55**:183–194.
40. Swammerdam, J. 1737–1738. *Bijbel der Nature.* Leyden.
41. Thorson, J. 1966. Small-signal analysis of a visual reflex in the locust. *Kybernetik* **3**:41–66.
42. Trujillo-Cenóz, O. 1965. Some aspects of the structural organization of the intermediate retina of dipterans. *J. Ultrastructure Research* **13**:1–33.
43. Tunstall, J., and Horridge, G. A. 1967. Electrophysiological investigation of the optics of the locust retina. *Z. vergl. Physiol.* **55**:167–182.
44. Vowles, D. M. 1964. Models and the insect brain, in *Neural Theory and Modeling*, R. F. Reiss (Ed.). Stanford University Press.
45. Washizu, Y., Burkhardt, D., and Streck, P. 1964. Visual field of single retinula cells and interommatidial inclination in the compound eye of the blowfly, *Calliphora erythrocephala. Z. vergl. Physiol.* **48**:413–428.
46. Waterman, T. H., Wiersma, C. A. G., and Bush, B. M. H. 1964. Afferent visual responses in the optic nerve of the crab, *Podophthalmus. J. Cell. Comp. Physiol.* **63**:135–156.
47. Wiedemann, I. 1965. Versuche uber den Strahlengang in Insektenauge (Appositionauge). *Z. vergl. Physiol.* **49**:526–542.
48. Wiersma, C. A. G. 1966. Integration in the visual pathway of crustacea. *Symp. Soc. Exp. Biol.* **20**:151–178.
49. Wiersma, C. A. G., Bush, B. M. H., and Waterman, T. H. 1964. Efferent visual responses of contralateral origin in the optic nerve of the crab, *Podophthalmus. J. Cell. Comp. Physiol.* **64**:309–326.
50. Wiersma, C. A. G., and Yamaguchi, T. 1966. Types of multimodal integration in single units of the crayfish visual system. *Fed. Proc.* **25**:574.
51. Winthrop, J. T., and Worthington, J. T. 1966. Superposition image formation in insect eyes. Abstracts Biophy. Soc. 10th Ann. Meeting. *Biophys. J.* **6**:124.
52. Yamaguchi, T., and Wiersma, C. A. G. 1965. Interneurons selecting information from a fixed direction in space. *The Physiologist* **8**:311.

10

Touch, pain, and the chemosense of vertebrates

Vertebrate sense organs contain specialized cells or neurons, or their processes, some sensitive to light of certain preferred wavelength, others to movement, specific chemicals, temperature change, and so forth. Besides having a particular preferred, but not exclusive, stimulus to which it has a low threshold, as compared with other classes, every receptor is built into a specialized anatomical situation which is usually the critical factor for the ability of the whole animal to discriminate. In the vertebrate taste and auditory organs the sensory cell is a specialized nonnervous cell, and olfactory sensory neurons have peripheral cell bodies, but elsewhere the receptor is the peripheral process of a central or dorsal root-ganglion cell. Sometimes, as in the array of receptors in the retina, in the area-by-area innervation of the skin, or in the row of sensory endings along the cochlea in the ear, the most important feature to the animal is the position of the receptor in the geometrical pattern of ranks of cells the same kind. In addition, all sensory endings stand in a location that orients, protects, and modifies their input.

In the 1830's Johannes Müller enunciated the principle that the sensation depends on *which fibres are excited* and not on how they are excited peripherally. That they are excited appropriately is a matter entrusted to the filtering action of the sense organs. Reinterpreting the sensation in terms of nerve impulses, we infer that the kind of response of the central nervous system to impulses in the sensory fibres depends upon which incoming axons carry the impulses. Subsequent work has amply confirmed that this concept of specificity, as dependent upon line-labelling, applies in numerous sensory systems and is especially clear-cut in arthropod mechanoreceptors. In the tongue, nose, ear, retina, and skin of vertebrates, however, and in the compound eye of arthropods, there is a great deal of overlap of the sensory fields of numerous receptors, with a range of thresholds at any one point to a variety of different stimuli. It has been postulated with substantial supporting evidence in some instances that the central effect depends on the pattern of nerve impulses as a function of time, and their distribution among a number of fibres. As single units, these vertebrate sensory neurons show an ambiguity of response and overlap of the receptive field that is typical of most interneurons.

However, it is not at all clear to what extent Müller's law is true for neurons of the central nervous system. For analysis of this question further material is required, and we introduce this with a discussion of typical interneurons from the pathways of the special senses in mammals.

The spinal organization of mammals illustrates two general features in which vertebrates differ from invertebrates. First, there are large numbers of sensory fibres, interneurons, and motoneurons, which fall into definite classes, but there are no features that enable a single neuron to be recognized individually. These classes make their own sets of connexions, join certain tracts, belong to definite modalities, and are usually laid out topographically with reference to the body surface. Perhaps only because they cannot be individually identified, the connexions seem not to be absolutely predetermined at the cell-to-cell level, feedback seems more important than constancy of amplification at junctions, and the circuits are rather nonspecific with reference to segmental position. This fits in with the large numbers of motor units in most vertebrate muscles, the innervation of limb muscles from several segments in tetrapods, and the existence of a control of the effectiveness of the sensory input by the brain. The second feature characteristic of the vertebrate segmental pattern is the presence of rather specific feedback loops by which the motor output is in part controlled by proprioceptive impulses from receptors in or near the muscles themselves, and in which the inflow of sensory impulses on entry to the loop is also controlled. Because they have been dealt with fully in great detail elsewhere, the spinal proprioceptive circuits to motoneurons will not be touched on here, but the control of the inflow of the somatic proprioceptive pathways illustrates well the subtlety of mechanism achieved by interneurons acting in concert at even the lowest spinal levels (see [13] and [22], p. 419). Where the fibres can be considered only as a group, Müller's principle cannot be applied to single ones, although it may apply to the group as a whole.

PERIPHERAL SOMATIC SENSORY FIBRES

Our representation of the outside world by touch, temperature, pressure, and pain has been determined in relation to the physical requirements that have exerted certain demands of selection in the course of our evolution, but the basic pattern is one which is common to all the vertebrates. The elements of our skin sense are probably not very different from those of a frog, and certainly close to those of a cat, although what happens to this excitation afterwards may be different. Apart from frog skin and the lateral line system of fish, not a great deal can be said on lower vertebrates; by contrast, the situation in the mammals, including man, has been the subject of much controversy in recent years [4].

Unlike the insects and crustaceans, among which specialized sensory endings of many kinds abound, mammalian skin has no variety of sensory end organs. There are basketlike networks around the necks of the hair follicles, each network giving rise to several fast medullated axons. In nonhairy areas the basket endings are replaced by compact entanglements of fibres that often lie within capsules. Apart from these, there is only a diffuse arborization of nerve fibres ramifying through the dermis and basal layers of the epidermis. They have axons of less than 5 μm, usually of the order of 1 μm or less. With very small, localized stimulation, we can evoke sensations of warmth, cold, touch, itch, and pain in slightly different, overlapping areas [4].

Recording of impulses in peripheral fibres confirms that delicate touch excites the large fast fibres, which are distinguished above. In addition, there are both large and small fibres, which have a low threshold to touch, pressure, warmth, cold, damage, or a pinprick. Some are bimodal or multimodal; the receptive fields overlap, and there is a range of thresholds, especially to touch. In general, thinner fibres have higher thresholds and adapt more slowly. There is no obvious grouping of kinds of adequate stimulus according to velocity of conduction or size of fibres. There is no special feature of the thinnest fibres except that they often continue firing after the stimulus has stopped. The response of mechanoreceptors is abolished by vigorous rubbing or scratching. Some of the thin fibres are quite specific, in particular to temperature changes, justifying a distinction between cold and cool receptors and between hot and warm (at least in the cat).

No fibres certainly specific for pain have been found. There is, however, in all animals a technical matter regarding interpretation of this problem: stimulation that is strong enough to cause pain necessarily excites many endings. In mammals the injection of chemicals that cause pain in man excites no specific group but only a cross section of fibres, which are also sensitive to other stimuli. The few examples of fibres apparently specific for pain may be ones of rather high threshold to any stimulus [4].

The picture we have then, of the nature of the sensory endings of our skin, is of the overlapping receptive fields of a spectrum of fibres, which can be divided only rather arbitrarily into sets with marked differences in thresholds and kinds of adequate stimulus.

As in the vertebrate visual and auditory systems, a great deal of lateral interaction between fibres as well as consideration of the temporal patterns has to be considered before the facts of sensory discrimination and apparent specificity—of pain, for example—can be explained.

In this context it is well to repeat that at the place we feel a sensation of heat when a drop of hot water falls on the skin, numerous sensory nerve fibres of several kinds are stimulated. Physiological analysis does not uphold the view that specific heat receptors alone are excited, or that active fibres project to a centre in the brain which perceives "hot." There is no invariant relation, like a telephone line, between adequate stimulus and sensation.

SPINAL CORD

What happens when the sensory impulses arrive at the spinal cord is not well understood, and the situation is extremely complex. There are numerous accounts [2, 7] more detailed than the rather inadequate and superficial one given here, which is designed only to convey the general features of the main interneurons, via which everything carried to higher levels must pass.

Sensory axons from the periphery enter the spinal cord by the dorsal roots, divide, and send an ascending branch up the cord. In fish the latter is thought to form local spinal connections; only in lower tetrapods do we have evidence of a sensory projection as far as the medulla, where in mammals the primary fibres end in the dorsal column nuclei (n. gracilis and cuneate n.). This could account for the importance in fish and amphibia of lateral line sensory nerves that run even from posterior regions directly to the brain by another route. Tracts ascending and descending the spinal cord, although not well known in lower vertebrates, show a progressive development of specificity and regionalisation in the series up to mammals, and the interneuron connexions in each segment have evolved from unspecialized, diffusely spreading dendritic fields in fish to topographically localized and spatially organised circuits with closer tolerances in birds and mammals.

Leaving aside the proprioceptive pathways and their concomitant ascending pathways, there are three main systems by which excitation conveying touch and thermal stimuli are conveyed into and up the spinal cord in mammals (Fig. 10.1). The most primitive, and perhaps the one associated with generation of the pain sense, is the column of cells at the dorsal tip of the dorsal horn, the substantia gelatinosa, and its associated Lissauer's tract, which seems to be composed of short fibres, partly sensory and partly from spinal neurons of the dorsal horn. Most of the sensory fibres that enter this area from the dorsal roots are very thin. They divide and send one branch up and one down the tract, with a total segmental spread of only 2 or 3 segments. Their endings terminate in the substantia gelatinosa or on nearby cells, many of which also send fibres into Lissauer's tract (Fig. 10.2 A). Other dorsal horn neurons send decussating

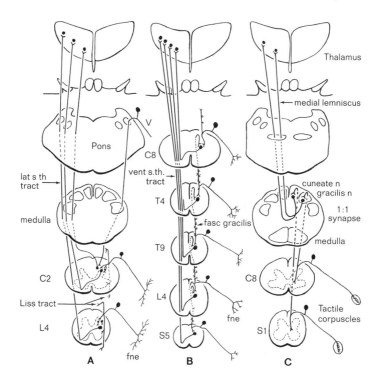

Figure 10.1

Tactile, thermal and pain pathways up the spinal cord to the thalamus.

A. Free nerve endings (fne) to Lissauer's tract and thence through synaptic pathways to the lateral spinal-thalamic tract (*lat. s. th. tract*).

B. General tactile sensibility via fasciculus gracilis and ventral spinal thalamic tract.

C. Fine discriminating sense from tactile corpuscles via primary fibres in the dorsal columns to the cuneate and gracilis nuclei in the medulla, thence to the thalamus. The projection from the thalamus is to the somatic sensory cortex. [Adapted from Crosby, Humphrey, and Lauer, 1962.]

axons across the cord (Fig. 10.1) and directly to the thalamus. There is thus a kind of paired longitudinal plexus, each region of which projects up to the thalamus.

Superimposed on the above is an ancient touch system fed mainly by larger sensory axons, each of which divides as it enters the cord and gives rise to ascending and descending branches that cover 7 or 8 segments. They synapse with higher-order neurons, which send decussating axons up the cord in the ventral spinal thalamic tracts. There is strong evidence (see below) that the more dorsal layers of the dorsal horn neurons and the other thin fibres of the sensory inflow modify the synapses of the large touch fibres in the dorsal horn before the sensory excitation reaches the spinal thalamic tract. The ascending interneurons have surprisingly wide receptive fields, which may include more than one limb, or areas on both sides of the body. Many interneurons discharge only when the stimulus is definitely injurious. Although this does not prove that these impulses are the ones by which pain is registered, they are the only ones excited by typical painful stimuli that project to the cortex, suggesting that they do actually participate in conscious painful sensations.

Where the ascending spinothalamic fibres terminate on cell bodies in the

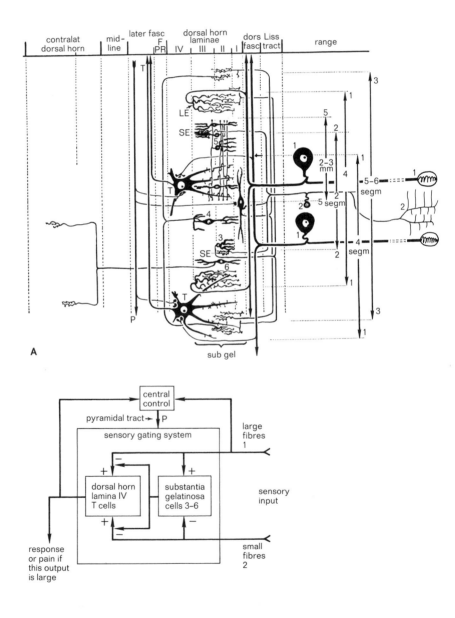

thalamus, there is no regular topographical representation of body form; that is, receptive fields of adjacent cells at this level are not spatially related. The typical activity pattern is a slow recruitment and a prolonged afterdischarge. The topography of inhibitory and excitatory receptive fields is very complex. Some thalamic cells that are activated by stimuli on one side of the body are inhibited by stimuli from homologous areas on the other side; some cells that are activated by a restricted field are inhibited by stimuli on almost any other part of the body.

The ascending sensory pathway with the finest discrimination is from hair endings and capsular touch endings. The relatively large sensory axons divide where they arrive at the cord and send one branch into the adjacent dorsal horn. The other branch ascends directly without intermediate synapse to the cuneate or gracilis nuclei of the medulla. Here there is a synapse which is the best known example among spinal sensory terminals as a site of presynaptic inhibition. The general effect of inhibitory interaction between vertebrate sensory pathways is that the size of receptive fields is thereby controlled by cutting out the weaker peripheral regions of each receptive field. The second-order neurons, with decussating axons, maintain their topographic representation of the body surface all the way to the thalamus (Fig. 10.1). They fire repetitively even to a single presynaptic shock, which causes an impulse in a few presynaptic fibres, and probably to a single impulse in a single presynaptic fibre. This repetitive discharge is characteristic of all mammalian sensory relays. When the thalamic nucleus at the head of this tract is stimulated in conscious humans, no pain is felt but only a localized tingling, so that the presence of pain must be signalled by some other pathway.

The chief region of interest in the above scheme is the dorsal horn complex, mainly composed of small interneurons arranged in laminae,

Figure 10.2

Theories relating to the connexions of sensory fibres in the dorsal horn of the spinal cord.

A. Anatomical relations inferred from Golgi preparations. The tracts of the cord are indicated above; the segmental ranges of the longitudinal connexions are indicated on the right; the diagram is laid out as a highly schematized horizontal section. 1, large touch receptor fibres with large endings (*LE*) in the substantia gelatinosa (*Sub Gel*), and synaptic knobs on large *T* cells of lamina IV; 2, thin receptor fibres with free endings in skin, and small endings (*SE*) in the *sub gel* and synapses on neurons of lamina I; 3, neurons of the *sub gel* with axons in Lissauer's tract (*lateral fasc propius*); 5, *sub gel* neurons with axons on the dendrites of *T* cells of lamina IV; 6, *sub gel* neurons with axons crossing to the other side. Descending pyramidal fibres in the lateral fascicle have endings upon the lamina IV *T* cells. [From Szentagothai, 1964.]

B. Scheme of the gate-control theory. The substantia gelatinosa cells presynaptically inhibit the inputs of all sensory fibres to the dorsal horn, but they are inhibited by small sensory fibres and excited by large ones. The resulting effect is that small fibre excitation leads to pain by further admission of all excitation, but large fibre excitation tends to cut off all excitation. [Adapted from Melzack and Wall, 1965.]

TABLE 7
Vertebrate interneurons of touch and taste

Somatic sensory cortex (area I): cat [Mountcastle, 1957]

Cells are arranged in narrow vertical columns, each of which is actuated by afferents of the same modality from almost identical receptive fields, often with inhibitory surround. Activated by:
1. Touch to hair
2. Pressure on skin
3. Joint movement
4. Light pressure in deep fascia

Somatic sensory cortex (area II): cat [Carreras and Anderson, 1963]

Two main types (nos. of units given).
1. Modality and place specific, contralateral.
   Forepaw 165, foreleg 26, hindpaw 148, hindleg 15, and body 5.
   Auditory 45, vibratory 7.
2. Unspecific with relation to location or modality.
   Contralateral 23, ipsilateral 17, bilateral 9.
   Specific field, but multimodal 12.
   Nonspecific field, multimodal 28.
   Purely nociceptive 12.
   Multimodal nociceptive 12.

Modality types are arranged in columns, no joint receptors. Type 1 have a simple inhibitory surround; Type 2 can be excited from one body area, but inhibited from quite a different area.

Taste units of tongue: frog [Kusano, 1960]

Totals ex 105 units in brackets.
1. Units responding to everything tried except Ringer solution (3).
2. To one specific substance, quinine, saccharin, water, acetic acid (11).
3. To divalent salts, sucrose, or water.
   (a) As above but not to NaCl, KCl, quinine, or acetic (27).
   (b) As above but not to monovalent salts (2).
   (c) As above and to NaCl, KCl, quinine, acetic (16).
4. To monovalent salts (8).
5. To quinine (9).
6. To acetic acid (7).

Taste units: cat, dog, monkey. (man and rat have no pure water fibre)
[Papers in Zotterman, 1963]

1. Acid
2. Bitter
3. Salt only
4. Sweet only } Spectrum of relative strengths of responses to different substances and mixtures.
5. Sweet-salt
   mixtures
6. Pure water

Some substances (e.g. alcohol) stimulate nontaste trigeminal C fibres.

TABLE 7 (Continued)

Tongue stimulation at thalamus: rat [Benjamin in Zotterman, 1963]

A. Single class of substances: 1. Sweet. 2. Acid. 3. Salt.
B. Several classes of substances including bitter in combination with one or more of the others.
C. Unimodal temperature.
D. Multimodal, e.g. 10% to temp. and taste in monkey.
E. Multimodal with mechanoreceptors (although the axons have taken different routes).

Tongue stimulation at cortex: cat [Landgen, 1959]

Unimodal

Thalamus		*Cortex*
Touch	32	32
Stretch	4	29
Cool	20	12
Warm	1	1
Taste	1	5

Touch signals arrive at cortex 10 msec before the others

Multimodal

touch and cool	8
stretch and cool	9
touch, cool, warm	3
stretch, cool, warm, taste	3
stretch, cool, taste	1
stretch and taste	1
touch and taste	2

---

at least in the cat. The dorsal horn is arbitrarily divided into nine layers, of which the first six divide the dorsal horn into horizontal strata (Fig. 10.3, A). Lamina II is the substantia gelatinosa, of small neurons; laminae I to IV are the sites of termination of primary sensory fibres. Axons of some of the cells in laminae III, IV, and V probably form the spinothalamic tracts. Descending fibres from the cortex project mainly on laminae IV and V.

After years of doubt concerning the origin of the potentials recorded at the sensory roots, we now have a new theory that accounts for most events in the dorsal horn, making use of new findings concerning presynaptic inhibition (Fig. 5.10). The effectiveness of the large cutaneous fibre input is partly determined by the balance of previous activity of large and small fibres, which seem in part to oppose each other. The potentials recorded are attributable to the depolarization of the terminals of

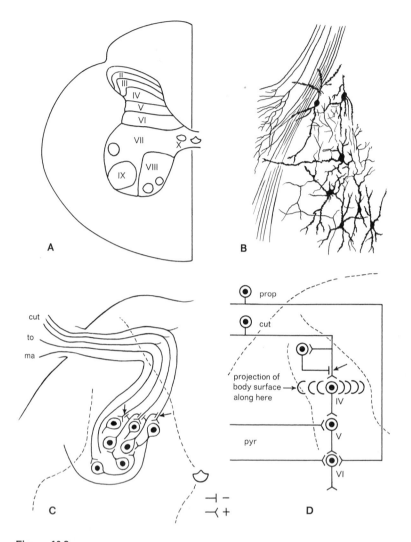

Figure 10.3

Dorsal horn of the lumbar segments of the spinal cord of the cat.

A. Divisions into lamina I–X, which are somewhat arbitrary though convenient. [Rexed, 1964.]

B. Neurons from a Golgi preparation of the kitten, mainly of cells of lamina V and VI.

C. Interpretation according to Eccles, Schmidt, and Willis (1963) to explain the presynaptic inhibition of primary terminals. *to,* tendon organ fibres; *ma,* other muscle afferents; *cut,* cutaneous afferents. Note the position of the presynaptic inhibition, as indicated by the arrow.

D. Interpretation according to Wall (1966) showing influence of pyramidal tract. The chain of neurons on the cutaneous pathway is in fact reduplicated to produce a topographical projection of the skin. *pyr,* pyramidal tract; *cut,* cutaneous afferents; *prop,* proprioceptive afferents.

the large sensory fibres by presynaptic terminals of thin sensory fibres. Depolarization inhibits by preventing the spike invasion of the sensory terminals. The inhibition is blocked by barbiturates and is more than an electrical interaction. On the other hand, impulses in large sensory fibres depolarize the terminals of other large fibres; depolarization also has an inhibitory effect because it reduces the amount of sensory transmitter liberated. The depolarization is mainly of cutaneous touch fibre endings by other touch fibres, but there is also a nonspecific depolarization of proprioceptive fibres by other proprioceptive and by cutaneous fibres. Details of interpretation differ (Fig. 10.3, C and D), but the main hypothesis to emerge is that endings of sensory fibres on dorsal horn neurons are well supplied with presynaptic inhibitory endings that control the effectiveness of the sensory inflow in a way not sharply related to modality or receptive field. One weakness of these theories is that the presynaptic connexions have not been described anatomically. In Chapter 14 it will be suggested that the actual pattern of presynaptic inhibition, even in the spinal cord, is a product of learning of a primitive kind at this level, and that inhibitory interaction between sensory pathways contributes to what we can conveniently call postural learning.

The interneurons of the dorsal horn on the somatic sensory pathways respond readily to a natural peripheral stimulus. This is partly because the sensory fibres from any particular area of skin are very numerous and the sensory fibres have a wide range of velocities, so that incoming excitation is well spread among fibres and also dispersed in time. There is little evidence, in the dorsal horn, of excitatory reverberating circuits that would spread and amplify a signal, but all the evidence suggests a damping down of background discharge by mutually inhibitory fields and at the same time a loss of specificity by mixing of responses to touch, joint movement, pressure, and thermal stimuli. With reference to proprioceptors, the inhibition that is fed back to the sensory endings is not selective of muscles acting at any one joint, but is, however, somewhat selective according to the type of receptor, in that annulospiral spindle endings, Golgi tendon endings, and cutaneous touch receptors tend to inhibit the central terminals of fibres of their own kind. The results of all experiments can be interpreted as due to presynaptic inhibitory endings that shut down the excitatory action of sensory terminals. The most obvious result is that a powerful signal, with an intense burst of sensory impulses, will block out weaker signals and prevent them from entering the cord. This might occur for interaction between endings of the same kind or of different kinds, in innumerable possible combinations. This system, however, has not only to deal with sudden bursts. The consequences of its activity will be intricate and presumably rather labile with small changes in background discharge. Probably the normal function is to restrict the size of the receptive fields in normal bursts, so that only the "hot" centre of a cluster of excited fibres will get through to the next level.

Here, if anywhere at the spinal level, we can postulate circuits that theoretically would improve the coordination of movements and postures that are repeated and perfected with practice. Orders from the brain determine which movement is to be made. We can suppose that when a new task (standing, walking, skating, dancing) is being learned, over many repetitions excitation from the brain acts, together with local pain, as a reward or punishment until the exact interneuron balance is achieved. As will be seen, an inhibitory feedback circuit is a pattern with different degrees of specificity in the closure of the loop, but a pattern that is not formed easily by growth of axons, so that some powerful advantage, such as ability to learn, must account for its evolution.

Recording from single cells establishes a consistent topographic mapping of skin and joint receptors upon dorsal horn cells of laminae II through V in the cat. Cells in lamina IV all have small receptive fields, which are, however, about an order of magnitude larger than those of the corresponding primary sensory fibres of touch to hairs, skin pressure, or joint movement. Although there is convergence of several types of large and small sensory fibres on to each second-order cell, the perfect spatial mapping is maintained as to location. Working away from the midline in the cord, we find multimodal cells of adjacent sensory fields, outwards across the foot and up the outside of the limb. There is no known effect of stimulating the cerebral cortex, but a complete block of the cord by cooling of a section higher up causes a large increase in sensitivity, showing that a tonic suppression of both excitability and receptive field size normally decends from the brain.

In lamina V the units are higher-order interneurons and there is a latency increase of 1.5 msec. These units habituate rapidly but then respond to a novel stimulus. Cooling the spinal cord now makes the receptive fields much larger and the "novelty" feature disappears; this does not imply that the novelty element is distinguished by the brain. Receptive fields can show inhibitory surrounds, and the spatial mapping of the skin topology persists at this level. In lamina VI are multimodal units that respond to joint movement as well as to touch of hairs or skin or pressure. The combinations of adequate stimuli are the expected ones; extension of toe, for example, goes with flexion of ankle plus footpad touch, as in standing. Stimulation of the cortex has a strong influence here, in changing the weighting between cutaneous and proprioceptive effects. Cold block of the spinal cord higher up enlarges the fields as before. What we have, in fact, is a processing of sensory excitation at spinal level, a highly evolved product of the old segmental system, presumably with effects upon local reflexes and with partial control from the brain.

THE SENSATION OF PAIN

A recent theory of how the sensation of pain may be abstracted from excited skin fibres illustrates how great a transformation can occur even at the first sensory synapses [15]. As set out in the hypothetical scheme (Fig. 10.2, B), it is supposed that one group of fibres—mainly those of large diameter from hairs and touch corpuscles—excite the first-order interneurons of the substantia gelatinosa (SG) and also other first-order cells (T cells) of the upper laminae of the dorsal horn. Small sensory fibres—mainly C fibres responding to a variety of effective stimuli—excite the T cells but inhibit the SG cells. The SG cells are supposed to inhibit the afferent fibres that terminate on the T fibres and thereby act as a gate guarding the input to the T cells. Background activity in small fibres normally inhibits the SG cells and holds the gate open. A sudden arrival of impulses in large fibres will immediately get through, but as the stimulus continues the later large-fibre impulses find the gates closed. A large proportion of small-fibre activity will open wide the gate and cause an avalanche of activity at the next stage.

The suggestion is that each T cell integrates a particular group of afferents, as modified by this gate, strictly in relation to the localization on the skin. Strong combinations of small-fibre impulses will be adequate to excite certain T fibres of high threshold, and it is the excitation in these when projected to the thalamus and cortex which is felt as pain. Some of the evidence for all this theory is as follows.

Anatomical studies and direct recording in the dorsal horn show that the pathways described are probable, but does not demonstrate them in detail. The sensation of pain involves a mechanism at spinal level which takes a long time—certainly up to 100 msec—to develop. Lesions in the substantia gelatinosa or its local longitudinal tract cause loss of the pain sense in that segment. Pain is relieved by rubbing, itch by scratching, and these are the very actions that would provide a continued stimulation of the large touch fibres and so close the gate to small-fibre activity. Pain in phantom limbs can be explained by imbalance between large and small fibres, and tapping the stump of the limb is a stimulus that would excite large fibres and so close the SG gates. Loss of the fast fibres, as in tabes dorsalis, is followed by inexplicable pain. Moreover, at the lowest spinal level this mechanism is modifiable by tracts from the brain, although as yet experimental evidence on this point has not been related to actual behaviour. It is not clear whether dogs which learn to ignore pain inflicted when a reward is regularly given, or people who succeed in "thinking of something else," are controlling pain at the spinal or the cortical level.

Pain, on this theory, is a disproportionately large discharge by numerous small sensory fibres, none of which is specifically a "pain" fibre. However, just any disorganised input to the spinal cord cannot be guaranteed to produce pain. In fact, electrical shocks (or a knock) to a peripheral nerve cause a tingling feeling that is different from pain.

This theory of pain—as arising from imbalance in the sensory excitation—agrees with our notions of the evolution of spinal mechanisms. It provides an obvious function for the very ancient chain of small dorsal horn cells, which is typical of all the lower vertebrates as well as mammals. We suppose that the same type of system causes spinal frogs to make appropriate reflexes when pinched. Perhaps primitively it is the motivating system by which spinal cord segments take care of local

Figure 10.4

Response profiles of primary and secondary taste units, showing the arbitrary nature of categories, and the lack of clear-cut specificity. The diagrams are not histograms but simply show responses (in **A**) or sensitivities (in **B**) to a standard set of stimuli.

A. Intracellular responses of seven taste receptor cells of the tongue of the rat to constant standard stimuli as shown by the arabic numbers. [Converted from data of Kimura and Beidler, 1961.]

B. The diversity of responses among 27 different higher-order taste units of the thalamus of the squirrel monkey. Except for the three on the right, where warm and cold are included, the four stimuli were salt (1.0 M NaCl), sweet (1.0 M sucrose), bitter (0.01 M quinine hydrochloride), and acid (0.1 M HCl). Plotted vertically is a measure of the sensitivity to each stimulus, with the value of 100 taken as the above concentration. [After Benjamin in Zotterman, 1963.]

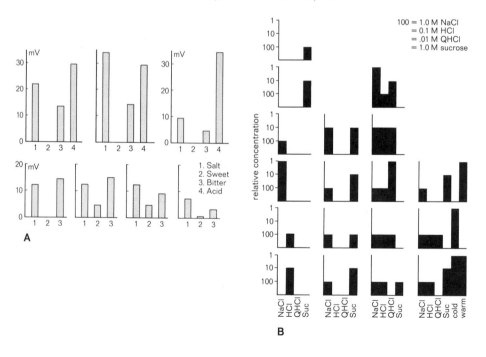

posture, and by which the whole animal is aroused by any unpleasant stimulus anywhere along its length. If so, we have started with a diffuse system that is segmentally nonspecific and superimposed on it other more specific interneurons, at the same time retaining the old system. This is the same kind of progression that is noted from polyp to medusa and from annelid to arthropod, as well as in the cephalisation of all axial nerve cords in which more specific pathways develop in the more anterior levels and then interact with the lower centres in progressively more distinguishable longitudinal tracts.

THE SENSE OF TASTE

The sensory fibres, with cell bodies in dorsal roots, innervate groups of specialised receptor cells called taste buds (Fig. 13.7), sometimes with single branches to more than one bud. There is probably only one anatomical type of cell in the taste buds, but the cells in each are usually separately innervated by numerous different endings, and probably each bud contains cells with different sensitivities. Intracellular records from the receptor cells record a depolarization upon stimulation, and the sensory cell is presynaptic to the nerve terminals; the synapse, however, if such it be, is not understood either with reference to vesicles, synaptic cleft, or current flow, and is rather variable in structure in different vertebrates.

The concept of four taste qualities (sweet, salt, sour, bitter) has for a long time coloured all research in this field, and there have been repeated efforts to discover a mechanism of discrimination that distinguishes sharply between these four commonly used stimuli. The facts, however, show that every pathway and element in the taste sensory mechanism responds to more than one taste quality. Different spots on the tongue are sensitive to acid, sweet, salt, and bitter, but the stimulation has usually been chosen with deference to the old theory. It was shown in the last century that each cluster of human taste buds responds to more than one taste quality. Later experiments have shown single taste nerve fibres of mammals behave in the same way. Microelectrode penetrations of single receptor cells now show that each of them has response profile to a number of different tastes, and every cell appears to be unique. Recent work demonstrates progressively greater variety of receptor types. The frog, cat, dog, and monkey have fibres specific for pure water, although these have not been found in man or the rat. There is more diversity and more specificity in mammals than in the frog. A problem arises because taste stimuli cannot be arranged systematically, as can sound or light, but if we plot a measure of the response of a unit (number of impulses in the first second of stimulation) to a constant sequence of chemicals scattered through the above four main classes at standard concentrations,

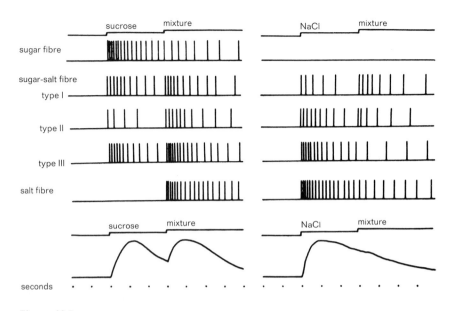

Figure 10.5

Responses of some primary taste receptor fibres of the dog, showing the interaction between common salt and sucrose when a mixture of the two substances is applied immediately after one or other of them alone. Specific sugar and salt fibres (top and bottom) do not show the interaction. Sugar-salt fibres show various responses to the mixture (types I–III) when one substance is already present. The smooth curves at the foot show summed potentials from the whole nerve. [Anderson et al. in Zotterman, 1963.]

we find that almost every fibre has a different response profile (Fig. 10.4). Further examination of latency, time course, and threshold shows that previous or simultaneous stimulation with other substances affects the fibres diversely. For example, some sugar receptors of the dog are specifically inhibited by previously applied salt (Fig. 10.5), and a range of amino acids and similar substances present in food gives a wide range of time courses of impulses in different isolated fibres. In the cat all types are sensitive to acid, none specific to sugar, and the water fibre is not specific to water alone. Clearly there is a great deal of information available in the numbers of impulses in a variety of fibres. We can infer only that the higher centres have a mechanism for taking weighted sums and differences from the input excitation, and each species investigated does this differently with its own distinct primary data.

There is more to the sense of taste than just the excitation of taste buds. Free nerve endings of the trigeminal nerve to the tongue and inside of the mouth are also excited by chemical stimuli. Strong alcohol, for example, exerts an effect beyond the tongue; there are reports that human patients with both chorda tympani cut, and therefore presumably without all taste bud fibres, can still discriminate by taste. There are many other examples of chemoreception outside the special organs; endings in the cornea, for example, are good receptors for the odour of onions.

In the thalamus the pure taste units are spatially located in a slightly different place from those of mixed modality. Pure taste units are projected from several areas of the tongue region to the somatic sensory cortex. In the thalamus and cortex there are at least two classes of tongue fibres: ones with small and others with large receptive fields, the latter (with some bilateral fields) being especially abundant in the cortex. The unimodal group (counting all taste as one modality) comprised 94% in the thalamus but 75% in the cortex. Cortical taste cells respond to more than one but not to all of the four qualities of taste. The columnar organization in the taste area of the cortex is not known but cells responding to heat, to cold, or to taste are found close together, suggesting that they will be integrated together at the next stage. We have no clue as to how or where tastes are discriminated.

THE SENSE OF SMELL

Innumerable different odours, most of them nonbiological, are somehow distinguished, first by the receptors and again centrally. In the frog, which is the only animal in which numerous recordings have been made, single primary olfactory fibres have a continuous but rather irregular background activity. Each single unit is inhibited by some odours, excited by others, and unaffected by yet others. The important result of a survey of numerous units is that we can always find a fibre that is influenced in opposite ways by any pair of substances, although other fibres may respond in identical ways to the two substances [8]. The evidence suggests that there is an innumerable variety of receptors. There is an enormous number of them—about 10^8 in the rabbit.

The fact that each receptor is either inhibited or excited, and in a graded way, makes it possible to represent an enormous number of odours by combinations of them (Fig. 10.6). A large proportion of the fibres are sensitive to any given odour, so that discrimination between odours must depend upon some kind of estimate of differences between the responses of numerous receptors at later stages of integration in the olfactory bulb.

In the olfactory bulb the primary olfactory fibres end in glomeruli and excite the dendrites of an ordered array of large cells (mitral cells), between which there are numerous small cells (Fig. 10.7). Mitral-cell responses are extremely diverse; again, every cell seems to be different from its neighbours in response profile, and for any pair of odours there can be found a mitral cell that will distinguish between them. The question of how these first- and second-order fibres are stamped with this extraordinary and centrally recognizable individuality will reappear in Chapter 13.

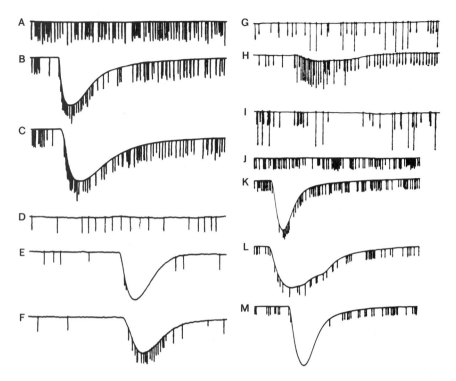

Figure 10.6

Responses that show the discrimination of odours by primary olfactory receptors of the frog. The spikes are from single cells; the large slow potential is from a large area of the epithelium.

A. The resting state of a unit (with spike slightly smaller than the largest shown), which responded similarly to menthone (B) and menthol (C). Both odours initially inhibit and then excite the unit.

D. The resting state of another receptor cell, which distinguished sharply between menthone (E) and menthol (F), which smell alike to man.

G. Two units, one with a large and the other with a small spike, which responded quite differently to diethylaminoethanol (H). The large spike increases frequency at "on," the small spike at "off."

I. Bursts of spikes as the units revert to their background discharge.

J. Background discharge of a unit that is inhibited to a short sharp puff (K), a long weak puff (L), and a strong puff (M) of limonene. The records are each 10 sec long. [Gesteland et al., 1965.]

THE SOMATIC SENSORY PATHWAYS, CORTICAL LEVEL

An important feature in the organisation of much vertebrate grey matter is that cells that are spatially adjacent to each other are the ones that are integrated together at the next stage, or are those that have a common

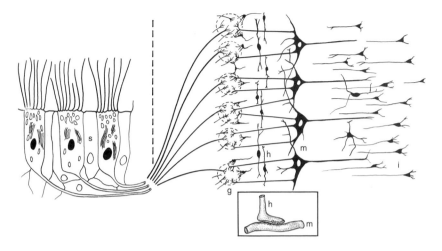

Figure 10.7

The principal connexions between the peripheral olfactory receptor neurons and their supporting cells (*s*) and the neurons of the olfactory bulb in a typical mammal. The very thin primary fibres end in glomeruli (*g*), which contain the dendrites of the mitral cells (*m*). Between the mitral dendrites are horizontal fibres (*h*), which end in anatomically two-way synapses (shown enlarged). Central to the mitral cells is a thick inner plexiform layer.

Figure 10.8

The columnar organization of the cerebral cortex. This is the visual cortex of a 25-day-old cat stained by the Golgi method. *a*, layer of giant pyramidal cells; *b*, layer of medium pyramidal cells with recurrent axons; *c* and *d*, pyramidal cells with descending and bifurcating fibres ramifying around giant pyramids; *g*, triangular cell with a recurrent axon and descending collaterals; *i*, pyramidal cell with a recurrent ascending axon, *j* and *l*, a star-shaped and a triangular cell of the fusiform or spindle-shaped layer; *j* has an ascending axon, *l* has a descending axon; *m*, spindle-shaped cell provided with a descending axon. [S. Ramon y Cajal, 1900–1906.]

Because several anatomical types of neurons are present, it is not possible to identify the electrophysiological units of the cortex as pyramidal cells. Typical responses are shown in Figures 12.12 through 12.14.

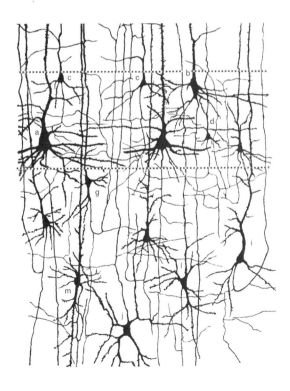

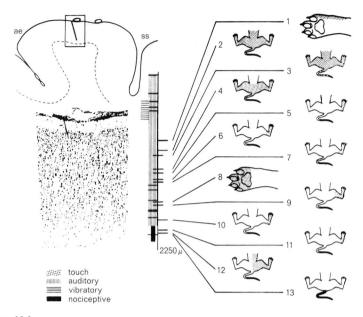

Figure 10.9
Units encountered in a traverse of an electrode through the somatic sensory cortex of a cat. On the left is an outline drawing of the cortex, together with a section, in which part of the line of the track is visible. The locations on the animal of 13 units are shown on the right, where dots show the areas where touch was an effective stimulus. The depth in the cortex and the modalities are plotted along the line of the track in the centre of the figure. Note that many units also respond well to auditory stimulation. [Carreras and Andersson, 1963.]

reference to one attribute (usually position on the body) while being diverse in other ways. In mammals, the somatic sensory cortex, to which excitation from touch to the skin is projected, has a pattern of organisation that may prove to be representative of all cortical areas, though these differ enormously in the receptive field and in the modality of the fibres projecting into them. Cortical cells are arranged in columns along the lines of the apical dendrites (Fig. 10.8). In the 1st somatic sensory area of the cat, there is specificity with reference to place and modality on the body surface, with four principal types of cell, which are responsive to one but never two of the following contralateral stimuli: movements of hairs, touch to the skin, movements of joints that indicate posture, and light pressure in deeper regions (Fig. 10.9). The cortical cells may be either excited or inhibited, but the important point is that within narrow vertical columns the cells at different depths are influenced by the same modality of stimulus. Neighbouring columns of the cortex are each distinct in some detail of their sensitivity, but across the cortical area there is a progressive drift in the topological reference to the body. The cells of a single column have receptive fields that are very similar but not identical; as shown by latencies, each has its own input from the thalamus.

This finely detailed representation at the unit level in the primary sensory cortex is surprising in view of the considerable divergence and widespread multiplication of pathways, which becomes evident when local strong or electrical stimuli are used to produce evoked potentials elsewhere. The natural cortical receptive fields, in fact, are similar to those of a single primary sensory fibres, although any stimulus excites many of the latter. Thus for any bunch of neurons excited by a given mixed stimulus it is only the "hot centre" of the bunch that excites cells at the next level. The pattern of excitation that gets through to the next stage is transformed by a maximum amplitude filter that allows the "hot centres" to pass at each relay station. On the somatic sensory pathway, if a signal starts out with a limited localisation on the skin, it finishes with an equally limited one on the cortex. This does not imply that the modalities recognisable at the cortical level are necessarily so sharp, or even present, or (if present) bear a one-to-one correspondence with those at the skin.

Figure 10.10

Projections of parts of the human cerebral cortex upon other parts. Certain areas (*dotted*) are regions where sensory interneurons arrive at the cortex. The tracks show the possibility of repeated projection of axons of cortical cells to further and further areas, and back again. This system therefore allows repeated transformation and abstraction of particularities or generalities, as explained in Figures 12.7 and 12.8 Details of the responses of units are only just being discovered for the primary sensory areas, and a fantastic complexity is possible for higher-order units anywhere in the cortex (see Fig. 12.8). **Left**, horizontal section; **right**, the left side of the cortex.

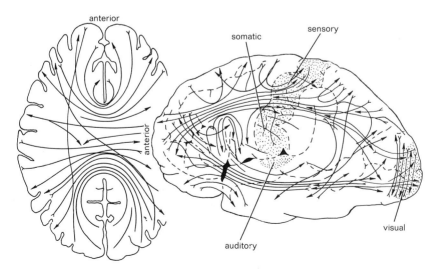

anterior

somatic

sensory

anterior

auditory

visual

As in other systems, a light stimulus to one area of the skin excites cells restricted to few columns on the somatic cortex and inhibits those of surrounding cortical areas. This inhibitory surround has the effect of sharpening the adjacent peaks of response that result from two adjacent stimuli. As in vision, however, lateral inhibition or inhibitory surrounds give an advantage to detection of movement of the stimulus; the finger, for example, has a more effective sense if it rambles over a surface that is being investigated. A natural stimulus such as the rotation of a joint during walking will excite cells in columns of all four modalities in a certain restricted cortical area, but the exact form of the movement determines very critically the exact location of the excited cells. What complex interactions occur between the cortical cells is unknown, but it seems certain that intercortical projections (Fig. 10.10) to other areas combine responses of units. We can expect summations, conditions, and exclusions similar to those in the projection from primary to secondary visual areas, or between auditory nuclei.

Auditory, visual, and somatic pathways each have two projections to the sensory cortex. The second somatic area in the cat (anterior ectosylvian gyrus) has cells of two main types. Units specific for modality or place are excited usually only transiently—by touch to hairs, touch to skin, by deep pressure, or by sounds—and to no other stimulation. They have small, continuous, contralateral place-specific receptive fields that do not change in properties when repeatedly stimulated. These units, like those of the dorsal columns, form an ordered representation of the body over this cortical area, with the proportions distorted by amplification of the extremities of the limbs in relation to the rest. The units of different modality types are stacked separately in vertical columns. The units are like those of the first somatic area except that joint receptors are absent. Units sensitive to vibration or noises are mixed indiscriminately with the others.

The second type of cell, less specific, is excited by a large receptive field of one or both contralateral limbs, or of both sides of the body, or by stimuli of several different modes, or by stimulation that is so strong or destructive as to be painful. Typically their spatial and temporal properties change with stimulation or with the level of anaesthesia; in fact they behave as if they had inputs from several cells of the specific type, and slight increase in anaesthesia causes a shrinkage of receptive fields. Numbers of each type are listed in Table 7. The pain-receptive units respond specifically to stimuli such as pinching and damage of the periosteum; most of these have very extensive receptive fields, and they are very sensitive to level of anaesthesia. Whether there are specific primary sensory fibres for pain, there certainly are some specific neurons of the cortex that behave as if they signal pain. The presence of these units is of great theoretical interest in considering the mechanism of reinforcement in learning, and in view of controversies as to whether pain originates at the peripheral or the central terminals of sensory fibres or elsewhere.

The unspecific cells behave quite differently from the specific ones with reference to inhibition. The latter have a typical inhibitory surround, which can be limited in area even to one foot-pad. Unspecific units can have inhibitory zones on the body surface which are far distant from the excitatory zones (for example, on different legs), and they clearly represent summation of earlier-order fibres that are not neighbours.

The general impression gained from these unit studies of the cat's cortex is that progressively more complex types of interaction will be found as cortical-cortical projection tracts are further explored downstream (Fig. 10.10). We can expect also that the arrangement of modalities in columns will extend to more and more subtle types; the most sophisticated of all should be the pyramidal cells in the motor cortex. The great problem, however, in the sensory systems, is that although behaviour leads us to expect evidence of *discriminations* by central cells, the records from units show mostly *summations*. Therefore discrimination must be a property of groups of interneurons right down to the motoneurons.

REFERENCES FOR CHAPTER 10

1. Adrian, E. D. 1953. The response of the olfactory organ to different smells. *Acta. Physiol. Scand.* **28**:5–14.
2. Albe-Fessard, D. 1967. Organisation of somatic central projections, in *Contributions to sensory physiology*, Vol. 2, W. D. Neff (Ed.) New York, Academic Press.
3. Carreras, M., and Anderson, S. A. 1963. Functional properties of neurons of the anterior ectosylvian gyrus of the cat. *J. Neurophysiol.* **26**:100–126.
4. Ciba Symposium. 1959. *Pain and Itch*. Foundation Study Group No. 1. Boston, Little, Brown.
5. Crosby, E. C., Humphrey, T., and Lauer, E. W. 1962. *Correlative Anatomy of the Nervous System*. New York, Macmillan.
6. Döving, K. B. 1965. Studies on the responses of bulbar neurons of frog to different odour stimuli, in *Symposium sur l'odorat. Rev. Laryngol. Oto. Rhinol.* Supplement for 1965.
7. Eccles, J. C., and Schade, J. P. 1964. Organisation of the spinal cord, in *Progress in Brain Research*. **2**. Amsterdam.
8. Gesteland, R. C., Lettvin, J. Y., and Pitts, W. H. 1965. Chemical transmission in the nose of the frog. *J. Physiol.* **181**:525–559.
9. Hunt, C. C., and Kuno, M. 1959. Properties of spinal interneurones. *J. Physiol.* **147**:346–363.
10. Hunt, C. C., and Perl, E. R. 1960. Spinal reflex mechanisms concerned with skeletal muscle. *Physiol. Rev.* **40**:538–579.

11. Kimura, K., and Beidler, L. M. 1961. Microelectrode study of taste receptors of rat and hamster. *J. Cell. Comp. Physiol.* **58**:131–139.
12. Kusano, K. 1960. Analysis of the single unit activity of gustatory receptors in the frog tongue. *Jap. J. Physiol.* **10**:620–633.
13. Mancia, M., Baumgarten, R. von, and Green, J. D. 1962. Response patterns of olfactory bulb neurons. *Arch. Ital. Biol.* **100**:449–462.
14. Melzack, R., and Wall, P. D. 1962. On the nature of cutaneous sensory mechanisms. *Brain* **85**: 331–356.
15. Melzack, R., and Wall, P. D. 1965. Pain mechanisms: a new theory. *Science* **150**:971–979.
16. Mountcastle, V. B. 1957. Modality and topographic properties of single neurons of cat's somatic sensory cortex. *J. Neurophysiol.* **20**:408–434.
17. Oakley, B., and Benjamin, R. M. 1966. Neural mechanisms of taste. *Physiol. Rev.* **46**:173–211.
18. Sherrick, C. A. 1966. Somesthetic senses. *Ann. Rev. Psychol.* **17**:309–336.
19. Szentágothai, J. 1964. Neuronal and synaptic arrangement in the substantia gelatinosa of Rolando. *J. Comp. Neurol.* **110**:117–134.
20. Zotterman, Y. 1963. Nerve fibres mediating pain: a brief review with a discussion on the specificity of cutaneous afferent nerve fibres, in *The Assessment of Pain in Man and Animals*, C. A. Keele and R. Smith (Eds.). London, Universities Federation for Animal Welfare.
21. Zottermann, Y. (Ed.). 1963. *Olfaction and Taste*. London, Pergamon Press.

11

Equilibrium and auditory interneurons

The equilibrium and auditory senses are closely associated in many animals, both vertebrate and invertebrate. In most lower animals it is difficult to distinguish between these senses, or to attribute one of these functions to organs that are known only anatomically. Detection of the direction of gravity and detection of vibrations in a fluid medium are achieved by some kind of displacement receptor, often associated with a calcareous otolith or statolith. Auditory receptors are usually rapidly adapting, but equilibrium receptors are not necessarily tonic because they may function by the mechanism called range fractionation (see T, p. 72) —small vibrations excite different neurons at different angles of tilt.

In many lower animals the primary displacement receptor cells bear nonmotile cilia, which seem to be concerned with the transduction process that ultimately depolarizes the receptor cell. In vertebrates, the underwater vibration receptors of the lateral lines, the auditory receptors and the gravity receptors are all developed from one embryological set of cells.

EQUILIBRIUM RECEPTORS

As an illustration of the limiting conditions set by the three-dimensional nature of the environment, the constancy of gravity, and the inertia of rotating liquids, it is instructive to compare the equilibrium receptors in a crustacean and in a vertebrate. The phasic and tonic receptor fibres that respond to a tilt of the head turn out to be quite similar.

The statocyst of the lobster is a hollow cavity formed by invagination of the cuticle in the basal joint of the antennule. It is lined with sensory hairs of two types, which are arranged around a central gritty statolith. Asymmetry in the attachment is presumably the basis of the directionality in the responses of individual hairs as they are moved by the shifting weight of the statolith they support.

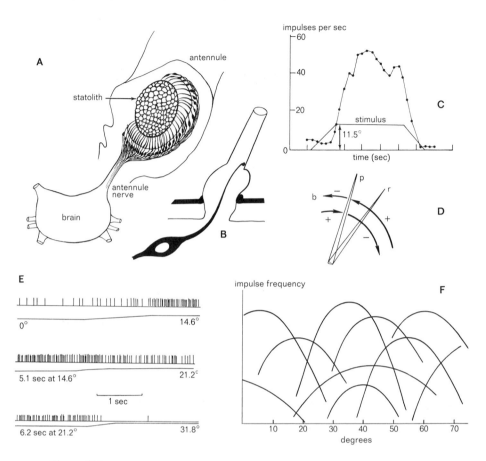

Figure 11.1

The statocyst of the lobster and the responses of its sensory neurons.

A. Plan of the organ and its nerve. A granular statolith is supported on bristles or hairs, each of which has a single neuron.

B. A single hair, showing the insertion of the sensory dendrite at one side, which presumably ensures the asymmetrical response.

C. The response of a single hair to a displacement of 11.5° and return after 10 sec, showing that the response is reasonably nonadapting; it is also repeatable.

D. The relation between position of the hair and the nature of the response. The resting position r is that when the hair is unloaded. The plus sign (+) indicates an increase in frequency when the hair is moved in the direction of the arrow, and the minus sign (−) indicates a decrease. Note that the resting position is not the same as the position p of the peak response. Steady movement of the hair will thus move it through the region of maximum response, as follows.

E. Movements (by the amounts shown) through the region of optimum response, showing the slightly irregular discharge and lack of adaptation.

F. Plots of impulse frequency against angular position for different hairs form a series of bell-shaped curves (as explained in D) with optima at various angles. [After Cohen, 1960.]

A nonadapting discharge is obtained from the neuron of each hair at rest, and a constant deflection causes a steady-state impulse frequency that is reasonably independent of the direction from which the deflection is approached [2]. The frequency rises from about 5 to about 40 impulses per sec over the first 20° of deflection. In their natural state the hairs are set at different positions in their response curves; this is necessarily somewhat fortuitous, because the statolith is an irregular mass of sand of external origin. But the 400 hairs are arranged in a crescent around the lobster statolith, so that tilting in any direction causes a unique change in the pattern of excitation in this arc. Presumably each hair is centrally represented according to its position in the circle, but we do not know to what extent the system depends upon learning with reference to the statolith, or whether there are fixed connections based upon the regional differences, or range fractionation, around the sensory crescent (Fig. 11.1).

The second type of neuron innervates very thin threadlike hairs, which move with the swirling of the sea water in the statocyst cavity. Bending these hairs posteriorly or ventrally increases the spontaneous impulse frequency of their neurons, without marked adaptation when the deflection is maintained. When the hairs are deflected naturally, however, their elasticity brings them back to their original position. They act, therefore, as receptors of the angular acceleration, which is the chief factor causing the wall of the statolith cavity to move at a rate different from its fluid contents. Because they lie within a curved cavity they necessarily cover the range of movements in different directions.

The lobster, then, derives two distinguishable modalities, absolute position and rotational acceleration, from two neuron types in one organ, and both are range-fractionated by virtue of the curved anatomy of the whole organ. As a mechanical consequence, the recorded sensory units fall into classes corresponding to forward, backward, or sideways tilting, but because it has an irregular statocyst of external origin the intact animal may have to learn the exact significance of every differently excited fibre cluster. Moreover, as the animal is slowly tilted through a full 360°, each individual neuron is brought into similar activity in several different segments of the full circle. We are reminded that the experimenter is trying to correlate the stimulus with a response, but the animal is trying to determine the stimulus. With the above-mentioned ambiguities it can determine its position by a rather sophisticated weighting of the excitation, which is summed. However, the net response of the whole animal shows no ambiguity at all, and a 1° tilt of a crab (in the dark) in any direction is almost corrected by a 0.95° compensatory tilt of the eyes.

THE INNER EAR OF FISH

In the most primitive vertebrate example that has been adequately investigated, the skate, we find the system of three semicircular canals arranged in the three planes, together with three position receptors of the otolith type—the utriculus, sacculus, and lagena. These receptors are well developed in the elasmobranch fish (Fig. 11.2), and function in them much as they do throughout the vertebrates. In these fish, which have no bony skeletons, it is possible to dissect out the organs for analysis [15, 16]. A strange feature is a considerable reduplication of receptors in different groups, and on each side of the head. The receptors of the semicircular canals of the ray each have a background discharge, which is increased by rotary acceleration in one direction and inhibited in the other direction. The horizontal canal is excited by rotary accelerations about the vertical axis when the ampulla end is trailing; the two vertical canals are both excited by rotary accelerations in all the appropriate planes (and to some extent also in the horizontal plane) but with the ampulla end leading.

Figure 11.2

A ventrolateral view of the membranous labryinth of the ray, showing the utriculus, sacculus, and lagena, which are vibration and gravity receptors, and the three semicircular canals. Although the example is from a primitive fish, its general structure is similar to that in a mammal, showing the remarkable stability in evolution of this particular combination of sense organs. *ant vert amp*, anterior vertical ampulla; *hor amp*, horizontal ampulla; *lag*, lagena; *post vert amp*, posterior vertical ampulla; *ram inf*, ramus inferior; *ram sup*, ramus superior; *sacc*, sacculus; *utr*, utriculus; *V–X*, 5th to 10th cranial nerves. [Lowenstein and Roberts, 1950.]

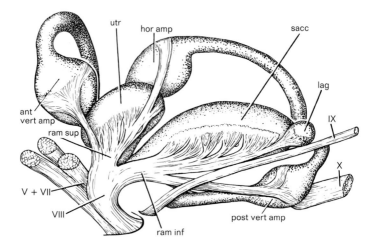

TABLE 8
Auditory system

Auditory receptors (tympanic organ): migratory locust

A. Peak sensitivity 4–6 kc/sec
B. Peak sensitivity 12–16 kc/sec
   Total 80 fibres each side.

Auditory interneurons: migratory locust [From Popov (Sechenov Institute) in press]

A. One paired fibre to brain, very sensitive. Graded response with intensity in the frequency range 12–20 kc/sec. But 1–3 spikes only in range 2–9 kc/sec.
B. One paired fibre to brain, very sensitive. Less response at higher intensities, in the range 12–20 kc/sec, but only 1–3 impulses in range 2–9 kc/sec.
C. Only ganglion T.II. Tonic, low threshold "on" units. No frequency discrimination.
D. Only ganglion T.II. High threshold, some inhibited by sound. Various types with reference pitch. Probably motoneurons.
E. Only ganglia T.II. and T.III. High threshold. Linear frequency characteristic. Input from hair receptors.

Semicircular canals: ray [Lowenstein and Sand, 1940]

Spontaneous active at rest.
1. Horizontal canal receptors, rotation about vertical axis
2. Anterior vertical canal, excited by rotation, ampulla-leading
3. Posterior vertical canal, inhibited when ampulla is trailing.

Otolith organs: ray [Lowenstein and Roberts, 1950]

Utriculus macula, units with diverse axes of sensitivity, covering the whole range of orientations (a) static (b) phasic.
Sacculus macula, similarly units sensitive to all tilts.
Lagena, units with maximum at normal head orientation.
Vibration receptors up to 120 cyc/sec in anterior sacculus.

Equilibrium receptors: cat

Similar to above for skate.
Spontaneous background + and − effects with opposite accelerations and tilts

---

Second order (vestibular) excited by the cupula endolymph system (rotation receptors): cat [Shimazo and Precht, 1965]

1. Tonic constant level of maximum frequency, proportional to log of rotational acceleration: not spontaneous background.
2. Phasic, no spontaneous discharge: high threshold: rapid adaptation to a new velocity of constant rotation.

Auditory nerve: bullfrog [Fishkopf and Goldstein, 1963]

Both types are probably primary sensory and they have sharp pitch dependency
1. Simple. Best frequency 1000 to 1500 c.p.s. not inhibited by any stimulus
2. Complex. Inhibited in the range 300–1000 c.p.s. Vary in sensitivity to vibratory stimuli. Best frequency for sound excit. is 200–700 c.p.s. Inhibition is not under efferent control.

TABLE 8 (Continued)

Auditory system

Auditory area in midbrain: bullfrog [Potter, 1965]

97% rapidly adapt to a pure tone. Response frequency increases with intensity only up to a maximum, thereafter declining. Many units not responsive to intenser notes, even of optimum frequency. All neurons are frequency-sensitive; some responded best to a note of specified duration. Some units respond to sound, others to vibration, others to both.

Auditory nerve: cat [Rupert et al., 1963]

1. Spectrum of properties, with each fibre sensitive to a narrow band of sound frequency which widens, and impulse frequency increases at higher intensities.
2a. Inhibited immediately by tones.
2b. Inhibited after a delay.
3. Spontaneous, impulses brought into phase with tones.

Cochlear nucleus: cat (second-order cells)
[Rose, Hughes, and Galambos, 1959; Moushegian et al., 1962]

1. Restricted band width to tones.
2. Few units with two response areas.
3. Some units excited by one note, inhibited by another.
4. Units only inhibited, not excited, by tones.
In general, dorsal cochlear units are on the click-sensitive fast pathway; ventral ones on a slower, frequency-analysing pathway.

Medial superior olivary nucleus: cat [Hall, 1964; Moushegian et al., 1964]

First centre for binaural interaction.
Units: 1. Inhibited ipsilaterally excited contralaterally (most abundant)
2. Opposite to 1
3. Excited from both sides
4. Complex varieties of 1–3 depending on timing at the two ears.
N.B. Time/intensity trading ratios (see text)

Medial geniculate: cat [Galambos, 1952]

1. Units sensitive to pure tones. No obvious spatial organisation. Band width at threshold is wide: complex response at onset.
2. Some spontaneous units inhibited by tones.
3. Units responding to clicks, not tones.
N.B. Failure to discover signs of differential pitch sense. A tone stimulus will suppress a response to a click.

Auditory cortex: cat
[Whitfield and Evans, 1965; Oonishi and Katsuki, 1965]
Arranged in columns, each with a characteristic frequency.

1. Responding to clicks and odd sounds only (21%).
2. Responding to tones (54%) (a) by sustained excitation, (b) by sustained inhibition, (c–e) by "on," "off," and "on-off," (f) to sliding tones only (4%).
3. Responding to visual stimuli (2.5%).
4. Responding to sound and visual (0.5%).
5. Having two or more peak frequencies.

On stopping the acceleration, the responses are reversed for a time because they arise from the movement of the wall relative to the fluid inside.

The three otolith organs of the skate, (utriculus, sacculus, and lagena) again show considerable overlap in sensitivity on each side. All three have units that respond to tilt and to linear acceleration: the utriculus has units for all planes of tilting, and each organ has units that duplicate others elsewhere except that the anterior part of the sacculus is particularly sensitive to vibration. Almost all units have a background discharge, and units responding to opposite directions are not regionally separated. The greatest uniformity of response is in the lagena, in which the majority of units have their highest frequency when the head is in its normal position. The lagena and the utriculus do not respond to vibration, but anterior sacculus units respond to various ranges of sound frequency up to 120 c.p.s. Apart from the vibration receptors, the functions of the three groups of static receptors overlap to a considerable extent, and it is broadly true that apart from the lagena most show their maximum activity when the head is out of its true position. All of these organs, together with the semicircular canals, are responsible for reflexes that govern the compensatory movements of eyes and appendages and the symmetry of the musculature at rest. Although we don't know any details of the pathways, whether genetically inherent or learned, the receptors sensitive to deflection in each of the possible planes must ultimately connect with the appropriate motor centres to elicit compensatory tonic responses of the muscles.

We should also note the remarkable resemblance between the results on the skate and those on the cat, even to the directionality of the angular accelerations with reference to the ampullae. This shows that the orientation of the sensitivity of the hair cells is constant over a very wide range of vertebrates, but presumably the whole system is conservative because in the radiation of the vertebrates to swimming, running, jumping, burrowing, or flying forms, there are no new types of forces imposed by motion or by gravity, and the system that is essential for a freely swimming fish is adequate for all.

Even in fish we find parts of this system specialized for hearing. In the teleost *Cottus*, responses to pure tones were obtained from almost all sacculus units, from two-thirds of those of the lagena, and from one-third of those of the utriculus. Units showed a variety of patterns of discharges: those with spontaneous activity responded to sound frequencies up to 200 c.p.s; units with irregular activity responded to 300–500 c.p.s.; ones with bursty activity followed up to 200–300 c.p.s. Units not responsive to sound are those which serve the position sense [5].

The mechanism of the undoubted pitch discrimination in fish and other lower vertebrates seems to be based mainly on the ability of groups of auditory neurons to follow the sound wave with synchronous impulses in phase with it. In minnows the range extends towards higher frequencies with increase in temperature. As noted above, two of the types of unit in *Cottus* differ in range, which could provide a crude discrimination of pitch. But behavioural discrimination is quite good; in the minnow, 9% change in frequency at 150 c.p.s., 12–15% change at 300 c.p.s., 30% change at 600 c.p.s. The inference is that this is based on frequency following by groups of cells, and therefore dependent on an unknown central mechanism. Presumably this is the primitive system from which the mammalian one, with a cochlea, has evolved. The primitive method of frequency analysis of the sound has been transformed into a mechanism for the analysis of arrival times and localization of the sound.

Mechanoreception in the lateral line and equilibrium organs requires shearing of the jelly that fills the cupula or otolith, but the transduction mechanism remains a puzzle. Two types of cilia (one kinocilium with the normal (9 + 2) pattern, and the others, stereocilia without fibrils) project into the jelly from the surface of the sensory cells. This is one example of the widespread specialisation of cilia in mechanoreceptors; we do not know their function (see p. 6 and Fig. 2.1, e).

The directional sensitivity of these cells is related to their orientation. For example, the lateral line organs of *Xenopus* have two types of unit that are sensitive to water movements in opposite directions. The asymmetrically placed kinocilium is towards one side in half of the cells, towards the other side in the other half (Fig. 11.3). The ampullae of the semicircular canals have a constant directional sensitivity in all investigated vertebrates. Bending the sense hair towards the side of the kinocilium in the ray excites the nerve fibre, and opposite deflection inhibits it [3].

The irregular pattern of disturbances in the water, as caused by natural objects in movement near a fish or a crustacean, are certainly detected by the sense organs, but they have not been found to be integrated centrally by a stereotyped system of interneurons. This may be for want of looking,

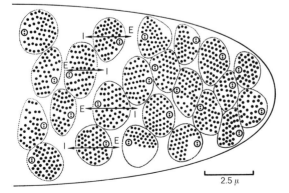

2.5 μ

Figure 11.3

Orientation of mechanoreceptor cells in one of two principal directions in a neuromast of the lateral line of the toad *Xenopus*. Each sensory cell bears a single cilium, of normal 9 + 2 pattern, together with a number of smaller stereocilia, which have no fibrillar structure. The arrows show the directions of depolarization or excitation (*E*) of nerve impulses, and of hyperpolarization or inhibition (*I*) (see also Fig. 11.4). [Dijkgraaf, 1963.]

but it seems more likely that the characteristic patterns in the water must be learned by the animal for each environment. It will be interesting to see whether the mechanism for the analysis of arrival times is related to that which localizes sound in higher vertebrates.

THE MAMMALIAN AUDITORY PATHWAY

There are about as many central synapses on the auditory as on the visual pathway of the mammals, and it provides an excellent example of transformations at successive stages along an interneuron chain. By necessity the auditory system has to operate quickly and at the same time to extract different kinds of information simultaneously from the sound signal. From the first-order cells through successive relays to the cortex, this system illustrates how many neurons in parallel abstract and carry different features of the stimulus, relating to intensity, tone, onset, change of tone, direction relative to the head, and so on. The following account refers to the cat—the animal in which the system is best known.

Hearing and the cochlea   The receptor cells are two distinct rows of hair cells, an inner and an outer, along the length of the tapering, coiled basement membrane. The endings of the nerve fibres upon the ciliated sensory cells are also diverse, some having knoblike, others platelike terminals. So far the only clear organization is that there is an array laid out along the cochlea; on the inner row two or three nerve fibres connect with each hair cell and two or three hair cells with each nerve fibre. Even after intense study, the process of transduction and impulse initiation is not clear.

The primary auditory nerve fibres (30,000 in the cat) have endings that are excited at the bases of the hair cells of the organ of Corti (Fig. 11.4) by so-called travelling waves in the basilar membrane [1]. High-frequency sound deflects the membrane at the basal end of the spiral; low-frequency sound deflects it further towards the tip of the spiral (Fig. 11.5). Recordings from single fibres in the auditory nerve show that fibres respond to only a narrow range of sound frequency when the intensity is just adequate to excite. The whole pitch range of the animal is covered by the superposition of overlapping ranges of individual units. For a hair cell and its nerve fibre at a given place on the spiral membrane, the best frequency is that which at lowest intensity deflects the membrane by the threshold amount at that point.

When the fluid displacements of the perilymph are initiated in the *apical end* of the cochlea through an artificial opening, the normal pattern of travelling waves moves *from the base to the apex*. In fact, the time of travel of a sound wave through the whole perilymph length is about 25

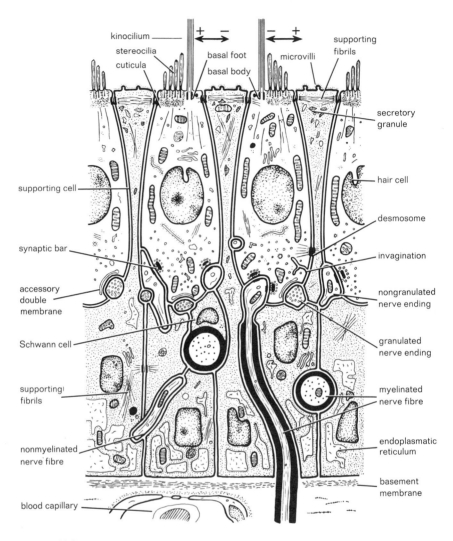

Figure 11.4

Schematic drawing of the ultrastructure of the sensory epithelium of the lateral line of the teleost *Lota vulgaris*. A group of several stereocilia and one kinocilium that projects from each cell is sensitive to shearing of the contents of the lateral line canal. The two orientations of cell are sensitive to shear in opposite directions, so that the stimulus is divided at source into two channels of opposite reference. Shear in the excitatory direction (+) causes depolarization of the receptor cell, and impulses in the myelinated sensory fibre. This general anatomical plan and physiological sensitivity seems typical of all the vertebrate lateral line organs, the equilibrium sensory cells of the vertebrate ear, and the acoustic receptors of vertebrates. The actual mechanism of the strongly directional transducer action is not known. [Flock, 1965.]

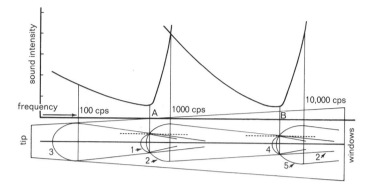

Figure 11.5

Simplified explanation of how the primary auditory neurons are line-labelled with reference to the frequency of a sound, relative to the movement of waves of different frequency along the basilar membrane of the cochlea. High-frequency waves cause a displacement only a little way from the window on the right; low-frequency ones displace the membrane further along, where it is narrower but less stiff. Threshold displacement to excite the neurons is represented by the horizontal dashed line. For a unit at A on the membrane, the best frequency causes a deflection that just reaches threshold, as for the contour 1. A wave of higher frequency has to be much stronger, as for contour 2, to reach threshold at the same place, and a low-frequency wave, as for 3, has to be a little stronger to reach threshold. For a unit at B on the membrane, of best frequency corresponding to contour 4, the lower frequency wave 2 and the higher frequency 5 are just adequate to reach the threshold.

μsec (at 1.4×10^3 m/sec through 35 mm). This is two orders of magnitude shorter than the delay in propagation of the travelling waves along the membrane. Therefore the travelling waves are not sound waves, and in fact energy is not transposed from one region of the membrane to the next, because the membrane is not in tension along its length. The location of the deflection is determined by the differences in stiffness of the membrane in different regions, the apex being more flexible, the base stiffer. The energy distribution takes only about 25 μsec, as above, and the wave of deflection appears to travel only because the latency of the response is progressively longer towards the apex, where the membrane is more flexible. The shapes of the contours of membrane deflection give rise to the frequency/intensity relations of the primary neurons, with a relatively sharp cutoff at the high-frequency side and a flatter curve towards the low-frequency side. With the onset of a steady note at constant pitch, the impulse frequency declines as in typical sensory adaptation. Although there is some efferent inhibition, it does not have a large rapid effect, for adaptation is little changed when the auditory nerve is cut. The impulse frequency is a function of sound intensity up to about 450 per sec. All fibres have a spontaneous background frequency, in which the distribution of intervals is exponential, although the significance of this is unknown. A greater amplitude of deflection necessarily activates auditory units over a wider area of the basilar membrane. Many of the (all primary) sensory fibres in the auditory nerve of the cat and bullfrog are inhibited by sounds of a pitch adjacent to that which best excites, or even simply inhibited by any tone. In different primary fibres the inhibition is of two kinds, rapid or delayed in onset, and its mechanism is not known. We cannot rule out physical effects such as current flow upon hair cells from adjacent receptor cells or antagonistic shearing of the receptors caused by opposing mechanical forces, but peripheral lateral inhibition between receptor endings has not been demonstrated.

All primary fibres are so thin that their conduction delays are up to a hundred times the temporal discrimination that can be demonstrated in the third-order cells of the olivary nucleus. Therefore, although the connexions in the lower auditory nuclei may be genetically governed, the system is quite susceptible to a tiny error of growth at this level; thus it is arguable that the exact connexions are formed partly on the basis of the nervous activity itself, not entirely genetically, and that the resulting binaural discrimination of sound frequency, direction, and patterns, although depending on fixed pathways in the midbrain, is in some way learned at a higher level.

Although they do not necessarily fire at every oscillation of the sound wave, the auditory impulses appear with a definite phase relation to the sound up to about 1500 c.p.s., with different units alternating. This explains how man can have a mechanism whereby a continuous pure tone up to about 1500 c.p.s. (supplied by headphone to avoid an intensity effect) can be localized in space by the use of the two ears, and why he can detect one tone in a random noise that is chopped on and off at frequencies up to about 2000 c.p.s. For clicks, which are sudden pressure changes containing a large number of frequencies, the situation is different. The time differences of 1 to 10 μsec involved in the optimal binaural localization of clicks by man (without intensity effect) are about a hundred times less than the figures for tones might suggest, showing that clicks are processed by a faster system than tones. For eventual discrimination of tone, however, a sound pulse need not last long; at 2 kc/sec a pulse need be only 2 cycles long (1 msec), and the precision does not improve with more cycles.

The cochlear nucleus Many of the second-order cells in the cochlear nucleus have narrower band widths than primary fibres in the auditory nerve (Fig. 11.6). As in the auditory nerve, some units are excited by notes of one pitch but are inhibited at a neighbouring pitch. Such units, showing excitation and inhibition, necessarily discriminate against white noise, and therefore they must contribute to our ability to operate with unsaturated tones. They have been found as far up as the inferior col-

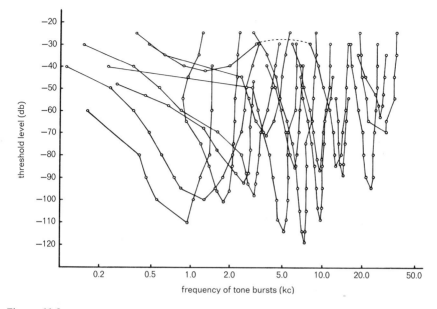

Figure 11.6

Sensitivity of 16 different units of the anterior ventral cochlear nucleus of the cat, as a sample of second-order auditory interneurons that are line-labelled according to best frequency. The exact shape of the curves depends on the stimulating conditions and the arbitrarily chosen adequate response. [Kiang, 1965.]

liculus but no higher. A few units, unlike any in the auditory nerve, respond to more than one narrow band. Occasionally band widths are far narrower than those in the auditory nerve; for example, one unit had a band width of 40 cycles/sec at 4.5 kc/sec; some units are inhibited by loud sounds even at the frequency to which they are most sensitive when excited by soft notes. These are all properties of neurons that must be excited or inhibited simultaneously by first-order units of different frequency characteristics. The operations that result in complex frequency curves are more typical of the ventral cochlear nucleus, with much convergence; higher-frequency and click-sensitive units are situated more dorsally. The dorsal cochlear nucleus, with large calyx synapses (Fig. 11.7, A), seems to be the rapid pathway that preserves the accurate timing of the onset of clicks, which are so beautifully analysed in the medial superior olivary nucleus.

There is a premium upon the prompt and complete analysis of the information in the primary neurons, and this is achieved by spreading it as early as possible into numerous parallel channels. Lorente de Nó describes the primary auditory fibres as dividing to thirteen different areas of the cochlear nucleus in man, with topographical representation

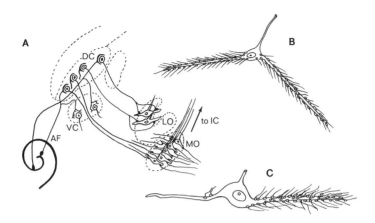

Figure 11.7

Connexions on the pathway where time and intensity differences between the two ears are first brought together at the median superior olivary nucleus in the cat. The features illustrated in the next figure are based upon these connexions.

A. Primary auditory fibres (*AF*) from neurons of the spiral ganglion of the cochlea end in the dorsal cochlear nucleus (*DC*) at large calyciform synapses upon secondary neurons. Branches of the same primary fibres project with ramifying terminals to numerous other neurons in the ventral cochlear nucleus. Axons of the dorsal cochlear nucleus of one side project to one dendrite of the two horned neurons of the median olivary nucleus *MO*, which in turn project to the inferior colliculus. Axons of the other side project to the other horn. The lateral olivary (*LO*) has a different projection.

B. A two-pole cell of the median olivary nucleus.

C. A similar cell after destruction of the cochlear nucleus of one side. Together with the distribution of slow potentials, this pattern of degeneration confirms that excitatory impulses from one side arrive at one horn and inhibitory ones from the opposite side at the other horn. [After Stotler, 1953.]

in each; that is, the cochlea is mapped out thirteen times in the cochlear nucleus. Presumably each of these takes a different aspect as may be judged from the dendritic structure, which is different in each. This is quite a feat of morphogenesis.

The accessory (median superior) olivary nucleus The fast pathway from the dorsal cochlear nucleus meets that from the opposite side upon the two-horned cells of the accessory olivary nucleus, which is concerned mainly with binaural localization, for which very accurate time preservation is necessary. Some at least of the two-horned olivary cells have all the fibres from the cochlear nucleus of one side upon one horn and all from the opposite side on the other horn (Fig. 11.7, B and C). Slow potentials suggest that inhibition predominates at the ipsilateral horn and excitation at the contralateral one; in fact, about 50% of cells in this area in the cat are inhibited by ipsilateral clicks and excited by contralateral ones (Fig. 11.8).

Units of the accessory olivary nucleus demonstrate the interplay of excitation and inhibition with a strict reference to the time of arrival of stimuli at the two ears. Clicks are the best stimuli. Frequency-response curves are diverse for these units and may or may not be similar for stimuli at the two ears. Some units are excitatory for both ears (with clicks), so that subthreshold stimuli sum between the two ears if presented close enough together in time (Fig. 11.8, A). Many units are inhibited from one side and excited from the other (Fig. 11.8, D). A few show either a sum or a difference between the stimuli on the two sides, depending on the exact timing. The difference units, in which inhibition from one side counteracts excitation from the other, have a critical relation between timing and relative intensity [10]. The cell shown in Figure 11.8, C, was more likely to respond when the click on the contralateral side was made stronger and less likely when the ipsilateral click was stronger. It was also less likely to respond when the ipsilateral was leading by a fraction of a millisecond than when the contralateral click was leading. There is therefore a "trading ratio" between equivalent intensity differences and time differences at the two ears, and the trading ratio improves with average intensity, up to a limit. Trading ratios for the most efficient cat neurons correspond closely with those obtained by sensory psychologists working on man—optima of about 15 μsec per decibel. Although the medial olivary cells are thus ambiguous with reference to time and/or intensity differences at the two ears, they can be classified into groups having different optimum delays or alternatively into groups showing different optimum intensity differences between the two ears. The range of time delays that these cells can manipulate corresponds to the range of delays in sounds reaching the two ears from different directions, but the intensity differences operate over the intensity range caused by the head shadowing of each ear from sound from the other side. Therefore sharp sounds arriving naturally from different directions are necessarily classified into different sets of neurons, and their origin in space outside the animal becomes line-labelled. Moreover, frequency can be taken into account in the directional localization. As shown in Figure 11.8, F, some neurons are best inhibited at the ipsilateral ear by the same frequency that best excites at the contralateral ear. This means that sound of the same frequency will converge upon the same cell after passing through both ears; thus different frequencies from different directions can be localized separately, even when occurring at the same time. Moreover, the intensity difference caused by the head shadow is taken into account. This mechanism shows how we may pick out one sound from several simultaneous ones, as in a room full of people, and how bats can discriminate objects of different auditory reflection properties.

In the establishment of connexions, the frequency characteristics of the second-order endings in Figure 11.7, B and C, which are in turn derived from the first-order neurons, have an influence in determining which cells

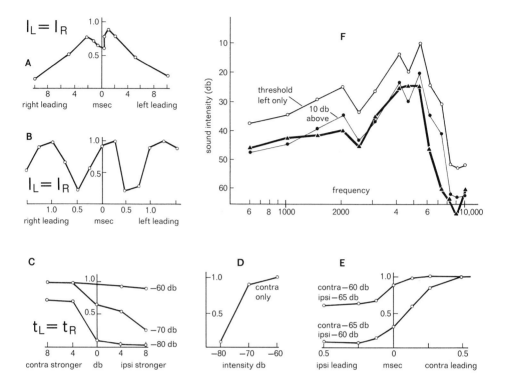

Figure 11.8

Features of the lowest-order binaural units on the auditory pathway of the cat, presumably based upon the anatomical connexions illustrated in Figure 11.7.

A. Probability of firing of a unit for which subthreshold stimuli sum between the two ears, plotted against the interval between a click delivered to each ear.

B. A unit as in **A** but with two troughs showing inhibition for two different lead/lag relations on each side of zero. There is therefore a fairly symmetrical input of both inhibition and excitation with different time relations for the two sides.

C. Probability of firing, plotted against the intensity difference for two clicks presented simultaneously at the two ears. Three curves for different average intensities show that intensity discrimination by this unit is best at the lowest average intensity.

D. Probability of firing plotted against intensity for a unit that was excited from the contralateral ear and inhibited from the ipsilateral ear.

E. The same unit as in **D**, showing the effect of varying the lag/lead interval of clicks at the two ears. Note that the curve is steepened (performance improved) when the contralateral intensity is 5 db above the ipsilateral value. [A–E from Hall, 1964.]

F. The two thin lines (*circles*) show points at threshold and 10 db above threshold for a unit that is driven by the left ear with tone pulses of different frequency. The thick line (*triangles*) shows the required intensity of a note at the right ear to provide just complete inhibition of the left ear stimulus for various frequencies at the right ear. The coincidence of the two effects shows that units of the cochlear nucleus of the same frequency characteristics project, with opposite effect from the two sides, to this third-order neuron. [Moushegian et al., 1964.]

they, in turn, terminate upon. Once again we find that detailed connexions of interneurons are fixed in some way according to properties of the receptor far up the line.

The proportion of inhibitory and excitatory endings upon an olivary cell influence the way in which the latency to a click changes with increasing intensity. Some cells, with predominantly excitatory synapses, show a shortening of the latency to clicks of increasing strength, because more inputs to the cell are then excited. Others, inhibited more, show a lengthening of latency. It is remarkable that one class of olivary units show no change of latency with intensity, and therefore must be in balance in this respect. Consequently they preserve the time relations of onset of a sound irrespective of loudness. Such a unit would be of great use to a bat, which is concerned with the delay preceeding an echo as well as the intensity. These neurons in the cat provide an apt illustration of how single features of neurons that seem so limiting when only the membrane properties are considered have most subtle consequences when they participate in relatively simple interactions.

The inferior colliculus Where third- and fourth-order auditory neurons predominate (see Fig. 11.9), we find that all the properties of the units lower down are now superimposed in different combinations, together with a wide variety of rates of adaptation to pure tones. At this level there is still a strong suggestion of the tonotopical arrangement of units (in the cat) with respect to best frequency, but integration between the two ears is almost complete. Although the band widths of many individual units are now much wider than at lower levels (proving convergence), their orderly arrangement in space suggests that units adjacent here are those which will interact still further at higher levels, as occurs in the laminae of the dorsal horn in the spinal cord and between columns of cells in the sensory cortex of the cat. Units with complex binaural interaction in this part of the auditory system, have e.p.s.p.'s from stimuli at one ear and i.p.s.p.'s from stimuli at the other, as in the accessory olivary nucleus. A strange but possibly significant finding is that while impulse frequencies may not be sensitive to the pitch of a note, the corresponding latencies can be extremely sensitive to pitch. The usefulness of having a minimum latency over a restricted frequency is not known but it fits in with the general picture that pitch is coded in different ways, not just by tone-labelled lines, at all levels in the auditory pathway.

The medial geniculate body Here fourth-order auditory fibres project to the auditory cortex (Fig. 11.9). At this level many units respond (perhaps spuriously) only to clicks or sharp noises, and responses can be suppressed by a simultaneous pure tone. Other units respond to pure tones but over a range of pitch that is much wider than for cochlear nucleus cells, and the response is complex at the onset of a note. Apparently the

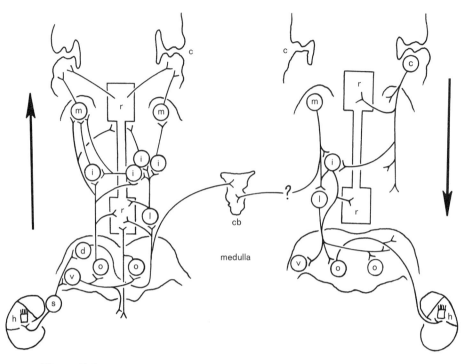

Figure 11.9

Ascending (*left*) and descending (*right*) auditory fibres of a typical mammal. *c*, cerebral cortex; *cb*, cerebellum; *d*, dorsal cochlear nucleus; *h*, hair cells of cochlear; *i*, inferior colliculus; *l*, lateral lemniscus nucleus; *m*, medial geniculate nucleus; *o*, superior olivary nucleus; *re*, reticular formation; *s*, spiral ganglion; *v*, ventral cochlear nucleus. [After Galambos.]

cat does not transmit the fundamental physical properties of the sound stimuli to the cortical level, and the most appropriate stimuli for units at this level have presumably not yet been discovered.

Responses to clicks and similar noises are obtained over wide areas of the brain, but units responding to pure tones occur only on the classical auditory pathway.

The auditory cortex Much electrophysiological evidence suggests that the actual steady pitch of a sound is of minor importance at the auditory cortex of the cat. Many units here respond better to a changing pitch than to a steady tone, and the behaviour towards one is not predictable from that to the other. Some units are excited only by falling notes, others only by rising ones, and some by both. The band widths are much wider than for primary fibres, as if they had several inputs from units of differing band width, some excitatory and others inhibitory—a situation exactly comparable to that in the visual cortex. Sustained excitation or inhibition is rare, and many units respond only to clicks or sudden noises. Many units respond to noises in the room, jingling keys, or talk, or so on, but not to pure tones. Some respond to weak but not to strong clicks. Some are novelty units, in that they soon habituate and then respond afresh to any novel stimulus. Although essential for classification and experimental analysis, responses to simple tones (Fig. 11.10) are not appropriate for the analytical neural mechanism at this level, just as simple lights are ineffective stimuli for units of the visual cortex.

Although the auditory cortex of the dog appears to be arranged spatially with reference to sound intensity in one direction and to frequency in the other, the cat's auditory cortex is not tonotopically arranged on a gross scale. However, the columnar arrangement characteristic of the sensory

Figure 11.10

Various types of unit responses to standard controlled stimuli. Because natural stimuli are difficult to control or define, the analysis of unit responses has proceeded by use of square wave, sine wave, or ramp function waveforms of controlled strength. These particular units are of the auditory cortex of the cat, in response to tone pulses as shown by a thickening of the lower line of each pair. From the top downwards there are (a) sustained excitation, (b) sustained inhibition, (c) "on" response, (d) "off" response, (e) "on-off" response, and (f) a unit excited only by changing frequency with the modulation at 10 c/sec of a 2 kc/sec sound shown along the bottom line. Horizontal time scale in each case is 0.5 sec. [Evans and Whitfield, 1964.]

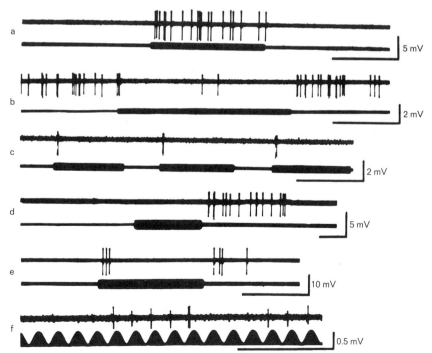

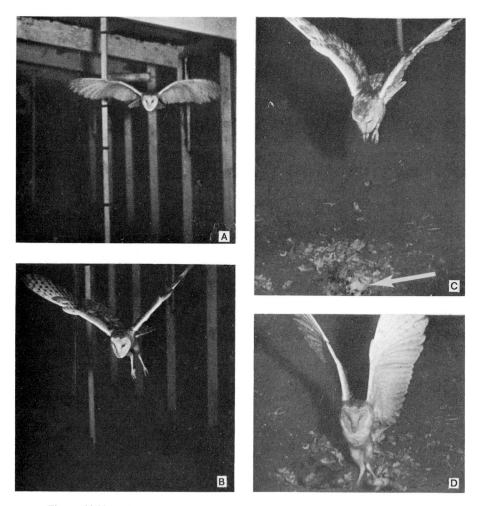

Figure 11.11

The pounce of a barn owl photographed by infrared flashes. The owl on its perch hears the rustle caused by the movements of a mouse, which lies at the point of the white arrow. The owl flies down when the movements stop, so that its flight must be made upon a schedule based upon sensory information that was complete before the movement started; for similar acts see Figures 8.8 and 12.19.

A. Just off the perch.

B. The feet come forward.

C. Feet now under its face, in readiness for the backward strike of both feet, which lifts the head and turns the body in flight.

D. The conclusion of the strike, with eyes closed, wings jerked up to give extra impetus, and the mouse beneath the left foot. [Photographs by Roger S. Payne.]

cortex is found in a pattern that is based partly on tone. Within a given vertical column the cells have similar best frequencies; commonly those deepest down have single sharp spectral peaks, those higher up have double or multiple peaks, and those nearest the surface have rather flat curves. Presumably the cells near the surface have inputs from lower down in their own or nearby columns, and some may be identical with those shown by some investigators to be especially sensitive to warble tones. In contrast to other sensory systems throughout the animal kingdom, a few cortical auditory units have been observed to change their response characteristics and become more sustained over a long period, but it must be remembered that the vertebrate auditory system is one in which efferent feedback occurs at every stage, including the rapidly acting regulatory muscle in the middle ear, which takes only 8 msec to complete contraction.

The location of nuclei where sound analysis occurs, as shown by recording from units, is mainly subcortical, but ablation studies show that the auditory cortex is necessary for discrimination of sound direction, change in note duration, and all sound patterns, even though these attributes are available in the impulse sequences at lower levels. Conversely, the fact that decorticate mammals can be conditioned to the onset of a sound, change of intensity, or change of frequency confirms that this other set of attributes are line-labelled in a learning mechanism at a subcortical level. We cannot say, however, that this simple learning occurs on the ascending auditory pathway, because auditory excitation spreads from it into the reticular system and even far down the spinal cord.

In general, the mammalian auditory system shows that a wide variety of attributes of a complex stimulus can be siphoned off into separate lines by a taking of sums and differences between fibres lower down. By this means some very narrow band widths, necessary for fine discrimination, can be achieved. Latency or phase in relation to intensity also becomes a channelling device for sounds from different directions in the third- and fourth-order cells. Perhaps cortical units that select sounds of certain patterns will turn up when deliberately sought. However, the indications are that apart from sliding tone units the true stimulus parameters for cortical auditory units have not been found. After all, in man, there are about 500,000,000 auditory cortex cells that carry the attributes of the signals from a mere 100,000 primary cochlear fibres.

ECHOLOCATION IN BATS

The bat is a particularly interesting specialized case where certain attributes of the auditory sense are known to be important in behaviour. Units of the cochlear nucleus are similar to those of the cat, many being in-

Figure 11.12

A bat catching a moth in flight in the dark near branches of a tree. The bat emits pulses of ultrasonic sound. The weak sound reflected from the moth enables the bat to localize the moth relative to its own flight path. The moth has ears sensitive to the high-frequency note of the bat, and the moth takes avoiding action. Some moths have ear fleas, which would make the moth deaf, and so all would perish together were it not for the fact that the fleas live in only one of the moths two ears, thus ensuring their own survival with the moth. The photograph is taken with a stroboscopic flash; successive positions of the bat are at 1 to 4, of the moth *a* to *f*. [Photograph courtesy Frederic A. Webster.]

hibited by one tone and excited by nearby ones, but with sharper distinctions than in the cat [9]. At the level of the inferior colliculus the units have very phasic responses, some with broad frequency-response curves. From knowledge of the cat auditory system this is clearly appropriate for a mechanism in echolocation which depends upon latency only, and in fact these units show the greatest changes in threshold upon movement of the stimulus location. Some colliculus units can be stimulated only from certain angles. Other units have response band widths much sharper than those of units lower in the system; some, which are particularly effective in the presence of extraneous noise, are tuned to the bat's own vocal frequency. Other units respond only over a limited rather *faint intensity range* even at the optimum pitch, and many bat auditory units differ from those of the cat in being very sensitive to slight changes in intensity. Many units, with binaural inputs, are sensitive only to sounds from certain directions, which is clearly helpful in location of objects in the presence of noise. The directional sensitivity is such that it would permit localization with an accuracy of 1–2° in the horizontal plane. Certain adaptations enable a bat to listen for the faint echo of its own vocal sound: (a) the rapid recovery of threshold within a period of half a millisecond following a loud pulse (blanking-out is 10 to 100 times shorter than in the cat); (b) abundance of faint-pulse units, which will not respond to loud noises; (c) the facilitation of some faint-pulse units for a short time, down to 1 msec, by a loud noise—echoreceptor units. Different units of this type give selective responses according to the delay of the echo, in the range 1–5 msec, and therefore sound pulses reflected from different distances are picked up by different units.

These results suggest that one way in which bats estimate the distance of a reflecting object is by having a population of echoreceptor units with differing optimum echo delays, so that stimulation of some acts as a measurement of the time delay to the echo. The results also suggest that the enormously developed accessory olivary nuclei of marine mammals serve a similar function, as yet untested. Directional sense in the bat seems to depend mainly on the time-intensity trading ratios, as in the cat. So far as several objects are simultaneously distinguished in space by the flying bat, each object could be centrally represented all the time by an excitation cluster of units, line-labelled by the same characteristic codes that are known for the cat. The variety of neural operations, the unlikelihood of genetic determination of every pathway, and the variety of environments and of ways of life among bats agree with the observation that young bats have to learn to perfect their locating system. There is every reason to suppose, however, that bats are able to build up an image of the objects surrounding them, just as we do with our differently coded visual units.

REFERENCES FOR CHAPTER 11

1. Békésy, G. von. 1960. *Experiments on Hearing*. E. G. Weaver (Ed.). New York, McGraw-Hill.
2. Cohen, M. J. 1960. The response patterns of single receptors in the crustacean statocyst. *Proc. Roy. Soc. B* **152,** 30–49.
3. Cold Spring Harbor Symposium on Quantitative Biology. **30,** 1965.
4. Dijkgraaf, S. 1963. The functioning and significance of the lateral line organs. *Biol. Rev.* **38:**51–105.
5. Enger, P. S. 1963. Single unit activity in the peripheral auditory system of a teleost fish. *Acta. Physiol. Scand.* **59:** Suppl. No. 210, 1–48.
6. Evans, E. F., and Whitfield, I. C. 1964. Classification of unit responses in the auditory cortex of the unanaesthetized and unrestrained cat. *J. Physiol.* **171:**476–493.
7. Frishkopf, L. S., and Goldstein, H. H. 1963. Responses to acoustic stimuli from single units in the eighth nerve of the bullfrog. *J. Acoust. Soc. Amer.* **35:**1219–1228.
8. Galambos, R. 1952. Microelectrode studies on medial geniculate body of cat. III. Response to pure tones. *J. Neurophysiol.* **15:**381–400.
9. Grinnell, A. D. 1963. The neurophysiology of audition in bats. *J. Physiol.* **167:**38–127.
10. Hall, J. L. 1964. Binaural interaction in the accessory superior olivary nucleus of the cat—an electrophysiological study of single neurons. M.I.T. Tech. Rep. 416.
11. Hall, J. L. 1965. Binaural interaction in the accessory superior olivary nucleus of the cat. *J. Acoust. Soc. Amer.* **37:**814–822.
12. Katsuki, Y. 1965. Comparative neurophysiology of hearing. *Physiol. Rev.* **45:**380–423.
13. Kiang, N. Y. S. 1965. Stimulus coding in the cochlear nucleus. *Ann. Oto. Laryngol.* **74:**463–485.
14. Lorente de Nó, R. 1933. Anatomy of the eighth nerve. The central projection of the nerve endings of the internal ear. *Laryngoscope* **43:**1–38.
15. Lowenstein, O., and Roberts, T. D. M. 1950. The equilibrium function of the otolith organs of the thornback ray (*Raja clavata*). *J. Physiol.* **110:**392–415.
16. Lowenstein, O., and Sand, A. 1940. The individual and integrated activity of the semicircular canals of the elasmobranch labyrinth. *J. Physiol.* **99:**89–101.
17. Lowenstein, O., and Wersäll, J. 1959. A functional interpretation of the electronmicroscopic structure of the sensory hairs of the cristae of the elasmobranch *Raja clavata* in terms of directional sensitivity. *Nature* **184:**1807.
18. Moushegian, G., Rupert, A., and Galambos, R. 1962. Microelectrode study of ventral cochlear nucleus of the cat. *J. Neurophysiol.* **25:**515–529.
19. Moushegian, G., Rupert, A. L., and Whitcomb, M. A. 1964. Processing of auditory information by medial superior olivary neurons. *J. Neurophysiol.* **27:**1174–1191.
20. Oonishi, S., and Katsuki, Y. 1965. Functional organisation and integrative mechanism on the auditory cortex of the cat. *Jap. J. Physiol.* **15:**342–365.

21. Potter, D. D. 1965. Patterns of acoustically evoked discharges of neurons in the mesencephalon of the bullfrog. *J. Neurophysiol.* **28**:1155–84.

22. Rupert, A., Moushegian, G., and Galambos, R. 1963. Unit responses to sound from auditory nerve of the cat. *J. Neurophysiol.* **26**:449–465.

23. Shimazu, H., and Precht, W. 1965. Tonic and kinetic responses of cat's vestibular neurons to horizontal angular acceleration. *J. Neurophysiol.* **28**:991–1013.

24. Stotler, W. A. 1953. An experimental study of the cells and connections of the superior olivary complex of the cat. *J. Comp. Neurol.* **98**:401–432.

25. Waltman, B. 1966. Electrical properties and fine structure of the ampullary canals of Lorenzini. *Acta Physiol. Scand.* **66**: Suppl. 264.

26. Ward, W. D. 1966. Audition. *Ann. Rev. Psychol.* **17**:273–308.

27. Weiss, T. F. 1964. A model for firing patterns of auditory nerve fibres. M.I.T. Tech. Rep. 418.

28. Whitfield, I. C., and Evans, E. F. 1965. Responses of auditory neurons to stimuli of changing frequency. *J. Neurophysiol.* **28**:655–672.

12

The vertebrate visual pathway

Among all the systems covered, the vertebrate visual pathway provides the most sophisticated examples of patterned stimuli that excite single nerve cells. The patterns are not only the actual patterns of contrast cast on the retina, but relate also to movement and colour. But there is no reason to suppose that the interneurons of the visual pathway are exceptional in their ability to respond to sums and differences of the inputs that fall upon them in a particular array. Examples have been described from invertebrates and from the vertebrate auditory and somatic sensory pathways. The auditory system is pre-eminent in its ability to handle signals exactly with reference to time. The somatic sensory pathways, and especially the chemosensory systems, showed that sensory neurons and interneurons differ individually, and therefore they must be treated as if in separate dimensions where they converge. Every neuron signals a unique message. The visual system best illustrates the abstraction of patterns of illumination with reference to space, colour, and timing. These differences between interneuron properties in the major sensory systems arise from two causes, which are not fundamental to the interaction of nerve cells. First, the nature of the effective stimulus pattern is determined by the physical properties of the sense organ; second, the different stimuli can be technically manipulated only in certain ways, and all the experimental findings depend upon accurate stimulus control.

An outstanding feature of the vertebrate visual system is the relative isolation of the retina from the brain; thus its anatomy and activity can be more easily studied. On this account, the exact anatomical connexions between the retinal neuron types will probably be drawn out as a wiring diagram before any other place in the vertebrate nervous system, just as the connexions of the first-order visual fibres were the first in arthropods. Regularity, as in a retinal array, greatly assists analysis.

However, the small size of the visual units, especially the rods and cones, has greatly limited physiological advance. Again the nature of the available techniques limits the advances that can be firmly made. It is therefore highly satisfactory to be able to describe visual units (in frog or monkey) that are easily recorded but have such complex properties that analytical advance is limited only by the ideas of the investigator in his design of suitable stimulus situations. As with all interneurons, the effective stimuli usually turn out to be rather different from what might be expected from our own introspection, although they must be highly adapted to the natural environment and behaviour of the animal. This suggests that our greatest frustration will lie in understanding why certain patterns are abstracted by particular cells; a behaviour pattern that is required to explain the peculiarity of units is not necessarily elicited by most of the stimuli that excite them.

THE RETINA

The rods and cones of the vertebrate retina are so small that it is only very recently that records have been obtained from single units, which appear to be primary receptors. The direct recordings suggest that the primary receptors fall into different classes with respect to spectral sensitivity, and all give "on" responses, like the better-known visual receptors of insects. Curiously, however, the potentials are apparently not depolarizations, as might be expected, but hyperpolarisations. It is abundantly clear, though, that the primary receptors fall into different classes, of which the cones are less sensitive than rods in dim light. Three different classes of cones, having different spectral absorption curves, have been directly observed by microspectrophotometer in certain fish, in which they are conveniently large [23]. Electrophysiological data on colour vision in fish and monkeys show that the outputs from these primary receptors are either inhibitory or excitatory, and in their effects upon higher-order units different colours are usually opposed to one another.

The distinction between rods and cones, upheld for many years, is beginning to break down, as more are carefully examined with the electron microscope in different vertebrates. For example in the retina of the guinea pig, there are no typical cones, but two types of receptor, A and B, are distinguished morphologically. Type A, like the cones of some other vertebrates, has several processes that grow out and make a contact (without synaptic vesicles but with specialised membrane) with receptors of both types of receptor. Sometimes these contacts are upon the base, where there are synapses with the bipolar cells (Fig. 12.1). Whether this pattern of contacts has anything to do with vision, or with mechanical or trophic function, is not known.

Numerous fibres connect with the synaptic base or pedicel of each receptor, notably dendrites of the bipolar cells upon their centres and of hori-

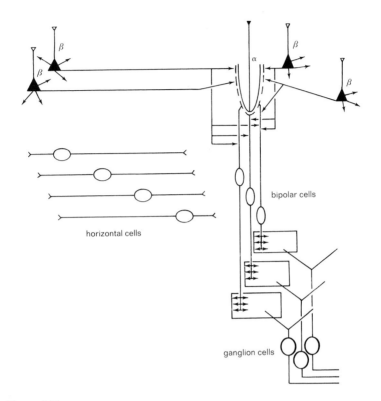

Figure 12.1

Scheme of connexions that are possibly synaptic between α and β types of receptor cells in the retina of the guinea pig. Many fibres from β cells converge on each α cell, and upon each other. Bipolar cells also form synapses in the same region at the bases of the receptors, which in this animal cannot be classified into rods and cones. At the electron microscope level, the connexions of the other neurons are not known; however, see Figure 12.4. [After Sjostrand, 1965.]

zontal cells upon their sides (Fig. 12.2). The direction of excitation in horizontal cells is unknown. A single receptor connects with many bipolar cells and a single bipolar with many receptors, except in the central area of the primate retina, where midget bipolars connect with one cone (which may also make other connexions) and single midget bipolars connect with a single midget ganglion cell. This is not a private line from a single cone because horizontal and amacrine cells also contribute synapses. The synaptic area of cones lies within a deep pit within the base of the cone. The ratio of bipolar cells to primary receptors is as great as 30 to 1. Bipolar cells in turn connect with third-order neurons, called ganglion cells, which have axons in the optic nerve (Fig. 12.3). None of the primary receptors is known to have a private line to the brain except for the "centres" in the fovea of primates, which seem to correspond to single cones.

Colour coding in higher-order units implies exact coding from the receptors onwards. One physiological evidence relevant to colour coding is that a lateral interaction between spectrally similar cones and between rods can be inferred in man from the effects of differential bleaching. It is possible that both horizontal cells and amacrines are colour-coded in primates but possibly additional effects arise from the lateral connexions between the primary receptors. The rods connect with one particular type of bipolar, the cones with two other types in the primate retina. The connexions of the receptor cells with the bipolar cells and with the horizontal cells (Fig. 12.4) are not mapped quantitatively, but we can be sure that the key to the coding of the retinal ganglion cells lies in the pattern of connectivity in this region. Each central terminal of a bipolar cell makes

Figure 12.2

A. Numerous dendrites of bipolar neurons (1) within a pedicel of a single receptor cell, as found in the retina of many vertebrates. The pedicel (2) is the central terminal of the rod or cone; it contains vacuoles (3) and synaptic ribbons (4), which are enclosed by the deeply penetrating ends of the dendrites (5). The dendrites, which emerge from the hollow of each pedicel, travel in all directions in the outer plexiform layer of the retina.

B. Responses of three different receptors in the retina of the carp, to a scan of monochromatic light through the spectrum. The spectral output of the lamp has not been allowed for, but the three responses are clearly in different regions of the spectrum. The *negative* monophasic potentials are thought to originate from penetrated single cone cells. [A from Pedler, 1965; B from Tomita, 1965.]

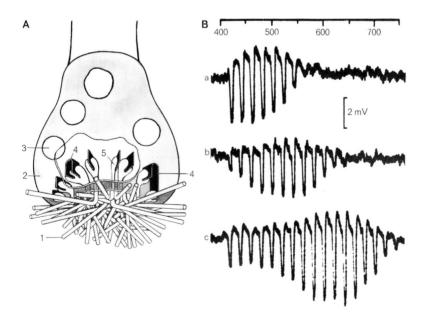

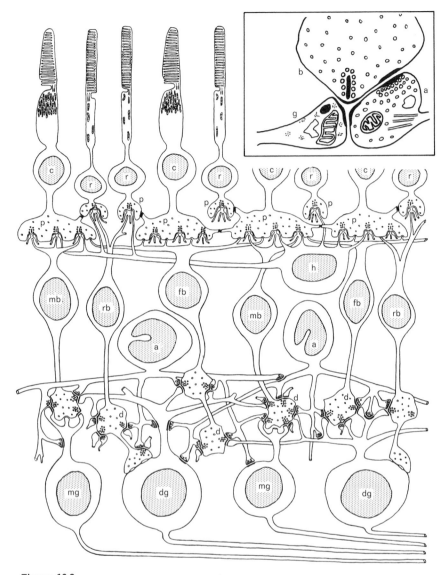

Figure 12.3

A summary of the nature of the connectivity pattern of the primate retina, showing the synapses between the different types of cells as observed with the electron microscope in serial sections. Note the contacts between receptors, the widespread connexions of the horizontal cells and of the amacrine cells, and the vertical arrangement of the bipolars. The swollen central terminals of the bipolar cells form so-called dyad synapses with a ganglion cell and simultaneously with an amacrine cell. In comparing this figure with Figure 12.4, the problem is to explain the considerable overlap and convergence, which cannot easily be correlated with the inferred physiological pathways. *r*, rod; *c*, cone; *mb*, midget bipolar; *rb*, rod bipolar; *fb*, flat bipolar; *h*, horizontal cell; *a*, amacrine cell; *mg*, midget ganglion cell; *d*, dyad synapse; *dg*, diffuse ganglion cell; *p*, pedicel. The inset at top right shows details of a typical dyad synapse. [From Dowling and Boycott, 1966.]

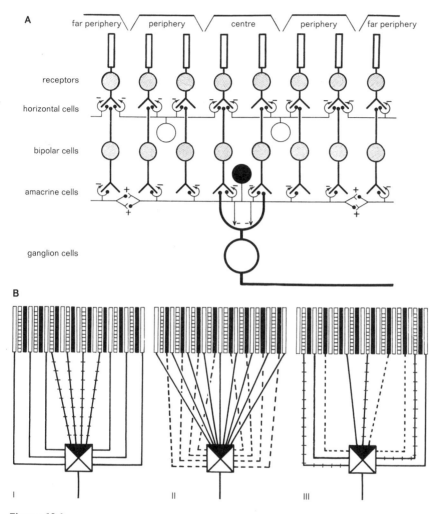

Figure 12.4

Inferred idealized pathways in the primate retina.

A. A wiring diagram for a ganglion cell, based upon both anatomy and physiology. Inhibitory synapses are represented by arrow points and those of the principal excitatory pathways by inverted V's.

B. The inferred contributions of three types of cones to three different types of unit that can be recorded in the lateral geniculate body of the rhesus monkey. The intervening synapses are not shown. Type I has excitatory or inhibitory centre with contrasting surround of a different and opposing colour sensitivity. Type II has opposing colour responses from two types of cone uniformly over the whole field. Type III has an "on" centre and an "off" surround with a similar contribution from each class of cone. The separation of these pathways to different ganglion cells must occur in different examples of **A**. [A from Dowling and Boycott, 1966; B from Wiesel and Hubel, 1966.]

a three-unit (dyad) synapse with a ganglion cell dendrite and simultaneously with an amacrine cell near by (Fig. 12.4, B). The amacrine cells are those with several short processes that spread sideways, and with no definite axon. The next most common synapse is of the presynaptic amacrine cell upon a bipolar terminal [8]. The bipolar cell terminals in the periphery of the retina also make tight junctions with ganglion cell bodies. These may be electrical junctions or possibly contact points having a trophic function in labelling the ganglion cells. Amacrine to amacrine synapses are abundant in bird retinas of pure cones, and in all retinas studied there is evidence of lateral interaction over long distances.

We cannot anatomically separate circuits for colour perception, for movement discrimination, or for the pattern of centres and surrounds of the ganglion cells, although there have been theoretical derivations of the geometry of the connexions to the different types of ganglion cell in the primate and frog retinas (Figs. 12.4 and 12.15). For the monkey, in which colour vision is well established, careful work reveals different ganglion cells, which can be inferred to have quite different input patterns from the classes of cones (Fig. 12.4, C).

Vertebrate retinal ganglion cells show a Purkinje shift (of spectral sensitivity with dark adaptation), showing that both rods and cones feed into them. Adaptation of one part of the receptive field of a ganglion cell affects all parts of the field, although the spread of the ganglion cell dendrites corresponds only to the "on" centre. Circuits responsible for particular functional operations of different types of retinal ganglion cells can be invented conceptually, but at present no corresponding and geometrically complete wiring diagrams are known anatomically (for arthropods, see p. 156 and Fig. 9.12). Although the visual pathway shows to a wonderful extent the capabilities of single neurons, we know less about the synaptic and membrane mechanisms than we do for the auditory system.

ACUITY AND RELATED PHENOMENA

A measurable feature of the visual system as a whole is its acuity. It becomes clear from the following measurements that the nervous mechanisms (partly in the retina and partly in the brain) ensure that we do not see the imperfections of the image that is cast on the retina. A point source of light can be focused optimally so that it covers a minimum of about 3 cone widths on the retina; a smaller size than this cannot be achieved on account of chromatic and spherical aberration and diffraction at the pupil. Moreover, when one colour is in focus the other colours are not, and when the image is focused on the ends of the cones it is out of focus for their middle regions. A cone subtends about 25 sec of arc on the retina, which is approximately the optimum resolution for separation of grid

TABLE 9

Vertebrate visual interneurons

Retinal ganglion cells: frog [Maturana et al., 1960; Muntz, 1962]

1. Sustained edge detectors.
2. Convex edge.
3. Changing contrast.
4. Dimming. ⎫
5. Dark.   ⎬ Further details in text
6. Blue detectors, "on" response, to diencephalon.

Retinal ganglion cells (*N.B.* There are efferent fibres to the retina): pigeon [Maturana, 1964]

Five colour-blind classes, not spontaneous, blind to "on" and "off."
1. Verticality. Up to 100 spikes/sec even to stationary vertical edges in the receptive field. No response to small objects. Field size about 1°. Units few.
2. Horizontality. As for No. 1, but rotated by 90°.
3. General edge. Slight response to "on" and "off"; strong response to any edge moving across the field or to a small spot dark or light within the field.
   (a) with fields of ⅔°
   (b) with fields of ½°
4. Directional moving edge. Selectively directional to any moving edge irrespective of contrast reversal. "On"-"off" to minute spots of light. Field ½–1°, with no asymmetries.
5. Moving convex edge. Not selectively directional but independent of contrast reversal (unlike frog). Respond only to small curvatures and points. Field size about ⅒° (about 10μ on retina).
With maintained discharge, sensitive to colour.
6. Rate of firing proportional to luminosity. Several diverse subgroups not described.

Retinal ganglion cells (pure cone retina): ground squirrel *Citellus* [Michael, 1966]

1. 18%. One-way movement, not due to stimulus moving from inhibitory into excitatory area. Range 0.1°/sec to 30°/sec. All possible orientations found.
2. 19%. Opponent colour units green/blue, with centre/surround basis. Some inhibited by green, others by blue. No red/green antagonism.
3. Remaining units not defined but most are of the typical mammalian centre/surround type, as in cat, insensitive to total luminosity changes.

Retinal ganglion cells: rabbit
[Barlow, Hill, and Levick, *J. Physiol.* **173**:377; **178**:477; and **188**:285.]

1. Concentric field. Equal nos. of "on" and "off" centre with opposing surround. Latency from a surround is greater than from a centre.
2. Directionally selective movement perceptive. Mostly "on"-"off" responses to flashes, mainly with horizontal or vertical direction of axis; all are inhibited by stimulation of a surround.
3. Large receptive fields, sensitive to fast movement, nondirectional.
The following in a horizontal visual streak across the retina.
4. Orientation selective units, sensitive to horizontal or vertical extended objects, acting like extended concentric units.
5. Local edge detectors, respond to appearance or movement of a contrasting edge, inhibited in a surround by an edge stimulus.
6. Uniformity detectors with a high level of activity inhibited by any stimulation in their field.

TABLE 9 (Continued)
Vertebrate visual interneurons

Retinal ganglion cells: goldfish [Wagner et al., 1960]

1. Some units had "off" centre, sensitive to long wavelengths, surrounded by an "on"-"off" annulus and a large "on" surround. The latter was sensitive between 400 and 550 mμ, i.e., reverse of 2.
2. "Off" responses at short wavelengths, "on" responses at long ones.
3. Units inhibited by maintained illumination.

Retinal ganglion cells: monkey (*Ateles*) [Hubel and Wiesel, 1960]

1. "On" centre with inhibitory surround.
2. "Off" centre with excitatory surround. Smallest field 4' of arc, -20μ on retina.
3. Out of 100 units, 3 gave "on" response to blue light but "off" response to red light, transition at 500 mμ.

Retinal ganglion cells: cat

1. "On" centre with inhibitory surround.
2. "Off" centre with excitatory surround.
   The surround in 1 and 2 disappears in dark-adapted eye. Not selectively sensitive to direction of movements. Inference of an antagonistic colour response as in fish, but there are no chromatic spatial differences.
3. A few other types, see Fig. 12.14.

Retinal ganglion cells: rat [Brown and Rojas, 1965]

1. "On" centre with inhibitory surround.
2. "Off" centre with excitatory surround, as above with varying effectiveness of the surround and with varying adaptation rates. Bursting activity synchronized over large areas.

Lateral geniculate cells: cat [Kozak et al., 1965]

1 and 2. Similar to retinal ganglion cells but not identical. Stronger effect of suppression by the "surround." Can be modified by other inputs, e.g. arousal.
3. "On"-"off" centre.
4. Binocular.
5. Large receptive field.
6. Directionally selective.

Lateral geniculate cells: rabbit [Arden, 1963]

1. Inhibited by light. "On," "off," or "on"-"off."
2. Excited by light spot. "On," "off," or "on"-"off," with most fields oval, radial, or tangential axis and field size about 6°.
3. Very large receptive field: excitatory in some regions, inhibitory elsewhere.
4. Elongated receptive field: excitatory in some regions, inhibitory elsewhere. Movement much more effective than intensity change. Some units especially sensitive to shift across a boundary. Many directionally selective. Sometimes movement sensitivity not corresponding to flash-receptive field. Some with receptive field that changed with stimulation. Seven types of spectral response, some inhibited by one colour, excited by others.

TABLE 9 (Continued)

Lateral geniculate units (colour vision): macaque monkey
[De Valois, Abramov, and Jacobs, 1966]

"On" responses. Units in sample 147.
1. Spectrally nonopponent, i.e. no antagonistic interaction between different colours. 1. Excitors, 22. 2. Inhibitors, 22.
2. Spectrally opponent cells: classification difficult because they are diverse.
   a. Long wavelength excitation, 54.
   b. Short wavelength excitation, 49.
Latency 50 msec. "Off" responses also complex. Nonopponent excitors probably carry luminosity information. Properties of opponent units agree with human colour-naming data.

Lateral geniculate units (colour vision): rhesus monkey [Wiesel and Hubel, 1966]

Type I.
Concentric field with excitatory or inhibitory centre and opponent surround, the centre and surround having different spectral sensitivities, therefore giving "on" responses at one wavelength and "off" responses at another. This type most common, some with connexions to rods as well as cones. Smallest field centres of 2' (= 10 μm).
Type II.
No centre-surround pattern but with uniform opponent colour responses over the whole field: green "on," blue "off," or green "off," blue "on." Not common, no connexions to rods.
Type III.
Concentric field as in Type I but the centre and surround have identical spectral properties. Some with similar connexions to rods as well as to several types of cones.
Type IV.
On centre and a very large "off" surround sensitive to longer wavelengths than the centre.

Striate cortex: cat [Hubel and Wiesel, 1959, 1962]

1. Elongated units (1° by 4°) with inhibitory central strip flanked by excitatory areas.
2. The converse of 1. Wide variety of relative sizes of flanks and centre lines. The stimulus must be specific in form, size, position on eye, and orientation, but a line stimulus can be any length. Many units binocular, with interaction between areas on the separate eyes. Many units selectively sensitive to direction of movement; transverse movement of a slit is effective at one orientation in space.
3. Complex. Responses not predictable from a survey with a small spot. Activated by (a) narrow $\frac{1}{8}$° slit, not uniform field edge, (b) slit, uniform field edge, (c) edge, (d) dark bar. The slit, edge, or bar must be correctly oriented and somewhere on the visual field, but can be any length. For these specific forms, as appropriate for each cell, movement is an additional stimulus.

Nonstriate visual cortex area 18 and 19: cat [Hubel and Wiesel, 1965]

4. Complex as in striate cortex.
5. Hypercomplex, in which the slit, edge, or bar must have a termination on the receptive field of the cell.
   (a) Single-stopped edge (corner)
   (b) Double-stopped edge (tongue)
   (c) Slit (double-stopped)
   (d) Dark bar (double-stopped).
   All these can discriminate the orientation and direction of movement.
6. As in 4, but responding to two orientations at right angles.
7. As in 4, but responding to movement of a tongue over a field much larger than the tongue, i.e. generalized movement sensitivity within the form category.

---

lines when these are cast on the retina by a double-slit pupil, thus avoiding the diffraction limit set by the normal pupil diameter. With such a stimulus, every row of cones—not every alternate row—carries a band of light; therefore the cones must be in staggered rows. Another indication that interaction between cones increases acuity is that a dark wire subtending 1 sec of arc is visible against a bright sky ($\frac{1}{4}$-inch thick at a distance of about $\frac{1}{4}$ mile, or $\frac{1}{25}$ of the width of a cone). The minimum observable offset in vernier acuity is about 2 sec of arc. We can therefore see detail that is much finer than the cone pattern or the fuzz caused by bad optics. No matter how closely we examine a sharp edge between black and white, as in any reasonable print, we never can make out the area of coloured fuzziness, which is certainly present and which is about 2 cones wide on our fovea. Finally, the small movements of the eye are of such an amplitude and frequency that in every 0.1 sec of time the eye typically moves by about the width of a cone on the fovea. Over longer periods, the eye wanders further, with occasional larger saccadic movements during which vision is suppressed and is also ineffective because the brightness of the image falls below threshold during the move. Voluntary control of the human eye, as in fine searching, is accurate to about 1 minute of arc, whereas each ganglion cell presumably has a receptive field larger than this. In a study of lateral geniculate cells of the rhesus monkey, the smallest "centre" of a visual field of a single cell was 2 minutes of arc, corresponding to 10 μm on the retina, and possibly the input was derived from a single cone. Ganglion cells of the cat have minimal centres of about 0.5°, but the cat can resolve about 5 stripes per degree with normal pupil and bright light. We see immediately that acuity is achieved in the brain by abstraction of information from numerous retinal ganglion cells with fields that overlap strongly. Superb discriminations in all higher animals seem to have this in common, and discrimination by the line labelling in a single unit is never sufficiently acute. What we do not understand quantitatively is how discrimination is maintained together with convergence of neurons.

RESPONSES OF OPTIC NERVE FIBRES

From each eye there are about 10^6 ganglion cells and optic nerve fibres in man, from a retina containing 10^8 rods and 5×10^6 cones. But the million optic fibres spread out to five hundred million neurons of the visual cortex, and thereafter to other "silent" areas of the cortex. In all vertebrate sensory systems there is opportunity for the information in the ganglion cells to be processed many times over in parallel overlapping and in channels [30].

Fibres of the optic nerve of vertebrates are of cells that are at least third order. The typical ganglion cell, found from fish [36] to mammals, has a receptive field with a "centre" of low threshold, as tested by a small spot of light, and around this is an annulus-shaped "surround" for which the response is opposite to that for the centre (Fig. 12.7). One type has a centre in which illumination inhibits; the other type has a centre in which illumination excites. In the cat, these two most abundant types are similar in abundance, distribution, and spontaneous background discharge in the dark. One type cannot be converted to the other, although the relative contribution of the surround is decreased progressively by higher levels of illumination. In the cat, but not in the rhesus monkey, when the eye is dark-adapted the surround disappears and the whole field assumes the properties of the centre. This is apparently not a change in the synaptic connections of rods and cones, and is certainly not a consequence of pigment bleaching. Changes at dark adaptation appear to arise by neural feedback in the bipolar layer.

The best model of the organization of the visual field of an "on" centre ganglion cell has two components. First, there is a peak sensitivity of the "on" mechanism at the centre, extending to a low level at the periphery. Second, there is a much flatter sensitivity of the "off" mechanism extending over the whole centre and periphery. These two components have different latencies and vary in relative contribution according to the prevailing state of dark adaptation. The two components differ in spectral response in animals with colour vision, and clearly they represent two different types of input to the ganglion cells (Fig. 12.4, A). In units with irregular visual fields, there is a remarkably exact return of the outline of the same irregularities at each adaptation, suggesting that one dendritic pattern in each is involved each time [33]. Summation between excitation and inhibition can be linear or highly nonlinear. Because of the unequal effects of activation and inhibition over the centre and surround, diffuse light usually causes some response, both here and in lateral geniculate neurons; this effect is in contrast to cortical cells, which no longer respond to diffuse light or stationary patterns. The receptive field centres of "off" and "on"-centre units of the cat are 0.5–4.0° and the surrounds 4.0–30.0° in diameter, and only the centre corresponds to the spread of the cell's dendrites. The background discharge is constant irrespective of the state of adaptation but is sensitive to a 1% change in intensity. The typical mammalian retina is a mixed array of these units, with an enormous overlap of the receptive fields, so that even the smallest light spot has effects in many axons of the optic tract. The information content cannot be considered as that of a single unit, for it is subsequently abstracted by interaction between axons from neighbouring ganglion cells.

The direction in which a spot of light crosses its receptive field has no effect on the responses of the above types of ganglion cell in the cat, but there are types that are selectively sensitive to lines or edges (Fig. 12.14).

In the area centralis there is a small proportion of cells sensitive to movement. Therefore caution must be exercised in the interpretation of responses of cortical visual units of the cat in terms of centre/surround units only.

The most carefully analyzed retinal ganglion cells, of a mammal having some variety of units, are those of the rabbit, which turn out to be somewhat intermediate between a frog and a cat. About two-thirds of the recorded units are of the concentric type, with a centre that is inhibited by light in one subtype and excited by light in the other, with a surround of opposing properties. The shorter latency to responses initiated from the centre, as compared to those elicited by the surround, agrees with the theory that the spread of the dendrites of a ganglion cell corresponds to the field size of its centre, and the surround involves an additional synapse. The responses from the surround are much stronger in the light-adapted than in the dark-adapted state, perhaps because lateral inhibition is much more pronounced in the light-adapted state.

A second type of retinal ganglion cell of the rabbit responds to the motion of a contrasting stimulus irrespective of contrast reversal. This is quite different from the response of a unit with adjacent excitatory and inhibitory areas, which responds to movement in the opposite direction if the stimulus is changed from a white to a black moving target. Most directional units respond at "on" and at "off" to a stationary spot of light, and they have a weak surround in which movement causes inhibition of the main response area. The response to apparent motion by successive stimulation of two neighbouring regions within the field is strong when the two are separated by no more than $\frac{1}{2}°$, if the apparent motion is in the preferred direction. When the two stimuli are presented in sequence in the null direction, the effect is much less than when either are presented separately, showing that inhibition occurs between parts of the visual field of the ganglion cell. The mechanism is further discussed on page 271. It is likely that these units serve to stabilize the eye against the average movement of the visual field, exactly as is inferred to happen in the crab (p. 339). The units respond to stripes down to $\frac{1}{2}°$ period.

The third type, the large field units, give "off" responses over a rather large area, with an eccentric "on" region of the field. These units are sensitive to motion of a black or white target, irrespective of direction, with a marked preference for motion of a particular, usually high, velocity.

Other types are found in the visual streak, which is a horizontal elongated area of the retina along the line at which the image of the horizon falls in normal posture [22]. Here there are many units with elongated fields, which are therefore selectively responsive to elongated targets. There are two types, one selective to horizontal, the other to vertical targets, and it is clear that the rabbit does not depend on these for discrimination of direction of an elongated target because it can readily distinguish between lines sloping at 45° to the right and others sloping at 45° to the left.

In the visual streak there are units that respond to the appearance or movement of a contrasting edge in their visual field, irrespective of contrast. They have properties that match exactly those of the selectively directional units and act as if their inputs are the same except for the specific feature of directionality. Each unit has a surround in which movement of an edge strongly inhibits. This has the interesting consequence that when the eye moves so that contrasting objects cross the surrounds, the units are inhibited. With the eye at rest, the best stimulus is a moving contrast, sufficiently small that it does not overlap too much upon the surround. Some of the effects of this surround could account for the "erasability" reported for the frog [21] when a sustained response to a small target was abolished by a transient darkening. This might serve a useful function in that blinking the eye would wipe clean the map of the visual world that is provided by these units. The first subsequent movement of a small target would then occur upon a blank background. Another effect of this surround is that the edge detectors in fact make no response to movement of a fine grating (black and white stripes) on account of the overlap upon the surround, although, in fact, gratings down to about $\frac{1}{2}°$ are resolved if the effect of the surround is blanked off.

The last type of unit isolated in the rabbit retina is the uniformity detectors, which have a brisk background discharge when nothing is happening in the visual field but are inhibited by any change in the visual field. Stationary contrasting edges or lights, black spots, or gratings down to 0.35° period all inhibit, but after some minutes the discharge starts up again and slowly returns to its former level. In normal life we might suppose, therefore, that these units would be inhibited for most of the time when the animal is above ground in daylight.

An interesting question is what we would see if only "off"-centre units were excited on our retina. We cannot make such a stimulus, but when the illumination of an area on the retina is suddenly raised except for one central spot we see a spot of blackness. This is not because a cell in that spot is stimulated by light but presumably because the excitatory surrounds of one or more "off"-centre units are excited. This can be taken as evidence that impulses in "off" units are interpreted as a seen blackness, and extending this bold assumption to a retina with colour vision leads to the conclusion that white is inferred when no opponent-colour units are excited, and introduces other, more complex problems.

Even from this cursory summary it will be evident that much of the psychophysiology of vision, for example in connexion with afterimages, may eventually find explanations in terms of the activity of retinal neurons, but that day is still far off.

LATERAL GENICULATE BODY

The next cells on the visual pathway are those of the lateral geniculate body. In the cat their responses to white light spots are similar but not identical to those of retinal ganglion cells, with a similar concentric arrangement of centre and surround, but with fields of 1–2°. The cat's lateral geniculate nucleus has three thick layers of neurons (Fig. 12.5). Cells of layers A_1 and B are driven by the contralateral eye; cells of layer A_2 (which lies between A_1 and B) are driven by the ipsilateral eye, but binocular interaction is rare, although it is common at the next stage. In fact the function of the complex synaptic patterns and feedback arcs in the lateral geniculate are not understood (see Fig. 16.4). The peripheral surround is stronger in these cells than in ganglion cells of the retina, so that they discriminate more against diffuse light. The spatial arrangement of cells is very exact, and the retina is projected upon each major geniculate layer. In addition to the two common types of unit with "on" and

Figure 12.5

The chief input (*left*) and output (*right*) of part of the lateral geniculate body of the cat. There are three layers or zones, A, A_1, and B, which are outlined by dotted lines. The basket-shaped arborizations of axons of the optic tract (coming in from the right) form synapses upon multipolar cells, which have thin axons (going off towards the left) that in turn project to the visual cortex. Terminations and dendrites are restricted to their own layers in the geniculate body, but with considerable overlap within these layers. Each of the thicker optic fibres divides and only one branch ends, as shown, so that this is not the only projection of the optic fibres in the brain. [O'Leary, 1940.] See also Figure 16.4.

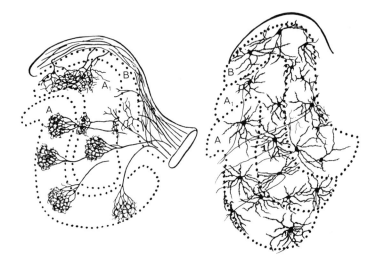

"off" centres, there are others. "On-off centre" units respond when either a black or a white figure is moved in or out of their field, and they must have inputs from both "on"- and "off"-centre units. They achieve a generalization in that they detect movement irrespective of contrast and, since they require summation from several retinal ganglion cells, they can achieve accurate localization. Between the three principal layers of the lateral geniculate are a few cells with inputs from both eyes, with receptive fields at corresponding points on the retina (within experimental error). A few units have abnormally large receptive fields with 10–20° centres, and a very broad surround. A few others have poor responses to movement of a black disc in one plane but a directionally sensitive response to a similar movement made at right angles to the first [19]. This latter group may descend from the visual cortex, or they may be related to the few selectively directional units of the area centralis in the retina of the cat.

In the rabbit, with directionally selective movement detectors and orientation-selective slit and bar detectors in the retina, the lateral geniculate cells require more experimental time to define than those of the cat [1]. There is no obvious anatomical division into layers, as in carnivores; the cells often fail to have visual fields with an annular surround and instead the receptive field may be a long rectangle. Moving stimuli are far more effective than stationary flashes. Histologically about 10 optic nerve fibres converge on each lateral geniculate cell, with a progressive shift in the overlap of neighboring dendritic fields, as is characteristic of all visual systems. Some cells, similar to the "newness" units of frog tectum, respond only to a novel stimulus; conversely, the "sameness" units in both animals respond better to a stimulus when it is familiar. In some units, which must have been infuriating to analyse, the receptive field, and even the presence of areas of inhibition depends on previous stimulation by a moving target; others, which responded well to the operator walking past, had no visual field that could be plotted with small spots of light. This is reminiscent of the situation in the cortex of the cat or the deep layers of the insect optic lobe (p. 189). Colour vision at this level in the monkey is treated on page 275.

CORTICAL VISUAL UNITS

At the cortical level, data from the cat outweighs that from other mammals [14, 15]. Analysis without the customary barbiturate anaesthesia reveals the presence of a large number of centre/surround units like those of the retina but with an input from corresponding points in the two eyes. In man such units would fit well with the psychological data on the binocular perception of dot patterns in depth. These units have not been reported by Hubel and Wiesel, who, moreover, find no response to diffuse illumination, stationary contrast, or lights, and cells are all spontaneously active. The so-called "simple" cortical visual cells have receptive fields that are in part inhibitory and in part excitatory when tested with a light spot. Commonly there is a central elongated region flanked by areas that give the opposite response: sometimes the field is divided by a line into an excitatory and an inhibitory region. The orientation of the central band or line, called the axis orientation, is critical for effective stimulation. Normal eye movements are quite adequate for excitation by stationary contrasts. The optimum direction for movement of a stimulus is at right angles to the axis orientation of the cell, which acts as if receiving inputs from a row of one type of ganglion cell of the retina (Fig. 12.6). Some cells are monocular, others binocular, with varying degrees of dominance between the two eyes. The responses of simple cells can be predicted from the results of tests with an exploring spot of light, and, apart from selective directionality and failure to respond to diffuse or stationary light, there is no indication of stimulus generalization.

Complex cortical visual cells, in contrast with the above, have properties which cannot be predicted from the responses to a light spot, which commonly has no effect, even when moved or switched "on" and "off." Complex cells are activated by a slit, edge, or bar, and different cells are specifically selective for one of these three forms, with critical orientation but with little attention to the position on the receptive field (Fig. 12.7). For cells that respond to slits, the most effective width is about $\frac{1}{8}°$; accuracy of orientation is $\pm 5°$ and optimum movement rate is $1°/\text{sec}$.

Figure 12.6

A possible scheme of connexions that would agree with the properties of the cat's cortical visual cells with simple receptive fields. A large number of lateral geniculate cells, of which four are illustrated in the upper right in the figure, have receptive fields with "on" centres arranged along a straight line on the retina. All of these project upon a single cortical cell, and the synapses are supposed to be excitatory. The receptive field of the cortical cell will then have an elongated "on" centre, which is indicated by the interrupted lines in the receptive-field diagram to the left of the figure. If strong summation is necessary, only a correctly orientated line or edge will be an effective stimulus. [Hubel and Wiesel, 1965.]

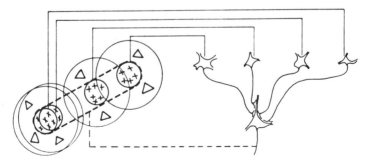

In one case a unit was sensitive to a vertical edge within a field of 16°, with excitatory responses in one side of a straight line and inhibitory ones on the other. One aspect of the stimulus may be generalized: the orientation is critical but the position is not. In this instance reversing the contrast reversed the form of the response, suggesting that the input is all from ganglion cells of one type. Another cell responded to a black rectangle ⅓ ° wide with a critical horizontal orientation anywhere in a field of 5° × 5°, especially when this was moved at right angles to its axis in one direction, but not in the other. The requirement for optimum stimulation does not change over many hours of observation, showing that the connexions are fixed, although they have necessarily crystallized during a formative period. Cells similar to the above are found in the corresponding area of the cortex of the monkey and presumably of man.

Complex cortical visual cells exactly comparable to those of the adult are found in the visually inexperienced young kitten. Therefore the highly complex neural connexions are formed without benefit of visual experience. The visual responses, however, are not mature until many days have passed, suggesting that higher-order units have not developed connexions.

Hypercomplex units, even more interesting than the last group, are found in the nonstriate visual areas (II and III), which in the cat are lateral to the striate cortex. The majority of the cells in area II and half the cells in area III were "complex," but 5–10% of those in II and

Figure 12.7

Possible scheme to explain the properties of the cat's visual cortical cells that have complex receptive fields. A number of cortical cells with simple fields, of which three are shown schematically, are imagined to project to a single cortical cell of higher order. Each projecting neuron has a receptive field, as shown on the left, with an excitatory region to the left and an inhibitory region to the right of a vertical straight boundary. A vertical-edge stimulus falling across this rectangle, regardless of its position, will excite some simple-field cells, any one of which excites the higher-order cell. [Hubel and Wiesel, 1965.]

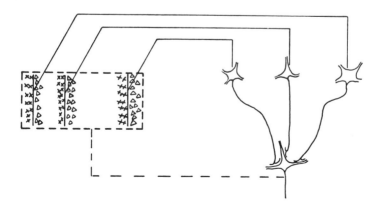

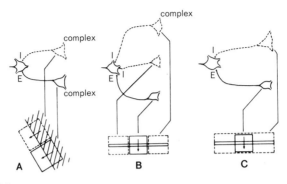

Figure 12.8

Model systems that account for the properties of hypercomplex cells of the cat's visual cortex.

A. The hypercomplex cell responding to a single stopped edge receives projections from two complex cells, one excitatory (E) and the other inhibitory (I), which refer to the two rectangles in line in the visual field, as shown on the left.

B. Hypercomplex cell responding to a doubly stopped slit, with the two antagonistic areas in line on each side referring to inhibitory complex cells.

C. Alternative explanation for B, with the inhibitory input from a single cell, which has a large antagonistic field surrounding the excitatory field. [Hubel and Wiesel, 1965.]

50% of those in III were hypercomplex, and a few cells in area III merit the term higher-order hypercomplex. The adequate stimulus for a lower-order hypercomplex cell is a critically oriented line within a given "activating" region, so long as a similarly oriented line does not fall over an adjacent "antagonistic" region (Fig. 12.8). This condition is most readily met by a slit or edge with a definite termination at one or both ends, which must be within the receptive field, but more demanding criteria must be met for some units (Figs. 12.9, 12.10, and 12.11). Higher-order hypercomplex cells behave in the same way except that they respond to a line stimulus limited at one or both ends in either of two orientations 90° apart, and the position on the receptive field is even less critical (Figs. 12.12 and 12.13). They behave therefore as if excited by any one of a large number of hypercomplex cells of lower order (Fig. 12.8).

As to the effect of the normal continual small eye movements on the responses of cortical cells, two features are relevant. First, illumination of a stationary pattern in front of the eye causes no change in the background activity of any cortical cells, and eye movements are essential and adequate for a signal, although vision seems to be reduced during large eye movements [38]. Second, only contrasting edges excite units, so that without further information a solid shape might subjectively appear hollow. During a voluntarily jump of the human eye, vision is cut off, but, as in the crab, information about small eye movements is apparently not fed back to higher levels; thus at any time the instant and the direction in which the tremoring eye crosses the contrast are not available to the cortical mechanism. However, when a repeated movement of an edge is caused by representative eye movements, it has been observed experimentally that the temporal sequence of impulses in a responding unit in the cortex depends upon whether the centre of the

Figure 12.9

Properties of a hypercomplex neuron of the cat's nonstriate visual cortex III, driven by the contralateral eye only. The visual field is about 12° long, 5° wide, and the best responses to moving edges are in the long axis. The numbers by each figure give the numbers of impulses in response to comparable movements (shown by arrows), of a doubly stopped edge in the direction shown. A thick horizontal bar means "no response."

A. No response to a long edge.

B–F. The response was maximal in D when the edge subtended 2.5°, with a weak response to movement upwards.

G–I. A rotation by 30° almost eliminates the response.

J–O. The effect of the side regions in antagonizing the response over the middle region, until a 2.5° tongue must be critically placed to produce any response, as in O.

P–T. Shift of the tongue even one-half degree laterally reduced the response by loss of activating area and simultaneous inclusion of inhibiting area. [Adapted from Hubel and Wiesel, 1965.]

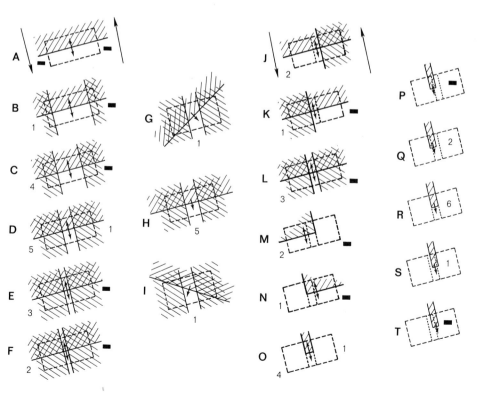

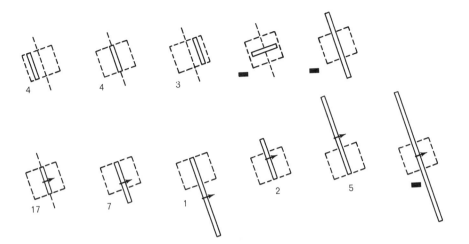

Figure 12.10

Hypercomplex neuron in area III, responding to a slit one-eighth degree wide and 2° long anywhere in a 2° field, driven by both eyes but best ipsilaterally. A one-half degree slit was ineffective, and the one-eighth degree slit had to be stopped at both ends to be effective, as shown at upper right. Responses to movement as shown in the lower row was about equally effective in either direction, with optimum at 3°/sec. Note that the inhibitory area extends 2–3° around the excitatory field. The horizontal bar shows "no response" and the numbers show impulse counts, as in Figure 12.9. [Adapted from Hubel and Wiesel, 1965.]

field for that unit is on the light or on the dark side of the edge [6]. Irrespective of the actual brightness at their centre, such units responded with a larger number of short intervals between impulses when centred on the relatively brighter parts of the visual field than they did when centred on the darker side. The movement of the contrasting edge is the same in each case and does not cross the centre of the unit (Fig. 15.4). Of course, there may be another more sophisticated coding in the pattern of impulses, but this is the simplest adequate pattern for a visual signal that depends on unpredictable eye movements. The important feature is that only the intervals between impulses are important in the code and also available to the neurons. The observation also shows that local periods of high frequency in the sequence of impulses must be the feature of interest to the next neuron down the line, as might well be expected. The above interpretation, however, has recently been thrown into jeopardy by the discovery of directionally sensitive edge and line detectors among the ganglion cells of the cat's retina (Fig. 12.14) [33], and also of the centre/surround units that are abundant in the visual cortex when no anaesthetic is used.

A unit that responds as if to a line stimulus when there is almost a complete line, but with a small break in it, would fit very well the common experience of vision, in which small defects are completed. The filling

in of the centres of continuous areas away from edges, the filling in of
the blind spot, the sharpening of edges, the straightening of lines that
are curved on the periphery of the retina, the binocular fusion in depth

Figure 12.11

Properties of a hypercomplex cell of visual area III of the cat cortex. Some stimuli
are black bars, others are white slits. The activating region is 4° long and 3–4° wide,
as shown by the dashed rectangle, with long axis 15° to the horizontal. The horizontal
bar indicates "no response," and the numbers show impulse counts for a constant
movement.

A–D. Responses to an illuminated 1° slit moving at 3°/sec, showing unidirectional
properties and inhibitory effect of the surround.

E–L. Responses to a black bar are almost as effective as those to a bright slit, but
show how critical the optimum length can be.

M–Q. When a second bright slit is moved in line outside the activating field, it
always inhibits the response, and in all hypercomplex cells an optimum stimulus
never produces any response if outside the activating region. The position on the
cortex is shown in R. [Adapted from Hubel and Wiesel, 1965.]

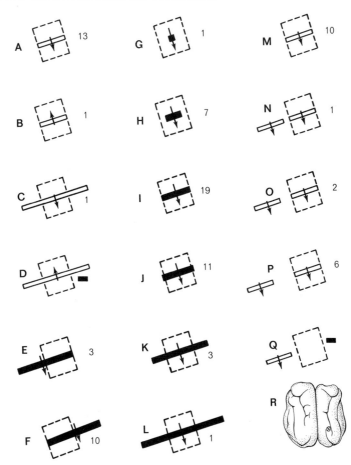

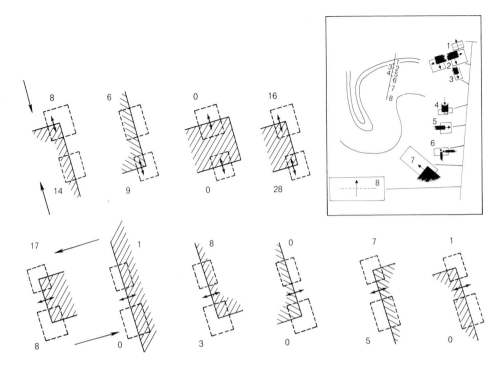

Figure 12.12

Responses of a higher-order hypercomplex neuron of visual area III (unit 2 in the inset at right). This cell responded bilaterally and behaved as if having inputs from two sets of hypercomplex units. With an edge stopped at one end, the activating region was a rectangle of 3° times 4° in size. With the edge stopped at the other end, the activating area was a second rectangle on the same long axis. Responses were to movement either way in two directions at right angles, as shown by the upper and lower rows of diagrams. The numerals show the numbers of nerve impulses evoked by a standard movement at 0.5°/sec in the directions shown by the single arrows on the left. The responses to each corner were rather uniform over each of the rectangles. A tilt of 15–20° was sufficient to abolish responses. The inset (*top right*) shows fields of other units found in the same electrode traverse. [Adapted from Hubel and Wiesel, 1965.]

of two nonidentical images, and many other features are of interest in this connexion. It seems probable that properties of units in the cortex must eventually explain these and other features of perception in terms of sums and differences of earlier units. We can only guess how many further stages of analysis there are beyond those at present known. There is no doubt that many abstracted features of the stimulus are line-labelled as unit properties, but this does not mean that all are so distinguished.

The cells of the visual cortex are arranged in columns in such a way that cells of one column have a similar direction of the axis of orientation of their elongated visual field. This applies also to area III, in which columns contain hypercomplex cells and complex cells having similar axis orientation but differing in precise position and arrangement of receptive fields. Some vertical columns of cells, reaching from white matter to the surface, contain complex cells with their orientation axes in two directions at right angles, together with hypercomplex cells that combine these directions. In the monkey, units of neighbouring cortical columns differ

Figure 12.13

Responses of a higher order hypercomplex neuron of area III (unit 6 in Figure 12.12). The activating region was a rectangle 4° times 1.5°, inclined at 15° to the horizontal.

A–D. A dark tongue one-half degree wide introduced from below and advanced at 0.5°/sec, is equally effective (30–40 impulses) anywhere in the activating region. Note the narrowness of the optimum stimulus in relation to the field width. A slit or dark bar was equally effective.

E–H. A movement at 1°/sec in one direction at right angles to the first was also effective, irrespective of the level at which the field is crossed.

I–N. Responses to various widths of tongues, showing the optimum at one-half degree. This unit showed novelty properties in that it rapidly habituated to repeated movements of the one-half degree tongue at one place in the field but responded anew with full vigour when the tongue was moved to a new place in the field. The inset (O) shows the position of the recording. [Adapted from Hubel and Wiesel, 1965.]

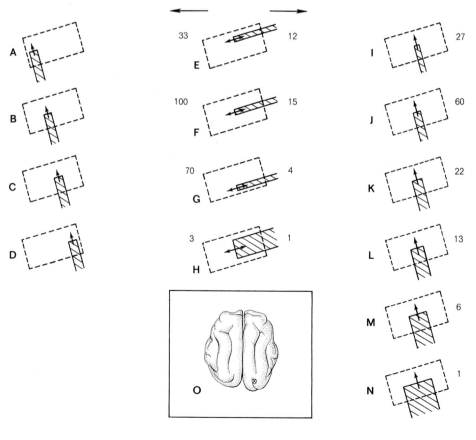

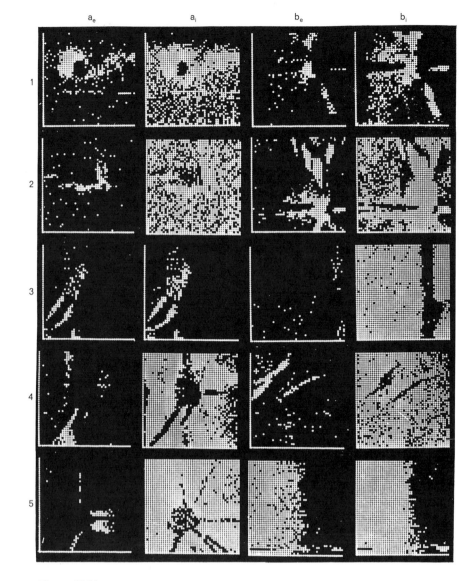

Figure 12.14

Receptive fields for ten ganglion cells of the retina of the cat. The excitation columns (a_e, b_e) show as white—the points where a white disc 0.2 in diameter on a black background caused an impulse frequency of more than 3 standard deviations above background activity. The inhibition columns (a_i, b_i) show as white those areas where one or more impulses occurred with the same stimulus, thus showing as black the inhibited areas.

Several important points emerge from observations by this method. The receptive fields are remarkably irregular and their long thin arms suggest that they are caused by the shapes of dendrites. The receptive fields are of various shapes; $a1$ is circular, $b3$ is a slit, $b5$ is a straight edge, and others are irregular. After changes such as the increase in the "centre," which is caused by dark adaptation, exactly the same minor irregularities reappear when stimulating conditions return to the former state. [Spinelli, 1966.] For subsequent discussion of these results see *Science*, 154, p. 920, 1966.

in their dependence on which eye is dominant, and columns also differ in axis orientation. In the hypercomplex cells these aspects are brought together at binocular units, which are sensitive to a line of critical orientation in any position in the receptive field of that cell for either eye. The cortical column therefore brings together just those cells that are likely to activate a common cell at the next stage.

In reviewing the abstraction of pattern along the visual pathway, we see that the convergence of incoming geniculate fibres onto a cortical unit of the simple type produces a maximal effect only when a certain aligned group are all excited, such that a single spot is a weak stimulus but an appropriately oriented slit is a strong one (Fig. 12.6). This results in an enormous increase in selectivity at this stage, so that each first-order cortical cell now has a narrow set of requirements of shape, orientation, and position. Different cortical cells can select different directions from one group of geniculate cells. At the next stage, however, many simple cortical cells of similar orientation feed into one complex cell in such a way that any one is sufficient to activate it. This has the effect of maintaining the requirement for the orientation but relaxing that for position, a feature to which the term stimulus-generalization has been given in the psychological literature. In the integration by a hypercomplex cell there is a summation between two mutually antagonistic influences that come together: these cells respond to a properly oriented line within a certain area so long as the line does not continue into an adjacent area— that is, it must be appropriately terminated. A line or edge crossing the whole combined field has no effect. We may call this kind of response a rejection of the redundant but it is more attractively considered as an acceptance of the significant by that particular cell. The same mechanism of summing an excitatory and an inhibitory response is found in the cat retina (which discriminates against diffuse light in favour of patterns of light), in the fish retina (which discriminates against white light in favour of red or blue light), and in numerous cited instances on the auditory pathway. In the responses of the higher-order hypercomplex cells we again see stimulus generalization; a doubly stopped edge can here be effective at any part of a rather large receptive field. The property of picking out a particular pattern in any part of a large field is achieved by a unit that is excited by any one of a number of small field units. At the present time we can only suppose that our ability to recognize a given form at any point in the visual field depends on just this ability of single units. In the case of recognition of letters of the alphabet and similar signs, we learn by a few repetitions, and we must be prepared for the finding of units (in human cortex, but hardly in cats) that respond to a symbol of a certain kind. It requires very little more summation beyond what is already known before we would reach a unit that would respond to a symbol or a face in any position or orientation. It is perhaps worth adding that when their visual cortex is removed, monkeys can still learn to discriminate brightness, but all form vision, colour, and perception of space and movement disappears.

At the conclusion of their important study of hypercomplex cells, Hubel and Wiesel stress two points. First, a proper understanding of the function of an interneuron depends on knowledge of how the information it conveys is made use of at higher levels. This is the surest way to avoid spurious responses from inappropriate strong stimuli. The very highest units are motor and cause an observable adaptive behaviour. Second, the known properties of even hypercomplex units in the cat go only a little way towards accounting for human perception.

The cat and the pigeon can discriminate the orientation of rectangles and have no difficulty with delicate discriminations involving oblique lines or movements. In fact, if an animal runs, flies, jumps, or pursues objects in space, it must excel in discrimination of angular movements. The electrophysiological units that are sensitive to the direction of edges (retinal in the pigeon and cortical in the cat) are presumably the abstracting system in this discriminatory behaviour. To demonstrate their involvement, however, would require closely correlated quantitive behavioural and electrophysiological work.

The fixed inclination of the axis of orientation of visual units sensitive to movement of edges leads to an immense problem when placed side-by-side with the apparent constancy of the position of the world around us, despite head movements. When the head is tilted, the direction of an image on the retina is changed and yet the object is still recognizable and in the same orientation in space. Much of this is a learned habit in man, but we cannot disregard the apparent fixity of the axes of the receptive fields of visual units. If we extrapolate from existing findings on hypercomplex cells of the cat, we conclude that units sensitive to edges feed into units sensitive to particular shapes, and that units that respond to all shapes of a kind then act as input for a unit that responds to that shape irrespective of its inclination and position on the retina. A tilt of the eye upsets the whole basis of abstraction, by moving a different collection of units into line, and yet we see no perceptual interference.

Of all the properties of the units on the visual pathway, the importance of the extensive surrounds in the fields of all visual cells in vertebrates cannot be overexaggerated. The stimulus in the surround strongly affects the response of the centre; this is especially true for units at higher levels with large receptive fields, and it must underlie the ability of the human eye to set its own contrast scale and colour balance, as indicated by the following example.

A board covered with a pattern of papers of black, white, and various depths of grey, and illuminated within a lantern-slide projector giving a uniform field, is seen in a full range of contrasts. The physical brightness of each paper as measured with a photometer will be found to agree with its subjective appearance. An optical wedge is now projected on to the pattern so that the illumination has a smooth gradient from one side to the other. The full subjective range from black to white remains, but a test with the meter shows that an area that now looks darker to the eye than another can actually be reflecting more light than an area that appears lighter, and vice versa. There are many variants on this theme, showing that apparent contrasts depend on the whole picture. If we look through a tube at a small spot on one of the grey papers, the subjective appearance then agrees with the physical measurement of the brightness. Moreover, in experiments of this type, the ability to make a cortical fusion of different presentations to the two eyes depends on what is perceived by each separately and not on the physical sensation received at the eye. Much of this can be explained by a reasonable interpretation of the known properties of visual units.

Even more remarkable examples of the regain of a balanced picture can be demonstrated when two different monochromatic lights illuminate a pattern of coloured papers, but here it is not clear how we can relate the properties of the nerve cells to what is perceived.

MOVEMENT PERCEPTION

When we analyse our visual perception of the world around us, we find that we can sensibly use nouns that represent abstractions—verticality, rotation, constancy of shape of an object as it moves in the visual field, fixity in space, and so on. One of these abstractions is seen movement. Each retinal cell responds to the intensity of the light that falls upon it, although complications may arise from the past history of the receptor and interactions from its neighbours. However, a nervous mechanism must infer movement of a body in space from the times of occurrence of similar responses with a delay at neighbouring points.

In the rabbit and ground squirrel, and probably in most mammals and birds, some of the retinal ganglion cells give a vigorous discharge of impulses when a stimulus is moved through their receptive field in one direction but not in the opposite, so-called null, direction. These units occur in the visual streak, which is a line across the retina in the region where the horizon is projected when the animal is in its normal posture. A single movement unit of the rabbit retina responds to objects that subtend an angle of about 3°, with considerable overlap of fields of nearby cells [2]. Most regions of this receptive field give responses to both "off" and "on" of a small testing light. The preferred direction of movement is the same for a black-white as for a white-black edge, and the directionally sensitive mechanism is distributed over all regions of the receptive field of the cell. Therefore movement sensitivity does not involve a shift from inhibition to excitation, as in typical centres and surrounds.

Several possible models of movement sensitivity are shown in Figure 12.15, any of which will abstract a movement with directional sensitivity when a stimulus is presented at input 1 and subsequently at input 2. Several of these model systems are externally indistinguishable so long as one can only vary the two inputs and read off some measure of the output. A disagreement between experimental results and the theoretical behaviour of a model may demonstrate that the model is an unsatisfactory description of the whole mechanism down to the level where the output is drawn off. However, the model is not thereby demonstrated as inadequate for the mechanism that detects the motion, because nonlinear and rate-limiting processes may lie in series with the model, and additional excitation may arrive in parallel with it. This last possibility means that the model may be an excellent representation of the mechanism of movement perception, but it may seem not to be on account of other factors such as adaptation and flicker fusion in the receptors and

Figure 12.15

Six "mathematically pure" forms of lateral interaction of receptor channels. The box H corresponds to a first-order low-pass filter; D denotes a delay, S a subtraction, and M a multiplication. In shunting inhibition, Q denotes an effect found by dividing that f input by one plus the value of the adjacent input, for example in **A**, $r_1 = f_1/(1 + Hr_2)$ and in **B**, $r_1 = f_1/(1 + Hf_2)$. All of the above models will produce selectively directional movement perception of a stimulus that shifts from f_1 to f_2, and there are many more possibilties and combinations that have not been considered. Therefore, even for this superficially simple example, a direct approach to the mechanism is at some stage essential. [A to E from Thorson, 1966; **F** from Barlow and Levick, 1965.]

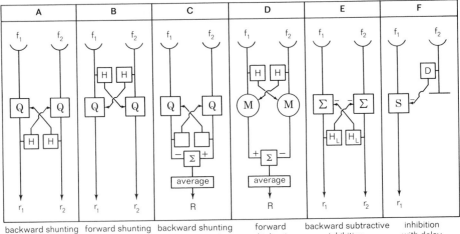

A	B	C	D	E	F
backward shunting inhibition	forward shunting inhibition	backward shunting compare and average	forward multiplicative compare and average	backward subtractive inhibition	inhibition with delay

inertia in the effectors. A model that represents the mechanism for perception of movement cannot in fact be proved or disproved by measurements, however exact, on the behaviour of the whole animal or of higher-order units.

The original work [2] on the rabbit favoured the mechanism of a subtractive inhibition with a delay, as in Figure 12.14, F, but later work on the class I detectors of the frog retina, which are superficially similar, favours a multiplicative mechanism [31]. In Figure 12.15, F, the preferred direction is from f_1 to f_2, because movement in the other direction is blocked by the lateral inhibition. A special delay mechanism can be replaced by the persistence of the inhibitory transmitter or the continued discharge of the inhibitory neuron. In the rabbit the following facts are known. (a) A small stationary spot produces a response when turned "off" and "on," at about the same brightness threshold as for a moving spot. (b) Anomalous responses at the edges of a receptive field are explained by the lack of an inhibitory lateral component, which would be present in the centre of the field. (c) A spot gives a large response when it first moves off in the null direction, evidently because the inhibition spreading out from it has decayed. (d) With a sequence between two separated places, the total number of impulses obtained when stimulating in the null direction is less than when each region is stimulated separately, showing that inhibition really occurs. These observations could equally well be explained by a cross-multiplication model, and direct electrophysiological analysis coupled with anatomical details is required to distinguish the different models. The directionality selective response, however, could not be predicted from a knowledge of the impulses in any one of the component neurons. Observations on the class I contrast detectors of the frog (see p. 278) are also relevant.

Discussion of these models cannot be allowed to pass without a comment on the possible nervous mechanism of multiplication. Presynaptic inhibition can theoretically provide a multiplicative effect, but only over a narrow dynamic range. Addition of two logarithmic functions can also give the effect of multiplication, and relations approaching logarithmic are not difficult to find in any nervous system.

INTERNEURONS IN COLOUR VISION

Animals with colour vision have different classes of primary receptor cells. For example there are three different kinds of cones in the goldfish retina, with spectral peaks at 455, 530, and 625 nm, and in the macaque monkey with maxima at 445, 535, and 570 nm [10]. In the bee there are primary receptors with at least three different types of spectral response curves having maxima at 340, 450, and 530 nm (drone) or four 340, 430,

460, and 530 nm (worker) [7]. In mammals, at any rate, there are lateral connexions between similar receptors (Fig. 12.1) and very complicated connexions with great convergence and many parallel pathways where the receptors meet the next layer, the bipolar cells (see p. 247). Somewhere in this region lies the basis of an opponent colour mechanism, which has the following effects.

In the goldfish, frog, rabbit, and monkey there are retinal ganglion cells with a much narrower band width than can be expected from the properties of the visual pigments. These units behave as if they receive

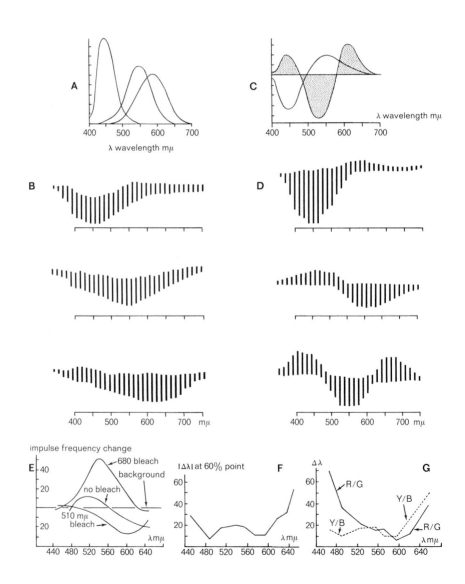

antagonistic inputs from at least two classes of other units, as suggested by recordings from large cells in the retina of fish (Fig 12.16). They are inhibited by light of one colour and excited by light of another colour, with little response to white light [7, 9, 10]. Ganglion cells of the goldfish of the three types "on," "off," and "on-off," when dark-adapted, have a spectral sensitivity corresponding to rhodopsin 533. When light-adapted, the ganglion cells can be classified with reference to colour. There are red-green units, red-blue units, and yellow-blue units, all of which are excited at one of the colours and inhibited at the other, with sensitivity curves that can be derived by taking differences between the absorption curves of the cone pigments. The optimum response is not obtained by stimulating the largest number of receptors. In the macaque monkey there are red minus green units and blue minus yellow (and vice versa) units in the lateral geniculate body. Besides subserving colour vision, the difference units have the effect of discriminating against white light and must contribute, here or in higher units, to the general ability, essential for the utilization of colour vision, of being able to operate with unsaturated colours. The quantitative discrimination of colours by the opponent colour cells accounts very well for the behavioural discrimination by the macaque monkey (Fig. 12.16). The primary colours or the visual pigments have no special importance once we get into the nervous jungle. Colours such as grey, brown, and purple could be represented centrally on exactly the same basis as the colours of the spectrum. The nocturnal owl monkey has more than one visual pigment, but the whole of the visual information is summed irrespective of colour, so that the animal sees by total luminosity, which is evidently its special adaptation to night vision.

Figure 12.16

A trichromatic mechanism of colour discrimination by three types of receptor cells with transformation by sums and differences at later stages.

A. Curves of spectral sensitivity of three hypothetical primary retinal receptors.

B. Responses from three different glial cells (morphologically the equivalent of horizontal cells) near the receptors in the retina of a fish.

C. Theoretical curves produced by taking sums and differences of the curves in A.

D. Responses of glial cells further from the receptors in the fish's retina. They could be produced by sums and differences of the responses in B.

E. Spectral sensitivity curves of a unit in the lateral geniculate body of the macaque monkey. The unit is sensitive to green minus red, with no bleaching. Bleaching at 510 and 680 mμ have different effects.

F. Wavelength discrimination ($\Delta\lambda$) of the macaque monkey at different spectral points by a behavioural method.

G. Wavelength discrimination by two cells of the lateral geniculate body of the macaque monkey at different spectral points. One cell responds oppositely to red and green, the other oppositely to yellow and blue. [A–D from Svaetichin, 1964; E–G from De Valois, 1965.]

Interneurons that are sensitive to movement in the visual field can be expected to have inputs from only one colour class of photoreceptors (as in the frog); otherwise, colour would be confused with movement.

As in other vertebrates, rod and cone excitation converges upon single ganglion cells in the primate retina as the histology suggests (Fig. 12.4). This has the effect that at low intensity the spectral sensitivity of single ganglion cells in the fish and the macaque monkey follows the scotopic curve for rods, with long latency of spikes (> 50 msec), but at higher intensity the spectral sensitivity of the same ganglion cells is that of the cones, with short latency. This is a good illustration of how the spectral sensitivity is a useful tool for plotting pathways of interaction in the visual system. By the same token the existence of colour vision means that there must be a mechanism by which colour coding is posted inwards along the pattern of connexions.

There are two opponent processes in vertebrate retinal ganglion cells, and they interact to different extents as is seen in the units of the lateral geniculate body of monkeys, which have colour vision [37]. One is the spatial opponent system of centres and surrounds. As illustrated by the properties of units of the visual cortex, this concentric pattern is adapted to subsequent synthesis by sums and differences to provide an analysis of edges, corners, and perhaps other figures, irrespective of general brightness. Its full potential is not known. The second opponent system is that between different colours. The two opponent systems are found side by side in the same cells and some units are concerned less with colour, others less with the spatial aspects. Both systems make individual ganglion cell or geniculate units specialized with reference to colour rather than white, or with spatial contrast rather than diffuse illumination. Stimulation of all the receptor input of a unit is the least, not the most, efficient stimulus for it.

Three types of units have been distinguished in the lateral geniculate body of the rhesus monkey. They illustrate one or other or both of the above opponent systems. In the simplest, type III, all three cone types act as input for both the centre and the surround, with inhibitory effects in one area and excitation in the other (Fig. 12.4, B). The analysis is consequently of spatial contrast irrespective of colour over a broad range of the spectrum. Diffuse light of any colour fails to stimulate. For type II units there is no clear centre and surround, but receptors of one colour act as excitatory and those of another colour as inhibitory input over the whole receptive field of the unit. This pattern of connexions is inferred because these units react most readily to a particular colour however it is distributed in their field and because diffuse coloured light is as effective as a single coloured spot. Finally, the most complex units, type I, are inferred to have two sets of receptors, separated spatially as well as by colour, for example, a red "on" centre and a green "off" surround.

Other workers with the macaque monkey [9] find a less obvious classification into types of unit in the lateral geniculate nucleus, but the light stimulated a large area of the retina uniformly. Under these conditions, which eliminate the spatial organization, some units are inhibited, others excited by light of any colour; others are inhibited at one wavelength but excited at another. These spectrally opponent units are very diverse; some are inhibited by red and excited by blue light, and others respond in the opposite sense. The crossover point between excitation and inhibition can occur anywhere from 450 to 700 mμ. It is not easy, therefore, to classify the units arbitrarily into types, although one has a strong inclination to classify in this way, since it would limit the number of channels upon which colour vision is based. Because each unit in the pathway transmits a slightly different information from every other cell, it is not easy to understand how two monochromatic lights side by side can appear equal, and yet human discrimination is extraordinarily accurate in a test of this type. De Valois and his group consider that information is averaged over a number of cells in the determination of colour. They do not suggest how the deeper connexions know which units to average together. The possibility that every unit is really unique, as indicated for neurons in arthropods and even for muscle fibres in some parts of crustaceans, and that somehow each pathway passes on the properties of its own input, has not been worked out. There seems no a priori reason why each relay nucleus should not contain some primitive learning mechanism which is adapted for the purpose of coping with this diversity among its input units.

The higher-order units derived from colour-coded units of the lateral geniculate body have not been described. Strangely, most units in the visual cortex of monkeys with colour vision are *not* colour-coded. Possibly the cortical information about colour is coded in some other form, or is carried elsewhere. Only a small fraction (10%) of colour-coded units in the cortex is sufficient for behaviour that is indistinguishable from our own with reference to colour discrimination. Although introspection leads us to suppose that the image on the retina is somehow reconstructed in the brain, the increasing diversity and complexity of units at the higher levels suggests that there cannot be a single reconstruction, but that many unexpected features of the visual field are abstracted in many parallel representations.

RETINAL GANGLION CELLS OF THE FROG AND PIGEON

In strong contrast to those of the primates and carnivores, the retinal ganglion cells of the frog have sophisticated responses, which reveal that a considerable processing of the primary image has already occurred in the retina. Five classes of units are distributed among the ganglion cells of the retina and all can be found in particular layers of the optic tectum. The optic fibres do not transmit a point-to-point pattern of light on the retina, but give the result of an analysis in terms of four attributes—variations in light intensity, moving edges, curvatures, and standing contrasts—together with a measure of illumination. The following six classes of cells have been distinguished.

1. *Sustained edge detectors.* These have a small field of 1–3°, unmyelinated axons, with conduction velocity 0.5 m/sec, and terminals near the surface of the tectum. Their response is to a contrasting edge in their visual field, with bursts of impulses when the edge moves and a sustained response when it is stationary. The response is independent of the shape of the edge. There is an optimum velocity and an optimum position for the sustained response. When the lights are turned off and then on again, the response reappears after a delay of ½ to 1 sec, although the edge has remained stationary. Some units continue to respond for some seconds in the dark. Large changes in general illumination have no effect. The last detail eliminates the possibility of backward inhibition (Fig. 12.15, A, C, D, E). The long delay when the lights are turned on again favours a multiplicative model. The maximum distance over which lateral interaction occurs is about 2.5 receptor units. The receptors are apparently typical rods, as shown by the spectral sensitivity to movement, but the lateral interaction is probably between bipolar cells and not between the rods themselves. Multiplicative properties would be provided by presynaptic inhibition and the dynamic range of the class I receptors is not great; the model of Figure 12.15, D is a likely candidate [31].

Eye movements of the frog, caused by a regular respiratory rhythm, are adequate to cause stationary contrasts to move across the retina sufficiently to stimulate these cells. The responses caused by the respiratory rhythm are, however, filtered out by the habituation to the stereotyped movement.

2. *Convex edge detectors.* These cells have fields of 2–5°, unmyelinated axons with conduction velocity 0.5 m/sec, and terminals immediately beneath the first group in the tectum. They respond to any small dark object having a sharp edge in the visual field of the cell. In the absence of movement the response wanes after some seconds, disappears when the light is turned off, and does not reappear on reillumination. The small object must move into their visual field before these cells respond, and they will not do so if it arrives during a dark period before the light is turned on. The greater the curvature of the edge, the larger is

the response, which is maximal to small spots of about 1° or to sharp corners. Movement of a light object on a dark background is not very effective, and there is no response to a chequerboard or a large pattern of spots. Even two moving spots can cause less response than one. Movement of the background while a small object remains stationary has little effect, but movement of the small object against the patterned background is very effective. Changes in general illumination have no influence.

3. *Changing contrast detectors.* These cells have fields of 7–12°, myelinated axons with a conduction velocity of 2 m/sec, and terminals in an intermediate layer in the tectum. They respond to any sharp edge, dark or light, moved across their field. There is an optimum direction and speed of movement; changes of general illumination cause only small responses at "on" and at "off." Unlike the previous classes, there is never a sustained response when the edge comes to rest.

4. *Dimming detectors.* These cells have fields up to 15°, myelinated axons with conduction velocity up to 8 m/sec, and terminals deeper in the tectum, just below those of the last group. At "off" they give a prolonged response which may last for many minutes, or even indefinitely. The initial spike frequency can be up to 300 per sec, and then the spikes appear in a series of bursts at a characteristic burst frequency of about 20 per sec, with bursts synchronized between different fibres. Any dark object moving across the field excites the fibre, without regard to direction or presence of edges, but the response arises only from the percentage dimming.

5. *Dark detectors.* These have very large fields and are continuously active, even under bright light. The frequency of spikes increases sluggishly with falling light intensity. There is no response to movement.
    There is an additional class of blue-sensitive optic fibres, which run not to the tectum but to the diencephalon.
    These classes remain distinct and constant under all conditions of illumination and background. They clearly represent a species-specific set of transformations by which the representation on the optic tectum is made quite different in kind from the two-dimensional image on the retina. What the brain receives is a set of signals that have been specially digested; we don't know their particular purpose because their fate in the tectum is not known. Because cells of different types from the same area on the retina have endings that are vertically beneath each other in the tectum (and arguing from the arrangement of the mammalian cortex in columns), it seems reasonable that cells of different types having

the same receptive fields will interact further in the tectum. Thus a small object such as a moving fly will be represented not by a single unit but by a dense cluster of active units upon a distinct background, much in the same way as a pinch of the skin is represented in a cluster of units in the ascending sensory tracts in mammals. The form of the cluster in space and time and its distribution in the different dimensions that are units of different classes must determine its effectiveness at the next stage.

The retina of the pigeon has even greater complexity and subtlety, perhaps not yet fully explored [24]. Six classes of ganglion cells have been distinguished, as set out in Table 9 and Figure 12.17. Five of them, apparently without colour discrimination, run to the tectum as in the frog and the sixth class may be heterogeneous, certainly with a colour sense, and perhaps like the blue receptors of the frog. In complexity the five classes rival the simple cortical cells of cats.

Figure 12.17

Characteristics of the patterns that excite five types of ganglion cells of the retina of the pigeon.

A. General edge detectors (a) of large field, (b) of small field. Both see movement of a small object down to a few minutes of arc.

the field.

B. Horizontal edge detector, responding only if the horizontal edge spreads outside

C. Vertical detectors, as for B; note the response to a stationary edge.

D. Selectively directional movement detectors.

E. Convex edge detector. [After Maturana, 1964.]

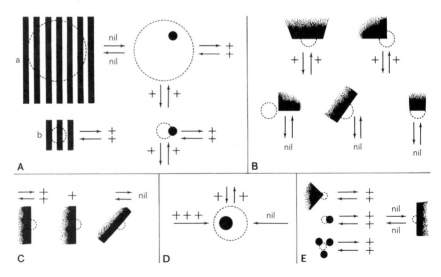

Their constancy in the pigeon and the approximate agreement of their field size with the dendritic spread suggests that the ganglion cells of the bird have a rigid set of connexions, which as peripherally as possible in the visual pathway analyse the inputs into categories appropriate in the life of this animal. We would very much like to know, however, the way in which these units interact at the next interneuron stage. In particular, we must note that some of these units take into account features lying outside their field as tested. For example, the horizontal and the vertical edge detectors fire when an edge of the appropriate direction lies across their field, so that there is summation from some directions outside the field and inhibition from other directions. As elsewhere in sensory analysers, only a certain configuration of input is acceptable. We can only guess that the reason lies in the spatial pattern of connectivity of the neurons all the way along the sensory pathway.

FROG TECTAL UNITS

Considering the complexity of the units in the frog optic nerve it is not surprising that those at the next stage, in the optic tectum, are difficult to characterize [21]. Only two main groups have been distinguished, both with complex properties and large receptive fields. "Newness" units respond to the jerky movement of an object across the visual field; some of them, with overlapping receptive fields of about 30°, respond best to particular sizes of objects, but they only respond to novel movements. Repetition of a movement over the same path as before, with less than 5 to 10 sec delay, fails to cause a second response. Even with a wait of 20 sec the second response is reduced, but the habituation is only to movement along that path. In some units the habituation can be erased by a moment of complete darkness.

"Sameness" units all see most of the total visual field but each has a null patch where stimuli are ineffective. The following description of the properties of these units is so characteristic of the stage we have reached in recording brain mechanisms at work in single cells (without understanding them) that it is reproduced in full. "Let us begin with an empty gray hemisphere for the visual field. There is usually no response of the cell to turning on and off the illumination. It is silent. We bring in a small dark object, say 1 to 2 degrees in diameter, and at a certain point in its travel, almost anywhere in the field, the cell suddenly 'notices' it. Thereafter, wherever that object is moved it is tracked by the cell. Every time it moves, with even the faintest jerk, there is a burst of impulses that dies down to a mutter that continues as long as the object is visible. If the object is kept moving, the bursts signal discontinuities in the movement, such as the turning of corners, reversals, and so forth, and these bursts occur against a continuous background mutter that tells us the object is visible to the cell. When the target is removed, the discharge dies down. If the target is kept absolutely stationary for about two minutes, the mutter also disappears. Then one can sneak the target around a bit, slowly, and produce no response, until the cell 'notices' it again and locks on. Thereafter, no small or slow movement remains unsignalled. There is also a place in the visual field, different for different cells, that is a sort of Coventry to which a target can retire and escape notice except for sharp movements. This Coventry, or null patch, is difficult to map. The memory that a cell has for a stationary target that has been brought to its attention by movement can be abolished by a transient darkness. These cells prefer small targets, that is, they respond best to targets of about 3 degrees.

"There is also (we put this matter very hesitantly) an odd discrimination in these cells, which, though we would not be surprised to find it in the whole animal, is somewhat startling in single units so early behind the retina. Not all 'sameness' cells have this property. Suppose we have two similar targets. We bring in target A and move it back and forth along a fixed path in a regular way. The cell sees it and responds, signalling the reversals of movement by bursts. Now we bring in target B and move it about erratically. After a short while, we hear bursts from the cell signalling the corners, reversals, and other discontinuities in the travel of B. Now we stop B. The cell goes into its mutter, indicating that what it has been attending to has stopped. It does not signal the reversals of target A, which is moving back and forth very regularly all the time, until after a reasonable time, several seconds. It seems to attend one or the other, A or B; its output is not a simple combination of the responses to both" [21].

Frogs show an interest in and approach small moving objects that are below a critical size of about a centimetre, and avoid things that are larger. The critical size is greater for bigger frogs, but we have as yet no knowledge of the properties of the visual units in relation to size. In view of the fact that blue light stimulates pathways to the thalamus, not the tectum, it is of interest that frogs will approach larger objects if the background is blue. If sounds of 1500 c.p.s. are heard at the same time, frogs even fail to approach the small objects. These results [3] show that the determination of action involves several areas of the brain. When watching a frog that is about to feed on a fly, we cannot help noticing the long period required before the animal does anything. Electrophysiologically it would be very difficult to identify the neurons responsible for the decision in view of this long and uncertain latency. Whereas the animal is very easily frightened off, a much longer appraisal is needed before it strikes. If we can translate the word "appraisal" into terms of neurons,

Figure 12.18

The frog has a visual capacity adequate for discrimination between different types of food, and it learns to associate distasteful food with pattern. The unit analysis of the frog's visual system so far identifies no sign of this, but it should be noted that the frog requires a relatively long period of gazing before making its decision to grab one lure rather than another. [Photograph by Lee Boltin, from *Natural History*.]

Figure 12.19

When it finally decides to grab its prey, the frog hurls itself forward with its hind legs and scoops in the prey with its forelegs, at the same time ejecting its long prehensile tongue. During most of this action the frog can no longer see its prey. Therefore the maneuver must be centrally controlled as a result of information obtained earlier. In case the prey is distasteful and the frog learns to avoid it, a visual impression of the prey must at the same time be retained until the consequences of the decision to pounce has filtered back to the learning mechanism. [Photograph by Mervin F. Roberts, from *Natural History*.]

perhaps it would be best rendered as the requirement of a long series of impulses in a particular pattern of higher sensory interneurons before an easily inhibited premotor command fibre will fire. The patience of an angler would be necessary to demonstrate that command fibre electrophysiologically.

GENERAL DISCUSSION

Each group of animals clearly has interneurons that reflect the common environmental patterns and objects significant for its way of life. Within the complexity of releaser mechanisms, which ethologists have shown are specific to particular groups, there are undoubtedly many fascinating neurons—even though very difficult to find—which are specific filters for remarkably complex patterns. If so, we are about to witness a period when the neurophysiologists will encourage the behaviourists to seek out releaser mechanisms (see Fig. 12.19), which may then be recognized electrophysiologically in the animal as individual interneurons, rather than by patterns and constellations of neurons.

From the very few animals so far studied (Table 9), it is evident that among vertebrates there is a diversity of the location where movement and contrasts on the retina are analysed, as well as a wide diversity of the combinations and types of visual units. There are already signs that the retina will be the first area in the nervous system in which different patterns of neural connexions will be found to correspond to different physiological properties. In this correlation of structure and function the comparative approach is of great value because differences of function can be correlated with differences of structure. The cat and the monkey differ from the lower forms in having a great many ganglion cells; in primates there are as many as there are primary receptors. These are not especially sensitive to movement or to edges; the output of each is ambiguous, because it has a surround of opposite effect from the centre. It is unspecific with reference to pattern and the information is conveyed only by groups of cells. In the vertebrates that do not rely on binocular vision of objects in depth, we find ganglion cells that have outputs with a more particular message to the brain. Such cells may still operate in groups but it is not a necessary consequence of their properties that they should do so, as it is for the ganglion cells of the cat. These differences are no more than those that are abundantly illustrated by interneurons everywhere.

In the system found in the higher mammals, much more primary information from the retina is carried relatively untransformed to the cortex, where there is a vast amplification in the number of cells that correspond to each region of the visual field. The transformations at each interneuron stage are not any more wonderful in the mammal; they are astonishingly precocious in the frog. But processing in the retina means loss of detail and freedom to manoeuver later, and learning demands manoeuvering between pathways. The frog throws away the information in the retinal image that is not specifically relevant for the few types of unit that run to its brain. Having available a cortex with great learning power, the mammalian retina can retain details that may turn out to be relevant. Moreover, the cat and the primates have binocular vision, and any form of pattern abstraction derived from congruent information at the two eyes would be seriously impaired by pattern abstraction performed by the retina.

REFERENCES FOR CHAPTER 12

1. Arden, G. B. 1963. Complex receptive fields and responses to moving objects in cells of the rabbit's lateral geniculate body. *J. Physiol.* **166:**468–488.
2. Barlow, H. B., and Levick, W. R. 1965. The mechanism of directionally selective units in rabbit's retina. *J. Physiol.* **178:**477–504.
3. Biersner, R., and Melzack, R. 1966. Approach-avoidance responses to visual stimuli in frogs. *Experimental Neurol.* **15:**418–424.
4. Brown, J. E., and Rojas, A. R. 1965. Rat retinal ganglion cells: receptive field organisation and maintained activity. *J. Neurophysiol.* **28:**1073–1090.
5. Burke, W., and Sefton, A. J. 1966. Recovery of responsiveness of cells of lateral geniculate nucleus of rat. *J. Physiol.* **187:**213–230.
6. Burns, B. D., and Pritchard, R. 1964. Contrast discrimination by neurones in the cat's visual cerebral cortex. *J. Physiol.* **175:**445–463.
7. Ciba Foundation Symposium. 1965. *Colour Vision.* A. V. S. de Reuck and J. Knight (Eds.). Boston, Little, Brown.
8. Cold Spring Harbor Symposium on Quantitative Biology. 1965. Volume 30.
9. De Valois, R. L., Abramov, I., and Jacobs, G. H. 1966. Analysis of response patterns of CGN cells. *J. Opt. Soc. Amer.* **56:**966–977.
10. De Valois, R. L., and Abramov, I. 1966. Color vision. *Ann. Rev. Psychol.* **17:** 337–362.
11. Dowling, J. E., and Boycott, B. B. 1966. Organization of the primate retina: electron microscopy. *Proc. Roy. Soc. B* **166:**80–111.
12. Gouras, P., and Link, K. 1966. Rod and cone interaction in dark-adapted monkey ganglion cells. *J. Physiol.* **184:**499–510.
13. Hill, R. M. 1962. Unit responses of the rabbit lateral geniculate nucleus to monochromatic light on the retina. *Science* **135:**98–99.
14. Hubel, D. H., and Wiesel, T. N. 1963. Receptive fields of cells in striate cortex of very young, visually inexperienced kittens. *J. Neurophysiol.* **26:**994–1002.
15. Hubel, D. H., and Wiesel, T. N. 1965. Receptive fields and functional architecture in two non-striate visual areas (18 and 19) of the cat. *J. Neurophysiol.* **28:**229–289.

16. Jacobson, M., and Gaze, R. M. 1964. Types of visual response from single units in the optic tectum and optic nerve of the goldfish. *Quart. J. Exp. Physiol.* **49:**199–209.

17. Jones, A. E. 1966. Wavelength and intensity effects on the response of single lateral geniculate nucleus units in the owl monkey. *J. Neurophysiol.* **29:** 125–138.

18. Jung, R, and Kornhuber, H. (Eds.). 1961. *The Visual System*. Symposium at Freiburg. Springer-Verlag.

19. Kozak, W., Rodieck, R. W., and Bishop, P. O. 1965. Responses of single units in lateral geniculate nucleus of cat to moving visual patterns. *J. Neurophysiol.* **28:**19–47.

20. Kuffler, S. W. 1953. Discharge patterns and functional organisation of the mammalian retina. *J. Neurophysiol.* **16:**37–68.

21. Lettvin, J. Y., Maturana, H. R., Pitts, W. H., and McCulloch, W. S. 1961. Two remarks on the visual system of the frog, in *Sensory Communication*, W. A. Rosenblith (Ed.). New York, Wiley.

22. Levick, W. R. 1967. Receptive fields and trigger features of ganglion cells in the visual streak of the rabbit's retina. *J. Physiol.* **188:**285–308.

23. Marks, W. B. 1965. Visual pigments of single goldfish cones. *J. Physiol.* **178:** 14–32.

24. Maturana, H. R. 1964. Functional organization of the pigeon retina in *Information Processing in the Nervous System*, R. W. Gerard, (Ed.). Amsterdam, Excerpta Medica.

25. Michael, C. R. 1966. Receptive fields of directionally selective units in the optic nerve of the ground squirrel. *Science* **152:**1092.

26. Nye, P. W. (Ed.). 1966. *Information Processing in Sight-Sensory Systems*. Symposium at Pasadena. California Institute of Technology.

27. O'Leary, J. L. 1940. A structural analysis of the lateral geniculate nucleus of the cat. *J. Comp. Neurol.* **73:**405–430.

28. Pedler, C. 1965. Rods and cones—a fresh approach. In a Ciba symposium, *Colour Vision*, A. V. S. de Reuck and J. Knight (Eds.). Boston, Little, Brown.

29. Peters, A., and Palay, S. L. 1966. The morphology of lamina A and A$_1$ of the dorsal nucleus of the lateral geniculate body of the cat. *J. Anat.* **100:**451–486.

30. Polyak, S. L. 1941. *The Retina*. Chicago, University of Chicago Press.

31. Schipperheyn, J. J. 1965. Contrast detection in frog's retina. *Acta Physiol. Pharmacol. Neerl.* **13:**231–277.

32. Svaetichin, G. 1964. In *Information Processing in the Nervous System*. R. W. Gerard (Ed.). Amsterdam, Excerpta Medica.

33. Spinelli, D. N. 1966. Visual receptive fields in the cat's retina: complications. *Science* **152:**1768–1769.

34. Thorson, J. 1966. Small signal analysis of a visual reflex in the locust. I. Input parameters. II. Frequency dependence. *Kybernetik* **3:**41–53, 53–66.

35. Tomita, T. 1965. Electrophysiological study of the mechanisms subserving color coding in the fish retina. *Cold Spring Harbor Symp. Quant. Biol.* **30:** 559–566.

36. Wagner, H. G., MacNichol, E. F., and Wolbarsht, M. L. The response properties of single ganglion cells in the goldfish retina. *J. Gen. Physiol.* **43:** Suppl. 2, 45–62.

37. Wiesel, T. N., and Hubel, D. H. 1966. Spatial and chromatic interactions in the lateral geniculate body of the rhesus monkey. *J. Neurophysiol.* **29:**1115–1156.
38. Zuber, B. L., and Stark, L. 1966. Saccadic suppression. Elevation of visual threshold associated with saccadic eye movements. *Exp. Neurology* **16:**65–79.

13

Establishment of neuron contacts

The complex interwoven fabric of axons and dendrites has come about by a process of growth, but how is the choice of synaptic connexions made? More specifically, how does a given axon "know" in which direction to grow, when to branch, when to stop, and upon which fibre to differentiate a synapse? We then ask whether the causes operating during the orderly development or regeneration continue to maintain the synaptic connexions for all the life of a nerve cell. The conventional circuit diagram for illustrating nervous connexions has to be considered as a steady state with the possibility of minor connexions continually growing and shifting.

FLOW OF SUBSTANCES ALONG AXONS

Films of living axons, speeded up a hundredfold, reveal a flow of particles in both directions along the inside of the nerve fibres. In addition there is a back and forth streaming of the axoplasm, which has the net effect of moving the whole contents towards the tip. Phospholipids labelled with isotopes move at 3–6 mm/hour; visible particles move along the axons at 0.5–2 mm/hour. The rate of elongation of growing axons is about 2 mm/day, which seems to reflect the difference between the mass movements in the two directions. This flow causes the accumulation of particles and enzymes of all kinds at a blockage of the fibre, and there is strong evidence that it is a normal feature of intact nerves and not associated only with tissue cultures or regenerating and growing axons. In vertebrates one of the consequences of cutting off this flow is the marked increase in mitosis of the glial cells, and a manyfold increase in protein synthesis by the glial cells [37]. These processes are inhibited as the neuron completes its regeneration. One puzzle of the nervous system is where the flow ends, and what types of active substances it carries to other cells downstream; another is the function of the fluid-filled vesicles that are continually taken in by the tips of growing nerve fibres [1].

Flow of some factor toward the cell body is necessary to explain the onset of the cycle of cytological changes called chromatolysis in the soma of most neurons of vertebrates and some invertebrates when the axon is cut at a distant point. During chromatolysis there is little change in the electrical excitability of cat spinal motoneurons, but the longer dendrites disappear and those remaining are capable of spiking. Synaptic transmission often fails when the postsynaptic neuron is chromatolysed following section of its axon. After transection, vertebrate motor axons continue to conduct impulses for 50–80 hours, but their neuromuscular junction fails in about half this time. It is curious that section of the peripheral branch of a vertebrate sensory cell causes intense chromatolysis but section of the central branch of the same cells causes little change in the dorsal root ganglion. Evidently the flow from the periphery is the more vital. Flow of factors in both directions is required to explain many different aspects of the maintenance and establishment of patterns of connexions [38].

GROWTH OF NERVE FIBRES

Merely watching the process of growth tells little about the causes that underlie it. More is learned from operations or other experiments when individual nerve fibres are given an abnormal choice, which is preferably a critical one. In fact the causes that determine axon pathways will only be found by studying these choices under experimental conditions. In our present ignorance we must assume, until proved wrong, that the same forces act on nerve growth throughout the animal kingdom. A great deal must at present be inferred from the few examples that have been studied. A variety of methods has been employed, including direct staining of pathways and inference of pathways from electrophysiological tracing. However, theories are at present built upon insufficient evidence, and the coming decade will see a much-needed stage of data collecting. While maintaining an open mind and governed by the experimental results, we exercise the mediaeval method of argument by making distinctions as to what is and what is not an applicable analogy. This, in its modern form, is the exploration of how far our models are valid.

The following details are from Speidel's observations of nerve fibres in transparent amphibian tissues [39]. At the tip of each growing fibre is an enlargement called the growth cone, which advances by amoeboid movement, spinning a nerve fibre behind as it goes. The growth cone is provided with delicate pointed pseudopodia that actively extend and retract in the tissues ahead (Fig. 13.1). Barriers to growth cause a re-

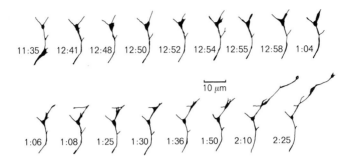

Figure 13.1

The outgrowing tip of an advancing axon in the transparent tissue of the tail of a tadpole. The numbers show the successive times of day. The axon is a regenerating one from a stump that had been cut four days previously. [Speidel, 1933.]

traction of the ending, followed by a change in direction or by branching. Growth cones may move simultaneously in different directions at the same place, a fact that has important consequences for any theory of how their direction is controlled by factors in the medium. The rate of advance is up to 10 μm in 10 minutes in spurts, with a mean of about 200 μm per day. There is an obvious difference in acceptability of outgrowing fibres to Schwann cells, which form myelin sheaths upon some of them but not upon others. Fibres put out numerous branches, some of which thrive while others regress; this natural selection of the strongest branches and the retraction of others can lead to major changes in direction. On the other hand, terminal arborizations are branches that persist. In sensory terminals in the skin there is a continual regression and advance of the fine-branched terminals, and any wound or irritation causes a burst of growth and regression [39].

In this process of growth there is full opportunity for exploration by the advancing tip of the area immediately ahead and to each side; the final pathway of the axon is determined by the outcome of this "feeling its way along," and in the central nervous system the postsynaptic dendrites form after the arrival of the presynaptic fibres. Nerve fibres grow only in contact with existing surfaces, and they tend to run along the lines of orientated structures in their path. Therefore they follow other fibres and so form tracts and nerve bundles. In tissue cultures the mechanical factors are dominant, and they are clearly important in normal growth, as may be judged from the abundance of axon bundles. However, at crucial choice points other factors override them. One very relevant but unexplained feature is that some fibres, both peripheral and central, never cross the midline, but others do. The complex configurations of the finely

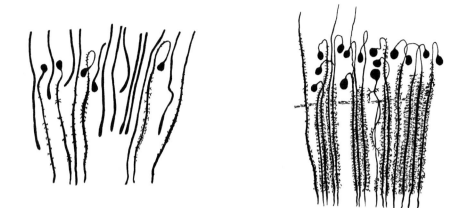

Figure 13.2
Development of the ganglion cells of the first optic neuropile in the pupa of the butterfly, *Pieris*. The left illustration shows the short axons of the retinula cells are in process of growing into the lamina. The long axons and the initial segments of the ganglion cell axons are already putting out side branches, which from electron microscope studies we know to be the sites of the first synapses on the visual pathway. On the illustration at right an older specimen shows the side branches of the ganglion cells much more developed. The terminals of the short retinula axons and arrangement in optic cartridges is not shown; however, see Figures 9.7 and 9.10. [After Sánchez y Sánchez, 1919.]

branching endings, and all the multiplicity of patterns of fibre interlocking, are the result of the growth processes. Neurons that fail to make connexions usually eventually degenerate and disappear, and in vertebrate embryos a large proportion of the growing neurons do not survive into the adult. When motor axons are cut, at least half of the cells die because they fail to form new connexions.

TISSUE CULTURES

Synapses have been established in tissue culture. When two very small explants of 14-day foetal-rat spinal cord are placed 1 mm apart on a collagen-coated coverglass, axons grow from one to the other. After a few days it is possible to work with microelectrodes and, with precautions against stimulus spread, to record responses from one explant when the other is stimulated [12].

An advantage in working with tissue cultures is that there is no blood-brain barrier, which in vertebrates prevents many otherwise active substances from reaching the nervous tissue. We can look forward to the time when it may be possible to infer from the formation of synapses that selected and individually different neurons in tissue culture retain their specific distinctness as they grow. However, it is more than likely that tissue culture studies will be defeated by the tendency of cells to dedifferentiate in the very features that are of interest.

GROWTH OF MAUTHNER CELLS

In the medulla of those lower vertebrates that have swimming tails, there is a pair of large neurons (the Mauthner cells) with axons that always decussate immediately and then run down the length of the spinal cord. Their large size makes them distinctive, so that individual cells are recognizable. Before their axons have grown out in the early embryo, an additional pair of Mauthner cells can be grafted on, together with the surrounding auditory region of the brain from another animal [24]. When the graft is correctly oriented with respect to the host, the extra axons cross from their side of origin and grow down the cord in the usual way. However, when the graft is rotated, so that its anterior/posterior and left/right axes are reversed, the Mauthner axons first grow forward as long as they are surrounded by nervous tissue that came with the graft. After a short distance they turn through 180° and grow in the opposite direction through the graft to the true posterior end of the animal (Fig. 13.3). In this process of growth there are several points of choice that are influenced by distinguishable factors. Only some of the phenomena have so far been defined, and none of the mechanisms are known.

The initial outgrowth of the axon is always towards the midline, showing that the cell is polarized, either intrinsically or by interaction with the cells immediately surrounding it. Its turning towards the longitudinal axis may be a mechanical influence of the longitudinal fibres the growing axon encounters, or may result from a chemical gradient. After having grown so far incorrectly with reference to the animal, it turns round, so providing real evidence for a controlling factor that conveys the anterior-posterior gradient. Now travelling in the properly oriented direction, the axon continues to grow, making synaptic contacts that are specific for that neuron. With formation of its synaptic contacts the growth stops, perhaps because the secretion of raw material for growth is stopped. In films of nerve cells in culture we can readily see a simultaneous movement of particles and vesicles in both directions in the axons, and the inference is that messages that control growth are carried by the particles and vesicles. However, it is feasible that growth is slowed when synapses are formed, because an increased permeability at the synapses would then let through substances that formerly maintained the increase in volume of the terminals.

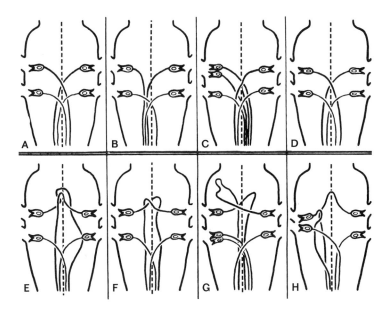

Figure 13.3

The course taken by axons of Mauthner cells in the medullas of eight operated newts (*Pleurodeles*). All the animals had an extra segment of medulla and an extra otic capsule grafted immediately anterior to those of the host in the tail-bud stages.

A–D. The graft normally oriented.

E–H. The graft rotated around a vertical axis so that the anterior-posterior orientation is reversed. The axons of the reversed cells change their direction during the course of their growth. [Hibbard, 1965.]

The factors that determine leftness and rightness remain a great puzzle. When Mauthner cells are disturbed or grafted, their axons grow down either side of the cord, irrespective of the side of their true origin or grafted position. It is possible that the normally growing axons produce a substance by which they repel each other and so keep to their own sides, but we have no clues as to why they adopt that side in the first place. The same problem—how one side is almost a mirror image of the other—applies to the whole animal kingdom.

DENDRITIC GROWTH

A neuroblast cell develops its neurite and becomes a neuron presumably because it is driven by genetic factors that lead to the appropriate rapid protein synthesis. The neurite eventually branches and the dendritic pattern is the outcome (Fig. 13.4). A branching arthropod bristle grows out in a similar way from a single hypodermal trichogen cell, and mutants are known in which the pattern of branching takes a different form. For the bristle, the branching in different directions to form a final fan or brush can be followed because the structure is external. For neuron arborizations we can only infer their growth from fixed preparations. In tissue culture the normal growth of neurites seems very difficult to achieve, presumably because many subtle influences are lacking, and studies of axon growth in tissue culture led to an overemphasis of the importance of contact guidance by mechanical factors in the medium. However, observations of abnormally oriented pyramidal cells of the mammalian cortex suggest that contact guidance plays but a small part in the ordering of the regular pattern of dendrites.

Pyramidal cells of the mammalian cortex are usually arranged with their apical dendrite pointing towards the pia mater (Fig. 13.4). In every preparation, however, 15–20% of the cells have an abnormal orientation (Fig. 13.5). The important feature is that, for these disoriented cells, the pattern of both of the two distinct sets of dendrites is in line with the

Figure 13.4

Development of the three most common cortical neurons in the newborn kitten.

A. Newborn.

B. At 15 days.

C. At 60–75 days. The stellate cells (s) with short axons generate increasingly dense dendritic and axonal arborizations, reaching maturity between 60 and 90 days. Meanwhile, the terminal fibres of the specific afferent fibres (a) and the pyramidal cells (p) are also reaching maturity. The latter develop spines where some of the synapses are situated. [After Scheibel and Scheibel, 1964.]

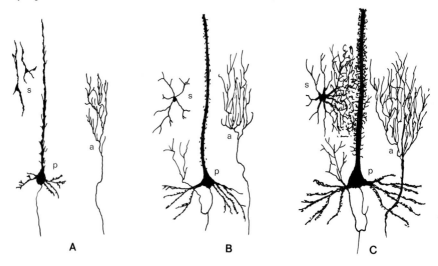

A   B   C

orientation of the cell, and not with the surroundings [46]. The cell is clearly tilted before its processes grow out, and their general form is determined by intrinsic factors within the cell, not by the mechanical or chemical orientation of the milieu in which the cell lies. But the course of the axon is not intrinsically determined. Usually the axon emerges from the pole opposite the apical dendrite (but in inverted cells it may even grow out from the apical dendrite itself), and eventually the axon takes a pathway directly away from the pia, although it may have to curve round to do so. Evidently the direction taken by the axon is controlled by extrinsic factors, which in some as yet unknown way act over considerable distances (Fig. 13.6).

The growth of a complex arborization and the connectivity pattern of synapses depend on the epigenetic interaction of the material of inheritance, represented in that neuron, with the environmental factors derived from the milieu of each of the separate growing branches. The total

Figure 13.5

A normally orientated pyramidal cell (1), with apical dendrite pointing towards the pia mater, adjacent to another cell pointing in the opposite direction (2). The picture on the right shows how, in an inverted pyramidal cell, the axon grows from its normal position upon the cell and curves round towards the normal direction. These cells are in Golgi preparations of the cortex of the rabbit. *ad*, apical dendrite; *ax*, axon. [Van der Loos, 1965.]

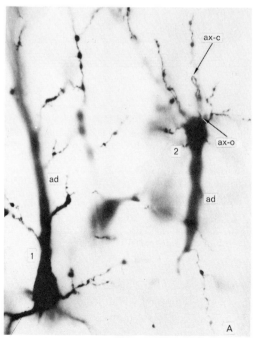
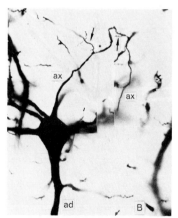

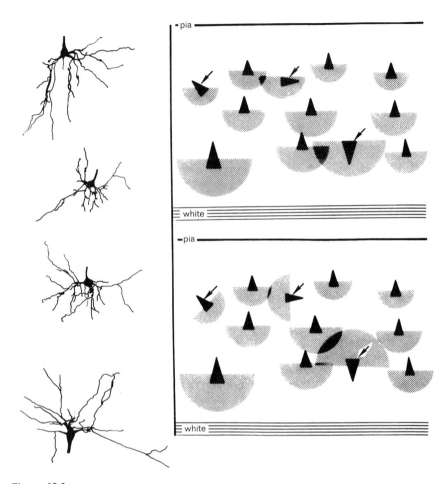

Figure 13.6

Evidence that the pattern of dendrites of a cortical pyramidal cell depends on factors within the cell and not upon the milieu in which their growth occurs. On the left are four pyramidal cells of the cortex of the rabbit, with various orientations of the dendrites, each with a typical dendritic spread that is disorientated in the same way as the cell. Note how the dendrites mainly grow away from the thick apical dendrite (see also Fig. 10.8). The upper figure on the right represents a hypothetical state with dendritic patterns controlled by the tissue surrounding the cell. The lower figure on the right shows the actual form of dendritic patterns as seen in disorientated pyramidal cells. The directions of the axons, on the other hand, are controlled by factors outside the pyramidal cells. [Van der Loos, 1965.]

interaction, which leads to the possible stabilization of a neuron's form and connexions, must be fantastically complex. The following experimental evidence indicates only a few scratches here and there in the surface of an immense problem of how the synaptic pattern forms.

SENSORY FIBRES

The specialized integrity of most vertebrate receptor organs seems to depend upon their sensory innervation. Most receptors—including taste buds, lateral line organs of fish, muscle spindles, and those cutaneous receptors that have been carefully studied—all disintegrate (at different rates, depending on age, species, temperature, and so on) when their sensory nerves are cut. They redifferentiate, especially if still surviving in a rudimentary form, as the nerve supply regenerates back to them. So far as experiments have been made, especially upon taste buds, it appears that the trophic effect is not specific, and that any type of sensory nerve will suffice for any organ. Similarly, any motoneuron seems to be effective in preventing the degeneration of denervated muscle, at least in amphibia and mammals [52], though not in the embryonic chick.

In vertebrates, one end of the sensory neuron has a specific effect on the connexions made by the other [50]. There is a refined local specificity in the skin, which is picked up by the sensory arborizations that grow into it, so that their central terminals make correct connexions. On a gross scale, but dramatically, this is shown in the following experiment, which is statistically correct and repeatable. A large piece of skin stretching from the back to the belly is cut off a tadpole and turned around so that the belly skin is on the back, and vice versa. After healing in situ, followed by metamorphosis when limbs are developed, the animals scratch reflexes are reversed; tickle to the back now causes wiping of the belly, and vice versa [29]. Therefore the topography of the skin has been impressed on the peripheral endings of the sensory nerves and conveyed to their central endings, which have thereby grown with a reversal of their normal connexions. This experiment does not suffer from one common objection, that homograft reactions that come into effect at metamorphosis may cause rejection of grafts.

The outcome is not always as clear as this, however, and there has been some dissension over these results, although no outright disproof. Conflicting evidence comes from the control of two reflexes in young newts [42]. One, the lowering of the gills when the skin around them is touched, is controlled via sensory fibres of the vagus nerve. The other, the corneal reflex, which is a withdrawal of the eye when the cornea is touched, by contrast depends on trigeminal sensory fibres. Animals with two vagal ganglia (transplanted in place of a trigeminal ganglion in tail-bud stages) give an abnormal gill lowering response when the larval cornea is touched. Therefore the transplanted sensory neurons find their normal vagal motor connexions. After metamorphosis the transplanted vagal sensory cells participate in an apparently normal trigeminal corneal reflex. The cornea seems to have modulated the sensory nerves that were transplanted to it. With the converse operation, with a trigeminal ganglion planted in place of the vagal ganglion, the gill lowering reflex is normal in the larva, showing that the sensory cells fit in with their new situation at both ends of their fibres. After metamorphosis the corneal reflex is normal but is not elicited by stimulation of the vagal region, and the transplanted trigeminal fibres do not form reflex connexions that would correspond to their original character.

On a finer scale, the problems of sensory-central connexions are even greater. For example, the taste buds of a vertebrate are continually shedding new cells from the centre of the bud and growing new ones at the periphery. The average lifetime of a single taste bud cell is only about one week. These cells are each innervated by a taste fibre (Fig. 13.7), which has its cell body in the cranial sensory (petrosal) ganglion of nerve V and its central terminals in the tractus solitarius of the

Figure 13.7

The vertebrate taste bud.

A. Each cell in the capsule is in contact with a plug at the external opening and forms synapses with nerve fibres below. The cells have a life of only a few days, those at the centre being continually replaced by new ones that migrate inwards. Therefore the connexions with the nerves are in a continual state of flux. Either the nerve determines the class of sensitivity of the receptor cell, or conversely, and in either case there must be an appropriate control of one cell by the other.

B. Section of a taste fibre terminal in the tongue of the rat, surrounded by the base of a receptor cell, with a few presynaptic vesicles.

C. A similar section in the frog, showing presynaptic dense core vesicles and smaller "empty" vesicles in the nerve fibre. [A from Cajal; B after Farbman, 1965, and Gray and Watkins 1965; C after Uga, 1966.]

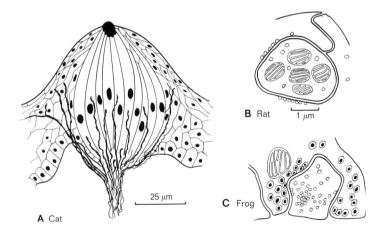

B Rat   1 μm

25 μm

C Frog

A Cat

medulla. Taste buds can regenerate as long as they have their own nerve supply, but they disappear soon after the nerves are cut, only to reappear when the nerves grow again. Taste buds can be removed surgically and then new ones reappear only if nerves are present. The results of crossing nerves and allowing regeneration, and the fact that one axon can serve more than one papilla, suggest that the taste cells are modified by the sensory nerves, which then need not repeatedly form new central connexions.

Regeneration of sensory fibres to the tongue after crossing of two different nerves is particularly convenient in the rat, in which the chorda tympani nerve to the front and the IX nerve to the back of the tongue differ in their responsiveness to cooling and taste chemicals. Electrophysiological recording 15 weeks after the operations show that while a simple cut nerve regenerates its normal functional properties, the cross-innervated nerves develop characters more typical of the area which they innervate, in response to cooling as well as to taste [31]. Whichever way it occurs, one cell must clearly modulate the other, and the peripheral coding must in some way be centrally represented.

REGENERATION OF CENTRAL CELLS IN LOWER ANIMALS

The problems of how individual neurons assume their shape and connexions are nowhere so baffling as in the regeneration of parts of the central nervous systems of lower animals. Flatworms, annelid worms, and molluscs achieve spectacular replacement of groups of central cells and even of whole ganglia. The highest percentage of successful regenerations is found where regeneration may well be necessary in normal life, as in the arms of octopus and the anterior ends of tubiculous worms. The whole central collections of interneurons can regenerate in these instances, complete with connexions, central rhythms, and neurosecretion. The process has frequently been described histologically but almost nothing is known of the mechanisms of re-establishment of the neuron connexions.

Among lower vertebrates there are also remarkable abilities of central regeneration and continuous growth. The forebrain of fishes will regenerate almost entirely so long as some ependymal cells remain; so will the forebrain and optic tectum of some amphibians. This ability almost certainly is possible because the matrix tissue or ependymal cells are continually dividing and forming new nerve cells for the whole life of the animal. Some amphibia are able to regenerate new retinal tissue and most can re-establish functional connexions across severed parts of the central nervous system, including the optic tract [36]. In higher (especially warm-blooded) vertebrates, regeneration in the central nervous system is limited by lack of a growth-promoting factor and hindered by growth of scar tissue.

REGENERATION IN THE SYMPATHETIC CHAIN

In the cervical sympathetic ganglion of the mature cat, preganglionic fibres activate different postganglionic pathways, such that stimulation of one preganglionic nerve root (T_1) produces dilatation of the pupil and stimulation of another (T_4) produces dilatation of blood vessels of the ear [19]. Upon section of all preganglionic fibres, with subsequent regeneration, the normal situation outlined above is restored. However, when only T_1 to T_3 were crushed, and T_4 was left intact, it was possible for some months to dilate the pupil of the eye and blood vessels of the ear by stimulation of T_4 alone. These abnormal connexions persisted until the fibres of T_3 regenerated, when normal relations were again established. This shows that the postsynaptic fibres are plastic but they prefer a certain input if they can get it; possibly the reallocation of connexions depends on multiterminal innervation (see p. 311). The rules defining the connectivity are permissive in a way that leaves no cells without an input of some kind. This is a useful idea when we consider later the formation of connexions between the innumerable cortical cells, for which there are an inadequate number of rules for specifying each separately.

REGENERATION OF THE OPTIC TRACT

The next step in increasing complexity occurs when a group of axons that are spatially related grow to a set of terminals, where they form a projection of their origin. The best-known example is the regeneration of the connexions between the retina and the contralateral optic tectum in fishes and amphibians after the optic nerve has been cut [15]. Even after the nerve is crushed to destroy a possible order in it, there is usually complete recovery of function, including colour vision in fish. In the subsequent regrowth, fibres from different parts of the retina invade the midbrain and terminate in the particular areas of the tectum they occupied before the operation. This has been demonstrated histologically and functionally.

Growing optic nerve fibres that arrive at the tectum pass by a series of vacant slots and settle on their own proper resting places. The techniques actually show that fibres are ordered on a gross scale, not that every individual one becomes distinctly connected or how it becomes connected. Axons from the central area of the retina terminate in the central zone of the tectum (and similarly for other areas), as is shown by removing parts of the retina and allowing fibres from only the remaining parts to regenerate (Fig. 13.8). At first sight the tectum contains a representation of the retina that is independent of the presence of the eye [3]. The central-peripheral correspondences in adult fish have been repeated with embryonic amphibia, with a different result in that embryonic fibres from a half retina spread over the whole of the tectum, not over half of it as regenerating adult fibres would in the adult fish. The results for amphibia show that although chemical affinity plays some part in the decision by the neuron to form a synaptic termination and stop

Figure 13.8

Preferences of destination shown by regenerating axons of retinal ganglion cells from different parts of the retina when they regrow into the optic tectum in the brain of the goldfish. The figure at bottom right shows the anatomical relation of the eyes, optic tracts, and optic tectum. The other diagrams show the relation between the positions adopted by fibres that arrive in the tectum and the region of the retina (shaded) from which they originate. Nothing is known of the formation of new connexions by the regenerated fibres. The terminals do not grow all over and then redistribute themselves afterwards. a, anterior; d, dorsal; p, posterior; v, ventral; l, lateral; m, medial. [From Attardi and Sperry, 1963.]

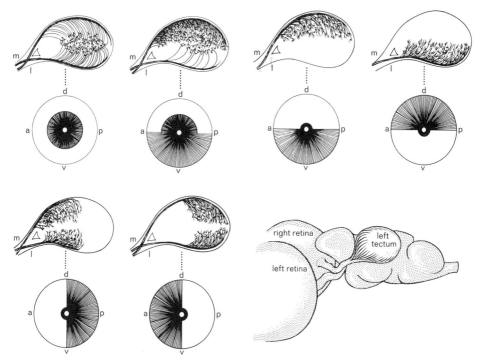

growing, the landmarks are not necessarily fixed before the prospecting axons first stake out their claims [15]. If an area between the far side and the near side of the tectum is filled in by axons in rank order and if the axons spread away from each other to fill the whole area, the result will appear to be determined by a gradient, although the gradient is one that never can be apparent to the observer except by observation of the neuron pattern in this experiment. It should be borne in mind that the tectum is a very complex structure (Fig. 13.9).

Not only the spatial projection of the retina on the midbrain but also the different units responsible for discrimination of colour and brightness in fish regrow to connexions that are specific for these classes; this has been shown behaviourally but not as yet physiologically. If we wish to explain the decussations at the optic chiasma on the same basis, it is necessary to postulate that there are left-right differences operating at

Figure 13.9

The principal types of neurons of the optic tectum of a typical teleost, based mainly on the salmon and goldfish, showing the layers of intrinsic cells with their stratified dendrites. Axons of retinal ganglion cells enter along the outer (upper) surface in strata *D* and *E*. The numbers show neuron types that are multiplied many times over. The diagram illustrates a stratified neuropile and the great complexity of this region. Neither the physiological analysis (discussed on p. 281) nor the studies of growing fibres (p. 311) achieves the necessary detail that so complex a structure suggests. [Leghissa, 1955.]

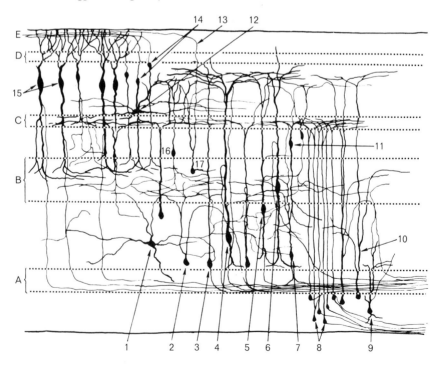

the region of the chiasmata during the critical period of embryonic growth. Numerous experiments show that neurons accept or make connexions that are normal except for being on the wrong side, and so evidently left-right differences do not necessarily operate during the formation of terminal synapses. They may well connect on the wrong side, however, because they find nothing more suitable among a range of priorities.

The regeneration of old connexions or the growth of embryonic ones is not mechanistically related to function at the time, at least for amphibian optic nerve. When the adult eye is rotated and the optic nerve is then cut, the regeneration always results in a correspondingly rotated vision, as is shown by the direction in which the animals snap at food. Therefore the topographical relation between retina and tectum is previously determined. If the rotation experiment is done before the late tail-bud stages, vision is erect and normal, whereas after this stage vision is rotated; moreover, determination of the retinal ganglion cells occurs independently along the two axes of the eye, the nasotemporal axis being fixed before the dorsoventral axis.

With reference to left and right, the normal situation in lower vertebrates is that all fibres in the optic chiasma form a contralateral projection from which other fibres return through the chiasma to an ipsilateral projection. In frogs and toads this ipsilateral projection is mainly from the tempero-inferior quadrant of the retina (nasosuperior field of view) and goes mainly to the rostral half of the ipsilateral tectum. The contralateral projection, in contrast, covers almost the whole of the contralateral tectum. All this will regenerate, with a percentage of anomalous patterns in adult frogs.

Because we have two organized patterns, the retina and the tectum, which interact, further analysis depends on watching the consequences of experimental alteration of one but not the other. So far this has been done by grafting together half eyes in different combinations in the late embryo, allowing the axons to grow to the brain, and then plotting the projections on the tectum [15]. It is not clear how the homograft reactions, which follow metamorphosis in frogs, have been overcome in these cases.

When two nasal half eyes are fused and allowed to mature, each half retina projects to the whole area of tectum that received optic fibres from the whole retina in the normal animal, with each projection correctly arranged topographically. In other words, there is a superimposed projection, and each half retina has spread itself to the borders of the tectum. With two temporal retinal halves fused together, the situation was exactly reversed, but this time the dividing line between the two half retinas was projected to the posterior of the tectum (Fig. 13.10). The areal magnification factors are greater than those for the normal animal, but it is possible in the absence of a suitable control that parts of the tectum

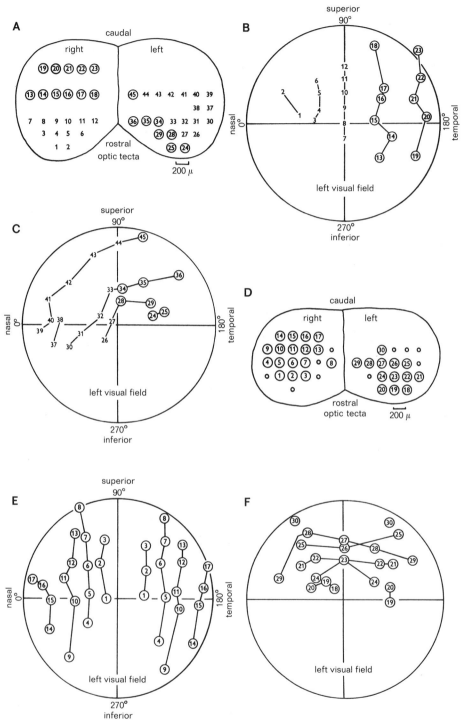

with no corresponding retinal region have degenerated and that the residue has expanded into the remaining space [15].

That parts of the tectum have not degenerated in this way, however, is suggested by the ipsilateral connexions, which are all *normal*, despite the existence of a double retina. The ipsilateral projection from the normal eye on the area occupied on the tectum by the double projection, however, is abnormal, and in two cases was inverted along the rostrocaudal axis, as if following only the direction set by the reversed half retina (Figs. 13.10 and 13.11).

These results are compatible with the view that the retinal fibres sort themselves out by rank order and spread out to fill the whole area of the projection available to them, the temporal border of the retina going to the front and the nasal border to the back of the tectum, with the rest in order between. They do not go to particular places on the tectum but arrange themselves like soldiers forming ranks, on the next man, and then settle down. This order of settling down then carries an influence to the fibres that connect with the opposite tectum and can impose a rank arrangement on them.

A question arises as to whether optic fibres from double eyes form functional connexions in the tectum. Eyes with double temporal retinae behave as if blind after destruction of the rostral part of the contralateral tectum, as do also eyes with double nasal retinae after destruction of the caudal half. In other words, the region of the tectum corresponding with the side of the retina that is displaced to become the seam down the middle doesn't function in visual responses. This implies that the afferent and efferent fibres in the tectum have some kind of congruence, or matching, that has to be met, and that this requirement is fulfilled in normal development, although it may depend on function.

Experimental findings are consistent with the view that each retinal neuron regenerates to its proper place in the tectum by some place-specific chemical means. But individual fibres differ in their degree of

Figure 13.10

The projection of the retina upon the optic tectum in the toad *Xenopus*.

A. The optic tectum, seen from above; the numbers are electrode positions.

B. The left visual field, showing positions that correspond to the electrode positions on the right (contralateral) tectum.

C. The left visual field with stimulus positions corresponding to the electrode positions on the left (ipsilateral) tectum.

D, E, and F. The visual projection from a retina that consists of two nasal half-retinas (double temporal field). The small circles in D are electrode positions from which no responses could be obtained. E shows the projections to the contralateral tectum; F shows the ipsilateral ones. The chart of the visual field in each circle extends symmetrically to 100° outwards from the centre. [Gaze, Jacobson, and Székely, 1963.]

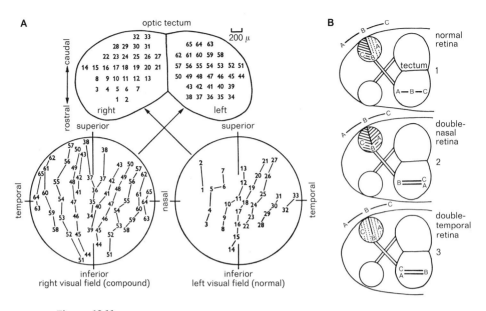

Figure 13.11

Optic tract fibres from each half of a double-nasal compound eye spread over the whole tectum in *Xenopus*.

A. Maps of the contralateral projection from retina to tectum for a double-nasal eye (two nasal halves fused) and for the normal eye of the other side. Each number on the tectum represents an electrode position at which an optimal response was evoked by a visual stimulus at the corresponding position in the visual field. The visual fields extend 100° from the centre. The projection from left eye to right tectum is normal, but that from the double-nasal eye shows a reduplication of stimulus positions about the vertical meridian. In the horizontal plane each half of the visual field reaches over the whole tectum. This contrasts with the situation in the fish (see Fig. 13.8).

B. Areas of the retina with simplified projections on the tectum: 1, normal; 2, double-nasal; and 3, double-temporal eyes. [Gaze, Jacobson, and Székely: A, 1965, B, 1963.]

specificity as well as in the place-specific label. In the newt, for example, fibres from the centre of the retina are more likely to establish earlier contact with the proper tectal location. The degree of specificity is also improved with time; when fibres first arrive at the tectum they make connexions reflecting wide retinal fields, but in a period of 5–12 months the field sizes are progressively reduced, suggesting an increased specificity of connexions (there is no evidence that the field sizes are physiologically reduced, for example, by inhibition). This finding agrees with the reduction and movement of axon arborizations when they have regenerated to muscle fibres with polyneuronal innervation, and it suggests that the invading fibres compete upon a background of preferences of the cells that they innervate (see p. 311). Little more is known on these topics but it is obvious that, where parts of the nervous system develop in isolation and later join up, each side has prepared slots that are filled as ordered infiltration proceeds, and yet there can still remain a residuum of detailed connexions that depend for their development on normal function.

The importance of function is clear in split-brain baby monkeys, in which visual guidance of one hand is not able to develop if prevented at an early stage when it would normally occur; with the normal brain, transfer occurs.

When young kittens open their eyes at the 6–10th day, they are visually inexperienced, and yet the responses of complex units of the visual cortex appear to be normal. Therefore complex connexions, at the unit level, are not dependent on visual experience. Projections of these units to further parts of the cortex may, however, require visual experience of patterns.

The following of a moving stimulus by the eyes and visual placing appear only at 20–25 days, and therefore some connexions further down the line require more time for their establishment in kittens ([14] of Chapter 12).

Of fundamental importance, in all the experiments on the formation of connexions by fibres of the optic tract, is that these axons are not of primary sensory, but of about third-order interneurons of several types (p. 250); in fish and some other animals they are coded for colour vision. They lie in the middle of a chain, which continues into the central nervous system. Therefore the chemical individuality that can be demonstrated in the axons of the optic tract is already several stages downstream from the retinal elements from which it must partly originate.

NEUROMUSCULAR JUNCTIONS

The actual establishment of synapses is best known for the neuromuscular junctions of the newborn mammal. Nerve fibres arrive in their neighbourhood but appear not to influence the muscle cells before the latter differentiate and fill with myofibrils. Vertebrate embryonic muscle fibres are slow; some develop into fast fibres later. Motoneurons of vertebrates will innervate any muscle if the normal nerve supply has been removed. There is no question of incompatibility, and cholinergic somatic motor fibres of the hypoglossal nerve of the cat will even replace the adrenergic postganglionic sympathetic innervation of the nictitating membrane, forming a physiologically effective neuromuscular junction [47]. Some unknown mechanism regulates the number of muscle fibres in a motor unit, and in higher vertebrates another mechanism prevents multiple innervation of each muscle fibre. When a mammalian muscle is partially denervated, the remaining nerve fibres sprout and supply new endings to the muscle fibres lacking them. The mechanism is again unknown. Miniature end-plate potentials are found at the earliest established end plates but at only about a hundreth of the adult frequency.

When motoneurons to slow muscle fibres of vertebrates regenerate to fast muscle fibres, and vice versa, the muscle fibres change several of their properties to come into line with their new innervation. They change their speed of contraction and their characteristic enzyme contents, but the fine structure that is characteristic of slow and fast muscle fibres does not change [6, 7]. Denervated fast muscle fibres first revert to the "embryonic" slow condition, and denervated vertebrate muscle eventually degenerates altogether if motoneurons of some kind fail to reach it. The motor end plates are recognizable by their cholinesterase for up to a year after denervation in mammals, and the old endings are preferentially reoccupied by the regenerating nerves. New end plates are formed only with difficulty unless the muscle has been damaged. Muscles of the developing chick rapidly degenerate if they are innervated by nerves of the wrong segment, but in other groups any motoneuron seems to join with any muscle.

Foetal muscle fibres are uniformly sensitive to acetylcholine (ACh) along their length, but after they are innervated there is a progressive diminution until only the area immediately around the developed end plate is sensitive. The muscle fibres again develop ACh sensitivity away from the end plate after they have been denervated in the adult, when transmission to them is blocked by botulinum toxin for long periods, or when they are severely damaged even if still innervated. A long muscle fibre with an end plate at each end becomes sensitized to ACh only around the end plate that is denervated, and even there to a less extent than when both are denervated. Therefore intact nerve endings cause the whole of the muscle fibre they innervate to become less sensitive to ACh. This shows again that an influence on the postsynaptic cell appears to be transferred from a nerve terminal.

At this point we ask: What is the function of the large amounts of RNA and protein synthesis in nerve cell bodies? What is the function of RNA at synapses [5]? What is the fate of the protein, which is carried at about 2mm/day towards the tip of the axon? Retinal ganglion cells of the rat lose at least 1½ times their volume every day as axoplasm [44]. One suggestion, which would at one stroke account for many observations, is that proteins pass along nerve fibres and carry a long-term stimulus that helps to retain synaptic relationships, to modify the postsynaptic cells, and to promote regeneration. Besides the above changes, vertebrate muscle fibres eventually atrophy if deprived of their nerve supply. Limb stumps in newts are able to regenerate a new limb only if they have some nerve supply from any spinal cord region. There are many little-known but widespread examples of degeneration of neurons (called transynaptic degeneration) when all their synaptic input is removed. Vertebrate sensory cells usually degenerate eventually when their sensory nerves are removed. For example, when the lateral line nerve of amphibia is cut, the lateral line organs disappear after 6–12 months. When the nerve regrows, the new sense organs form only by division from old ones under the influence of the invading fibres [39]. The somatic muscles of the adult moth fail to grow if their nerve supply is removed in the pupa, in contrast to cuticular structures and peripheral sense organs, which develop normally. All these facts emphasize the importance of a flow of active substances in both directions between the nerve fibre and its end organ.

CONNEXIONS TO SPINAL MOTONEURONS

The artificial crossing of nerve trunks in mammals is followed by regeneration, leading to a chaotic situation with loss of function. For certain nerves, crossed in the newborn kitten, changes in the synaptic connexions of the relevant motoneurons can be recorded with microelectrodes 6 months later [13]. Nerves of two muscles are crossed and months later the synaptic relations on their motoneurons and on the untouched synergic pair are tested. As a control the same nerves are severed and reunited without being crossed. The result is that the number of fibres in a monosynaptic reflex pathway can be reduced and a new pathway can become prominent (Fig. 13.12).

The numerous failures may be due to some peculiarity of mammals, but the efferent fibres may have to be within a very short distance of the motoneuron if they are to make an appropriate new connexion. About half the motoneurons with severed axons die. No new synaptic connexions were detected upon motoneurons that never have their axons cut, suggesting that the disturbance in the cell body caused by section of its axon is necessary before the motoneuron becomes plastic. We might suppose that the sensory terminal initially "smells out" the appropriate motoneuron, and after the nerves have been crossed the motoneuron changes its smell. It can only have done this if some message has conveyed the identity of the muscle up the axon with an effect meaningful to sensory axons, which also have connexions in the spindles of the same muscle. That messages travel from a muscle to its nerve under different circumstances is shown by the degeneration of motor axons that fail to make contact with muscle cells during development or regeneration.

There is a considerable literature, some of it controversial, on the reformation of functional nervous connexions during regeneration of nerves or muscles in amphibia. There is a parallel literature on the

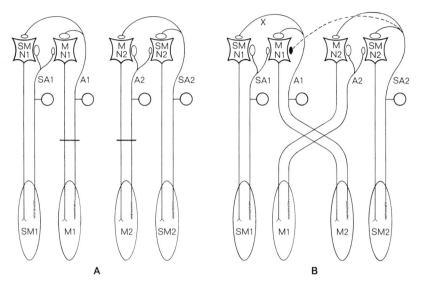

Figure 13.12

The effect of crossing peripheral nerves upon central synapses in young kittens.

A. Monosynaptic pathways for two pairs of synergic muscles, $M1$, $SM1$ and $M2$, $SM2$. The afferent fibres $A1$, $SA1$, $A2$, and $SA2$ from the annulospiral stretch receptors of these muscles make monosynaptic connexions to motoneurons of their own and of the synergic muscle. The larger knobs signify a more powerful action.

B. When nerves are sectioned and allowed to regenerate in a crossed condition, a new synaptic connexion, as indicated by the dashed line from $SA2$ to $MN1$, can be inferred by recording synaptic potentials. At the same time the connexion indicated by X is weakened. [Eccles et al., 1962.]

embryonic establishment of connexions between the spinal cord and the muscles in embryonic amphibians. It is not my purpose to review this work, because the principal results are collected in the summary by Weiss [49]. However, it is important that a new interpretation of these results should be outlined.

After transplantation of limbs to a region where the limbs' own spinal nerves can reach them, the muscles of the transplanted limb take part in the locomotory cycle according to their names, even if the resulting movements are ridiculous. As many as five additional limbs can be planted upon the appropriate region. Functional or proprioceptive feedback from the muscles seems to play no part. A postulate that explains how the motoneurons become connected with their appropriate muscles during development is that they first grow out from the developing cord, make contact with muscles, and then modify their central connexions as is appropriate for those muscles, being guided in this by chemical signs acquired by contact with the muscles. Similar *modulation* of motoneurons by their new muscle will explain why grafted limbs make movements in which abnormally located muscles move at the same time as normal muscles of the same name. The limb muscles are clearly differentiated from each other and presumably contain individually different proteins, so that a mechanism of transfer of information via the particles and pinocytotic vesicles that move up motoneurons to the cell body is quite possible. Acceptance of this concept implies that motor regions of the spinal cord in turn acquire synaptic inputs as influenced by the muscle connexions of the motoneurons their terminals encounter. In other words, modulation by the periphery as the mechanism for the motoneuron stage implies that the imposed chemical differentiation of the motoneurons is passed back to other neurons, which in turn control the connexions of their own dendrites, and so on throughout the nervous system.

An alternative and much simpler explanation, only recently enunciated, is that each motoneuron is determined with a preference for a particular muscle, although it will connect with abnormal muscles if it fails to find its own. The fixation of the motoneurons may have occurred in the embryo following the formation of its first connexions. In mammals the muscle fibres are each innervated by a single motoneuron, which seems unable to leave once it has become attached. The growth of motoneurons into transplanted muscles or their regeneration into normal muscles after nerve section then leads to a chaotic loss of coordination, which can only be partially overcome by a long period of conscious training in mammals.

In the lower vertebrates, however, in which the muscles can assume a reasonably normal coordination if reinnervated by motoneurons of the appropriate region of the spinal cord, the motor innervation is polyneuronal and multiterminal. This means that every motoneuron branches to many muscle fibres and every muscle fibre is innervated by several motoneurons. The new hypothesis is that in this situation the different motoneurons can interact and compete where they meet on every muscle fibre, and, having a tendency to branch widely without stopping at the first unoccupied muscle fibre, they may find their own muscle and move entirely to it [27]. Additional transplanted limbs function in time with nearby normal limbs because specifically labelled branches of the same motor axons possibly innervate corresponding muscles in each. By extension, similar fixed tendencies, with multiterminal and polyneuronal innervation at the interneuron level, could make possible a great deal of interaction in growth in the central nervous system or in taste buds. The inference is that in lower vertebrates every motoneuron is differentiated to the extent that it is unique, and it corresponds to a particular muscle. This has been long recognized in the arthropods and in errant polychaete worms, but it is new as applied to vertebrates. Neuron differences originate in the embryo, though whether from the genes of the neurons, from the milieu of the spinal cord, or from the muscles themselves has not been determined. It will be interesting to see to what extent this idea of motoneuron specificity can be demonstrated experimentally and whether the postulated mechanism of competition between branches of different motoneurons can be applied generally to all neurons.

THE "STAMPING" OF UNITS IN THE VERTEBRATE OLFACTORY PATHWAY

The vertebrate olfactory pathway illustrates, by its very great specificity and complexity, the problem of how the outputs of differently specialized sensory fibres are recognized at the second- and third-order stages they excite. We have seen that primary olfactory receptor cells are probably all slightly different from each other in their responses, since theoretically there can be found a primary fibre that can discriminate between any pair of odours ([8] of Chapter 10). This diversity and specificity of the receptor cells must be matched by a specificity of the connexions of their central terminals; otherwise the elaborate sorting in the sense organ would mean nothing. Olfactory receptors in all animals characteristically have numerous peripheral cell bodies (Fig. 10.7). The specificity of the receptor presumably springs from a differentiation of some enzyme system or other protein within it, and the axoplasmic flow will carry a sign of this differentiation to the axon terminals. In this transport of protein, I believe, lies the essential clue to the ordering of the olfactory fibre connexions, and the differentiation of the mitral cells and other second-order cells from each other.

The mitral cells show as great a diversity as receptor cells, and mitral cell differentiation must depend on receptor differentiation, for unless the mitral cells are in some way tied to the specificity of the receptor combinations that excite them, a central chaos and mere random summation ensues. In fact, discrimination, not summation, is the final result.

The transfer of information inwards is carried on by second- and then third-order neurons, each of which *must acquire and pass on* the specificity of each receptor axon, which is different from its neighbours in the periphery. A central discrimination of many odours is only possible if each relay along the path is capable of keeping separate some aspect of the addressing system for posting information inwards. The connexions, from receptor to interneurons down the line, are laid down before the odour acts as a stimulus. If a chemical—such as a protein, with a peripherally determined specific reference to the receptor that secretes it—is passed on to the second-order cell, then the distribution of connexions made by them upon later interneurons could be a kind of image, or unique analysing system, of the peripheral odour. Because the stimuli are so varied, the odour-conveying interneurons, above all others, must have developed this ability to pass the appropriate connectivity pattern all down the line, over successive synaptic relays. The olfactory epithelium can be completely regenerated when destroyed; it is, after all, in a state of continual rebirth of new cells. Transneuronal degeneration is a feature of the olfactory pathway. Thus we are faced with a situation in which central interneurons may modify and switch about their central terminals in accordance with chemical messages that continually flow down axons from the periphery. As will be discussed later, this is exactly what is wanted for a mechanism that learns by formation of new connexions (see p. 368), and we remember that the vertebrate cortex has evolved from highest-order olfactory units. New rules of an extremely plastic nature had to be evolved for odour discrimination, in which genetic information could not supply an adequate number of clues either about total nerve connectivity or about possible odours in the environment. And these plastic rules seem to have been preadapted for formation of novel connectivity patterns in the cortex for other modalities also. We realize that all interneurons have to evolve in a context that includes the somewhat unpredictable sensations offered by a real world.

FORMATION OF NEURON CONNEXIONS IN INVERTEBRATES

Among the invertebrates there are numerous examples of regeneration of nerve cords and peripheral nerves, in which growing axons cross a lesion and re-establish normal functional relations. Sensory cells are usually peripheral in invertebrates and when their axon is cut they grow a new one to the central nervous system. So far there is no example in which a complex topological or multimodal peripheral pattern of regenerated endings has been traced, either histologically or physiologically. In invertebrates there are not many examples of definite projections, area by area, but on the other hand the obvious regularity of normal connexions as seen in histological preparations should allow a histological test of whether regenerated axons readopt their former connexions to exactly the extent that they are rigidly fixed by choices made during development (see p. 326). The possibilities are considerable because a cut across the central nervous system will regenerate in most lower invertebrates and some (especially juvenile) arthropods.

Intensive study of neuron distributions in annelids, arthropods, or gastropods occasionally turns up neurons whose cell bodies are out of place; invariably, however, on examination of the axon and dendrite connexions it is apparent that the connexions of the cell are normal, showing that connexions are more important than cell position in the survival of the cell through the process of development. In sensory systems, however, the position of the cell body in the periphery determines the differentiation. The remarkably constant bilateral symmetry of the neuron patterns in the ladderlike nerve cords must arise from their similar differentiation pathways, with symmetrical paired cells probably always the daughters of one mother cell.

Invertebrate sensory neurons almost always have a peripherally differentiated cell body from which the axon subsequently grows in to make its appropriate central connexions. When the antennule of a lobster (bearing the olfactory receptor cells) is cut off, it will eventually regenerate, and the newly formed peripheral sensory cells of the regenerate will send axons in to make connexions with the brain. It is curious, however, that when a whole eyestalk is cut off, the structure that regenerates is frequently similar to an antennule; in one way, at least, the animal treats it as an antennule, for when the heteromorph antennule is stimulated, the normal antennule of the same side makes a protective avoiding response [28]. Nothing is known about whether the olfactory fibres are re-established, but presumably they could be if they could locate the appropriate region of their normal terminals in the brain. This is not an example in which any neuron has been "modulated." The sensory cell bodies have differentiated in the periphery as part of the antennule. In the brain their terminals presumably make connexions that are typical if they can grow to the appropriate region. Doubtless numerous examples of this will turn up as peripheral regeneration is studied.

INSTINCTS AND INTERNEURON GROWTH

To the man in the street the instincts of animals seem to represent genetically built-in parts of behaviour that are comparable to hair or eye colour. However, careful analysis is necessary to establish that these actions are not learned. Sometimes this is clear for highly adaptive complex behaviour. The young European cuckoo, for example, having been reared by a foster parent of a different species, migrates *after* its parents. As an experimental technique, young animals are reared in complete isolation from any possibly relevant influence; when this is done it is found that some actions are nevertheless perfect and other actions less so. Birds will still sing (although the song is not perfected unless they hear their own species in song). Monkeys reared in isolation show a preference for models that resemble monkeys, although they may be incapable of even the most rudimentary social behaviour when introduced as adults to the colony. At a simpler level, actions such as eating develop in isolated mammals, but deeper analysis reveals that even the correlation of hand and eye or the visual recognition of objects, are achievements that are slowly perfected by a process in which maturation of interneurons and learning seem to be both involved. What happens in the visual pathway of the kitten (p. 322) may prove to be representative for mammals. In vertebrates that hatch from eggs, instinctive whole acts are more clearly laid down by the growth of interneuron connexions. Chicks, for example, will peck at spots at a certain time after hatching even if previously having never seen spots. Their accuracy nevertheless improves with practice. As long as the tendency is strong enough for survival, much can be left for improvement by learning, especially if the protected period of development is long. Of the few invertebrates studied, all seem to hatch or grow in isolation to a normal state without learning from their own species, except that some colonial activities are certainly perfected by learning. Baby squids attack the shape of their characteristic food without having previously seen it. The same must be true of most invertebrates, especially insects that emerge from metamorphosis, even though fine adjustment by learning can be expected. Bees learn the complex duties of the hive and dances of orientation from their hive mates under normal conditions, but they have the tendency to perform all these acts. This is shown, for example, by preventing the dance until an entirely new generation of bees has grown up that never had been in contact with dancing bees. When conditions favouring the dance are once more permitted, it takes only a few weeks before the standard rituals have been resumed. Resumption by trial and error is hardly likely. The only explanation of innate behaviour is that interneurons grow and mature their connexions in particular patterns, which are derived from their hereditary material. Sufficient has been said about the maturation of pathways to show that there are all degrees of specificity, and each individual case has to be examined to see how much detail is entrusted to subsequent learning processes. An unpredictable environment favours the latter. A simple quantitative question—such as how many synapses and neurons or which pathways are involved in the innate as compared with the learned part of any response—immediately reveals that the problems are understood only in the most general terms.

THE SIGNIFICANCE AND FORMATION OF NEUROPILE STRUCTURE

The complexity of neuron entanglements has not lessened since Bullock and I wrote the account in Chapter II of *Structure and Function*, to which the reader is referred. The last few years have seen a large number of electron microscope studies, which now begin to reveal a diversity of synaptic organelles at the electron microscope level, but few that relate to the challenging problem of the organization of neuropile. It is worth repeating that even an indifferently trained neurologist can distinguish between a histological preparation of the retina of a mammal, the neuropile of an insect optic lobe, or the plexiform layer of the optic lobe of an octopus, although these are all superficially similar regions of laminated neuropile that must perform comparable operations on the excitation from a retinal image. (In a compound eye there is still a spatial representation of the environment.) The differences between neuron patterns in different animals are obvious at family and sometimes at genus level.

In the formation of pattern, we suppose that each neurite branches as it grows through the neuropile during development and eventually forms its correct synaptic connexions by a chemical matching of its own cellular identity with appropriate partners. By such an expression we defer the question as to whether each synapse is determined genetically or in some other way. If chemical matching is the general rule, it follows that a patterned neuropile is not necessary, and that where it occurs it is an accident caused by repetition of growth processes. Organised neuropile would function equally well if the neurons reached their correct connexions by unspecified routes, to form a structure without recognizable pattern. Therefore the obvious spatial pattern of laminated neuropile, the constancy of position of cell bodies, tracts, and so on, may be of little significance except as a by-product of growth. Here, however, it is necessary to refer to the nature of the null hypothesis and the significance of a departure from randomness.

In science one method of approach is to assume the random situation and then infer that order exists by observing a significant difference from randomness. This is because there is less to specify about the random state. The enquiry, however, must be restricted to the topics of importance in the system under examination. The question of fibre directions is one of interest only to the observer, because the nervous system is directed by the way the fibres interact. An enormous departure from randomness has already been specified by the classes and subclasses of synaptic connexions, no matter which lies over or under which.

Although the evidence is sparse, it is a fair generalization to say that over the whole animal kingdom there is greater ability to regenerate the correct set of nervous connexions in ganglia with random neuropile than in those where it is obviously ordered. Where there are regularly repeated growth patterns, the number of rules that govern and limit the connexions can be reduced for the same number of fibres, but there is a greater chance of creating erroneous connexions when fibres regenerate in a sequence that is different from that in normal growth.

To see why this should be so, consider the case of a developing optic lamina in an insect. The retinal cells develop and grow their axons inward (Fig. 13.2). The retinula cells of one ommatidium of the fly obviously all differ from each other because they grow with regularity to different places (Fig. 9.12). Their neighbourliness in the ommatidium is replaced by a different arrangement in the cartridge of the optic lamina (Fig.

9.10). They grow laterally only a certain distance (for reasons that we do not understand, any more than we understand any of the morphogenetic factors), but the growing primary visual fibres evidently obey a few simple rules, which are the same for every ommatidium. Every cell No. 5 develops an individuality of its own, and its growing axon performs a certain contortion that brings it to the appropriate destination (Fig. 9.12). A feature of this and other similar patterns is that they develop progressively; the compound eye, for example, grows at its edge, and timing of the growth is important. Following a large lesion in an ordered system of this type, we would expect that some cells in No. 5 position in the ommatidium would make connexions intended for other No. 5 cells. If transplanted No. 5 cells managed to grow until they reached the intended terminations from their original places, we should have to admit the existence of additional rules. Certainly additional rules of some kind exist where long bundles of nerve fibres grow out *simultaneously* and still maintain a topographic representation of the area at one end as projected on a space containing their terminals at the other end. This is why the concept of rank order was introduced for regenerating fibres of vertebrate optic nerve (p. 305, see fig. 13.13). This, however, looks like being a rare state of affairs.

Figure 13.13

Types of projection from one region of the nervous system to another with reference to a theory of pattern formation by rank order, which depends upon the property of being adjacent to the next cell.

A. The cells *a* to *h* on the left project to the series on the right with no particular pattern. The only specification would be that a position on the right would no longer be available to a second fibre arriving upon it. Projections such as this are not known in any nervous system.

B. The cells here project in a reverse order upon the series on the right.

C. They project here in the same order, with an appropriate complex crossing of fibres. Projections like those in B and C occur commonly—for example, in the chiasmata between the neuropiles of optic lobes of arthropods. They could readily grow (and regenerate) if the connexions of each fibre were related to those of its immediate neighbours. The orderly projection could then be reformed in the new situation, whatever the size and pattern of the area over which they spread.

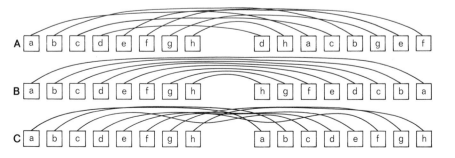

The point about simultaneity of growth is important. Compound eyes grow at their edges and we can imagine that the fibres that first arrive at terminals prepare adjacent slots for those that follow. In developing body segments with the same pattern of nerve fibres repeated in each, the anterior ones always grow first. Early maturing fibres land in early maturing slots, and presumably they modify neighbouring slots to receive a different class of fibre. This would constitute a simple rule. Instead of specifying every slot individually, a general rule can be based on pairing by rank order of age and by origin within the repeated unit. The rank-order concept—but in space rather than in time—is useful when considering examples in which long fibres, with simultaneous growth, regenerate a spatial projection, such as that of the vertebrate retina upon the brain.

Figure 13.14

Retinal ganglion cells of the rat, stained vitally with methylene blue. **Above:** camera lucida drawings of seven ganglion cells; **below,** the orthogonal projections of these cells. Cells A, C, E, and G are classified as "tight." Cells B, D, and F are classified as "loose." The dendritic expansions of the loose cells penetrate in depth to not more than 30 μm, whereas those of the tight type extend in depth from 30 μm to 60 μm. See also Figures 12.14 and 13.15. [J. E. Brown, 1965.]

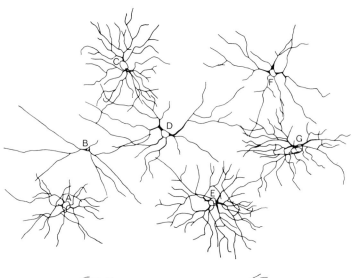

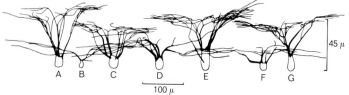

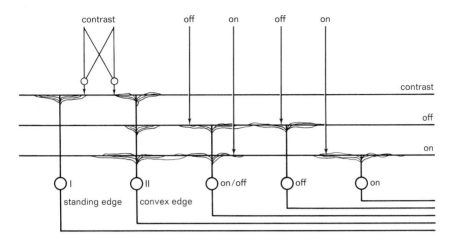

Figure 13.15

The importance of the distribution of dendrites in layered neuropile, as illustrated by a hypothetical interpretation of the types of ganglion cells in the retina of the frog by correlation of known functional types with anatomy. In the five main types shown, each is assumed to have a distinct pattern of dendrites; the known anatomical patterns consist of combinations of dendritic branches at different levels in the retina, as shown by the horizontal lines. The hypothesis that the peripheral layer of dendrites detects contrasting edges, the middle layer "off" signals, and the deepest layer "on" signals, agrees with the abundance of these functional classes. The system that is sensitive to contrasting edges is some kind of anticoincidence circuit, which must lie immediately behind the receptors. To be effective it requires small eye movements such as those normally caused by respiratory movements. [Schipperheyn, 1965.]

The second mechanism contributing causally to the ordered appearance of laminated neuropile is the repetition of arborizations. Like the same word written over and over again in script, the terminal of a particular class of neurons is always characteristic, but never quite identical in detail of twist and thickness (Fig. 13.14). In invertebrates, numerous individual neurons are frequently constant from animal to animal. The fabulous variety of diagnostic forms of nerve endings and synaptic contacts is one of the most impressive results of anatomy. Axons of different classes of cells that grow into the same region each develop their individual terminals, the form of which therefore depends on the individuality of the cell body, presumably determined by natural selection acting via the DNA and RNA of the nerve cells. The form and the function are, of course, inseparable (Fig. 13.15). Actual varieties are reviewed and illustrated in earlier works; in light microscopy, there are dozens of types: baskets, bushes, calyces, nests, tufts, interdigitations, climbing fibres, coils, clubs, or long threads, with rather less variety at the electron microscope level.

Bearing in mind much that has been said in Chapter 5, we may say that the pattern of arborization of a neuron has important consequences in its summation properties, acting via the space constant in each region, because each bit of every branch sums and conducts all potential changes electrotonically by cable theory. The space constant of most fibres is large compared with the size of synaptic terminals and small bushy arborizations. Although exact measurements are not available, it is still clear that large arborizations will not be depolarized uniformly or simultaneously. Another consideration, as yet of minor experimental importance, is that neuropile is sensitive in a consistent way to weak ionic currents (potential fields). Moreover, depolarisations in ordered arrays sum and generate fields. We just don't know whether mass effects, such as the large oscillatory potentials of insect optic lobes, are relevant to function. Field effects are not regarded as significant at the gross level in the mammalian cortex because inserted strips of foil have no obvious effects on behaviour. On a small scale, however, interactions cannot fail to be of significance. Many elongated pacemaker cells and endings are sensitive to potential gradients of about 1 microvolt per 10 μm and neurons in ganglia, if appropriately aligned, could be influenced by such gradients. The thresholds of spinal motoneurons are reduced by up to 30% by electrical field effects of short latency from active neurons in the immediate vicinity [30]. We are coming more and more to accept the notion that extracellular tissue currents have real effects on neurons.

One remarkable example of the ordered arrangement of neurons is in the mammalian cortex. Here there is vertical (radial) organisation into columns of cells, which have one feature of their receptive field in common. In the somatic sensory cortex those in a column are sensitive to one of the following: touch, pressure, joint movement, or hair movement. An adjacent area of the body projects to an adjacent group of columns. In the striate visual cortex, cells of the same column all have the same axis of orientation in responses to edges or slits. Within each column the projection is from approximately the same place on the retina. Striking differences have not so far been found between cells at different depths in the same column except in the auditory cortex (p. 239). Although there are lateral connexions by horizontal fibres, a curious property of the cortical system is that after vertical dicing by a large number of cuts down to the white matter, the behavioural discrimination of pattern appears normal, so far as subsequent behaviour shows. The necessary integration must occur between neighbouring columns and by deeply looping fibres that project through the white matter into other columns.

As described on page 269, we see more and more that ordered arrays of neurons in vertebrates serve a definite purpose: cells that are found close together are the ones that act together upon another cell at the next stage. The dendrites of the higher-order unit take a sum of the inputs upon them; the nearer together the groups of cells to be integrated, the fewer rules that need to be specified to determine the growth of their terminals. This is an explanation of the topographical layout of nuclei and within nuclei in spinal dorsal horn, spinothalamic nuclei, and sensory cortex.

SYNAPTIC CONNEXIONS DETERMINED BY FUNCTION

The formation of connexions has been considered so far in terms of sets of genetically determined rules, the operation of which need have no relation to the function of the final result. The remarkable results on the regeneration of the optic tract and the re-establishment of motor connexions to a limb in amphibians prove that the pattern requires no feedback from experience. But there is no reason to suppose that this mechanism is universal or occurs in the same neurons when they *first* connect in the embryo. In fact there is an excellent reason to suspect that connectivity of nerve cells in the cortex of mammals and perhaps at all relay stations from the primary sensory terminals onwards must be partly determined by some attribute of the normal excitation in groups of nerve fibres. It is known that normal input must sometimes be present for normal connexions to form in vertebrates, and must always be present for them to persist for long periods. The interesting question is whether the form of the connexions is determined by the form of the input *excitation*.

The mammalian cortex has an immense number of neurons. The genetic DNA is supposed to contain just about enough genes (10^5 to 10^7 cistrons) to determine the estimated 10^5 to 10^7 proteins and enzymes that ensure development. There is no possible way of seeing how 10^8 to 10^{10} cells of the cerebral cortex, each with possibly 1000 synapses, can be determined in all their combinations by genetic information. Expressed in another way, it took about a million years for the brain size of man to double in his evolution. This is very rapid, and could not have involved many mutations, but, if neuron numbers are approximately related to brain volume, 5×10^9 neurons were added to the brain in that time. Since not many new genes could be added in a million years, how could these extra neurons be genetically determined in their connectivity? It helps, but does not solve the problem, to suggest that numerous different connexions are determined by many relations between the effects of a few genes, because the nature of the relations must then be specified. One possibility is that the new connexions are just a reduplication of standard circuits that can learn or become adapted to the periphery; another way of expressing this is to say that the connexions are determined by the patterns of excitation. In all of his discussions of the subject, Cajal took the viewpoint that growth, which continues in neurons after the embryonic period, is activated by exercise or intensified function of those parts of the nervous system where it occurs. But only recently has good evidence for this appeared. Not surprisingly, the best evidence comes from the study of the establishment of connexions to cortical interneurons.

In the visual pathway of the kitten, fairly normal receptive fields can be plotted for single cortical "complex" cells of the striate cortex of the visually inexperienced newborn kitten. However, if one eye is sewn shut and the same area of cortex examined 3 months later, only a small fraction of cortical cells can now be excited by stimulation of the retina of the deprived eye. Furthermore, the cortical cells also progressively fail to respond to stimulation of an eye that sees only diffuse light without forms. Even those cells that respond are abnormal. Curiously, when *both* eyes are sewn shut, most cortical cells remain responsive and about half of them are apparently normal, although the remainder responded abnormally or not at all. At this stage the kitten acts as if blind (apart from a normal pupillary response), so that even though some cortical cells were excited, perhaps the units of still higher order failed to make proper connexions [51]. Apparently there is a period when plastic circuits are available for the development of the visual analysers, but the proper connexions cannot form with both eyes sewn shut.

Some groups of neighbouring cells in the striate cortex of normal cats are dominated by one eye, other groups by the other eye, with areas of mixed dominance. The division by ocular dominance is independent of the classification into receptive fields of different orientations. When the cat is prevented from seeing with both eyes simultaneously by covering each on alternate days, or when a squint is artificially introduced, there is a marked fall in the proportion of cells with binocular inputs. Evidently the convergence of signals from the two eyes failed to produce a meaningful pattern and convergence was eliminated. Even though one eye is dominant on a given cell, the connexions from the other eye are normally retained so long as they reinforce, although for real images in depth there cannot be exact duplication of signals from the two eyes.

In the cat this plasticity occurs only during the first three months or so of life. However, it immediately raises certain questions. Are such controlled modifications a feature of neuronal growth elsewhere? Is this learning? Could such changes on a smaller scale be the mechanism of all long-term learning? Evidently the formation of synapses on cortical visual binocular cells depends on the coincidence of incoming signals from the two eyes. We can add to the familiar concept of use and disuse something much more specific—the idea of the trophic interdependence of the synapses from different afferents on to one cell. The problem is how the cell knows when to reject synapses. Like the muscle fibres discussed on page 311, it may do so because it has a choice of several neurons, but the choice lies in the nature of their excitation, not in their history of growth. There-fore a neuron that finds itself over- or underexcited or on a nonsense schedule must be able to decrease or increase the number or change the distribution of its synaptic inputs in a direction that yields a more nor-mal pattern of its own activity. How might this come about?

POSTULATED CONTROL OF CONNECTIVITY
BY THE PRESYNAPTIC INHIBITORY PATH

Consider the problem facing a cell that is receiving an afferent supply from a variety of different axon arborizations, which refer to different receptive fields or modalities. The job of this cell is to respond to a par-ticular combination of inputs relevant for the further adaptive behaviour of the animal. First, how does it know the outcome of its own activity? Second, how does it pass a message back upstream to synapses between its dendrites and the incoming fibres, so that, if there is plasticity at all, more appropriate synaptic relations form? We must bear in mind that only a generally applicable explanation will suffice because it has to serve for an enormous variety of neurons at all levels in the mammalian CNS from dorsal horn and mitral ganglion to cortex. The only close-range feedback arc is the one typical of self-control by inhibition, and one such circuit is the presynaptic inhibition of sensory fibres, as described physiologically in the dorsal horn of the spinal cord (p. 204). When we inquire why the inhibition is presynaptic, we are given the answer that this circuit makes possible an inhibition of some inputs selectively, whereas postsynaptic inhibition would inhibit the whole cell. Apart from the theoretical objection that far out on a dendrite we might imagine that postsynaptic inhibition could also be local, we find that the presynaptic inhibitory circuit is a most interesting one. Here is an example of a purely nervous feedback circuit, although the examples known in the spinal cord have not shown themselves to be specific closed circles.

A feedback circuit composed entirely of neurons is easy enough to draw on paper or infer from experiment, but in the animal it has to grow. To do this, the circuit must somehow be able to join itself in a ring, which requires the recognition by a nerve terminal of another neuron that is in its own circuit.

The simplest hypothesis to explain how this could happen is that a chemical message, by which the neurons recognize each other, passes round the circuit. Consider a circuit (Fig. 13.16) having numerous inputs a–h, numerous principal integrating cells A–E, and numerous small cells 1–5. When cell A is too much excited, cell 1 will also be overworked, and it is not a long step to suppose that the overloading of the presynaptic

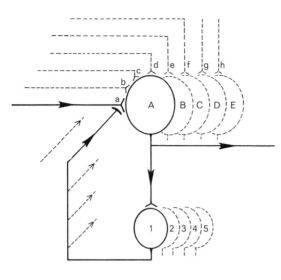

Figure 13.16

A simple presynaptic inhibitory circuit, the point of which is to draw attention to the passing of chemicals from cell to cell, which is necessary for such a circuit to be formed. In most known examples there are numerous endings on the cells and numerous afferent fibres, as suggested by the dashed lines. See also page 383 and Figure 16.4.

terminals will force some of the inputs a–c to leave and go elsewhere. This could regulate input qualitatively if specific substances that identified an individual circuit were passed from the first arriving terminals a–d to the cell A, thence to 1 and back to a, so regulating this feedback arc. It seems that a specificity of synaptic connexion in a feedback arc is possible only if there is a circulation of some chemical message of recognition around the arc, as postulated here. Similar arguments could be applied to any feedback loop, which necessarily requires growth in a closed circle.

We now have outlined a circuit (Fig. 13.16), which is inferred to be common in vertebrate sensory relays and which may apply to the cortex. The next step is to suggest that it is preadapted for learning: all that is required is a mechanism by which the small cells are suitably controlled by reinforcement to take up specific chemicals and thereby control those input fibres that are preferred in their connexions with the principal interneuron. That part of the story will be continued in the chapter on learning (p. 367).

DIFFERENCES BETWEEN NEURONS
IN THE EVOLUTION OF COMPLEX BEHAVIOUR

Vertebrates

1. Widespread trophic influences, including transneuronal degeneration, show that axon terminals can have morphogenetic effects upon nerve and muscle cells upon which they form synapses.

2. There seems to be insufficient genetic information to specify all possible synaptic connexions (possibly 10^{13}–10^{14} synapses in man) over and above the number of cistrons required for all enzymes and proteins. This is only one reason for supposing that synaptic connexions are governed by a limited number of rules we can hope to discover.

3. The vertebrate sensory cells lie in dorsal root ganglia and therefore are not differentiated along with their sensory field or labelled by their peripheral position, as in invertebrates. Necessarily, therefore, they evolved a mechanism whereby the chemical differentiation in the peripheral field is conveyed centrally along the fibre. Without such a mechanism there could be no central representation of the peripheral diversity with respect, for example, to dorsal and ventral or to responsiveness of chemoreceptors. Strikingly, the physiologically very diverse olfactory receptors retain peripheral cell bodies, from *Amphioxus* to man.

4. As a hypothetical general principle, chaos of neural connexions is prevented because one end of a fibre can make connexions in a way that is influenced by connexions made earlier at the other end.

5. This mechanism is supposed to have evolved progressively, so that more specific messages pass further and further from lower- to higher-order interneurons along a chain, with the result that line labels may be preserved in terms of relevant properties of peripheral receptors. For example, ganglion cell axons in animals with colour vision can form different classes under the influence of the different classes of receptors and retinal bipolars that are their inputs. There is no simpler way of preserving colour coding into fifth-order cells than by supposing a chemical coding passed from cell to cell.

6. The rules defining connectivity are permissive in a way that leaves no neuron without an output or input of some kind. This is, as least, the indication in vertebrates.

7. The same mechanism for limiting the formation of connexions has been applied to two other situations. (a) The ascending sensory interneurons form connexions at higher levels according to the chemical specificity of their input from primary fibres. (b) The dendrites of each motoneuron possibly make central connexions appropriate for the biochemical peculiarity of the muscle block that it first innervates in the embryo.

8. This ability to lay down a cell-to-cell sequence based on chemical specificity makes possible the progressive evolution first of reflex arcs and then of control from a brain, and of systems superimposed on more primitive locomotory methods, which depend on central rhythms.

9. In the primitive case, similarity of segments means a reduplication of the neuron sets in each segment, but the progressive evolution of distinctions between the segments, as cephalisation evolves, means that each segmental group necessarily develops its own individual chemical labelling. This longitudinal diversity can in turn be impressed on the inter-

neurons, thus making possible a separate central representation of each part of the longitudinal axis at a higher level.

10. Evolution of distinctions between segments means that motoneurons in different parts of the body axis can be chemically distinguishable along the long axis. Only then is it possible to evolve a mechanism whereby descending tracts convey commands from a brain to particular segments of the body, instead of a general arousal or a wave along axial muscles. With the possibility of making commands to different body levels, there is a selective advantage to a progressively better brain that perfects these commands.

11. The above conceptual framework suggests how the evolution of the connexions necessary for more complex behaviour patterns was made possible by a progressive increase of chemical differences between the neurons.

Invertebrates

12. The neuron connexions in most small invertebrates can probably be explained on the hypothesis that every neuron cell body differentiates epigenetically according to the site where it lies, and grows out an axon that makes connexions according to that differentiation. For many species, a fixed number of cells and a constant pattern is indicated by our present knowledge. Regeneration is always back to this pattern.

13. In higher invertebrates, there are lobes of numerous small neurons, thought to be concerned with learning, and this is where—if anywhere among invertebrates—flexible connexions occur.

To approach a readable prose, *presumably's* and *possibly's*, which by tradition betray the scientific writers' wariness, have been omitted throughout the above paragraphs. Neuron growth, along with the study of learning, is one of the most interesting fields of biology today.

REFERENCES FOR CHAPTER 13

1. Andres, K. H. 1964. Micropinozytose in Zentralnervensystem. *Z. Zellforsch. mikrosk. Anat.* **64**:63–73.
2. Arora, H. L., and Sperry, R. W. 1963. Color discrimination after optic nerve regeneration in the fish, *Astronotus ocellatus. Develop. Biol.* **7**:234–243.
3. Attardi, D. C., and Sperry, R. W. 1963. Preferential selection of central pathways by regenerating optic fibres. *Exp. Neurol.* **7**:46–64.
4. Birks, R. I., Katz, F., and Miledi, R. 1960. Physiological and structural changes at the amphibian myoneural junction, in the course of nerve degeneration. *J. Physiol.* **150**:145–168.
5. Bodian, D. 1965. A suggestive relationship of nerve cell RNA with specific synaptic sites. *Proc. Nat. Acad. Sci.* **53**:418.

6. Buller, A. J., and Lewis, D. M. 1963. The rate of rise of tension in isometric tetani of cross-innervated mammalian skeletal muscles. *J. Physiol.* **170**:67–68.

7. Buller, A. J., and Lewis, D. M. 1965. Further observations on mammalian cross-innervated skeletal muscle. *J. Physiol.* **178**:343–358.

8. Bunge, R. P., Bunge, M. B., and Peterson, E. R. 1965. An electron microscope study of cultured rat spinal cord. *J. Cell. Biol.* **24**:163–191.

9. Charlton, B. T., and Gray, E. G. 1966. Comparative electron microscopy of synapse in the vertebrate spinal cord. *J. Cell. Sci.* **1**:67–80.

10. Coghill, G. E. 1929. *Anatomy and the Problem of Behaviour*. Cambridge University Press.

11. Colonnier, M. 1964. The tangential organization of the visual cortex. *J. Anat. London* **98**:327–344.

12. Crain, S. M., and Peterson, E. R. 1965. Onset and development of functional relations within and between explants of mammalian spinal cord ganglia during differentiation in vitro. *Anat. Rec.* **151**:340.

13. Eccles, J. C., Eccles, R. M., Shealy, C. N., and Willis, W. D. 1962. Experiments utilizing monosynaptic excitatory action on motoneurons for testing hypotheses relating to specificity of neuronal connection. *J. Neurophysiol.* **25**:559–579.

14. Farbman, A. I. 1965. Fine structure of the taste bud. *J. Ultrastructure Res.* **12**:328–350.

15. Gaze, R. M., Jacobson, M., and Székely, G. 1963. The retinotectal projection in *Xenopus* with compound eyes. *J. Physiol.* **165**:484–499; **176**:409–417.

16. Gray, E. G., and Guillery, R. W. 1966. Synaptic morphology in the normal and degenerating nervous system. *Internat. Rev. Cytol.* **19**:111–182.

17. Gray, E. G., and Watkins, K. C. 1965. Electron microscopy of taste buds of the rat. *Z. Zellforsch. mikrosk. Anat.* **66**:583–595.

18. Guth, L. 1963. The problem of selectivity between nerve and end-organ following nerve regeneration, in *The Effect of Use and Disuse on Neuromuscular Functions*. E. Gutman and P. Hnik (Eds.). Prague. Publishing House of the Czechoslovak Academy of Sciences.

19. Guth, L., and Bernstein, J. J. 1961. Selectivity in the re-establishment of synapses in the superior cervical sympathetic ganglion of the cat. *Exp. Neurol.* **4**:59–69.

20. Gutman, E. 1964. Neurotrophic relations in the regeneration process. *Progress in Brain Research* **13**:72–114. Amsterdam, Elsevier.

21. Gutman, E., and Huik, P. (Eds.). 1963. *The Effect of Use and Disuse on Neuromuscular Functions*. Amsterdam, Elsevier.

22. Hamburger, V. 1962. Specificity in neurogenesis. *J. Cell. Comp. Physiol.* **60** (Supplement):81–92.

23. Harris, H., Watkins, J. F., Ford, C. E., and Schoefl, G. I. 1966. Artificial heterokaryons of animal cells from different species. *J. Cell. Sci.* **1**:1–30.

24. Hibbard, E. 1965. Orientation and directed growth of Mauthner's cell axons from duplicated vestibular nerve roots. *Exp. Neurol.* **13**:289–301.

25. Luco, J. V. 1963. The trophic effect of neurone activity. *Acta Physiol. Lat-Amer.* **13**:124–129.

26. Mark, R. F. 1965. Fin movement after regeneration of neuromuscular connexions: an investigation of myotypic specificity. *Exp. Neurol.* **12**:292–302.

27. Mark, R. F., Campenhausen, G. von, and Lischinsky, D. J. 1967. Nerve-muscle relations in the Salamander: possible relevance to nerve regeneration and muscle specificity. *Exp. Neurol.* **16**:438–449.

28. Maynard, D. M., and Cohen, M. J. 1965. The function of a heteromorph antennule in a spiny lobster, *Panulirus argus. J. Exp. Biol.* **43**:55–78.

29. Miner, N. 1951. Cutaneous localization following 180° rotation of skin grafts. *Anat. Rec.* **109**:326–337.

30. Nelson, P. G. 1966. Interaction between spinal motoneurons of the cat. *J. Neurophysiol.* **29**:275–287.

31. Oakley, B. 1967. Altered temperature and taste responses from cross-regenerated sensory nerves in the rat's tongue. *J. Physiol.* **188**:353–372.

32. Peterson, E. R., Crain, S. M., and Murray, M. R. 1965. Differentiation and prolonged maintenance of bioelectrically active spinal cord cultures (rat, chick and human). *Z. Zellforsch. mikrosk. Anat.* **66**:130–154.

33. Romanul, F. C. A. 1966. Reversal of the enzyme profiles of muscle fibres in fast and slow muscles by cross innervation. *Nature London* **212**:1369–70.

34. Sánchez y Sánchez, D. 1919. Sobre el desarrollo de los elementos nerviosos en la retina del *Pieris brassicae* L. *Trab. Lab. Invest. Biol. Univ. Madrid* **17**: 1–64, 117–179.

35. Scheibel, M., and Scheibel, A. 1964. Some structural and functional substrates of development in young cats. *Progress in Brain Research* **9**:6–25. Amsterdam, Elsevier.

36. Segaar, J. 1965. Behavioural aspects of degeneration and regeneration in fish brain: a comparison with higher vertebrates. *Progress in Brain Research* **14**:143–231. Amsterdam, Elsevier.

37. Singer, M., and Schadé, J. P. 1964. *Mechanisms of Neural Regeneration.* Vol. 13 of Progress in Brain Research. Amsterdam, Elsevier.

38. Singer, M., and Schadé, J. P. 1965. *Degeneration Patterns in the Nervous System.* Vol. 14 of Progress in Brain Research. Amsterdam, Elsevier.

39. Speidel, C. S. 1933. Studies on living nerves. II. Activities of amoeboid growth cones, sheath cells, and myelin segments, as revealed by prolonged observation of individual nerve fibres in frog tadpoles. *Amer. J. Anat.* **52**:1–80.

40. Sperry, R. W. 1958. Physiological plasticity and brain circuit theory, in *Biological and Biochemical Basis of Behaviour.* H. F. Harlow and C. N. Woolsey (Eds.). Madison, University of Wisconsin Press.

41. Sperry, R. W. 1963. Chemoaffinity in the orderly growth of nerve fibre patterns and connections. *Proc. Nat. Acad. Sci.* **50**:703–710.

42. Székely, Gy. 1959. Functional specificity of cranial sensory neuroblasts in Urodela. *Acta Biol. Acad. Sci. Hungar.* **10**:107–116.

43. Székely, Gy. 1963. Functional specificity of spinal cord segments in the control of limb movements. *J. Embryol. Exp. Morph.* **11**:431–444.

44. Taylor, A. C., and Weiss, P. 1965. Demonstration of axonal flow by the movement of tritium labelled protein in mature optic nerve fibres. *Proc. Nat. Acad. Sci.* **54**:1521–1527.

45. Uga, S. 1966. The fine structure of gustatory receptors and their synapses in frog's tongue. *Symp. Cell. Chem.* **16**:75–86.

46. Van Der Loos, H. 1965. The "improperly" orientated pyramidal cell in the

cerebral cortex and its possible bearing on problems of neuronal growth and cell orientation. *Bull. Johns Hopkin's Hospital* **117**:228–250.

47. Vera, C. L., Vial, J. D., and Luco, J. V. 1957. Reinnervation of nictitating membrane of cat by cholinergic fibres. *J. Neurophysiol.* **20**:363–373.

48. Weiss, P. (Ed.). 1950. *Genetic Neurology.* Chicago University Press. [Many of the main problems were posed in this volume, and there has been surprisingly little advance since.]

49. Weiss, P. A. 1955. Nervous system (Neurogenesis), in *Analysis of development,* B. H. Willier, P. A. Weiss, and V. Hamburger (Eds.). Philadelphia, Saunders.

50. Weiss, P. A. 1961. The concept of perpetual neuronal growth and proximodistal substance convection, in *Regional Neurochemistry.* S. S. Kety and J. J. Elkes (Eds.). Oxford, Pergamon Press.

51. Wiesel, T. N., and Hubel, D. H. 1965. Three papers on binocular vision in kittens. *J. Neurophysiol.* **28**:1029–1072.

52. Zelena, J. 1964. Development, degeneration and regeneration of sense organs. *Progress in Brain Research.* **13**:175–213. Amsterdam, Elsevier.

14

The electrophysiological approach to memory

THE PROBLEM

Memory is not well understood. We have little to guide us in the search for a mechanism, and the wide range of speeds and variety of learning suggests that there is not one universally valid explanation. An eventual solution can come only from analysis of the actual mechanisms at work by a variety of methods. Meanwhile, observations on behaviour of whole animals or models on a computer cannot be ignored; even electrophysiological analysis depends on a good previous knowledge of behaviour, and all plausible models are worth evaluation for whatever suggestions they may offer. Although great efforts have been made by workers in many varied disciplines, each discipline seems to look to another for a solution of the basic mechanism. Furthermore, the practical applications of a knowledge of learning mechanisms in man and animals are as yet almost unconsidered, though they will certainly be more far-reaching than the mere treatment of loss of memory or failure to learn.

So far as can be gleaned from the experimental psychology of whole animals, indications of physiological mechanisms are few, and they may be briefly summarized. Recall and recognition are so rapid that there would be insufficient time to run through the whole memory store. Parts and perhaps all of the store are stable structures; severe cooling, for example, does not destroy memories in animals that naturally withstand cooling. In mammals, stimulation of certain central pathways can produce a positive or negative reinforcement superficially similar to that produced by normal stimuli on peripheral sense organs. When given an opportunity to press a bar causing stimulation in some areas of the brain, experimental animals will persist in the activity until physically exhausted, even though all possible physical needs are satiated. This suggests that positive reinforcement circuits are directly accessible to stimulation. Learning is possible without a response or any movement on the part of the animal; in fact, there is no necessary coupling of stimulus and response. In retrogressive amnesia, which occurs in man after an accident, the memories that are longer-established often return in succession before the more recent memories, suggesting that they are laid down in successive layers. However, a common memory defect is the inability to say when a well-remembered event occurred in relation to other events, suggesting that memories, if laid down in layers, are not sorted through in the same sequence on recall. This is in close agreement with theoretical models based on many interneuron pathways in parallel. Sadly enough, most experiments on learning reveal nothing as to the nature or location of the mechanism: most of them achieve no more than a description of some aspect of a learned response.

Solving the mechanism of learning involves much more than discovering a "change in synaptic properties" or even a "formation of new connexions." From what we know already it is certain that changes must occur that can be so interpreted. Animals after learning behave as if they have some new synaptic connexions, but we are still ignorant as to whether this is in fact the case. If so, how are the changes in connexions controlled? What is the particular situation in which they exert their crucial effect? Exactly how are the changes derived from a particular set of variables in the outside world? Why have they an appropriate but no indefinite stability? One of the great difficulties is that in actual nervous systems a great many neurons are excited in any situation in which learning takes place. The activity of very many nervous pathways in parallel cannot be avoided even though it may not be essential for memory, and yet it remains a curious fact that the changes that are learned are reasonably independent of each other. All central nervous systems are composed of interneurons that influence to some extent the background activity of other interneurons. Despite this interaction and the use of each others' pathways, an anatomical pattern of interdigitating dendrites can classify, encode, and lay down a distributed engram, which then allows subsequent behaviour to be modified only by the relevant stimulus. The word "engram" is the name for the elusive physical change that must occur somewhere in an animal, which makes it different from other animals because it has learned something. The outstanding problem from the electrophysiologists' viewpoint is that engrams are remarkably separate from each other.

That the engram of long-term memory can be a stable bond we have no shadow of doubt, for it resists both electroconvulsive shock and cooling. Fundamental questions, however, remain. How do the partners in this bond come to be rearranged in the new combinations that must exist? Is the bond itself a new covalent link in a large molecule, a new adhesion between nerve fibres, or a physiological rearrangement (such as a change in resistance of an existing pathway)? The nature of the process cannot be inferred from the differences between trained and untrained animals because the formal design of a model does not relate to particular mechanisms; chemical, hydraulic, or electrical models can all be conceived. Therefore, to find out what happens during the process of learning, there is no alternative to a direct analysis during this time by a method that gives access to the appropriate region on a size scale suitable for the entities to be distinguished.

The training procedure for a freely moving animal involves many unknowable variables caused by its own movements, so that to define the total pattern of stimuli is completely impossible. In fact the stimulus situation has not been defined in adequate electrophysiological terms for any learning situation. An idea of the complexity involved will be gained from the mental effort of trying to define to oneself the information that a rat obtains from proprioceptors when running a maze or the information that an octopus obtains from its freely-moving eye when making a visual discrimination. When the experimenter records from units within the animal's nervous system he cannot abstract from the nerve impulses the relevant aspects of the complex stimulus pattern in the way the animal itself is able to. Only the next-higher-order interneurons do that.

APPROACHES TO THE PROBLEM

Pavlov's approach was to isolate a dog in a harness in a soundproof room and to reduce the background interference. He then presented automatically definable stimuli such as lights, electric shocks, the noises of a buzzer, and food. In such an experiment some of the variables can be isolated and controlled, but not the consequences of the innumerable fidgets of eyes and limbs. The simplification of the experimental procedure limits the analysis to reactions that do not make full use of the great complexity and subtlety of the dog's brain. Furthermore, in order to explain in terms of mechanisms, some aspect of the mechanism must be observed, and this cannot be done by working entirely on the externally observed responses.

Pavlov's method has been extended in the past two decades, first by recording evoked potentials on the surface of the dog or cat's brain, and then by recording from single units of the cerebral cortex in the region where impulses derived from the relevant stimuli arrive at the cortex and the evoked potentials are strongest. The results show that during the learning process there can be activity in the hippocampus that is not found at other times, and that units of the cortex can change their responses to the standard sensory stimuli that were used in the learning situation. However, it is still fair to say that the mammalian brain is a very complicated structure in which to try to distinguish the truly primary change during learning from *other derived consequences of that change*. All the neurons that we know fire either spontaneously or, so far as we can tell, when their dendrites receive an adequate synaptic barrage, which need be only a fraction of their optimum excitation cluster. If this is all we have to take care of, it follows that during the process of learning one or more neurons that were previously not spontaneous now become so, or they respond to an excitation cluster previously not effective. So far it has not been possible to isolate these neurons *and to know that they are the very ones that cause the primary change*. Many of the difficulties in doing so are inherent in the methods employed and in the properties of interneurons, as listed on page 407 and following.

The modern electrophysiological approach to learning is based upon the experimental observations on interneurons as they are known to act in places where learning is thought to take place. These studies, however, are as yet incomplete; most interneurons have not been recorded from, and the receptive fields of very few are known. In invertebrates, apart from a few examples of inhibitory interaction in arthropods and *Aplysia*, the interneurons so far isolated seem to be fixed in their receptive field, without nervous feedback loops that control their input, and without plastic changes that might be a sign of a process of learning. The electrophysiological evidence suggests that synaptic connexions formed during development of invertebrates produce a set of predigested messages, which are presumably those of most interest at the next stage down the line. Bursts of impulses in each pathway appear to be accepted on their face value as they are subjected to a further process of digestion. This relative fixity may be a product of our limited techniques, and named interneurons with adaptive changes will presumably be found that fit the requirements for learning in a creature with the performance of an octopus or bee.

In the mammal the size and complexity of the cortex leads us to assume that it is the seat of learning. A great deal of information is carried up to the cortex relatively undigested except for rather obvious transformations concerned with the exclusions of unsaturated elements in colours or sounds. Electrophysiology of units in the ascending auditory and visual systems of mammals, however, shows that below the higher-order cortical units there is little or no plastic behaviour or adaptive changes in the single units that have so far yielded to analysis. Most of the work on mammalian sensory systems has been done without reference to learning, and this initial analysis is far from complete or, for higher-order interneurons, even representative.

At the cortex *or not far away*, there must be a device, as yet unidentified, that can hold a register of a stimulus together with the corresponding interneuron response, until sufficient time has elapsed for the consequences to become apparent by a reward or a noxious effect. Furthermore, the same or a neighbouring device can isolate and go on holding a register that fits in with any engram surviving from the past. (By the term register I mean an excited group of interneurons, which, when they are active together, correspond to some particular stimulus situation.) A great problem is set by the awkward fact that the highest sensory inter-neurons, like those at lower levels, are only briefly excited by their adequate stimuli, often with only two or three impulses. It is also curious and noteworthy that only very strong or long-maintained stimuli have a long-lasting effect in the sensory cortex, although reinforcement can cause long discharges elsewhere. Sad to say—and despite a long history of theory—there is no evidence that temporary registers use nerve im-pulses, although there are no examples of a neuron using anything else.

Observation of units has shown that a particular "excited cluster" of interneurons is like a key that opens a lock, so allowing the next inter-neuron to be excited. A system of this kind will be rather difficult to analyse if the spatial organization of the excitation cluster is not reason-ably constant upon repetition of the stimulus. Although eminent neurolo-gists have warned us that analysis into fixed spatial patterns of rigid anatomical projections, especially in the reticular system, can never pro-vide an adequate explanation, I see their hesitation only as a statement that neurons are not individually recognizable, and that no experiment on a mammal is ever repeatable at the level of the interneuron. On each individual occasion there must be a definite spatial pattern of excitation arising from causes that presumably are not mysterious. We have strong evidence that each interneuron responds to a particular excitation cluster that feeds into it, and the excitation cluster must remain reasonably constant if the receptive fields and response properties of the interneurons are constant. Slight changes in any part of a synaptic array necessarily change the pattern of the excitational cluster that is passed on to the next stage. When it becomes possible to repeat a learning experiment in many single interneurons over long periods of time, we may have an experimental proof of what has long been suggested—that neuron con-nexions change.

Recently it has been shown that the responses of individual association neurons to a single modality stimulus are modified after exposure to pairings of that stimulus with one of another modality. Although the same phenomenon could not be found in insect optic lobes [16], it is clear that sensory-sensory association will be found in single units in appropriate brain lobes if sufficient experimental trials are run. Despite the formidable technical and overwhelming methodological problems, efforts to find changes in single units in the mammalian cortex during learning are proceeding intensely in several important centres in the world. Numerous reviews are available but actual startling results are few. One problem is to distinguish between primary causes of learning and secondary manifestations of it that spread from elsewhere. Changes will certainly be found, especially if the animal as a whole learns during the experiment, but it is difficult to show that they are relevant. The ultimate validation of the claim that any observed change is the cause of learning is to impose it artificially and produce a behaviour change. The point is that the learning may in fact have been established elsewhere. A technical problem is to identify cortical neurons again, once contact has been lost. The properties of enough units are not yet adequately defined—even in the sensory cortex—for us to hope to understand the function of higher-order units in the cortical association areas. Finally, from this large and complicated field it is not yet possible to abstract any general statements having explanatory value, which at the same time have a reasonable faithfulness to the known abstracting properties of the single units as set out in previous chapters.

Although the cortex of mammals is generally accepted as the seat of learning, it is necessary to stress that this may be so because it is the seat of sensory analysis. Undigested sensory data is not suitable to be learned, whereas the highly abstracted excitation of higher-order sensory interneurons can be considered as produced for the purpose of sensory-sensory association and coupling with reinforcement, internal or external. Perhaps analysis is inseparable from storage, but we must remember one of Lashley's most outstanding but most awkward observations. Bilateral removal of the visual cortex of the rat causes the loss of a brightness discrimination that had previously been learned, which *can then be relearned at the same rate*. Subsequent removal of the whole neocortex after relearning fails to eliminate the second memory, showing that certainly the second (and perhaps the first) memory was not located in the cortex [12, 25].

In a discussion concerning the mammalian cortex it is essential to stress that the difficult literature on the effects of lesions on behaviour and memory has not been integrated with the modern data on the receptive fields of units. Some of the difficulties set out by Lashley [25] are now even greater obstacles to understanding than they were when first enunciated. The so-called specific motor cortical areas were not (in 1950) an essential part of any known conditioned reflex arc. Conditioned reflex arcs do not extend across the cortex as well-defined paths. They are either diffused or pass by subcortical paths or do not exist. Memory traces, at least of simple sensorimotor associations are not formed or stored within the associative areas supposedly concerned with each sense modality. Learning is independent of particular sensory pathways and the response is to a pattern of stimuli that may vary widely in position or size and therefore in cortical projection. Similarly, a learned motor response is not a predetermined activity of particular motoneurons but is an act in which the objective is paramount. We can disallow some of Lashley's conclusions because the cues available to his experimental animals may have been more subtle than was thought at the time, but his general conclusions have not been overthrown. Now that interneurons that respond to generalized features of the stimulus pattern have been described, it is possible to suggest that they participate in learning to respond to a generalized stimulus. It is still true, however, as Lashley pointed out, that any sensory discrimination must involve thousands and perhaps millions of cells in the mammalian cortex and that "the learning process must consist of the attunement of the elements of a complex system in such a way that a particular combination or pattern of cells responds more readily than before the experience" [25]. Interference by lesion must be gross before a function defect is noticed in long-term learning experiments.

Some part of the success of the mammals is attributable to their development of special sensory projections direct to the cortex, thus bringing finer, less digested detail to a place where it may be dissected and for a time remembered. However, this does not mean that perfectly good learning cannot occur at any interneuron, so long as the result of its abstracting operations can be fed back to it by reinforcement interneurons. The mechanism need not lie in a higher learning centre. In the octopus there are pathways by which fibres from the mouth and skin reach the optic lobes directly, and there may be acts of learning without the upper lobes of the brain. Most vertebrates have little cerebral cortex. Ganglia of the insect ventral cord are capable of adaptive changes with an element of association [16, 18]. To me there seems every reason to suppose that any system of interneurons, however near the periphery, can be regarded as a potential learning system so long as there is an input from reinforcement neurons. The existence of each, however, has to be separately proved.

ATTEMPTED SIMPLIFICATIONS

Another approach is to look for the most elementary and primitive forms of learning that can be found with cleanly defined stimulus situations, either in relatively simple nervous systems or in small parts of a larger nervous system. Some of the lower animals might yield convenient material, but most of the lower invertebrates are not attractive subjects when we take into account the electrophysiological requirements. Neurons in nerve nets are difficult to locate and record from, and no nerve-net animal has proved capable of making a learned response of sufficient precision and repeatability, or provided fruitful concepts of general application. Flatworms, on the other hand, have provided some remarkable results: it has been claimed not only that they learn but that the learning is embodied in ribonucleic acid (RNA), which can be transferred by ingestion or injection to other individuals [27]. But flatworms have very small nerve fibres, which are not convenient for present methods of recording. Interesting learning changes there may be in flatworm ganglia but we cannot approach them. The same is largely true for annelids and molluscs: the majority of axons are too small for recording, and giant fibres, when tested, are not involved in associative phenomena. Soft-bodied animals are inconvenient for the attachment of electrodes, and thus are almost impossible subjects for the electrophysiology of learning, for when learning the animal performs best when free to move. Apart from the following, there is as yet no example of learning in an isolated part of a vertebrate nervous system.

In 1929, Di Giorgis noticed in a number of mammals that an asymmetry in the posture of the legs, caused by an appropriate lesion in the cerebellum, would persist after the spinal cord had been cut, thus isolating the limbs from the source. Other experimenters made similar findings for the frog and pigeon, and the topic has been recently reinvestigated in the rat [4]. The spinal cord must be intact for about 45 minutes after the lesion is made in the brain before the asymmetry becomes impressed on the leg centres. After this the postural asymmetry persists for many hours after spinal section. The mechanism is not yet known.

The learning situation itself must be selected to be amenable to analysis in terms of neurons. Such achievements as maze running by ants or homeward flight by bees do not lend themselves to convenient study, and the clear road of analysis runs too early into the sand of model building. The change in the neurons must be one that occurs over a relatively short time, unlike imprinting should be reversible, and should be one that can be started off at any time in an animal readily obtained in any laboratory.

The presence of large numbers of neurons is not a fundamental disadvantage if one has sufficient detail about their anatomical arrangement, about the regularities of physiological pathways, and about how to identify individual neurons when searching to encounter the same neuron more than once. These difficulties are as yet insurmountable in vertebrates, but some invertebrate preparations are more attractive. The special feature of the two systems to be described is that they have a persistent trace like a memory, but without the requirement for a temporary register while the results of a response to the stimulus are evaluated. The orientation memory of homing insects, the synthesis of seen objects from contours and the imprinting of the "mother" image by young ducklings may also turn out to have conveniently identifiable automatic recording and holding mechanisms that operate without reinforcement.

OPTOKINETIC MEMORY

An insect that walks along a bent grass blade and is thereby constrained to turn relative to its visual field tends to keep to the direction of its former track when given an opportunity at the next intersection; such behaviour reveals a persistent memory of the earlier rotation of the visual field. Movement perception by insects, and especially by crabs (*Carcinus*), is effective down to angular speeds of rotation around the animal of one revolution in three days. Perception of such a slow movement could possibly be based upon a memory of the position from which a contrast-

Figure 14.1

The arrangement used for making and recording drum and eye movements of the crab. In the actual experiment the crab is clamped with its eye at the centre of the drum and all the apparatus except the tiny photocell is outside the drum. A flag (*f*) cuts across a parallel beam of infrared light that shines on a pair of photocells (*p*₁). The photocells are clamped to the same adjustable support *s* as the infrared lamp, which contains a filter of black glass (*g*). The drum can be moved in a controlled way by a modified pen writer (*w*), which is activated by a low-frequency waveform generator, and movements may also be made between the adjustable magnetic stops (*m*). Drum movement is recorded by the photocell *p*₂, which is shaded from a small bulb (*b*) by an obliquely cut card (*c*). The dark period in memory experiments is marked on the pen recorder by a double switch (*d*). Records appear as in Figure 14.2. [Horridge, 1966.]

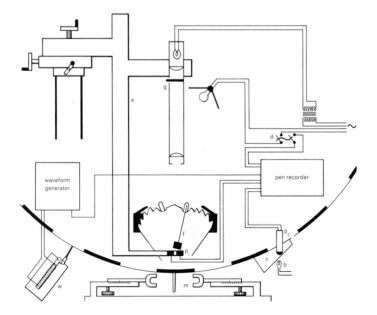

ing object has moved over a reasonably long period of time. It was this idea that prompted the following experiments [17].

A crab is clamped by its carapace in the centre of a striped drum (Fig. 14.1). The movement of the left (seeing) eye is recorded while the right eye is covered. The crab sees a stationary striped drum for a short time, its eye position becomes stabilised on the stripes, and the eye drifts when the light is turned out. When the striped drum is reilluminated after a short time in the dark, the eye moves back towards its former position. If the stripes have been moved during the dark period, the eye follows them (Fig. 14.2).

The crab remembers in some way the previous position of the image on its retina. About one minute of vision is required to build up the full memory of the first position of the striped drum, and this memory decays slowly during the dark over a period of fifteen to twenty minutes, as is shown by the progressive reduction of the response after longer periods of darkness (Fig. 14.4, C). A small movement of the drum during the dark period is equivalent to a drift of the eye in the opposite direction, and when working with short periods of darkness of ten to fifteen seconds the drift in the dark is small enough to be ignored. It is then possible to plot the response as a function of the angle through which the drum has been turned during the dark, as in Figure 14.3. The stimulus situation, for various fractions of the stripe period, is shown in Figure 14.4, A, in which each pair of lines represents the positions before and after the dark period. A human observer would interpret a shift of up to half a stripe period to the right as a movement to the right, and a shift of a half to one stripe period as a movement to the left. The periodicity of the response plotted against the angle of drum movement would have the same periodicity as the stripes. Locusts and some crabs behave in this way, suggesting that they "remember" areas of black and white as we ourselves would in the same circumstances. Other crabs, however, behave differently.

If the edges—irrespective of which side of the edge is black or white—are the feature of interest to the animal, the periodicity of its response will be twice the stripe period. When *only the edges* of the stripes are considered, a shift of $3/8$ of a stripe period to the right in the dark must be interpreted as a movement of $1/8$ stripe period to the left. This assumes that the animal makes no distinctions between the left and right sides of a contrasting stripe. When their eye is free to move, some crabs give responses that indicate a partial dependence on edges rather than areas. In experiments in which a striped pattern is continuously illuminated, the edges and areas move at the same speed, so that no distinction between them is then available.

Small movements of the eye on a scale similar to normal saccades can enhance contrasting edges relative to the areas, as follows. The right (seeing) eye of the crab is clamped to the carapace and records are taken

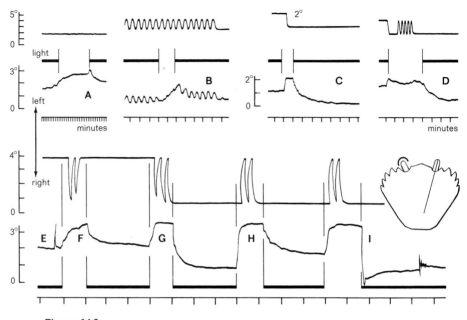

Figure 14.2

Eyestalk movements (*lower traces*) in response to drum movements (*upper traces*), which are completed during a period of darkness so that movement is inferred from the memory of the former position together with the new position after the drum is reilluminated.

A. Drift of the eye in the dark when the light is turned off, without drum movement, and recovery upon illumination. The eye moves across a stationary drum.

B. As before, but with a small oscillation of the drum. The eye responds to the shift of drum position when the light returns and at the same time follows the small oscillation.

C. A movement is made in the dark; the eye drifts in the dark and then responds on reillumination.

D. As before, but with an oscillation that is not seen during the dark period.

E. Spontaneous eye flick with return to the base line.

F–H. Responses with or without drum movement. The large movements of the drum during the dark period were to test for visual responses, which do not appear.

I. The response is here in the opposite direction on account of the large flick at "on." [Horridge, 1966.]

from the left eye, which is painted over. There is no visual feedback (see Fig. **8.7** and **14.5** for explanation), and therefore the blinded eye is now driven through an angle much larger than the apparent motion across the seeing eye. However, this arrangement allows a controlled tremor to be introduced at will into the motion of the stripes. With the stripes stationary relative to the seeing eye, the response is plotted for various

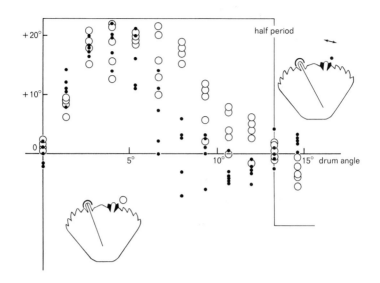

Figure 14.3

Movements of the left (blinded) eye of *Carcinus* in response to movements of a drum across the right (seeing) eye, which is clamped. Under these conditions there is no visual feedback and the response angles can be many times the stimulus angles. In this experiment the responses were plotted (*open circles*) for different movements of the drum when the crab, the seeing eye, and the drum were kept absolutely still while the light was on. The observations were then repeated with a constant tremor of 0.5° imposed on the drum at a frequency of 1 in 3 sec. The responses (*filled circles*) are now different, and this shows that tremor of the eye relative to objects in the visual field sharpens up contrasting edges relative to areas of light and shade. [Modified from Horridge, 1966.]

angles of shift made in a standard dark period. The experiment is then repeated with a sinusoidal oscillation of the drum of amplitude 0.5° at 1 per 2 seconds, applied both before and after the dark period. Comparison of the sets of results shows that oscillation causes enhancement of edges relative to areas (Fig. 14.3). Natural eye and body movements presumably act similarly, and this theory is based upon the assumption that the crab takes no account of the direction of its own small eye movements. In mammals the cells of the visual cortex respond only to changing visual stimuli, and known cortical responses depend on eye movements. However, as inferred on page 264, mammals have a mechanism by which the response of an individual cortical cell depends on which side of a tremoring black-white edge its receptive field is centred.

Although the optokinetic memory may reside in the long time constants of the movement detectors at a peripheral stage in the optic ganglia, this has yet to be proved, and it must always be borne in mind, as in much

neurophysiology, that distant parts of the nervous system might participate in what appears at first sight to be a simple local system. The
memory may be nothing but a long persistence in a system that lies in
parallel with the movement perception system and which carries a spatial
projection of the pattern on the retina; however, experiments designed
to reveal two separate systems always fail. Therefore, for economy of

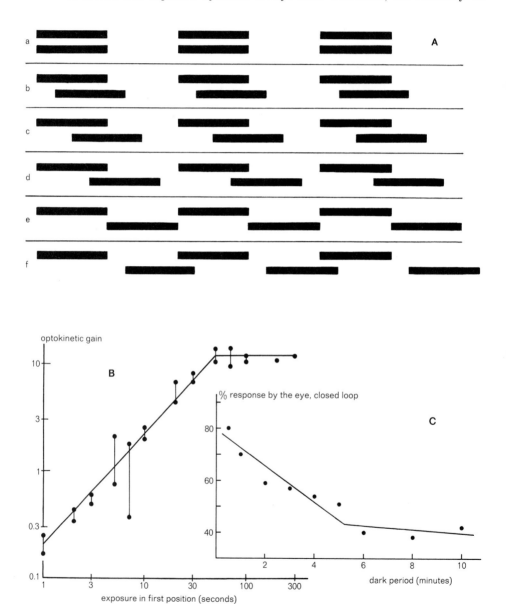

hypothesis, the memory is regarded as being dependent on the system that detects slow movement, as set out in Figure 14.5.

In any animal with a specialized eye, the necessity of assembling, from a background of irregular eye movements, a coherent pattern of signals from the outside world, means that short-term storage elements would be very useful on the visual pathway. The optokinetic memory of the arthropods is such an example as a system for detecting motion. The sustained edge detectors of the frog retina have a comparable feature (see p. 278). There are indications elsewhere of short-term visual memory in which reinforcement is not a consideration, even in man. If a contrasting shape 2.5 cm long passes behind a slot 1 mm wide in 0.2 to 0.5 sec, a reasonable impression of the whole outline can be seen, even though only a narrow slice of it is visible at any one instant [29]. In normal vision, when we scan a scene rapidly, we still get an impression of the world as stationary and entire. Such phenomena can be readily explained if there is an assembly of excitation for which exact time of arrival matters as little as exact location on the retina. If so, there must be some kind of automatic holding of registers without reinforcement in the visual pathway. The short-lived responses of units in the cortex of the cat suggest that if there is an automatic holding of short-lived memory it must be of higher order than the hypercomplex units or be in a separate parallel pathway.

In those instances in which there is evidence of a stored trace in a system that requires no reinforcement, the word "memory" has not been avoided, although the term "learning" has not been used. There is no reason why the mechanism should not lie in the long time-constant of a relatively simple system, but at present we have no idea of its nature.

Figure 14.4

Optokinetic memory.

A. The stimulus situations. Each pair of lines shows the position of the striped drum before and after the dark period. The crab eye sees the stripes in the first position and then moves to the right when the lights come on with the stripes in the second position after the dark period. Pairs of lines (*a–f*) show movements by 0, one-eighth, one-quarter, three-eighths, one-half, and five-eighths stripe period. For different reasons no movement is apparent in *a* or *e* and to the human eye the movement in *f* appears to have been to the left—that is, three-eighths. The actual stimulus to the crab is more complicated than this because edges can be accentuated relative to contrasting areas.

B. The buildup of the memory with time of exposure to the drum as seen in the first position. A period of about a minute is required for the full memory effect to be observed. The drum movement was about 1° throughout.

C. The decay of the memory with time, as tested by varying the dark period during which a standard drum movement was made. In **B** and **C** the ordinate shows a measure of memory. [A and C from Horridge, 1966; B by kind permission of P. B. H. Shepheard.]

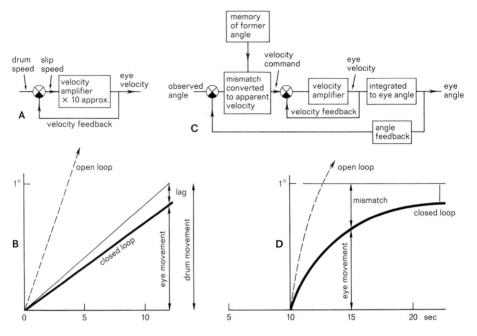

Figure 14.5

The optokinetic response (**A** and **B**) compared to optokinetic memory (**C** and **D**).

A. Box diagram of the response of an eye free to follow a moving stimulus.

B. The response and the stimulus plotted against time. The angles through which the stimulus and the eye move are plotted upwards. The response of the eye is shown as a *thick line,* and under closed loop conditions (when the eye is free to move) the eye always lags behind the stimulus. The open loop response (when the feedback from eye movement is eliminated), shown as a *dashed line,* is greater than the stimulus at some stimulus velocities.

C. The block diagram that represents the memory experiment, including the diagram **A**, which represents the response to a continuously moving stimulus.

D. The response plotted against time in the memory experiment. The stimulus is a movement made during a dark period, which must therefore be inferred when the illumination returns. The drum is always stationary when seen, but the response is nevertheless explained as a consequence of the mechanism of the perception of movement.

POSTURAL LEARNING IN INSECT THORACIC GANGLIA

When a large insect is suspended in the air by the thorax, the legs make spontaneous stepping movements from time to time, and it can be arranged for the leg to receive a shock whenever the foot falls below a specified level. A convenient experimental arrangement is to hold the animal over a dish of saline, which delivers shocks to it at about 1 per 2 sec for as

long as the leg (or rather, a bit of thin wire attached) dips into the
saline (Fig. 14.6, A). Locusts, stick insects, or cockroaches learn in a
few minutes to hold up the experimental leg for long periods. The arbitrary
height of the saline solution can then be raised, so increasing the "demand," and the leg will be held higher. The result is similar whether the
head is removed or not, and an isolated ganglion with a leg shows the
same change [16].

The change in behaviour could conceivably be caused by the repetition
of the unconditioned stimulus (the shock), whatever the position of the
leg, and might have nothing to do with the position at which the shock
is consistently received. As a suitable control, experiments use animals in
pairs. One member of each pair, the P animal, receives shocks when the
leg falls below a definite level. The electrical current of this shock flows
through a thin flexible wire to the tarsus of the second animal, called the
R animal, and so back to the stimulator to complete the circuit. The two
animals are in series and receive identical sequences of shocks; the P
animal gets a shock whenever its leg falls and the R animal gets the same
shocks as the P animal, no matter what it does with its own leg. In fact,
the P animal changes its behaviour and holds up its leg, but the R animal
does not hold up its leg, or at least not so much. After running them together in series in this way, the performances of the P and R animals
are tested separately, each in identical conditions over its own dish of
saline. The P animals now give themselves few shocks, just as at the end
of their period of training, but the R animals usually perform worse than
naive ones (Fig. 14.6, B).

The animals can be allowed to walk about between training and testing,
and the improved performance on retest remains after several hours. Animals trained on one leg and then tested on a different leg performed better
than naive animals, showing some degree of transfer between legs.

There are a variety of different movements by which the leg can be
raised, and if one movement is prevented the animal will quickly adapt
and use a different one, apparently by trial and error. The one thoracic
ganglion in the segment of the leg is sufficient to make significant differences between P and R animals. The static posture of the leg is of little
importance in comparison with the improved ability of the ganglion to
behave adaptively when the animal is placed once more over the dish
of saline. All these experiments work in the absence of the head.

In the cockroach the giant fibre response is modified along with the
other changes in leg movement. In a naive animal a puff of air to the anal
cerci causes the hind legs to flick downwards and backwards so that the
animal jumps forwards. When trained not to move downwards, the metathoracic leg instead moves only backwards or even upwards. This shows
a change in emphasis between motoneurons to the different leg muscles.

The leg of an animal trained over the saline sometimes controls its
movements in a remarkable way in relation to the level of the liquid

surface. After training to a given level, a P leg is lowered extremely slowly towards the point where it touches the surface. The leg may even be lifted by an apparently spontaneous withdrawal just before it actually touches the surface (Fig. 14.7). In fact, the dish can be removed altogether and the leg will sometimes go on responding by a withdrawal when it falls to the position at which it formerly received a shock. The precision of

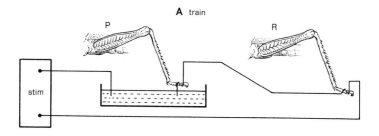

A train

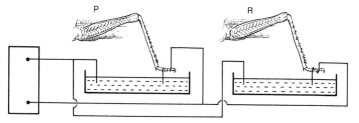

B test

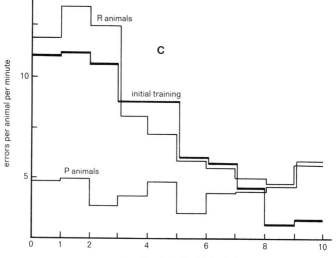

R animals

C

initial training

P animals

errors per animal per minute

time after start of test (minutes)

this "remembered" position in relation to all possible positions is accurate to about 1 part in 2^3 or 1 part in 2^4, and therefore would be achieved by a memory of 3 or 4 bits.

An electrophysiological continuation of the leg learning has been made by Hoyle [18], who recorded the frequency of motor impulses in one of the principal muscles, the anterior coxal abductor, which holds up the leg. Fortunately this muscle gives a train of impulses of constant height from one motor axon. The leg can be removed, or the attachments of the muscle cut, so that there is no movement or possibility of proprioceptive control. A stream of impulses flows spontaneously from the ganglion to this muscle; a fall in frequency of these impulses causes a fall of the leg, and a rise in their frequency lifts the leg. The stump of the leg nerve can be given an appropriate electrical shock, just as the whole leg was shocked with bipolar electrodes in the experiment with the whole animal. When a shock is given to the leg nerve at times of spontaneous falls in impulse frequency, there is a gradual rise in frequency after a few repetitions. The frequency below or above which a shock is given corresponds to the adjustable height of the saline in the dish. Similarly, when a shock is given at each rise in frequency, the frequency eventually falls. A ganglion can be "trained" to produce a frequency between two given limits, by combining an upper and a lower demand level. When the same average number of shocks is applied at instants that are not correlated with output frequency, there is no change in the frequency, and ganglia so treated do not learn so well if subsequently placed on the normal learning schedule (Fig. 14.8). The frequency range over which control is possible is 10 to 50 per sec. The time course of the change in the electrophysiological experiment is about the same as in experiments on whole animals, but the process is not necessarily steady or consistently in one direction.

The shocks cannot be applied successfully to any other nerve except the one functionally related to the muscle.

Figure 14.6

Postural learning of leg position by the metathoracic ventral ganglion of a headless locust.

A. The arrangement of the connexions to P and R animals from the stimulator. In the initial training the two animals are arranged in series and both animals receive shocks when P lowers its leg below the critical level.

B. For retest, the animals are separated and each receives a shock when it lowers its leg below the critical level. Any of the six legs may be employed, and the animal may be trained on one leg but afterwards tested on a different leg.

C. Results from an experiment in which right metathoracic legs of locusts were trained and tested on the same leg. The numbers of shocks for twenty P and twenty R animals are plotted for each minute interval following the start of the retest. The corresponding numbers of shocks received by the naive P animals when first trained, shown by thicker lines, are similar to those made by the R animals on retest. [Horridge, 1962.]

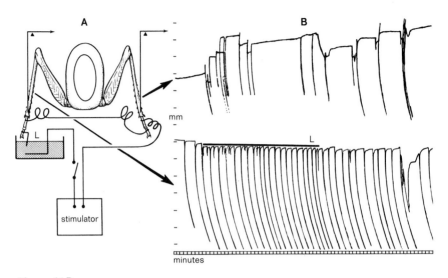

Figure 14.7

Simultaneous recording with a light isotonic kymograph level (loading weight 0.02g, magnification 9:1) of the two metathoracic legs of a headless locust.

A. One leg receives shocks whenever it falls below a definite level (L) and makes contact with the saline solution (as shown by the horizontal line on the trace in B). The other leg is connected in series with the first leg so that it receives the same shocks whatever its position.

B. Simultaneous records from the two legs as indicated by the broad arrows. Upward movements of the legs are downwards on the figure. The switch was closed only for the period shown by the horizontal line (L), during which time about 25 shocks were received, as shown by the numerous downward strokes on the trace, each followed by a gradual drift back to the level of the shock.

After the current is switched off, the leg that could learn the position of the shock holds itself at about the same level as before, with intermittent movements, as shown at the right hand of the lower trace. The other leg, which had no opportunity to associate the shock with any particular level, shows irregular changes in position throughout. Large downward arcs are the traces of spontaneous leg-lifting movements.

From this experiment we can infer several things. First, a part of the control of the muscle that raises the leg is achieved by a mechanism that takes into account only the frequency of the efferent output of motor impulses to the same muscle. This implies an ability to measure the efferent frequency in some way, and, moreover, to associate its spontaneous changes with the reinforcement. This mechanism now has to be borne in mind as possible in other long-term behaviour changes, and especially as contributory to the control of posture in arthropods, and perhaps elsewhere. Perhaps it is the most appropriate means of detailed adaptive control in a system in which the occurrence of centrally controlled sequences means that proprioceptive information is not immediately required for the coordination of movements. If other examples appear, the phenomenon will merit the special term of postural learning. Second, not many neurons can be involved because the ganglion contains only about 2000 of them, most of which must be concerned with other aspects. The cell body of the relevant motoneuron lies in a constant, verifiable location and—even if not related to other forms of learning—any changes in this cell, or other parallel changes, will be of interest. Third, the results suggest that if the proper technical approach can be

Figure 14.8

The frequency of motor impulses to the muscle that will raise the metathoracic leg of a locust, showing the different effects of shocks applied to the leg nerve with and without opportunity to make an association. A low frequency of motor impulses corresponds to a fall of the leg if it were free to move, but the experiment works as well if the leg apodeme is cut, or if the leg is removed altogether. Each dash represents the mean frequency in a 10-sec interval.

A. Responses when shocks are applied (as shown by the inverted V's) at periods of low impulse-frequency, with progressively higher demand frequencies of 12, 15, 20, and 30 per sec, as indicated by the dotted lines. There is a progressive increase in frequency, which keeps above the demand level. The arrows show spontaneous inhibitions arising in the ganglion.

B. Responses when shocks are applied (as shown by inverted V's) at instants that do not correspond to particular changes in impulse frequency. The average frequency remains approximately constant and then subsequent efforts to use first a controlled lowering and then a rise in the frequency (as shown by *solid triangles*) do not lead to significant changes. This corresponds to the observed failure of animals to perform reasonably over a saline dish after they have acted as *R* animals with shocks not related to leg position. [Hoyle, 1965.]

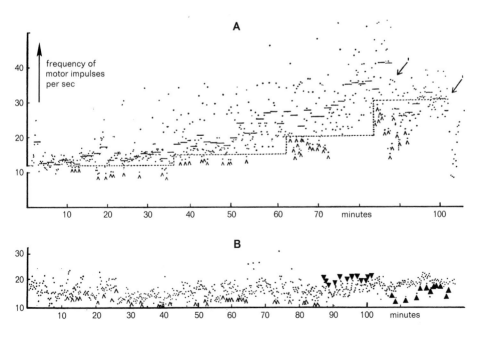

discovered, long-term changes with adaptive consequences may be found in many small groups of neurons, irrespective of their position in the nervous system or in the animal kingdom. Finally, a line can still be drawn between habituation or threshold changes and the examples in which there is a definable association of two variables. The insect leg preparation had the opportunity to associate a shock with the position at which the shock was consistently received; the corresponding isolated ganglion preparation associates a nonspecific punishment with an immediately preceding change in background rate of efferent impulses. Let us persist in calling these changes *learning* by virtue of this residual element of association. Since association requires convergence of two kinds of information, the electrophysiologist knows that a point of interest lies where the convergence is physically located. Whatever the ultimate cause of learning, the next step is to discover the changes in detail in this ganglion, and to investigate whether the same technique may be applied to interneurons as well as motoneurons.

INTERNEURONS AND MECHANISMS OF LEARNING

Ideally we seek situations in which single neurons exhibit some property that is acceptable as learning. Then we attempt to discover the mechanism. To simplify the problem of choosing a stimulus, learning is defined as the formation of an association between two aspects of the stimulating conditions. One direct approach is to pick out interneurons from a likely area of a brain that learns, and then test them with combinations of controlled stimuli. This has recently been achieved in the mammalian cortex and is discussed on page 334. Although we surveyed a variety of interneurons of the locust brain and optic lobes in an effort to find neurons that illustrate the association of sound and light or of two visual stimuli, we failed to find anything acceptable as learning [16]. However, in the course of the study we met numerous general problems that influence all efforts of this kind. First, when changes are observed, their source is never known to lie in the cell under examination. Second, even if the animal as a whole is learning, it does not follow that any of its component neurons will illustrate learning of the same kind. Whatever change occurs in the individual neurons, it may be quite a different phenomenon from what we may expect from the action of the whole group. Finally, when units are found with changes that can be accepted as association, as in the mammalian cortex, this is essentially one step too late in the process. We are not really looking for the effect, but for changes that cause it, and they are not likely to be recognized as connected with the learning.

These comments apply if recordings are made blindly with unidentified cells. However, if the anatomical wiring diagram is already known, the behavioural output secure, and the function and interaction of all neurons of the pathway known in detail, it may *then* be possible to isolate the critical change in a well-defined learning situation.

Of the long-term changes readily observed at unit level, the most common is habituation. Some units in the optic lobe of locusts take many hours to recover their full sensitivity after being stimulated. On the other hand, as an example of a much rarer phenomenon, some units of the mammalian cortex continue to respond for hours at an abnormally high rate after a very bright flash or 5 minutes of stimulation. Novelty units are so called because they respond with a few impulses to a novel movement in the receptive field, but are then silent until a new movement is introduced elsewhere in the receptive field. This behaviour, which is known in frog optic tectum, arthropod visual systems, octopus arm units, and mammalian sensory systems, even at spinal level (p. 206), need have no element of association. It is most easily explained as local habituation in a neuron that has a widely ramifying dendritic field, so that some of the inputs can habituate and leave the rest fully sensitive. The common occurrence of wide-field units strengthens the view that they have an important function, such as arousal or reinforcement.

Direct observation of long-term synaptic changes while two or more inputs are coupled together is becoming feasible as more is known about the connections between identifiable cells in certain convenient animals. In some *Aplysia* neurons it is possible to produce long-lasting changes in the effectiveness of presynaptic impulses, either by repeated use of one synapse or by heterosynaptic activity [23]. Changes that are brought about by one synapse alone are always a waning of responsiveness with repeated stimuli at each 10 or 20 sec. When two or more inputs are combined, some particular patterns produce a progressive facilitation, and with a few known cells the augmentation of the synaptic potentials is specific to the pairing process. In other cells it is less specific and resembles a sensitization. The increased sensitivity lasts ½ to 2 hours. A very powerful inhibition, with effects lasting for ½ hour, is caused by synaptic activity of certain cells upon others in *Aplysia*, and the wave forms suggest that a persistent substance is released. Interpretation, however, depends on the assumption of the simplest circuit. It is difficult to see how these studies are related to learning in *Aplysia* because no behavioural correlate is available. However, we can readily imagine that long-term changes in other situations are caused by persistence of transmitters or specific chemicals. The problem is to find a definitive test to show that this is the mechanism of association if we already know that the primary causative change of a well-defined learning situation occurs in that particular neuron connexion. An example is known in the cockroach, in which a change in a synapse of the metathoracic ganglion has the same time course as a change in leg usage after removal of the prothoracic legs [26], but again it is not clear whether this is the primary change, or how the observed synaptic change plays a part as a causative agent in modifying the complex postural behaviour. At present there is no way of deciding how long-term synaptic changes, habituation in interneurons, and its cancelling by other stimuli, are related, if at all, to the phenomena to which the term learning is more acceptably applied.

THE ORIGIN OF LEARNING

The detail of the circuits necessary in any learned response cannot be suddenly produced, and they must have evolved readily from pre-existing circuits. The capacity to evolve learning may exist in all interneurons, especially those involved in feedback loops (see p. 367). A selective discrimination of movement of a stimulus in visual or tactile systems necessarily involves a delay mechanism; if very slow movements are perceived, the time constants may be so long that the term "memory" is acceptable. In the case of the octopus, which learns to attack or ignore a visual stimulus, the learning must be built into and upon the visual interneurons at the most peripheral level where they distinguish one generalized stimulus from others. The touch sensory system of all animals must be organized in such a way that it operates the muscles that cause the appendage or whole animal to draw away from an object which, if touched, causes an accompanying unpleasant reaction. In these examples, the learning must depend upon interneurons where the discrimination occurs. There would be great economy if the interneurons that achieve the discrimination are the ones that learn. By some means, a system based on immediate pain or pleasure is then evolved to give a special response to those discriminated stimuli that were coupled with past pain or pleasure. This is why considerable importance is attached to the idea that the pain circuits of the spinal cord are primitive learning circuits, and that these have been progressively more elaborated anteriorly as head sense organs became more dominant in behaviour. In numerous animal groups, the neuropile areas and groups of small cells thought to be associatory have evolved from higher-order sensory centres.

That interneurons which achieve the abstraction to the level required are the ones where learning changes occur (at their *outputs*) is a hypothesis that agrees with many observations. There is abundant evidence that the optic ganglia of fish, arthropods, and octopus, for example, are analysers that are also the site of storage of visual memory traces. For simple auditory stimuli, a good deal of learning can occur in decorticate cats (see p. 239). In the tactile system, experiments with split-brain cats have shown that the learning is restricted to an island of the cortex in the tactile area; all the rest can be removed. For visual stimuli, however, leaving the island of the visual cortex but removing all the remaining cortex results in an animal that cannot learn visual cues; moveover, vision is practically absent. This difference between the various systems correlates well with the degree of abstraction achieved by the interneurons of the different systems at the different levels. Learning is not possible after removal of the interneurons that discriminate the complex cue. If we argue from Lashley's classical demonstration that the relatively small parts of the cortex remaining after ablation make relearning possible, it follows that all that is required is that one or a few interneurons *somewhere* must make an adequate discrimination and must do it in relation to the reinforcement neurons. This again suggests that reinforcement pathways can be identified with some widely ramifying interneurons.

TEMPORARY TRACES

Short-term storage of information, as studied by recall experiments with man, appears, from its time relations, to depend upon changes at the neuron membrane, which outlast the stimulus by only a few seconds. Persistent transmitters, graded depolarizations, or trains of spikes may all be involved, but there is no clear-cut positive evidence as to the mechanism. The short time scale favours a theory of physiological modification of existing pathways and not the formation of new pathways. Evidence that every stimulus sets up a temporarily persistent change, which is then disturbed and overlaid by subsequent signals, is provided by numerous demonstrations that recall is possible only if a further stimulus is not superimposed within about one second. The temporary change evidently lasts only for about a second, and is not recalled unless the animal makes some behavioural or internal perceptual response in this time. The neurons involved seem necessarily to be the ones that respond to patterns. This is the basis of the theory, expressed in this chapter, that longer-term memory is the result of a consolidation by a temporary additional activity of a widely ramifying reinforcement neuron. The time course of this short-term memory agrees reasonably well with the length of evoked bursts of spikes or rebound phenomena in many neurons scattered throughout the animal kingdom. From this point on, the consolidation can be a trophic or secretory phenomenon, and there we are even further from reliable signposts as to its nature.

MAINTAINING THE ADDRESS IN A MEMORY SYSTEM

A stream of sensory impulses flows all the time in most sensory axons. Some excitation clusters (for definition, see p. 396) excite interneurons or combinations of them that can be distinguished as analysers or classifiers. Before a classical type of association can be established in learning, there must be an interaction between the pleasant or unpleasant consequences of an action and the sensory pattern that gave rise to the response and had been represented some time previously in these analysers. Therefore, whenever more than one signal can be discriminated in a learning task, a temporary trace must be held for a short time in order that the signal fed back from the consequences can contribute towards making a permanent consolidation only at the appropriate place in the analysing mechanism of the association centre. This labelling of a temporary trace at the appropriate sensory analyser is called maintaining the address. For example, in learning to associate a warning colouration with an unpleasant flavour in an insect, an animal has to remember the appearance of the insect until it has been out of sight in its mouth for some time. *Before the reinforcement*, the animal must remember the visual impression of the insect it takes into its mouth. Similarly on the motor side—for example, in learning to walk or skate—the detailed pattern of an order to move must be remembered for a short time after it has been made, before the consequences come in. One of the difficulties of improvement lies in remembering exactly what was done. We can reasonably suppose that the same principle applies for interneurons, wherever a difference in the effectiveness of some inputs relative to others would exert a crucial effect upon the features they abstract. There is evidence from work on mammals and from human psychology that short-term memories are numerous and qualitatively different from long-term memories, and also that short-term memories are important in the establishment of long-term ones. Many theories of conditioning [3, 9] ignore the requirements set out in this section.

MNEMONS

In his Croonian lecture for 1965 Young proposes a unit that he calls the mnemon [36]. He derives this concept from a simplification of a hypothetical interneuron pathway leading to either advance or withdrawal behaviour in the octopus. The mnemon is a minimum circuit that learns a yes/no decision, based upon interneurons that classify sensory excitation. To be a useful concept it should, of course, be applicable to other animals. Examples of classificatory systems have been amply illustrated in previous pages, but the optic interneurons of frogs and arthropods, the auditory, tactile, and visual interneurons of the cat, and the central interneurons of arthropods provide the best examples. As yet few of these have yielded indications of learning, but I believe that as the appropriate experimental tests are made, more and more examples of associative learning will be discovered in interneurons.

If excitation in interneurons leads to more than one possible output, there must exist a switching system that changes the probability of action of the various output pathways. Learning implies only that this probability is modifiable by the consequences of the action that was the result of that particular switching. The mnemon is simply a reduction of this circuit to the bare essentials, consisting of the choice point and the positive and negative feedback from the pleasant or unpleasant consequence of the choice (Fig. 14.9). By the choice of output I mean not only motoneurons but also (and more especially) higher-order premotor interneurons or "command fibres."

Figure 14.9

The components of a mnemon and the suggested mechanism for maintaining the address during learning.

A. A single mnemon. The classifying interneuron responds to a particular type of event and has two outputs, which produce opposite motor effects—attack and retreat. Following one action, a signal that returns to the same mnemon can either reinforce or inhibit the action, with opposite effect on the antagonistic action. The small inhibitory cells, which inhibit the unused pathway, must have synapses that can be modified, but it is not clear how this is supposed to occur.

B. A mnemon of the optic lobe of the octopus connected with four parts of the vertical lobe of the octopus brain, in a way that could ensure that a signal for a good taste or a pain could come back to the appropriate mnemon. This presupposes that the nervous system can differentiate purely neural loops, which itself implies a peculiar form of recognition between growing neurons. *VU* and *VL,* upper and lower vertical lobes of the brain. [Young, 1965.]

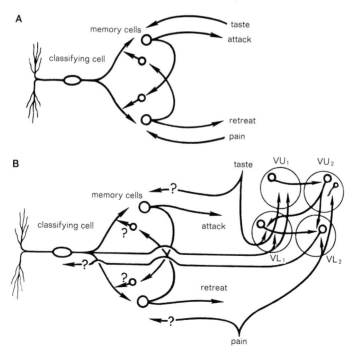

The central assumption is that each of the classifying cells must be able to operate the switching for a negative or for a positive response. To quote Young, "This would be achieved if its axon divides and makes synapse with output cells of the two types" (Fig. 14.9). The system is biased towards the output, which promotes exploration, attack, or approach to an unfamiliar object. The result of this action is fed back, either by a pathway that reinforces what was done or by an alternative pathway that has the opposite result. Young suggests that collaterals of the smaller cells bring in inhibitory cells with a long-lasting effect that breaks the unused pathway, thereby increasing the tendency for the positively reinforced pathway to be dominant.

It is unarguable that a system bearing some formal resemblance to this must be present because the results of an action are certainly fed back to a point preceding the premotor interneurons that make the ultimate decision to act. It cannot be otherwise, although reinforcement may be fed back to other places as well. But several aspects of the model are doubtful. First, the small cell components of the mnemon (Fig. 14.9) are generators of inhibitory transmitter, whereas their great numbers in association areas suggests that they act in some way as a store. Second, repetition of an action without reinforcement would keep closed the pathway leading to the alternative action, and there is no evidence that this occurs. Third, there is no evidence that the minimum memory circuit has so few cells, or that classifying cells have as few as two effectively distinct axon terminals; rather the opposite is true—they act in clusters. Fourth, reinforcements such as obtaining food or finding a mate are not so short-lived or immediate as to operate on the same time scale as the impulses in neurons. Reinforcement neurons must have effects on a time scale more in keeping with slower changes of the "excitational set" or the tendency of interneurons to be excited by one particular impulse cluster than another, as postulated below (p. 396). Finally, in all their actions, interneurons are not in a position to make choices: they act as they must with their given set of connexions, like Mrs. Bedonebyasyoudid in Charles Kingsley's *Water Babies*, and it takes time for the consequences of their outputs to work back to them.

A simple circuit of realistic interneurons which will make associations must satisfy the following requirements. (a) There must be a convergence between conditioning stimulus interneurons and positive reinforcement interneurons. (b) There must be convergence between conditioning stimulus interneurons and negative reinforcement interneurons (pain or abnormal or "unsatisfied" patterns of input), so that the latter "veto" the effector system. (c) Signals of the results of every action must be delivered back to the correct addresses—that is, must involve pathways that are the same as, or specifically related to, the interneurons that abstracted the sensory stimulus that led to the action in the first place. (d) Before there is any reinforcement, a record of events as they occur must be kept in a short-term memory by a mechanism in which they have little influence upon analysis.

The temporary memories must be subsequently identified if the decisions turn out to be "pleasant" or "unpleasant." Putting together (c) and (d), we infer the following. (e) There are a vast number of circuits by which certain patterns of inputs are temporarily connected to particular outputs; the results of these outputs are then fed back into the system of connexions so that responses which are rewarded are perpetuated and responses that are punished are abolished. The essential feature is that activity in a part of a circuit must be accompanied by a brief *persistent sensitivity* to punishment or reward. Every stimulus that excites a sufficiently large excitational cluster to be analysed at all must cause a temporary change in the responding circuits. This change will not necessarily be discernible by any neurophysiological test, other than one that repeats exactly the appropriate conditions. The point is that the effects of reward and punishment are widespread and not specific, but it is only recently active circuits that need be sensitive. If the period of sensitivity following activity were not both temporary and localized, the effects of reinforcement would spread to all circuits. In contrast to this method of maintaining the address of the reinforcement, back to the correct interneuron, Young proposes a specific line to each [36]. The difficulty about this approach is that a shape learned for one part of the visual field is learned also for the other parts. To explain this aspect, Young supposes that a specific signal carrying information about the nature of the successful discrimination spreads throughout a layer of neurons of similar function. I suppose, in contrast, that all interneurons on the analysing pathways are temporarily sensitized by their own activity, so that they subsequently respond to widespread reinforcement interneurons. The address the reinforcement acts upon is responsive and reveals itself because it has recently been active. The over-all feedback loops, carrying pain and reward —which are the universal teachers—must have access to all points that can learn or modify the stability of the system.

HOW DOES A SYNAPSE "KNOW" WHEN TO CHANGE?

Numerous mechanisms of learning have been suggested at the synaptic level, but they all suffer from the disadvantage that they are not specific. If interneuron connexions are modified, as changes in the behaviour suggest, the individual synapses effecting the change must "know" that they are the ones involved. This is why so much importance has been attached to the maintenance of the address, and one of the reasons why a mechanism for the control of growth of connexions of individual neurons is developed later in this chapter. Less specific effects on synapses are well known.

Post-tetanic potentiation is an increase in the ability to transmit, following repeated excitation at a synapse. A large number of impulses are required before minor effects are seen, and it is significant that in the newborn kitten the effect is reversed [32]. We are inadequately informed about other factors—such as the effect of repeated synaptic action on the movement of calcium and other ions, on active organic ions, on mobilization or persistence of transmitter substances, or on neighbouring glial cells—to be able to say whether any of these can be sufficiently sensitive and specific influences in modifying the pattern of synaptic connexions. Neurons and their synapses in tissue culture make movements in response to currents in the range 10^{-10} to 10^{-7} amps/μm^2, and current density at a synapse has been calculated as being in this range. These electrokinetic displacements form the basis of a recent hypothetical mechanism of learning [9], but the question at the head of this section remains unanswered.

Recently there has been an interesting suggestion that neurofilaments in some way carry information leading to the establishment of connexions. "The degree of specificity that would be required in different parts of the nervous system may be expected to vary; and it would not be unreasonable to suppose that the degree of specificity required in the spinal cord, where neurofibrillar boutons are common, is not required in the organization of the cerebral cortex, where they are rare" [14]. Although this hypothesis refers to genetically determined connexions, it emphasizes that learning by formation of new connexions implies that many circuits are genetically not determined, but remain to be established by functional events.

Whatever the nature of the postulated change at the membrane level, I cannot see how the region of the membrane that changes acquires from the nerve impulses the information that it is the region that must modify itself unless it receives some substance from the postsynaptic region. Postulated mechanisms based upon potentials fail by reason of their generality. Parts of a membrane, bearing many different synapses, are depolarized together. When every neuron responds to many stimulation patterns and every neuron is bombarded by many synapses, it is difficult to see how a particular pattern can be selected. Synaptic currents seem to carry insufficient information to determine the switching of one circuit rather than another. We therefore turn to mechanisms that involve differentiation and secretion of substances in individual neurons.

NEURON ACTIVITY, RNA, AND MEMORY

It has long been known that nerve cells are rich in ribonucleic acid (RNA), which has acquired a significance in the past decade as the carrier of genetic information from the deoxyribonucleic acid (DNA) of the nucleus into the cytoplasm in each cell. The information-carrying power and specificity of the RNA molecule is beyond doubt. When a mixture of the two from one species is prepared artificially, some forms of RNA will reversibly wrap themselves round the DNA, settling along those lengths of the DNA where the nucleotide bases of the RNA fit some sequence of those of the DNA. In the living cell the RNA from the nucleus in some way determines the sequence of aminoacids in the proteins that are synthesized in the cytoplasm [28].

We can presume that there is a good reason why nerve cells contain relatively large amounts of RNA—more RNA polymerase, weight for weight, than liver cells—and are so actively engaged in protein synthesis. One proposed explanation is that memory somehow finds a local habitation in the molecular sequence acting as a code in DNA, RNA, or proteins. This topic is singularly difficult to summarize at the present time, but it would be unreasonable to omit it from this account, even though full justice cannot be done. Curiously, it is RNA that has become implicated, although until recently it was assumed that only DNA has the low turnover rate that makes molecular coding an attractive proposition for long-term memory.

From the number of papers now appearing on the transfer of learning between small mammals by injection of extracts from one into another, there now seems no doubt of the reality of a phenomenon of some kind [27]. A wide variety of tasks, including operant and classical conditioning and discriminations, have been reported as transferable. The most recent studies, however, suggest that the active principle in the extract has a molecular weight of 1000 to 5000, that it persists after contact with RNA-ase but is destroyed by protease [30]. A doubting reader could still conclude that an active substance transfers a tendency for a particular kind of activity that would somehow fit the learning test rather well.

Changes (usually decreases) in the cytoplasmic RNA and proteins follow increased activity of neurons in both vertebrates [28] and invertebrates [7]. Changes in the RNA of large cells of the vestibular nuclei are found after prolonged vestibular stimulation, and it has even been shown that electrical stimulation has a smaller effect than natural stimulation [21]. Differences in the base ratio of the RNA of neurons have been found as a consequence of training and also a correlation between rate of RNA synthesis and the establishment of a learned response. However, the significance of changes in cytoplasmic activity is not understood, apart from the mobilization of cytoplasmic RNA caused by damage to the axon, which results in increased growth of the neuron.

The influence of antimetabolite drugs, which block various points in the synthesis of protein, is one of the few tools in tackling this problem. Guanine, one of the components of DNA and RNA, is mimicked by

8-azaguanine, which, when incorporated, blocks further synthesis of protein. When injected into the brain cavities of rats, this substance reduces their ability to learn but appears to have no influence on previous memories. There is some evidence that tricyanoaminopropene, which is supposed to increase neuronal RNA, accelerates an unknown central process whereby asymmetry can be impressed upon spinal neurons that coordinate posture in mammals [22].

Work on fish has followed the same lines. In one experiment a fish learns, at a signal from a light, to swim over a hurdle in order to avoid a shock. The antimetabolite drug puromycin, which blocks protein synthesis, prevents the fixation of a memory that would otherwise be readily demonstrable on retesting, but has no effect on a well-established memory trace. The time required for the memory to become immune to the puromycin is one to two hours at 18° to 19°C, but is longer at temperatures of 8° to 9°C. The drug has no demonstrable effect on the ability of the fish to swim and act normally. When puromycin is injected before the training begins, there may even be an initial short-term improvement in performance, but a long-term memory is never established and the fish return to the naive state. Therefore short-term memory and already established long-term memory are not sensitive to puromycin, but long-term memory fails to take over the information from the short-term system when protein synthesis is blocked. A criticism of this work is that the protein metabolism in mice has to be blocked so severely (80%) in both hippocampus and cortex that the failure to form a long-term memory might arise from any number of secondary effects. Moreover, other antibiotic drugs (such as acetoxycycloheximide) block protein synthesis but have no effect on memory; worse, they counteract the action of puromycin in mice [11]. Mice in which 96% of protein synthesis is blocked by actinomycin D learn and remember as though normal [5].

The claims of those who work on learning in flatworms have become extraordinarily difficult to evaluate impartially. Both head and tail sections will regenerate in flatworms, and there is some evidence that after being allowed to regenerate for one month both halves appear to learn faster on retraining than similar regenerates that were not previously trained. Doubt has been cast on the reliability of the results by others trying to repeat them. In another set of experiments, worms fed with chopped trained worms were found to learn more rapidly than controls fed with untrained worms. Here again there is a difficulty in finding substantiated repetitions by criticising scientists. It was inferred that a chemical substance carried the memory, and that the substance is RNA. Regenerates kept in dilute RNA-ase solution perform less well than those kept in pond water; injection of RNA-ase causes obliteration of memories, so that a complete retraining is necessary to bring to criterion once more;

finally, worms injected with RNA extracted from a trained animal learned faster than worms injected with RNA from pseudoconditioned or from naive animals. Moreover, the RNA from trained animals was no longer effective when treated with RNA-ase [27]. Although many critical scientists have attempted to *repeat* these experiments, there have been no reports of success. Whatever the final issue, the following comments seem pertinent.

What do we mean by statistical significance in a situation in which many groups are attempting to make experiments work, when success seems to depend on ill-defined details of arrangement, sliminess of mazes, and so on? If 100 experiments are performed and one of them turns out to be significant at the 1% level, is this proof or disproof?

When conclusions are based on rates of learning or number of trials required to reach criterion, it is impossible to say that the mechanism acts via the specific memory or via a general effect on the motivation or activity of the animal. So far no widely repeatable results on planarians meet this criticism.

Recently a report has appeared that RNA from brains of rats trained to take a left- or a right-hand choice caused a transfer of a tendency to turn in the appropriate direction when injected into naive rats that were tested in the same two-way choice situation [20]. This experiment escapes the previous criticism, which had suggested that sensitization and changes of motivation are the primary effects of the injections of RNA, because the transferred effect is specific for the task and is not just a general influence on set or motivation. A real difficulty at the present time is that many of these experiments cannot be repeated in other laboratories. For this reason alone it is too early to say whether the experimental result, let alone the interpretation, is valid. There is a notable letter in *Science* for August 5th, 1966, in which 21 authors from 7 major institutes report their failure to repeat the transfer experiments.

Other drugs unrelated to RNA also have an influence on learning. Mice exposed to a one-trial learning situation lose their retention of the experience if given an electroconvulsive shock 10 minutes later. However, those mice that have received a small dose of strychnine immediately after the training do not lose their retention when shocked 10 minutes after training. Strychnine and other analeptic drugs that bring the short-term memory more quickly into a permanently stored form are known to block postsynaptic inhibition, and therefore they cause more neurons than normal to be nearer threshold. Any treatment that acts at this point could modify the fixation of memory, and experiments intended to be upon RNA might have been influenced by this other system.

Apart from the suggestion that RNA injections can transfer a specific tendency to turn left or right, none of the evidence shows that RNA carries the memory code. In fact E. Roy John points out [22] that puromycin blocks protein synthesis for some hours but has no known effect on RNA synthesis. Therefore, if the information were coded into RNA, it should reappear when the protein synthesis starts up again after the puromycin effect wears off. Furthermore, blocking protein synthesis with actinomycin does not interfere with learning. The relation between RNA and learning seems to be this: any experience that makes the nerve cells more active makes them synthesize more protein, and during this activity the relative amounts of the different sorts of RNA in their cytoplasm can change drastically and rapidly; the memory could, however, still reside far away in the nerve terminals.

Taking all these results together, and arbitrarily rejecting some of their conclusions, it seems reasonable to distinguish three periods of time in memory experiments with mammals [1]. First, an initial phase of seconds or a few minutes, sensitive to electroconvulsive shock and analeptic drugs (strychnine) but not to antibiotic drugs. A second phase, of a few minutes, is inhibited by temporal lobe injections of puromycin in mice, but is not sensitive to actinomycin or acetoxycycloheximide. This suggests that growth or protein synthesis is involved, but there is no direct evidence as yet of the growth of nerve terminals (see p. 367). In the third period the memory is in a more permanent form and is insensitive to cooling, drugs, shocks, or anything except further training. This can be interpreted as a new distribution of synaptic effects, with neurons acting as if they have new connexions.

CRITICISM OF THE RNA THEORY OF MEMORY

Apart from the very real scientific doubt that the experiments are repeatable and the technical question as to whether they are properly controlled and interpretable in no other way, there are theoretical difficulties in accepting RNA as the substance that stores memories by the specific structure of a molecular code. There would be similar difficulties in accepting a protein molecule as a carrier of the code.

(a) The route by which a pattern of impulses in many neurons becomes coded into RNA is not imaginable as an extension of present scientific results, because RNA is replicated from DNA or RNA, which are rather stable molecules. The replication of RNA is known to be a flexible, impressionable system—for example, only in transforming experiments in which other DNA or RNA is involved. Outside circumstances acting at the time can influence the fidelity of the replication process, and in differentiating systems the control is exercised by the selective stimulation of some of the existing complement of cistrons. However, no process is known by which the information content of DNA or RNA can be "read in" from a system of a different kind. This is brought into focus by comparison of the velocities of learning and of information transfer in chain molecules.

(b) There is no reference as to whether a particular neuron makes only one RNA, corresponding to one memory, or whether all neurons make all kinds. Either way, we are faced with a problem of a message carrying no address of its location, and a read-in and a read-out problem for which no known mechanisms are available. Our survey in Chapter 1 of specialized transport mechanisms in cells revealed no channels that could feasibly carry the necessary amount of information between the synapses and the DNA or RNA and back again.

(c) The experimental situations have involved tasks in which there has been so little information content in the behaviour that a construct as complicated as RNA is not required to explain it.

(d) In the transfer experiments, when RNA is injected it is presumably immediately broken down by RNA-ase in the tissues. In mammals the individual nucleotide constituents would not penetrate the blood-brain barrier. Specific sequences of bases in the RNA molecule would not be retained. To add to the difficulties, it has been shown that radioactive RNA does not reach the brain when the standard methods are used. The RNA is not likely to have been pure in any experiments made to date, and an effect of a protein contaminant has already been demonstrated [30].

(e) In the transfer experiments, the injected RNA molecules would require a set of instructions comparable to a set of addresses, because to act within the nervous system each RNA molecule would have to arrive at its appropriate effective site. There is no reason why this traveller's guide for finding its destination in the brain should be built into the RNA molecule, because RNA normally is formed and acts within its own cell.

(f) The problems of read-out and read-in are even more acute for a transfer to a different species, which has been claimed.

(g) Mice treated with actinomycin-D learn and retain as well as controls, even though 94–96% of RNA synthesis is stopped. The brain is therefore not dependent on RNA synthesis for at least 4 hours [5]. The lobster stretch receptor neuron functions normally for many hours despite a complete inhibition of RNA synthesis [7].

Not only the neurophysiologists are shy of macromolecular memory stores. Much of the above criticism is based on the comments of biochemists: "there is no evidence justifying going beyond the statement that these cellular constituents are part of the whole metabolic system of the cell. None of the experiments demonstrate how the stimulus is carried from its entry, the synapse, into the cell, and how it is transferred to the cell nucleus, which is assumed to be responsible for the fixation of informa-tion received. Neither do any prove that nucleic acids or proteins are the primary substrate for the storage of information" [35].

Having now taken into account the work and ideas of others, the reader will perhaps not now be surprised if I produce my own theory of the learning mechanism, which is not related to any of the others and does not contradict them or the experimental data.

THE HYPOTHESIS OF "REINFORCEMENT" UNITS

When we turn away from the electrophysiological data, the biochemical evidence, and the computerized autocorrelation coefficients, and survey the enormous literature on learning from behaviour studies and psychology, we find another series of theories and controversies. Most are hopelessly naive when matched against the complexity of behaviour or the subtlety of the properties of interneurons, and all of them must incorporate the neurophysiological findings before the subject of learning theory can advance. However, one psychological concept that the neurophysiologist in his turn cannot reject is reinforcement, positive and negative. Within the nervous system there must be many reinforcements besides pain, elec-tric shock, food, drink, and sexual satisfaction, which we recognize as effective. Electric shock, the most widely used reinforcement in animal experiments, causes a burst of nerve impulses in a pattern that is not that of any normal stimulus. The next most powerful incitement to immediate action is the recognition of a sensory pattern previously associated with a favourable or unfavourable situation.

To be effective, the unconditioned stimulus (US, the reinforcement) must not precede the conditioned stimulus (CS, the one to be associated). Therefore, in some way the interneurons carrying the US can be distin-guished from those carrying the various possible CS's, and the US inter-neuron impulses must arrive after the CS impulses. Mere convergence is not enough for an association to be formed. In some instances, such as the formation of connexions to binocular cortical visual units of the cat from corresponding points on the two retinas, the motivation (if we can call it such) is the matching of impulse patterns of two sets of fibres that converge upon the one binocular unit. But in learning as normally con-sidered the impulses from the conditioning stimulus must in some way be consolidated by the subsequent arrival of impulses from a reinforcement of external origin. The two distinguishable inputs must be coupled by a physiological pathway already in existence.

The hypothesis of reinforcement interneurons that have a special power in establishing connexions from a new excitation cluster upon a cell, which thereafter recognizes and acts on that excitation, means that the learning problem is reworded in electrophysiological terms. A restatement, however, cannot be a solution, which will be reached only when such interneurons are demonstrated and the mechanism of establishing connexions found. If I had to hazard a guess, I would suggest that neurons with very widespread arborizations, as in Figure 14.10, must have an extraordinarily widespread function—such as reinforcement. Learning may be readily obtained in mammals when stimulation of the diffuse projection thalamic system is used as an unconditioned stimulus. During the reinforcement stage, either classical or instrumental conditioning techniques promote rapid learning.

Instead of postulating reinforcement interneurons, others have suggested that glial cells, electrolyte movements, or similar physical changes might ensure that a change "common to a set of cells in coherent activity changes the probability that the set will subsequently display coherence" and "such patterns of activity are released when retrieval of information occurs" [22]. Commenting on John's theory, suffice it to say that changes in glial cells are more likely to be consequences, not causes, of learning. Still influenced by Lashley, Roy John steers away from theories that suppose that particular neurons learn particular tricks, but I see no reason why the storage of memory cannot be the necessary response of particular cells, albeit distributed ones. Interneurons are necessarily excited in wide constellations as well as in tight clusters. The emphasis upon the "hot spot" in an excitation cluster, as amplified by a maximum amplitude filter, together with projections to other areas, implies that a large lesion in one place on the cortex will lead to new "hot spots" at other places. The ghost of Lashley can be circumvented, if he cannot be answered.

Figure 14.10

An extensive neuron of the reticular system of the brain of a 2-day-old rat, from a Golgi preparation cut sagittally near the midline. The axon has an anterior branch as far as the hypothalamus (*dotted outline*) and a posterior one to spinal cord nuclei, with ramifications in at least a dozen brain nuclei. [Scheibel and Scheibel, 1958.]

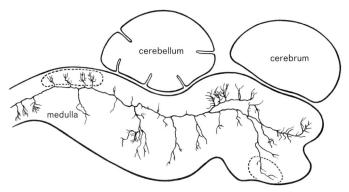

Reverberation in circulating feedback arcs has often been cited as a contributory means of converting short-term memory into long-term memory. Reverberatory circuits have never been observed in experiments, but this does not imply that none exist. As in the recognition of learning in single units, it may not be possible to identify a reverberatory circuit among a mass of other neurons, even if it were on the end of the electrode. The attractiveness of the reverberation theory really stems from its ability to carry over excitation of impulses and synaptic potentials from the 1–10 millisec range into a longer time scale of 10 msec to 10 sec. In fact any long-lasting effect will do as well, and persistent inhibition, particularly presynaptic inhibition, is equally attractive as an explanatory concept. It requires a very bright flash of light or peripheral or local electrical stimulation for at least 5 minutes before long-term increases in firing rate occur in the sensory cortex of mammals [10]. There is no evidence that short-term reverberation would be more effective.

A puzzling feature of the cortex is that direct stimulation of it in man must last for 0.5 to 1.0 sec or else a conscious experience is not reported by the awake human subject. Perhaps this much time is required to fatigue the inhibitory circuits that cut out meaningless combinations of impulses. Despite this finding, we can make an overt response in 0.05 to 0.1 sec to a sensory stimulus when a short reaction time has been acquired by practise. This suggests that most excitation clusters never find their way into consciousness, even if they excite a cortical circuit, because they are immediately blanked out by inhibition. The excitation clusters that persist are those that do not correspond with the pattern of inhibitory damping out. By definition, these are the learned, interesting, or important ones. By means of its persistent or successful activity an excitation cluster that is not damped out can have a special effect in the growth of a new circuit from that time onward. The question is what actually happens at this stage: what is the process of fixing a memory in place?

There is some suggestive evidence that cortical association depends on inhibitory feedback loops. Several workers have shown that direct electrical stimulation of the cortex causes long-lasting inhibition [24]. The shocks can be so weak that when applied alone they have no overt effect; however, when coupled with other stimuli, a direct shock to the cortex becomes associated, and subsequently a response is made directly to it [6]. The interesting feature, related to inhibition, is that positive shocks are reported as being more effective than negative ones. Inhibition is a common feature of responses of cortical cells.

Inhibitory feedback loops are a feature of vertebrate sensory nuclei and of fibres descending from the cortex (see Fig. 16.4). On page 324 it was proposed that the growth of a closed circuit of inhibition can be explained only by the passing of specific chemical messages from cell to cell around the ring of fibres. Once this mechanism is available it is preadapted to the learning situation, because the connexions to an integrating cell can now be controlled by trophic influences from the cell itself. Theoretically any unit has access to information as to whether it has the right set of inputs, because after being active it can recover from the periphery the consequences of its activity. This mechanism could operate in any closed neuronal loop with either pre- or postsynaptic inhibition. Only the former is considered in what follows. In Figure 14.11 the inputs are *a* to *f*, the integrating cells *A* to *D*, the small cells 1 to 8, and positive and negative reinforcement interneurons *P* and *N*. The effect of negative reinforcement could be no more than an increased transmitter output of existing connexions, or increased tendency to wander, until the afferent terminals finally settle on an integrating cell where their activity does not excite

Figure 14.11

A hypothetical learning system that incorporates the conclusions of this chapter. The central circuit is the inhibitory feedback loop with presynaptic inhibition. The growth of a purely neural feedback loop requires the passing of messages of recognition around the loop, as in Figure 13.16. The presynaptic inhibitory synapses are supposed to be maintained by a dynamic process that takes into account the individuality of the neurons and the influence of the reinforcement neurons. The latter are supposed to be widespread and to exert their influence upon those individual circuits of the kind shown here that have recently been active. The changes at learning are thereby brought about by growth, which is modified by the consequences of the circuit's own activity. *a* to *f*, afferent supply; *A* to *D*, integrating cells that respond to particular clusters of excited afferent fibres; 1 to 8, small cells that inhibit the afferent endings and influence their tendency to form synapses at all; O_1 and O_2, alternative outputs; *P* and *N*, positive and negative reinforcement interneurons.

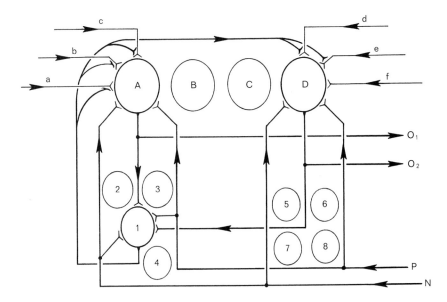

negative reinforcement neurons. The latter would be a trial-and-error type of mechanism of forming new connexions. The reinforcement need not originate in the environment but could be an output of a widely ramifying interneuron further down the line.

The postulated mechanism by which a purely neural loop could establish itself is by chemical messages passed from cell to cell round the loop, as in Figure 14.11. However, reinforcement fed back from the environment cannot be so easily line-labelled back to its appropriate register by the morphogenetic mechanisms that control the growth of nerve fibres. This is a problem that was faced by Young when he discussed the maintenance of the address (p. 354). On the other hand, the principal effects of reinforcement are very widespread, and the hypothetical reinforcement interneurons spread widely. The important additional point is that a widespread system is compatible with specificity if it acts on any classifying neurons that have recently been excited. The register is then a persistence in sensitivity, so that for a time any interneuron that has been active is influenced by a dispersed signal, and it acts as a single station replying to a general signal. (See reinforcement interneurons, p. 364.) This is a mechanism without the necessity for specific growth patterns of reinforcement interneurons back to the appropriate register.

The necessity for the unconditioned stimulus (the reinforcement) to follow the conditioning stimulus (which arrives in afferents a to f) and a previous rewording of the learning problem (p. 365) now become relevant. The influence of the reinforcement interneurons is subject to an evolutionary process. At first negative reinforcement can be imagined as merely provoking afferent endings to wander elsewhere, and positive reinforcement can be viewed as holding down endings still in the sensitive stage, when the feedback consequences are good or at least not intolerable. At a more advanced stage, reinforcement creates definite tendencies, by encouragement of certain afferents to stay and of others to move. Finally, by also stimulating the integrating and inhibiting neurons to grow in certain ways related to the input, the reinforcement interneurons can have an enormous variety of influences upon a circuit even as simple as that in Figure 14.11. Two types of transmission must be considered: the fast excitation pathway of impulses by which the circuit does its job in the animal, and the circulation of secretion around the feedback loop by which the arc is selected in the first place, modified and maintained as an active circuit.

Three comments are relevant. First, such a circuit takes no account of the statistical likelihood of making a correct choice, because at any time the input to an integrating cell is fixed. It responds willy-nilly to the excitation cluster in its afferent fibres, *but* it has its reward or retribution *afterwards* because its synaptic combinations are unsuccessful or otherwise. Second, although I have supposed that the vertebrate pattern of control of neuron growth, presynaptic inhibition, and feedback loops in sensory nuclei was adapted for a plastic adjustment leading up to the learning process, other mechanisms may exist side by side with this one, and no doubt other mechanisms of learning exist elsewhere. In invertebrate ganglia we have no sound evidence for either modulation of neurons in growth or any kind of feedback arc (presynaptic or otherwise) within the CNS. On the other hand, we have evidence of automatic sensory memory registers, as in motion perception and in the light-compass reactions, which require no reinforcement for memory to be built up.

A theory of memory by Griffith [13] has some similarities with the one just presented but has unfortunately appeared too recently to have had an influence on my account. Griffith's theory postulates substances that move across the cleft from postsynaptic to presynaptic cell when the two fire together. This substance is supposed to be effective or able to cross when two circumstances hold: there must be a persistent effect of the transmitter and also a subsequent influence from a nearby reinforcement axon. These postulates, like their counterparts in my theory, take care of the necessary sequence of events in learning and of maintaining the addresses. In Griffith's theory the unit is essentially an isolated synapse in which three axons are involved, long-term learning is an elaboration of growth processes, and short-term learning is a persistence of sensitivity at the synapse. In my theory the same features are present but I have in addition emphasized the properties of a feedback loop and set the whole against a background of excitational clusters. One critical difference is that contingent firing of the two neurons together is essential for the modification of the synapse between them in Griffith's theory, which is on that account perhaps more easily tested.

The test of any theory is whether the artifical introduction of the postulated change into the nervous system will induce the appropriate learned behaviour—and nothing besides. I see no other way of validating the claims that the experimental findings in this field always invite.

REFERENCES FOR CHAPTER 14

1. Barondes, S. H., and Cohen, H. D. 1966. Puromycin effect on successive stages of memory storage. *Science* **151**:594–595.
2. Bodian, D. 1965. A suggestive relationship of nerve cell RNA with specific synaptic sites. *Proc. Nat. Acad. Sci.* **53**:418.
3. Burke, W. 1966. Neuronal models for conditioned reflexes. *Nature London* **210**:269–271.
4. Chamberlain, T. J., Halick, P., and Gerard, R. W. 1963. Fixation of experience in the rat spinal cord. *J. Neurophysiol.* **26**:662–673.
5. Cohen, H. D., and Barondes, S. H. 1966. Further studies of learning and memory after intracerebral actinomycin-D. *J. Neurochem.* **13**:207–211.

✓ 6. Doty, R. W. 1965. Conditioned reflexes elicited by electrical stimulation of the brain in macaques. *J. Neurophys.* **28**:623–640.

7. Edstrom, J. E., and Grampp, W. 1965. Nervous activity and metabolism of ribonucleic acids in the crustacean stretch receptor neuron. *J. Neurochem.* **12**:735–741.

8. Eisenstein, E. M., and Mill, P. J. 1965. Role of the optic ganglia in learning in the crayfish *Procambarus clarki* (Girard). *Animal Behaviour* **13**:561–565.

9. Elul, R. 1966. Dependence of synaptic transmission on protein metabolism of nerve cells; a possible electrokinetic mechanism of learning. *Nature London* **210**:1127–1131.

10. Evans, C. R., and Robertson, A. D. J. 1966. Prolonged excitation in the visual cortex of the cat. *Science* **150**:913–915.

11. Flexner, L. B., and Flexner, J. B. 1966. Effect of acetoxycycloheximide etc. on cerebral protein synthesis and memory in mice. *Proc. Nat. Acad. Sci.* **55**: 369–374.

12. Goodman, D. C., and Horel, J. A. 1966. Sprouting of optic tract projections in the brain stem of the rat. *J. Comp. Neurol.* **127**:71–88.

13. Griffiths, J. S. 1966. A theory of the nature of memory. *Nature London* **211**: 1160–1163. Also *A View of the Brain.* Oxford University Press, 1967.

14. Guillery, R. W. 1965. Some electron microscopical observations of degenerative changes in central nervous synapses. *Progress in Brain Research* **14**: 57–76.

15. Hechter, O., and Halkerston, I. D. K. 1964. On the nature of macromolecular coding in neuronal memory. *Perspec. Biol. Med.* **7**:183–198.

✓ 16. Horridge, G. A. 1965. The electrophysiological approach to learning in isolatable ganglia. *Animal Behaviour, Suppl.* **1**:163–182.

17. Horridge, G. A. 1966. Optokinetic memory in the crab, *Carcinus. J. Exp. Biol.* **44**:233–295.

✓ 18. Hoyle, G. 1965. Neurophysiological studies on "learning" in headless insects, in *Physiology of the Insect Central Nervous System*, J. Treherne (Ed.). New York, Academic Press.

19. Hyden, H. 1959. Biochemical changes in glial cells and nerve cells at varying activity. Proc. 4th Internat. Cong. Biochem. **3**:64–89, O. Hoffmann-Ostenhof (Ed.). London, Pergamon Press.

20. Jacobson, A. L., Babich, F. R., Bubash, S., and Goren, C. 1965. Maze preferences in naive rats produced by injection of ribonucleic acid from trained rats. *Psychon. Sci.* **4**:3–4.

21. Jakoubek, B., and Edström, J. E. 1965. RNA changes in the Mauthner axon and myelin sheath after increased functional activity. *J. Neurochem.* **12**: 845–849.

22. John, E. R. 1965. The front stoop approach to memory. *Perspec. Biol. Med.* **9**:35–53. [See also paper by Agranoff in the same issue.]

23. Kandel, E. R., and Tauc, L. 1964. Mechanism of prolonged heterosynaptic facilitation. *Nature London* **202**:145–147.

24. Krnjević, K., Randic, M., and Straughan, D. W. 1964. Cortical inhibition. *Nature London* **201**:1294–1296.

25. Lashley, K. S. 1950. In search of the Engram. *Symp. Soc. Exp. Biol.* **4**:454–482.

26. Luco, J. V., and Aranda, L. C. 1964. An electrical correlate to the process of learning. *Acta Physiol. Latino-Amer.* **14:**274–288.

27. McConnell, J. V. 1966. Comparative physiology; Learning in invertebrates. *Ann. Rev. Physiol.* **28:**107–136.

28. *Nucleic Acid.* 1947. Symposium Soc. Exp. Biology, No. 1. C.U.P. [Papers by Bodian and Hyden emphasize how little reliable advance there has been in 20 years.]

29. Park, T. E. 1965. Post-retinal visual storage. *Amer. J. Psychol.* **78:**145–147.

30. Rosenblatt, F., Farrow, J. T., and Rhine, S. 1966. The transfer of learned behaviour from trained to untrained rats by means of brain extracts. *Proc. Nat. Acad. Sci.* **55:**787–792.

31. Scheibel, M. E., and Scheibel, A. B. 1958. Structural substrates for integrative patterns in the brain stem reticular core, in *The Recticular Formation of the Brain,*" Jasper, H. H., Proctor, L. D., Knighton, R. S., Noshay, R. S., and Costello, R. T. (Eds.). Boston, Little, Brown.

32. Skoglund, S. 1960. The reactions to tetanic stimulation of the two-neuron arc in the kitten. *Acta Physiol. Scand.* **50:**238–253.

33. Sperry, R. W. 1955. On the neural basis of the conditioned response. *Brit. J. Animal Behaviour* **3:**41–44.

34. Thorpe, W. H., and Davenport, D. (Eds.). 1965. *Learning and Associated Phenomena in Invertebrates. Animal Behaviour.* Supplement No. 1.

35. Waelsh, H. 1965. Biochemical interpretations of neurophysiological vectors. *Perspec. Biol. Med.* **9:**165–186.

36. Young, J. Z. 1965. The organization of a memory system. *Proc. Roy. Soc. London B* **163:**285–320.

15

Features of interneurons

Many far-reaching consequences flow from the discovery of the transforming and abstracting properties of interneurons as described throughout this book. These consequences relate to fundamental questions—the abstraction of universal qualities from normal stimuli in situations in which irrelevant features obtrude; the ability of some animals to recognize and react to signs specific to their species; the nature of a discrimination that was not present before it had been learned; the problem of what to look for when studying the brain. Basically, the properties of interneurons are an inescapable *a priori* of behaviour. Perhaps the whole mind-body relation depends on them.

The recognition of lines, shapes, words, or sentences must depend on the properties of pattern-selective interneurons or groups of them acting in concert. The slow and complex process of learning to see and to talk must involve the formation of interneuron circuits if not connexions; the former is a physiological pathway and the latter is anatomical. The limiting factors of this set of constituents are comparable to the limitations, such as knowledge of space and time, which Kant saw as confining our abilities of reasoning. What any man or animal perceives or does, and all human conceptions, are restricted by the limitations of interneurons. The converse—that all the wonders of behaviour and thought are made possible by the properties of interneurons—does not necessarily follow. Let us first summarize some of the properties of interneurons that have been described in previous chapters, and then suggest why mechanical explanations of the activity of brains are ultimately inadequate, even though they are all we can hope to derive.

INTERNEURON MECHANISMS

Accepting for the time being that neurons are separate cells that interact in the ways that have been described, the remarkable conclusion emerges that the only known level at which integration between simultaneous or successive inputs can occur is where the two or more inputs converge on one interneuron (Chapter 5). The postsynaptic potentials in response to two or more stimuli are summed algebraically in space and time by virtue of the time constant of the neuron membrane. Potentials spread with decrement to neighbouring regions in time or space. This is equally true for branching dendrites or for the more or less spherical cells, for branched sensory terminals or for a cylindrical muscle fibre bearing several motor axons. We find some peculiar types of responsiveness— inhibition produced at an electrical synapse on fish Mauthner fibres when current flows from the presynaptic fibres or, in some nematode muscles, contraction caused by hyperpolarisation of the muscle membrane—but nevertheless the same principle of summation applies.

Commonly, though not understood, the synaptic response to the second stimulus and later ones is not necessarily the same as to the first stimulus. The effect of the second excitation is to increase the amount of transmitter substances released per impulse and not to augment the excitability of the postsynaptic membrane. The principle seems to hold for a variety of synapses, including neuromuscular junctions, which are those best understood. The increased response at the second stimulus is said to be facilitated; the opposite effect, a diminution, is called antifacilitation. Both effects can sometimes be recorded in the same postsynaptic cell in response to excitation via different pathways. The nature of the progressive change with repetition depends therefore more on the nature of the presynaptic neuron than on the postsynaptic one. This is of critical importance in the present theory, in which short-term learning and maintaining the register consists of a kind of long-term facilitation of a postsynaptic cell upon which convergence occurs (see p. 367).

The nonlinear addition of polarizations that decay in time, together with the spatial pattern of dendrites and the arrangement of different types of synapses, determines how a neuron is stimulated by impulses that impinge upon it. A tree in the path of a hail of shot sustains on the trunk a force that depends on the spatial pattern of hits upon the outstretched branches. The arborizations of the dendrites are comparable to the branches of the tree, but in the case of the nerve cell the excitation at the ends of the dendrites has less effect than if nearer to the spike-initiating region. When the summed electrotonic spread of depolarization at the spike-initiating region is greater than threshold in that region, the neuron responds by firing, without choice. After learning it still responds in willy-nilly fashion, but presumably to a slightly different pattern. The spike is not necessarily initiated at the cell body and in most instances originates *far* from it. There are no known capabilities of neurons such as moments of decision, ability to wait and see, multiplicative properties, measurements of ratios, determination of points of balance or equalities, or choice of two different outputs. None of these desirable features can be given a physiological basis in a single cell. Therefore, wherever such features are shown by ganglia, they must be attributed to the pattern of organisation of groups of neurons.

INTERNEURON PATTERNS

In higher animals, especially in the arthropods and mammals, patterns of connexions, where examined, are genetically fixed in detail; in simplest central nervous systems ordered connexions are certainly present although more difficult to recognize. Every set of synaptic connexions is somehow a pattern, though not necessarily a significant one. The pattern, however, is of connectivity and not necessarily to be recognized in the spatial layout of the dendrites (see p. 316).

Only the two most elementary conclusions about the shape of dendritic fields have so far been clarified. (a) In order to have synaptic input from a receptive field there must be a fibre leading from that direction. However, since other interneurons may intervene on the path, any pathway is theoretically possible. (b) If a neuron has no input from a particular area, it is not likely to have dendrites in that direction. In general, a large spread of dendrites means a large receptive field. However, typical central nervous tissue with fibres running in all directions usually has an extremely well-ordered functional connectivity. Interneurons have sharply defined receptive fields and motoneurons have unambiguous adaptive responses. It is only when there is a spatial pattern consisting of many neurons, as shown by repeated traversing on a minute scale with an extracellular microelectrode, that we can say that the anatomical outline of a dendritic arborization is significant. For example, cells of the cortex are arranged in columns with similar receptive fields in each column, so that it now becomes important whether the *ascending* arborizations of other cells are restricted to a few adjacent columns. On the other hand, when the input to a neuron is projected from elsewhere, there are no known constraints to determine the dendritic form. Having thus cleared the air, we can then point to the numerous examples of topographical order—as in the lateral geniculate body, somatic cortex, spinal dorsal horn, and especially in the optic lobes of insects (Fig. 16.2)—but we cannot say whether the strict spatial plan helps the dendrites to grow in the first place, or subsequently allows certain regular and short patterns of cross connexions. No experimental evidence has yet shown that electrical field effects, which certainly would impose strict geometrical constraints, have to be taken seriously except in electric fish (where the tissue currents are large) and, of course, in electroreceptors.

An interneuron has a particular pattern of synaptic connexions (see p. 117), and this set of inputs is sufficiently depolarized to fire impulses only if a large fraction of the appropriate pattern of presynaptic terminals are excited together near a region that initiates impulses. This multidimensional maximum amplitude filter provides the means by which *most sensory excitation fails to excite higher interneurons,* and most patterns of impulses of interneurons in turn fail to excite motoneurons. However, in the same system, a relevant pattern of impulses is an immediately effective stimulus with no delay in sorting. A motoneuron is as effective a filter as any other neuron and the final integration of movement in all animals studied occurs upon the motoneuron dendrites and by the organized arrangement of joints and muscles.

Extrapolating from known detail of these patterns of connexions, a reasonable description of all the relevant inputs of all interneurons would fill existing books several times over. It is possible that the complexity of the structure of the human brain will continue for some time to rival the combined complexity of all its printed products, if we define complexity as information content or time required to describe.

PROPERTIES OF INTERNEURONS

Almost invariably the descriptions of interneurons have been of *types.* These do not necessarily exist in reality but are an average, a modal, or a construction based on a favoured or (more honestly) an idealized, rather than an average, type. Units "of one type" differ among themselves, even in cases in which other reasoning leads to the conclusion that they should be identical. For example, two primary visual cells, presumed to contain the same chemical photopigment, never have identical spectral sensitivity curves when measured experimentally. The boundary between statistical variation and real classes has to be laid down arbitrarily from a survey of the scatter of numerous single instances. In the vertebrates and in all small invertebrate cells this is prevented because the interneurons are anonymous (see Fig. 15.1). Classifications of interneurons, known by their authors to be unclear or fluid, soon become definitive by an intellectual foreshortening caused by the passage of time. We must therefore oscillate between scrupulous and methodical efforts to test whether what is believed is really so and new hesitant classifications that we believe to be representative. Moreover, the size of categories depends upon what acuity, and even rule of discrimination is accepted by the observer, rather than by the animal.

The *abstraction of universals,* like all known properties of interneurons, stems from an operation that is essentially a measure of the sums and differences of the weighted excitatory and inhibitory pattern within the sphere of sensitivity of the spike-initiating region. The outcome is converted to a spike frequency that goes elsewhere. The biological frame-

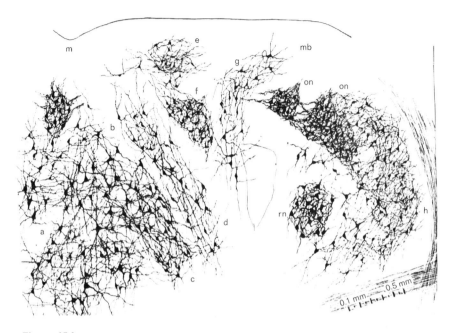

Figure 15.1

The appearance of interneurons in nuclei of the mammalian midbrain. This is a drawing of a longitudinal section of the medulla (*m*) and midbrain (*mb*) of an adult mouse stained by the Golgi-Cox method, which picks out about one neuron in a hundred. *on*, oculomotor nuclei; *rn*, red nucleus; *a* to *h*, various nuclei of the reticular formation, most of which (but not *e, f,* or *g*) are concerned with the control of eye muscles; *e, f, g*, autonomic nuclei. [Lorente de Nó, 1938.]

work for the abstraction of universals has its fine and its coarse structure. At the detailed level we have the distribution of synapses as neighbours along the dendrites, and to a lesser extent their absolute spatial arrangement, so far as this affects their distance from the region of spike initiation. At a coarser level we have the pattern of connectivity so far as this can be influenced by the size and shape of the dendritic field. For example, the presence of a line stimulus upon the retina is inferred from the excitement of an interneuron that has synaptic inputs from several units with receptive fields arranged physically along that line on the retina. If and only if most of its input cells are excited, the higher-order cell signals the presence of an entire line, with no accompanying mention of discontinuities that might really exist in the line. Note that the logic has the effect of smoothing over details; for example, summation has the consequence of synthesizing the line from a number of spots, some of which can be missing. If, over a larger receptive field, a number of line detectors feed into a higher-order unit that is excited *by any one of them* with no summation required, then any line in the field will excite (Fig.

12.8). This is the only experimentally demonstrated means by which we can contemplate the abstraction of universals. Interneuron connexions are not only appropriate for such a task: they can act in no other way when connected in simple combinations. Generalizations—the colour of an object irrespective of its shape, the shape irrespective of colour, the figure of a man no matter in what posture, the sound of an offspring's cry among other noises—must on our present evidence be abstracted in this way. The development of behaviour in higher vertebrates suggests that these abstracting abilities of higher interneurons mature slowly.

It is a small jump to suggest that an act of recognition, which consists of the excitation of an interneuron by one particular impulse cluster, improves when the same combination has previously been effective. We might suggest that recollection is the answering of its name by a wanted interneuron when a large number of memory circuits are excited and one of them finds the right combination. This hypothesis as to the mechanism of recollections agrees well with psychological findings. Abstraction, memory, and neuron connexions seem basically to be one topic, and, from the nature of the natural world, the effectiveness of a pattern recognition system depends on its learning power.

After a transformation by an interneuron we are left with a property of the environmental stimulus or of the previous excitational cluster that is not necessarily expressible in physical units. As universals it is possible to have colours such as purple or brown, which are not in the spectrum, and to perceive "black" and "silence," although they are not stimuli. Where numerous inputs feed into a widely branched interneuron, presumably it serves a basic function such as arousal or reinforcement, for which we have no name in our relationship with the outside world.

The nature of *species-specific abilities* in related animals becomes a question of differences between the connexions of their corresponding interneurons. In animals differing widely, we can already catalogue the interneuron types found in one and not in the others, but only the largest, most stereotyped, personality differences are as yet approachable at this level.

The problem of *what one should look for* when studying interneurons is thrown into the lap of the biologist, not the mathematician, biophysicist, or computer expert. Only the student long familiar with the ethology of owls, bats, seasnakes, porpoises, worker bees, or hunting spiders will know the special features of the environmental stimuli of interest to his subjects, and he is wise who studies specialized animals to which certain stimulus situations have a great survival value. This approach prevents a good deal of experimental floundering with inappropriate stimulus situations, which may lead to bizarre conclusions; as an example, we might with some justification say that cats have a visual system especially tuned to architectural drawings. The point is that analysis cannot proceed unless the choice of stimulus situations fits the set of filters that the animal's repertoire has imposed.

The optimum response of the interneuron becomes of the greatest significance as a guide in analysis. The temporary position of the optimum stimulus lies in an unknown direction in stimulus space, and we can never predict which dimension of the stimulus must be changed in order to approach it. To discover the optimum stimulus we must unfortunately also look at the response of the next higher interneurons. This necessity arises because the pattern of the excitation of interneurons at the level studied can be important in the excitation of the next higher interneurons, and even a strong response may be irrelevant if it excites nothing beyond itself. The exact phase or latency of a response may be important, as on the auditory pathway, and in other examples the spread of a stimulus into parallel pathways has an influence that is taken into account at the next stage. We can only guess what features are limiting when we find that lower-order interneurons (but not those of high-order) are excitable and that the subject fails to make a behavioural response. We must ask how long a courtship the higher interneuron requires, and with what special personal treatment and in how many dimensions. To switch lights on and off, to repeat the same series of clicks—or worse, to stimulate the afferent nerve electrically—is to miss the biological point.

Concerning ambiguity in the properties of interneurons, there are two opposite points of view: the first sees ambiguity as unfortunate and temporary, the second sees it as irrelevant in the animal's context. Every unit we examined in the locust central ganglia and optic lobes was sensitive to a variety of attributes of the visual stimulus, so that the quantitative, patterned, or temporal attributes of the stimulus are not recoverable by the observer from the impulse sequence in any unit alone. We found no truly specific recognition units for any particular stimuli among hundreds of visual units tested; those that respond rather well to general features such as movement in one direction, or to two clicks at a certain interval, always respond, though often at higher threshold, to some other stimuli not having these features. Even the best examples—the one-way movement detectors—show ambiguities in being influenced by flashing lights, stripe width, speed of movement, degree of contrast, and direction of movement in relation to direction or straightness of edges, besides being subject to adaptation ([24], p. 193).

If an animal is to derive from its neurons a pattern of its environment, we might expect that their responses would represent the outside world unambiguously. Clearly this does not happen, and ambiguity is the price paid for integration of any kind. When two or more inputs are integrated they are mixed in some way, and the mixture is now the signal for the next stage down the line. The separate inputs are no longer discernible to the experimenter who records from the higher unit, but other pathways containing the original information combined in a different way may proceed in a parallel course to the higher centres, where the true state of the environment can supposedly be recalculated. So stated, this is the first point of view, treating the activity of interneurons as responses that the experimenter relates to a stimulus. Higher-order interneurons, however, when examined, do not observe the stimulus and apparently make no attempt to recover it. In the clearest examples, actual interneurons make more and more involved transformations of the outside world at each successively higher unit. These transformations are those decided by natural selection as being meaningful in behaviour, and it is only in this context that the apparent ambiguity of responses of units is resolved. An animal that responds appropriately does so because the decisions at every neuron between sensory and motor are suitable for the life of that animal. Recovery of data and reconstruction of the environment may occur, but it is not essential that they should. In all the host of stimulus situations in which the animal makes no meaningful response, except perhaps to flee, his interneurons can be unresponsive or mimicking pandemonium and it will not matter at all, for no message gets through.

If we can accept that the principle of a selective filter applies universally and that only abnormally strong and properly patterned excitation gets through to the next stage, then the problem is to find effective stimulus situations. If the third-order interneurons are excited, we can infer that the stimulus conditions are reasonable for the second-order cells. When the animal as a whole responds, the problems of ambiguity, signal-to-noise ratio, and meaningful discrimination of stimuli are all necessarily solved at the neuron level. The problem of analysis is that within the nervous system we have only very indirect means of recognizing the combinations of neurons that are immediately of significance to the animal's own mechanism.

If our picture of interneurons is a reasonable representation, it implies that recording from sensory neurons will not tell us how the animal will respond, nor will recording from single interneurons tell what higher-order interneurons or motoneurons are likely to do. Recording from many neurons provides more data, but still does not tell us what patterns in this information are those of interest to the animal. Recording from motoneurons with natural stimulation only reaffirms that the animal responds to meaningful patterns. A complete inventory of every impulse in every axon over a period of time would not make it possible to construct a useful model of how the neurons interact, for it has already been abundantly shown that when even a few model neurons are linked together with a few feedback circuits to yield patterns of impulses, it is impossible to infer the pattern of connexions even when the pattern of impulses in all the outputs and inputs is known. If we record blindly without knowing the anatomy, it is not possible to determine which inputs correspond to which outputs. On the other side of the picture, building a complex picture of neuronal pathways and also anatomical patterns of fibres, when done in conjunction with physiological properties and normal activity at every point, provides a progressive attack on our puzzle, in the sense that the few actual physiological pathways become recognized in two ways. We can then assume that the basic physiological principles of summation apply on the anatomical dendritic patterns, and we can, at least in principle, suggest patterns of how the fibres interact.

LOCAL STIMULATION AND LESIONS

Two methods that ignore the individuality of interneurons but rely on the aggregation of neurons of a similar kind in tracts, nuclei, or small areas, are local stimulation by implanted electrodes or lesions made by knife or local electrolysis. When first applied, these methods gave rise to great hopes that the organization of the brain is amenable to this treatment; unfortunately, the technique is limited because of the relatively large size of the electrodes or lesions. Moreover, clear-cut responses are forthcoming only in a few places in certain groups of animals, and even these are difficult to interpret: First, it is not known how many effects are caused simultaneously by acting on several neurons of differing function; second, it is not known whether the real effect occurs at the experimental location or elsewhere, because long-distance tracts are excited: third, activation is indistinguishable from removal of inhibition, and effects may also be indirect because some factor such as motivation is changed.

Local stimulation of small areas of the thalamus in the mammalian brain can have astonishing effects in causing whole behavioural acts; when stimulated locally in these areas of the brain, the experimental animal eats, drinks, or voluntarily stimulates itself again by bar-pressing, for example, which is an action resembling eating or drinking. Stimulation of central areas of the brain stem of the hen can cause changes in attention, aggressiveness, or attitude to other chickens or to the cock, in a way which strongly suggests that definable parts of behaviour follow as a consequence of stimulating certain neurons. Similarly, stimulation of areas in the corpora pedunculata of crickets and grasshoppers releases a perfect chirping behaviour. In these instances the frequency and strength of the stimulus matters little so long as it lies within a reasonable range, showing that it is the pathway, not the pattern of impulses, that is important. These methods are significant for analysis, in which no tool can be disregarded; the method of lesions has led to much of our knowledge of the function of brain regions, but the resulting conceptual models must be treated with caution.

MISPLACED CONCRETENESS

One of the greatest pitfalls in the analysis of the nervous system, as in any experimental analysis, is the error that Whitehead called "misplaced concreteness." The tracing of physiological pathways leads, in the best examples, to diagrams of the flow lines of excitation. Translation of these flow lines into circuits, or substituting chains of interneurons for the pathways, always leads to a visualization of elements that appear more real than in fact they are. The neurons, which are traced anatomically by staining, degeneration, or electron microscopy, are primary and unshakable, but descriptions of them are in terms of types that are constructs of the mind. The physiological pathways, in contrast, are largely notional, but they are the functional interpretations that lead to explanations of behaviour. Also, the tracing of physiological and of anatomical pathways rarely goes hand in hand. It was ten years before the question of the anatomical form and position of Renshaw cells was seriously questioned [15]; it was ten years before the centre/surround pattern of retinal ganglion cells could be satisfactorily equated with the anatomical extent of their dendrites (Fig. 12.4). Moreover, these two regions of the mammalian nervous system have been studied more intensely than perhaps any other. In the vertebrate juvenile spinal cord every interneuron branches to many particular but functionally unidentified regions, and forms synapses with thousands of other neurons, all probably having unique receptive fields. Profusely branching sensory fibres account for only 1% of the total synapses. Except for short-latency two-neuron arcs, therefore, behaviour even at spinal level cannot be explained, because most of the possible models cannot be ruled out. Therefore diagrams of pathways that in principle explain how neurons interact are always temporary approximations, even though they have been checked against the morphological pattern of connectivity.

SELECTIVE PERCEPTION OF THE UNFAMILIAR

As judged by their behaviour, most advanced animals such as birds and mammals can apparently ignore or direct their attention to a particular stimulus. This applies especially to the temporary interest in the unfamiliar, and to the sudden arousal caused by a particular stimulus, however small, that is of especial selective or remembered importance. An important consequence of this is that most stimuli are ignored; this is almost always the result when a stimulus is repeated many times.

Numerous analyses of behaviour of whole animals show that when a specially significant message passes down a channel to which the animal is not at that moment attending, or if a clue is given in a channel to which the attention is already directed, or if there is a sudden change in the unattended channel, then such signals will very likely be noticed whereas they would otherwise have no effect. The question is, Where does the scrutiny of incoming messages occur? Only a partial answer can be given, even for mammals, and only for a few higher-order sensory interneurons in lower animals.

The capacity to deal with sensory information is very clearly limited. In man only one channel can be attended to at one time (observation of two channels of low-information content can be explained by alternation), and if a complex stimulus is overlaid by another within 1 sec of presentation it cannot usually be recalled. When two different sense organs are stimulated they interfere centrally, as judged by subsequent behavioural criteria.

Recording of units in lower animals has shown that so-called "novelty" units are common at about third- or fourth-order level on many sensory pathways. Thus, in the tracts along the arms of octopus (Chapter 6), the optic lobes of locusts (Chapter 9), and the optic tectum of the frog (Chapter 12), novelty units respond to a stimulus when presented for the first time, with rapid decay of the number of spikes at successive occasions. For each stimulus to be as effective as it was when novel, the necessary interval may range from 10 sec to 2 or more hours. Visual, auditory, tactile, and mixed modality units are found with these features. A clue to the mechanism can be inferred from the fact that all are wide-field units, and when the response has declined the presentation of the stimulus in a different part of the field brings back the response at full strength. Therefore novelty units behave as if they had many dendrites that can be separately adapted or inhibited. This is a simple and powerful property that explains many features of behaviour, but whether the mechanism is actually this simple remains to be seen. Among invertebrates there is no evidence of centrifugal control of the effectiveness of sensory endings or of any other mechanism that refers to the perception of the unfamiliar or exclusion of background sensory excitation in this context.

There is a rather generally held assumption that in mammals the amplitude of an evoked potential at the appropriate area of the sensory cortex is reduced when the animal is distracted from the stimulus, and increased when the animal attends to it. Critical analysis, however, suggests that the sensory pathways are not greatly modified in a selective way. Evoked potentials in all pathways are reduced when a cat sees a mouse on the first occasion, and changes in size of the pupil or direction of the ears must be carefully taken into account [6]. The potential evoked at the cortex certainly changes, but in a less predictable way—one that has been related to changes in the reticuloactivating system.

The sensory pathways to the cortex (except for some in the auditory system) are relatively little changed by repetition of the stimulus. Spontaneous units recorded in the thalamus, however, outside the direct sensory pathways, frequently act as novelty units, whether tactile, auditory, visual or multimodal. A consequence is that, as units are explored in one animal, new stimuli have to be continually found, and the level of anaesthesia suggests that the cortex is not responsible. In the cat lesions in the region of the spontaneous novelty units destroy spontaneous activity; an animal so treated will walk about slowly if stimulated but will fail to attend to anything in the environment. It seems reasonable to conclude that the novelty units are the appropriate mechanism in an attention-directing region of the brain. Whether there are any other mechanisms of selecting the unfamiliar it is too early to judge [6].

Not all this behaviour is innate, for it has been demonstrated that units that progressively fail to respond on repetition of the stimulus do so less rapidly if the stimulus is paired with a shock to the skin (perhaps even to the cortex). For visual cortical units, with a simple flash for the stimulus, the response of some units to the paired stimuli is greater and of others less than that to the flash alone [6]. There is no information as to the location of the association, or if the critical change even occurred on this pathway. However, when a large number of novelty units have been tested by pairing with shock, it may be possible to be less imaginative about the relation between attention-directing systems and arousal by a newly learned stimulus pattern.

LOCAL INHIBITORY FEEDBACK CIRCUITS

One of the outstanding features of the sensory pathways of mammals, and perhaps of all vertebrates, is the existence of sensory nuclei that act as relay stations where each sensory interneuron exerts an inhibitory action upon itself and others with neighbouring receptive fields. A circuit fitting most of the known instances is shown in Figure 16.4, B; the significant point is that the inhibitory interneuron is excited by branches of the postsynaptic and not the presynaptic fibres. A similar circuit has been proposed for spinal motor neurons, for the hippocampal pyramidal cell and its basket cell, for the relay in the thalamus on the somatic sensory pathway to the cortex, for the cortical pyramidal cell and inhibitory stellate cell, for the cerebellar granular cell and its small Golgi cell.

One effect of such a circuit is to modify inhibitory surrounds and to create new ones; another effect is to act as an automatic gain control for any strong local stimulus. The topological anatomical plan of the sensory nucleus, as a spatial representation of some aspect of the outside world, makes it possible for short inhibitory fibres to reach the units having neighbouring receptive fields. This is one way of looking at the problem of why vertebrate sensory nuclei are arranged in columns or layers. If the units are laid out topologically and the inhibitory feedback fibres are short, it may be possible that they act only on cells of a given class that are *within reach*. This would help dispose of the problem of how each inhibitory feedback arc is closed in an exactly specific way during the formation of synaptic connexions. It is also possible that the binding action of the inhibitory feedback loops acts in a trophic way to modify the formation and maintenance of the principal excitatory synapses on the ascending pathway in their correct and adjacent connexions. Some such feature is required to explain the long persistence of the geometrically laid out sensory nuclei during vertebrate evolution.

THE EVOLUTION OF COMPLEXITY

Whether interneurons do in fact interact in interlocked feedback loops becomes of special interest when we consider how central nervous systems might have evolved. From what little we know of the detailed organisation, it seems that at the jellyfish level the ganglia do not differ from nerve net condensations. By this I mean that neurons of a jellyfish ganglion could belong to few classes, and *within any one class* the neurons may form synapses indiscriminately with each other, act as alternative pathways, and be excited simultaneously. We do not know whether such a pattern forms a significant part of any proper central nervous system, but as we ascend from the lowest worms (or from the lowest members of each phylum to the highest), the number of classes of neurons increases and the dendritic patterns look more ordered. The same holds true if we compare the abdominal or visceral ganglia of most animals with their cephalic, and particularly their optic, ganglia; these last have the appearance of being more differentiated. Only in a few highly differentiated places have there been found purely neural feedback loops that require the unique identification of one cell by another for their formation. It must be stressed that even in the higher centres of mammalian brains certain cells seem to make contacts with any nearby members of a certain class in a way seemingly not referable to individual neurons; for example, in the hippocampus of the rabbit, each basket cell has axon terminals that surround about 200 pyramidal cells, with terminals on all of them. Our inability to discuss the exact wiring diagrams in any ganglion shows how relatively primitive is the art of neuranatomy, because in vertebrates the neurons are not recognized individually.

A negative feedback loop back to the same cell through another neuron requires a very special matching of specificity in growth. Cell A must make synapses upon cell B, which in turn must make synapses only upon cell A and not upon other cells of the class to which A belongs. Although there has been a great deal of work on recurrent inhibitory pathways in mammalian spinal cord and brain, examples as specific as the above don't come to mind. Usually the axon of the feedback loop makes synapses with cell A and neighbouring similar cells (Figs. 10.3, A, and 16.4). Our present inability to describe the anatomy of neuronal patterns in terms of individual cells emphasizes once more the histological precision required. For this work, completely new techniques will have to be devised.

The development of behaviour in vertebrate embryos, as the nervous system differentiates, reveals that general responses of large areas appear first; progressively more specific and localized patterns develop subsequently. This ontogeny mirrors the postulated phylogeny, implying that more specific connections evolve from less specific ones. With reference to the actual mechanisms in the ontogeny of behaviour, we have no information on the relative importance of the growth of new synaptic connections as compared with the shift of old ones to more specific sites.

VARIABILITY OF IMPULSE INTERVALS

The experience of many workers suggests that responses of individual central neurons to repeated application of physiological stimuli of the same intensity have a rather wide variation in impulse interval, as compared to sensory nerves.

The variability of timing of central impulses stands in contrast to the considerable precision with which the animals freely respond to the same stimuli. To average out the irregularities and recover the periodicities by summation over many neurons is sometimes possible and is certainly done in places, as in the achievement of accurate localization in the ascending auditory system of the mammal, in the smooth response of a muscle with many motor units, and in the cooperation of units at all levels in eye stabilization. In sensory systems we must frequently infer that an improvement of the signal-to-noise ratio has been achieved by smoothing inputs from a very large number of sensilla, as in the response of a moth to a faint odour or of a compound eye to a small optokinetic stimulus. But, if other means are available, this method of increasing numbers of units is one of decreasing returns, because the improvement in signal-to-noise ratio is proportional at best to the square root of the number of duplicates. A further improvement is to make averages over longer periods of time, but the value of doing so depends on the nature of the distribution of impulses as a function of time [5]. There are almost no experimental facts that define the periods of time over which averaging takes place in real nervous systems, or that suggest whether this period is controlled by some kind of compromise between urgency and accuracy.

The period over which a sequence of impulses is actually averaged depends upon the time constant of the next higher-order neurons and upon the form the summation takes. There is no question of a decision by the neuron as to whether a signal is distinguishable from background

Figure 15.2

The intervals between nerve impulses commonly have a smaller standard deviation at higher frequency that they have at a lower frequency in the same neuron. The significance of this is suggested by the diagram. On the left is a curve showing a typical relation between quantitative values of stimulus and corresponding quantitative frequencies of the nerve impulses. A small increment Δs of the stimulus s gives rise to a relatively large change in the frequency of impulses when the stimulus is weak. A similar stimulus increment gives rise to a much smaller difference in frequency when the stimulus is strong. As shown on the right, under these circumstances a constant standard deviation of interval has the effect of reducing the significance of a difference in frequency when the stimulus is strong. On the other hand, if the standard deviation of interval is a function of interval, a significant difference can be maintained over a wide range of frequency. In the theoretical example on the right the standard deviation of intervals between impulses was set at half of the mean interval. The data is from somatic sensory interneurons. [Werner and Mountcastle, 1963.]

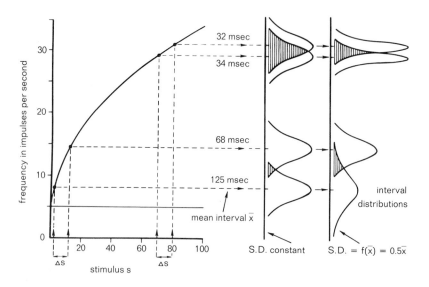

activity or whether there is a real increment in the signal. The neuron will be excited if and when its threshold is exceeded, willy-nilly: the question is whether external factors can influence the summation upon it.

To an observer outside the animal, one feature of interest is the standard deviation of the interval between impulses, which decreases with average frequency for many neurons [21]. The dependence of standard deviation upon frequency in some interneurons has the effect of making the signal-to-noise ratio consistently bad over a wide range (Fig. 15.2).

SYSTEMATIC IMPULSE PATTERNS

It has often been suggested that the same axon can carry two qualitatively different messages, distinguished by virtue of their pattern of spacing in time; certainly temporal patterns are readily generated in simple systems (Fig. 15.3). Apart from some cells of *Aplysia* and some crustacean muscles that are pattern-sensitive, there is little actual work to substantiate this idea. Spontaneous impulses are commonly spaced with a simple pattern, so that short intervals tend to be followed by long ones, as in the beat of a jellyfish ganglion or in visual ganglion cells of the cat. In the ascending somatic sensory system of the macaque monkey, Werner and Mountcastle found in a computerized survey that 50% of units had intervals with a statistically significant departure from randomness, but they could suggest no functional significance.

The reflex control of opening of the crayfish claw provides a curious example of systematic (temporal) pattern. With motor impulses at 12 per sec, more tension results in the opener muscle when the impulses arrive in pairs than when they are equally spaced. The significant point is that normal impulses in freely moving animals are frequently patterned in exactly this way [22]. In the *Aplysia* neurons, in which the pattern sensitivity has been analyzed intracellularly, it is clear that all preferences for particular patterns of intervals depend on the time course and summation of postsynaptic potentials as influenced by the proximity of synapses and the nonlinear nature of the facilitation that favours a short interval at a certain time in the pattern. Here we find once more the familiar influence of the time constant of the dendritic tree and the geometry of impulse initiation [17].

In the auditory system of the cat there are units that become more regular in interimpulse interval when stimulated by continuous tones, without change in the average impulse frequency. This can be called a meaningful response in that the impulses come into phase with the sound and make possible the method of localization that is based upon phase differences between the two ears. In the visual system the exact temporal spacing of impulses is less obvious but must be important in

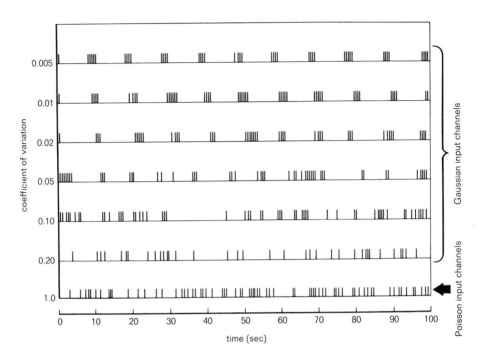

Figure 15.3

Nerve cells are commonly encountered with activity in a regular series of bursts, others with less regular bursts, and others with spikes apparently at random. One explanation of bursting is that the cell has two inputs, each with its own coefficient of variation of interval between spikes. The above traces show computed outputs, assuming synaptic potentials of typical size and decay rate, from two inputs for different values of the coefficient of variation of interval between *both* sets of inputs. The mean frequencies of the two pacemakers were 2.0/sec and 1.9/sec, giving a burst at 10-sec intervals. The burst pattern deteriorates quite rapidly with increasing variance. A coefficient of variation of 0.1 produces a pattern that is hardly distinguishable from a purely random distribution and looks like many patterns found in real neurons. Given an irregular burst pattern, however, it is not possible to recover any one unique explanation in terms of a few particular input frequencies, and no known neurons have only two inputs. [Perkel, 1964.]

reading and fast ball games. People who are both blind and deaf can nevertheless learn to tell the direction of a sound, after some training, by the aid of electronic receivers that vibrate in time with the sound on the skin of the arms or body. For this to be possible there must be a high degree of accuracy in phasing in the somatic sensory system, but we can only guess as to its normal function.

In general, the temporal aspects of excitation in interneurons are less important than the spatial ones, and the significance of impulse frequency seems to decrease the further we are from neuromuscular junctions and sense organs. In the control of flight rhythm of the locust, stimulation of the nerve cord near the metathoracic ganglion can be either random or patterned, but in either case it gives rise to a rhythmical and coordinated wing movement (without necessary proprioceptive feedback). Impulse pattern in the input seems to have no significance at all in this case.

The occurrence of neurons with regularly, randomly, or rhythmically spaced impulses, as judged by the rather haphazard and few cases studied, suggests that irregular intervals are a feature of the higher parts of the nervous system of higher animals, and that regular trains of impulses are a feature of sensory systems and ganglia with few neurons. Unless it controls an oscillatory effector, a neuron that gives bursts of high-frequency impulses is often suspected of being damaged or overstimulated.

The observer vaguely discerns the receptive field of an interneuron by working through numerous stimuli. To a higher-order interneuron, however, the impulses in its input are an indication of the situation in the outside world. None of the neurons have any knowledge of the instant when the stimulus occurs. Therefore poststimulus histograms are of no significance to the animal, although possibly useful to the observer (Fig. 15.5). Similarly, any measure of nervous activity involving a standard deviation, or features of a distribution such as measures of skewness or serial correlation coefficients over long periods, cannot be of any significance to the animal at the time, because its neurons cannot compute them.

Almost universally, impulses of constant mean frequency are more likely to excite when bunched; the feature of interest to a target neuron is whether it is excited above threshold. This again demonstrates the superior effectiveness of the excitation cluster that results in a maximum frequency filter [19]. The actual stimulus intervals that are most effective depend on the time constants and on the conditions of summation at the next junction down the line. When Burns and Pritchard searched in the responses of visual cortical neurons for some feature of the signal that would show whether the visual field was centred on the black or the white side of a contrasty edge [2], the feature that fitted best was the relative abundance of short intervals—that is, the occurrence of short bursts (Fig. 15.4).

Although little is known of the occurrence of temporal patterns in the interneurons, they are indicated by the facts of discrimination. We are wonderfully receptive to sequence—music, dance, tremor in the voice, a series of symbols such as words scanned into a time series; all of these are conveyed by groups of interneurons. Small nuances and errors of timing, if they are discriminated, must cause differential responses by different interneurons, somewhere. According to uniformitarian principles we can only suggest that the interneurons discriminate even complicated sequences by principles that have been amply illustrated at a simple level. Something must do it and we know of nothing else that can fill the requirement or could be imagined to act in this way.

As to the part played by the timing of impulses in the mind-body (or thought-brain) problem, we can say nothing yet that is worth saying. The interneuron accepts a stream of sometimes conflicting depolarisations, and emits a signal that for that line omits earlier discrepancies and noise. The whole mind accepts a stream of facts, errors, and memories and makes from them a series of decisions, feelings, and movements. As outlined later, each level of activity and each type of experimental

Figure 15.4

A possible significance of interspike interval distributions in conveying a signal by the proportion of short intervals. The frequency of occurrence of intervals between spikes from a neuron of the visual cortex of the cat. The proportion of short intervals in the spike train of a unit carries information as to which side of a contrasting moving edge that unit is centred upon, although the unit has no knowledge of the small eye movements that make it possible for it to respond at all. In this experiment the contrasting edge oscillates at 3 cycles per sec and amplitude 0.5° to simulate eye movements.

For the three figures on the left the centre of the unit's field (*black spot*) lay 2° from the contrasting border; for the three on the right it lay 0.5° away. In each case there is a relatively higher frequency of short intervals when the unit is centred on the light side of the boundary, irrespective of inversion and actual brightness. [Burns and Pritchard, 1964.]

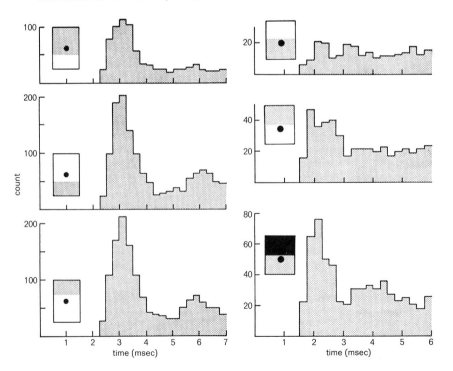

result can be used to explain the other in the sense of clarification, but the causal relations cannot be completely laid out because only a small proportion of the factors involved can be assessed. Still, every opportunity to unify knowledge of brains, behaviour, and the mind has to be grasped. There is no scientific reason to suppose that brain mechanisms have any unique feature in man even though, in their entirety, they are beyond the edge of the experimental universe.

COMPUTERS AND NEURONAL CONNEXIONS

The computer is distinctly complementary to and not a substitute for man's creative talent. The investigator can imagine a causal relationship or see an event in a new framework, but he is unable to explore the

Figure 15.5

Histogram plots of responses of two units, from the cochlear nucleus of the cat.
A. Histogram of about 4000 interspike intervals of various durations from 0 to 250 msec. The numbers of intervals are plotted vertically on a logarithmic scale with the typical result of a fairly straight sloping line along the tops of the columns.
B. Histogram of the occurrence of spikes at various intervals after a click stimulus.
C. Histogram of the occurrence of spikes at various intervals after a 25 msec tone stimulus at 14.7 kc/sec.
D, E, and **F.** Similar plots from a different unit, with a 25 msec tone stimulus at 25.6 kc/sec in **F.**
Histograms are useful for showing averages from many responses, but this kind of information is not available to the next unit down the line, which has to respond to whatever ongoing activity it receives. [After Kiang, ref. 13, p. 242.]

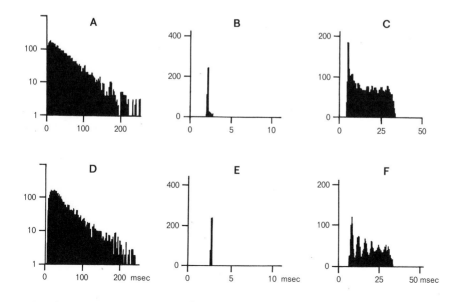

relations he has conjectured if there are many simultaneous interactions or if the channels of analysis go too deep. The computer, although unable to depart from its defined rules, can explore relations very quickly and systematically, but it can only work out the consequences of an idea, with no verification of its relevance to the animal. The computer functions as an extension of time-limited man, who uses it to evaluate his models. But even if a computer model simulates the behaviour exactly, we don't know that the mechanism has the formal structure that we proposed in setting up the model.

The other major use of the computer is to organize data. Anyone who owns a warehouse full of data, whether it be shipping office ledgers or bird-banding records, knows that the major problem is one of access and classifying. Once the material is on cards or tape, a computer performs these operations very well and will do arithmetic upon relevant parts of the data, with valuable conclusions that are really sophisticated summaries.

The problem we face is how to understand nervous integration—that is, the origin of the behaviour that emerges when the sensory background reacts with the nervous system. But when we open our eyes to what it is that we are finding out, rather than our aims, we observe that the most meaningful results are always structures. At best they are realistic structures, like patterns of synapses between neurons, but often they are model structures like a set of lines on paper, which is simply a representation of the pattern of interactions called physiological pathways. At any rate they are structures that theoretically can be built as working models. Nothing else satisfies us in this decade. When we digest the results of experiments to understand nervous organization (as distinct from nerve membrane function), we express the results as physiological pathways and represent synapses as connexions between lines of discharge. When we take any small entity—say, one synapse or a group of synapses, since they usually don't just come singly—we consider it geometrically as an object in space, with current flow causing spike initiation. Without this visualization of the real thing, a mathematical equation describing the relation between input and output, as produced by a summarizing computation, is a contribution that we do not accept as an explanation; an infinite number of other equations could provide reasonable approximations of the same input-output relations. Only one structural representation of what actually goes on will ultimately resist all efforts at disproof.

In view of the complexities of neuron interaction we can envisage an enormous potential for computer techniques within experiments. The two distinct roles of the computer come together at this point. By computations based on numerous simultaneous records of single units, the computer can produce mathematical relationships that are representative of the average interactions of the neuron population (Fig. 15.5). Qualitative experimental data of a different kind may then show the function of some of the neurons, such as the location of excitation and inhibition, in order to exclude some of the possible models of all possible inter-connections of the nerve cells. We can then proceed with model building. Some of the remaining conceptual or diagrammatic arrangements are then ruled out by a quantitative analysis of them as models, by further use of the representative data. By this method, coupled with progressively deeper experiments, we might hope to rule out all except one of all possible models. But the complexity of the nervous system means that, in practice, black boxes are successively opened to reveal more black boxes within. This general method is acceptable where there are many inter-neurons with similar properties and effects. It is much more difficult, however, to deal with the situation now common among the invertebrates, in which one neuron (perhaps for long unsuspected) has an overriding excitatory or veto effect. It has been shown that where there are few and individually identifiable neurons, as in the invertebrates, this identity matters very much. To identify cells singly has not so far been possible or been expressed as essential in vertebrates, but when that time comes we can anticipate a need for even more subtle and extensive data logging and exploration of models by computer.

Simulated networks of model interneurons have many disappointing features and so far have taught us little that is relevant to real neuron patterns. An increase in the number of connexions soon brings an in-superable computational complexity, and models become impossible to handle long before they approach the complexity of real systems. If the artificial net is too lively, any effects that are sought, such as learning, are submerged in background activity. An artificial net that is not lively enough tends to go dead and not recover. A reasonable liveliness has to be carefully achieved by tuning components to suit quite an artificial state of affairs, and even then the net tends to throb with pulses of activity. The conclusion from one detailed study was that an artificial net based on direct anatomical analogy will teach us nothing because it is too rich in connectivity and synapse types [12]. A systematic series of computations with various parameters becomes prohibitively expensive as the numbers of neurons in the net increases beyond the trivial [11].

INTERNEURON TRANSFORMATIONS AND VON NEUMANN'S ARITHMETIC

In his Silliman lectures, von Neumann wisely, and rather before his time, pointed out that brains are quite different from computers because the latter perform their operations many times over, and that such "in depth" or iterative methods make use of small differences between large numbers

[10]. They therefore demand an accuracy of better than one part in ten billion, whereas nerve cells rarely achieve one part in a hundred. On this account alone, the arithmetic performed by nervous systems must be "shallow," with few iterations.

Having now surveyed some interneurons we find that the operations performed at synapses have the logical components of arithmetic—conjunction, alternation, the conditional, exclusion, and negation—in that receptive dimensions of interneurons are recombined in this way. However, the operations performed by neurons are not hard-edged or unchanging as are the logical rules. A conjunction of two interneurons upon a third is usually weighted to give preference to one of them. A conditional element can be present at certain times but not at others, such that stimulation of another area, again weighted, is sometimes effective; moreover, the past history of all parts of the system may enter into the result. A great deal of interaction goes on together, often in a complex geometrical packet such as the optic cartridge of the arthropods or the olfactory bulb of the vertebrates. This fits exactly with von Neumann's concept of a "shallow" computation, which he inferred as necessarily present by an argument based on the relative importance of errors. Because many parallel paths are available, even quite subtle reflexes can be performed by three-neuron arcs. We can infer from the shortness of the latencies of learnt reactions in man that quite complicated predetermined discriminations can be achieved centrally in less than 100 msec. This inference eliminates the possibility of many successive relays, and it agrees with the properties of interneurons as set out in this book.

TWO UNSOLVED PROBLEMS, POSSIBLY RELATED

When we pick up a broken pebble and examine its fractured face, we can imagine that another part exists that fits against it exactly. Similarly, light may be thrown on some scientific problems by a realisation that an entirely different group of facts are complementary in an unexpected way.

The differences between interneurons have been abundantly described, each with its receptive field. However, the response of a neuron for a well-defined stimulus must also be considered as a function of time. Almost all exteroreceptors are phasic. Most neurons adapt when a constant stimulus is applied; all have a transfer function that defines the relation between the response and the stimulus (for maintained, oscillatory, or ramp-shaped stimuli) as a function of time. We know very little, however, about the variability of the time constant of adaptation or of variability of other features of the transfer function when the same neuron is examined in different individuals. There are slow and fast motoneurons in vertebrates, and well-defined features such as the slowly and rapidly adapting stretch receptor neurons of the crayfish abdomen (Fig. 8.2). Neurons of *Aplysia* are said to be remarkably consistent between specimens. Where individual neurons can be distinguished they usually have similar time constants from animal to animal. Differences between individuals occur, however, and I know of no accurate catalogue of them. Certainly the variance between animals for a given neuron is little studied, but is familiar to all who work with identifiable neurons of arthropods and *Aplysia*.

Careful mapping of receptive fields of individual neurons reveals numerous small irregularities in the responsiveness of the neuron as a function of stimulus variables other than change of intensity with time. Again accurate information is scarce, but that illustrated in Figures 10.5, 10.6, 11.6, and 12.14 come to mind. If we put these facts together with the variations in the time constant, we can no longer ignore the immense problem that faces the higher-order units, which have to act effectively in the face of this variability.

As soon as we postulate, however, that every sensory-analysing system contains a simple learning mechanism somewhere along its length, by which the animal adapts itself to the peculiarities of its own receptors and interneurons, then variation in the same neuron between individuals becomes of no significance. This applies to those invertebrates in which, it is reasonable to suppose, many of the neurons are individually distinguishable. In the vertebrates, with enormous variability between individuals at the level of individual neurons, and in all examples of irregular regenerates that manage to function normally, a theory that all sensory systems in some way compensate for the variability of their own inputs in very attractive. One conclusion of Chapter 14 was that vertebrate sensory pathways contain a potential learning or optimizing system in the feedback loop at the central sensory terminals, and possibly at every relay thereafter.

EXCITATION CLUSTERS, DECISION UNITS, AND MÜLLER'S CONCEPT

A problem that is technically and conceptually more difficult to tackle than the timing of impulses in a single neuron is the relative timing in different neurons, and especially in groups of neurons with adjacent receptive fields. Numerous channels of recording are necessary, and for repeatability the neurons must be individually identified. Motoneurons are convenient, and the correlations between them have been used for models of their interaction in insect ganglia during flight. This is one available and purely analytical technique for demonstrating interaction and seeking its causes. Sensory interneuron clusters are more easily appreciated in relation to the stimulus, of which, of course, the animal has no independent knowledge. In the auditory system, for example, although the units are individually sampled, constant relation of each to the stimulus shows that differences of sound intensity, direction, and frequency excite different groups of interneurons (p. 233). For the touch sense, the control of the stimulus is more difficult, although there are many indications that the exact relative timing of mechanoreceptor impulses in different neurons is their most important aspect. Several species of fish, such as the common minnow, are able to localize the source of a small vibration in the water and to turn at once to seize it. Along the sides of the fish is the lateral line system of directional water movement receptors, all of which connect via a long nerve directly to the brain. This system is related to the ear in vertebrates and presumably the localization depends on the relative instants of arrival of impulses from different sense organs along the animal. The footpad of the cat has numerous pressure receptors, each of which responds with only a single spike to the sudden onset of a maintained pressure at the surface. Depending on the *position* of the stimulus, a particular pattern of single impulses arrives at the spinal cord in a cluster of fibres, from which the final discrimination of position is somehow achieved by the pattern-selecting properties of interneurons. That this is a feature of the whole touch system of mammals is suggested by the fact that totally blind and deaf people can learn to localize sound sources or echos by vibrating devices attached around their chest and abdomen. This means that the exact timing of impulses relative to each other in the touch system can be recovered centrally if it becomes relevant. For an outside observer to discern a significant excitation cluster combines all the difficulties of function-finding in single interneurons with the immense technical problem of multiple-channel recording from the correct group of neurons. Two-point discrimination depends on the central differences between *groups* of sensory neurons with overlapping receptive fields.

Interneurons also have receptive fields with a different degree or kind of overlap. The simpler situation, with nonoverlapping receptive fields, is less common. Every stimulus causes an "excitation cluster" of impulses, which start out together but do not necessarily remain together when projected to a distant part. Only broadly speaking, each sensory fibre evokes a sensation that is typical of its end organ, because the exact timing and distribution within the cluster can make a crucial difference further down the line. For example, only certain patterns of primary visual impulses excite groups of visual interneurons that are sensitive to movement or evoke optokinetic reflexes. Again, different temporal patterns in the touch sense are interpreted as different sensations or switch into action quite different interneurons, as must happen in the performance of a skilled reader of Braille.

Müller's concept is that a neuron carries a signal that depends on the connections of the fibre and not on the nature of the stimulus to that fibre. Classically, it is the explanation of the flashes seen when the eye is knocked. By extension in recent times the concept implies that when a particular neuron is active the animal always gets the same kind of message. We now know, however, that temporal patterns can be important in the impulse sequence (p. 387) and that the effect of one neuron in an excitation cluster is modified by the activity of others. Therefore Müller's concept appears to be only approximately true for interneurons on sensory and central pathways.

In a sense, every neuron that reaches threshold has "decided" to become active, but this becomes a meaningless definition of decision units as all neurons. From the earliest phylogenetic appearance of two-point discrimination of a touch to different segments, in ladderlike nervous systems right up to man, only a small fraction of the interneurons are known to act individually. Giant fibres are specialized examples of this type, and some of the known descending premotor fibres in invertebrates cause definite effects when they alone are stimulated. However, there need not be one unique decision unit for each action, because the excitation cluster can proceed through the nervous system until it becomes a group of simultaneously active motoneurons and final integration is achieved mechanically by muscles. This appears to be the case in the eye movements of the crab, the leg muscles of the locust when walking, and in the posture of mammals. The exact form of a behavioural response is achieved by many equally effective alternative patterns of motoneuron impulses, although each of these alternatives may still be a rigorously predetermined set of instructions. In the case of locust walking, the choice of motor output may be influenced by proprioceptors, or the variations in motor output could be spontaneous irregularities. The exact line of demarcation as to just what is a predetermined response is in fact very difficult to define (see p. 135).

Even where single command fibres bring into operation whole patterns of behaviour, there must be a central switching between mutually incompatible responses, and we may well ask whether such a decisive role can be played by a single nerve cell. The idea of an appropriate excitation cluster suggests that a command fibre is excited only under conditions that include nonactivity elsewhere. Some extremely simple examples are known but not fully understood. For example, a single excited sugar receptor cell on the foot of a hungry fly causes the complex unrolling response of the mouth parts, whereas a single salt receptor cell can cause the opposite movement when stimulated. Again, walking and flight in insects are incompatible via a simple reflex; contact of the feet with the ground inhibits flight and loss of contact promotes it. But vertical muscles in the thorax of some insects act antagonistically in walking and synergistically in flight, with the same motoneurons in each case. Granted the contact with ground, the central command to "walk" divides the motoneurons into one set of antagonists whereas the command to "fly" divides them into a different set of antagonists with other rules of rhythmical control. The decisive activity that is observed experimentally can be of a group of neurons or, in other cases, of a single one.

THE POSSIBILITY OF A COMPLETE SOLUTION

Suppose that with the hopes of youth and the knowledge and skills of experience, we attempted a complete description of the nervous system of one animal, to show how its behaviour thereby originates. What kind of a work would this be?

To limit the problem to proportions that are manageable, we must choose a simple system. In the nerve net animals, ctenophores and coelenterates, one neuron of a net can act in place of another, neurons are indeterminate in number and far more numerous than seems necessary, responses are rather limited, and the results may not be applicable to other types of organization. These facts drive us to look among the lower phyla, in which some nervous systems have a supposedly fixed small number of neurons, which are mostly recognizable as sensory, motor, and central interneurons. Of these groups of animals the nematodes have a fixed number of cells, but their central neurons are accepted as being in cytoplasmic continuity with each other. Moreover, this group bears no promise of depth or diversity of behaviour. Therefore we turn either to one of the smaller free-living animals (a rotifer, gastrotrich, or tardigrade) or to a free-living larva (a nauplius or trochophore), or to a larger animal in which the problem is simplified by segmental repetition (an annelid worm or a myriapod).

The first problem is the exact anatomical description of the system studied. The enthusiastic beginner usually overlooks the fact that the object of study has a detailed anatomical form. Methods whereby nerve cells and their processes can be followed are few. Indeed, only three principal methods will enable even a reasonable proportion of the axon pathways to be followed. These methods are vital staining with methylene blue, impregnation by one of the Golgi methods, and following degenerative changes after a lesion. But, in small animals, only the larger neurons and axons will be revealed; fibres down to 0.05 μm diameter are abundant; this is probably the size range of fibres that interact in neuropile and they are mostly unresolved by the light microscope. Therefore we must reconstruct the system from serial electron microscope sections. This brings a major advantage if we are content to accept one useful assumption—not yet proved invalid—that definite clefts between two neurons in contact, with synaptic vesicles or other signs on one side, are really synapses in the physiological sense. If we assume also that the synaptic vesicles are presynaptic in the physiological sense, it may be possible to infer pathways of excitation. This assumption may have to be rejected if proved wrong more times than is tolerable.

It is feasible, therefore, that the nervous system of a small animal can be described completely in terms of the geometry of the outer membrane of all its neurons, together with all recognizable structural synapses or anastomoses.

Having achieved so much by nothing more than tedium and care of serial sectioning, the next problem is set by the fact that the resolution of our physiological methods nowhere nearly approaches that of the anatomy. Microelectrodes are essential to probe each region to discover what is actually going on, and our best microelectrodes record from axons down to about 2 μm in diameter. Most fine axons occur in bundles that are surrounded by tough glial sheaths, into which microelectrodes do not penetrate. Then, to correlate with the anatomy, the axon from which the recordings are made must be identified. To do this requires a knowledge of the constancy of the geometry and the certainty with which neurons can be recognized.

Anatomical recognition of individual neurons has proceeded much further in the invertebrates than in mammals, whose abundance of motoneurons and central neurons of each type makes it almost impossible to recognize individuals. In the best-known invertebrates it is clear that the same individual cell can be recognized in one anatomical preparation after another, on physiological and anatomical evidence. This, at any rate, holds true for the larger interneurons, most of the motor fibres, and to a less extent for the sensory fibres, in polychaetes and arthropods (p. 98). It is reasonable to suppose that higher-order interneurons on sensory pathways, premotor interneurons leading to motor systems, and motoneurons will be reasonably constant from animal to animal in a creature such as a rotifer or in the segment of a worm. However, no one has ever suggested a constancy in the small interneurons, especially in the special groups of globuli cells in higher centres. The above statements are in fact optimistic, because the physiological identification of individual neurons has hardly been achieved except in the crayfish, the motoneurons of the cockroach, and a relatively minute fraction of the larger cells in some other animals.

To find where an electrode marks a thin fibre of interest, we must search through serial sections, whether or not under the electron microscope, but in invertebrate neuropile it is then not possible to identify the sectioned fibre as one of those previously delineated in the reconstruction of the whole animal. In general, we would have to reconstruct from a number of serial sections until some feature in the geometry of that fibre revealed the individuality of the neuron to which it belonged. On a large scale, special selective stains for neurons might be combined with electrode markers to identify neurons individually. The best that has been achieved picks out individual marked cells, with luck, but fibres that are marked cannot be recognized as originating from particular neurons or even neuron types.

If we have a circuit diagram, there are several reasons why we cannot trust it from one minute to the next. We cannot prove that structural synapses are functional, that the endings may not actually move, and that some clear contacts may be purely trophic. Moreover, in all the lower animals there are neurons containing obvious secreted products (see Fig. 6.9). Our notions in this field are derived from neurosecretion, but that concept is widening rapidly. Many cells loaded with vesicles are undoubtedly neurons in that they may be pre- or postsynaptic, but no special end organ need be present to define a neurosecretory function; some of these neurons end in the glial sheath in molluscs. Nor need they stain by special histological techniques. We may even imagine that there are neurons that secrete and yet have no obvious collections of vesicles or droplets within them. It is widely known that different sets of neurons respond selectively to different active substances. If we were looking for a type of neuron that could account for integration over long periods of time or could cause a long-term shift of emphasis from one preferred circuit to another, then secretory neurons would stand out as appropriate. The trouble is that no one seems to have tested them. If secretions have any action at all on surrounding neuron activities, we will have to revise our concepts about long-term integration in ganglia and analyse the system only when the hormones are at a known level of activity (see Fig. 15.6). The relation between secretion, spike activity, and responses to other secretions will have to be examined in many individual cases before generalizations can be made.

In the rabbit hypothalamus two nuclei that show very similar anti-diuretic secretory activity show very different responses when their spike activity is examined. Supraoptic neurons are generally accelerated by intracarotid injection of hypertonic sodium chloride or glucose, but paraventricular neurons are inhibited. The majority of all hypothalamic neurons responsive to osmotic stimuli are not sensitive to touch or to auditory or visual stimuli [3]. For some reason, animals that have eyes and actively move around are more attractive for analysis than those in which the whole behaviour is restricted to secretion or cellular differentiation. Our attitudes are coloured by success in the analysis of rapid responses, but many animals manage well enough with almost none. We may well have been led far astray from the more germane pursuit of the control and effects of secretions.

Turning away from the relatively straightforward anatomical ques-

Figure 15.6

A characteristic long-term activity that depends upon the appropriate hormonal condition, which is in turn controlled by an annual cycle. A pair of English frogs, *Rana temporaria*, in amplexus. The motor centres of the spinal cord of the male maintain the grasp of the female even after the forebrain, midbrain, and all special senses of the head are lost. [Photograph by W. B. Pitt.]

tions, we find a series of logical and methodological problems in our complete analysis of interneuron activity. Many difficulties can be inferred from the accounts in Chapters 9–12 of what has been found; a condensed list follows this chapter. For a complete solution of the functioning of a ganglion of even a few neurons, these difficulties are formidable indeed.

Although we may trust that activity in a central neuron always conveys to the next stage down the line a message that depends only on the line-labelling of the neuron, it is necessary to record from all the other neurons simultaneously and to vary the external stimuli over all possible ranges, to prove that no pattern of impulses in other neurons will modify the effects of the one in question. Clearly this survey becomes ridiculous as the number of neurons increases, but enumeration of all possible interactions, coupled with rejection of all but one, is the only way to secure a proof of this type of question.

More hopefully, following a different path, we examine the behaviour first, and then try to account mechanistically for each act of behaviour. If the animal ignores over a certain time scale most of the continual activity of its sense organs and interneurons, we also may ignore them over the same time scale. The time scale, however, is important.

In the comparison between nervous systems and computers we came against the problem of iterative depth—that is, the number of successive operations required by the device to obtain its output or solution. It was inferred (p. 394) that in a small ganglion or even in the human brain there are not a large number of steps in the operation whereby behaviour is controlled by input, but that multilateral interaction of many simultaneous variables is more likely to approximate the real situation. We saw that this emphasized two features of real nervous systems: (a) the proximity of synapses of different kinds upon one neuron, (b) the geometry of the dendritic tree. Both features make multilateral synaptic interaction unavoidable and the interaction is all in the form of synaptic potentials. Spikes need not be generated at all in small cells.

For a complete solution of even a tiny piece of neuropile, let us consider what multilateral interaction implies. Although several examples of single synapses have been examined in detail, their properties have not been predictable from their geometry. That would be too complicated a task, and the physiological properties of the different regions of membrane must be measured from the preparation itself. Where two or more synapses lie in close proximity, either serially or in parallel, we might infer some of their individual properties if the physiological behaviour of the two together is known in a variety of conditions. When dozens of synapses occur within one space constant and are formed by contacts of numerous axons of different types (see Fig. 9.7), there seems no hope of inferring their separate contributions or the meaning of the arrangement by present techniques. Moreover, each measured feature is a statistical variable, whereas the input/output relations can depend critically upon one extreme value or a momentary change. A reasonable hope is to record the input on numerous channels together with the output of that region of neuropile and regard it as an impenetrable black box. Even this approach assumes all activity ultimately has an electrical effect. This assumption is evidently not justified when long-term behaviour and learning are included, because there is abundant evidence that synthesis and secretion are involved. Neither the physiological pathways nor the behaviour are predictable from the detailed morphological pattern of synaptic connexions, although the two aspects may be correlated if separately investigated.

REFERENCES FOR CHAPTER 15

1. Békésy, G. von. 1965. Inhibition and the time and spatial patterns of neural activity in sensory perception. *Ann. Oto. Laryngol.* **74**:445–462.
2. Burns, B. D., and Pritchard, R. 1964. Contrast discrimination by neurones in the cat's visual cerebral cortex. *J. Physiol.* **175**:445–463.
3. Cross, B. A., and Green, J. D. 1959. Activity of single neurones in the hypothalamus; effect of osmotic and other stimuli. *J. Physiol.* **148**:554–569.
4. Evans, E. F., and Whitfield, I. C. 1964. Classification of unit responses in the auditory cortex of the unanaesthetized and unrestrained cat. *J. Physiol.* **171**:476–493.
5. Fitzhugh, R. 1957. The statistical detection of threshold signals in the retina. *J. Gen. Physiol.* **40**:925–948.
6. Horn, G. 1965. Physiological and psychological aspects of selective perception, in *Advances in Animal Behaviour*, Lehrman, D. S., Hinde, R. A., and Shaw, T. I. (Eds.). New York, Academic Press.
7. Lorente de Nó, R. 1938. Analysis of the activity of the chains of interneurons. *J. Neurophysiol.* **1**:207–244.
8. Marler, P. 1961. The filtering of external stimuli during instinctive behaviour, in *Current Problems of Animal Behaviour*, Thorpe, W. H., and Zangwill, O. L. (Eds.). Cambridge University Press.
9. Murata, K., Cramer, H., and Bach-y-Rita, P. 1965. Neuronal convergence of noxious, acoustic and visual stimuli in the visual cortex of the cat. *J. Neurophysiol.* **28**:1233–40.
10. Neumann, J. von. 1958. *The Computer and the Brain.* Silliman Memorial Lectures. Yale University Press.
11. Paxson, E. W. 1962. An elementary cortical cylinder. *Rand Corp. Mem.* RM–3405–PR.
12. Perkel, D. H. 1964. Neurophysiological models; methods and applications. *Rand Corp. Mem.* RM–4247–NIH.
13. Rose, J. S., Greenwood, D. D., Goldberg, J. M., and Hind, J. E. 1963. Some discharge characteristics of single neurons in the inferior colliculus of the cat. *J. Neurophysiol.* **26**:294–341.
14. Scheibel, M. E., and Scheibel, A. B. 1958. Structural substrates for integrative

patterns in the brain stem reticular core, in *The Reticular Formation of the Brain*, Jasper, H. H., Proctor, L. D., Knighton, R. S., Noshay, R. S., and Costello, R. T. (Eds.). Boston, Little, Brown.

15. Scheibel, M. E., and Scheibel, A. B. 1966. Spinal motorneurons, interneurons and Renshaw cells. A Golgi study. *Arch. ital. Biol.* **104**:328–353.
16. Schipperheyn, J. J. 1965. Contrast detection in frog's retina. *Acta Physiol. Pharmacol. Neerl.* **13**:231–277.
17. Segundo, J. P., Moore, G. P., Stensaas, L. J., and Bullock, T. H. 1963. Sensitivity of neurones in *Aplysia* to temporal pattern of arriving impulses. *J. Exp. Biol.* **40**:643–667.
18. Shimazu, H., and Precht, W. 1965. Tonic and kinetic responses of cat's vestibular neurons to horizontal angular acceleration. *J. Neurophysiol.* **28**:991–1013.
19. Uttley, A. M. 1961. The engineering approach to the problem of neural organisation, in *Progress in Biophysics and Biophysical Chemistry*, Butler, J. A. V., Katz, B., and Zirkle, R. E. (Eds.). London, Pergamon Press.
20. Uttley, A. M. 1962. Properties of plastic networks. *Biophys. J.* **2**:169–188.
21. Werner, G., and Mountcastle, V. B. 1963. The variability of central neural activity in a sensory system and its implications for the central reflection of sensory events. *J. Neurophysiol.* **26**:958–977.
22. Wilson, B. M., and Davis, W. J. 1965. Nerve impulse patterns and reflex control in the motor system of the crayfish claw. *J. Exp. Biol.* **43**:193–210.
23. Wilson, D. M., and Wyman, R. J. 1965. Motor output patterns during random and rhythmic stimulation of locust thoracic ganglia. *Biophys. J.* **5**:121–143.

16

Limitations on interneuron studies

In the following pages I have tried to draw together some generalities, to be read en masse. In no sense do they form a summary of the book, for they will certainly become out of date sooner than many of the facts in the text. Let me suggest that they not only designate some of the stumbling blocks and potholes that will hinder future researchers and model builders, but they also sketch out the line of some of the hills between which the road must run.

A. *The problem of identifying structure with function*
1. Single interneurons can often be recognized histologically in invertebrates and they are constant in location, but usually one must record from their axons because the cell bodies are silent. However, stereotactic measurements cannot possibly resolve single axons because the neuropile is deformed up to 50 μm by the electrode tip. It is therefore difficult to recognize individual fibres in neuropile.
2. No example is known of a population of small neurons all of one set, as revealed by their similar responses. There is always an unknown mixture. Interneurons are most easily found where they are homogeneous (Fig. 16.1); this is why the main tracts have been analysed first, but the procedure prevents identification of individual ones.
3. Marking the position of an extracellular electrode with a dye or passing current to form a lesion in tangled neuropile is not sufficiently accurate to localize single fibres. In any case, named small neurons are only recognizable by specific stains, which are too capricious as an electrophysiological aid. It is only for the very largest fibres, giving the largest spikes, that a uniquely identified neuron of known anatomical form can be given a definite function, since large fibres give stereotyped responses.

4. Because synapses with one-to-one transmission are not easily inferred physiologically and are likely to occur anywhere, there is no reason to suppose that the extent of a physiological "unit" corresponds with the anatomical extent of a nerve cell. Conversely, a single cell may be more than one electrophysiological unit; it may have several all-or-none impulses in different branches.

5. With a number of dendrites entwined together, almost any structure is compatible with almost any input-output relations, so many physiological parameters are available. Spikes need not be present.

B. *The problem of function-finding of single units*

1. Many interneurons encountered in a routine probing are sensitive to a wide range of relatively strong stimuli, such as bright flashes, loud sounds, rubbing of the body, or shadows across the eye. These responses are probably all irrelevant to the "true" function of the interneuron because such strong stimulation causes the arousal

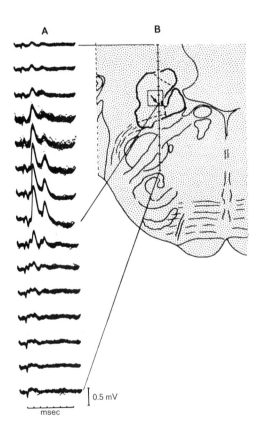

A
B

0.5 mV

msec

Figure 16.1

A method of locating the region where a large number of homogeneous fibres terminate. Field potentials from the brain stem of the cat are correlated with locations of electrode tip. The stimulus was a single shock of the vestibular nerve at each position of the electrode; upward deflection indicates negativity. About 20 superimposed traces were obtained from each of the locations indicated by the position on the scale. Scales on the vertical line of insertion of the electrode indicate intervals of 500 μm. The arrow indicates the site of maximum response where single units would be recorded with a finer electrode. [Shimazu and Precht, reference 18 on p. 404.]

of large numbers of units. Realistic responses of interneurons are distinguished by low thresholds.

2. The function of an interneuron can be discovered only by innumerable patient tests that define the contours of its response to many possible inputs. If interneurons really do abstract, in the sense that they respond only when a meaningful pattern impinges on them, the appropriate type of pattern may sometimes be partially guessed by inspection of the whole range of the animals' normal behaviour, but usually this is not yet known.

3. A single interneuron is in general not likely to control a specific response for the following reason. A response requires several motoneurons, and each motoneuron is excited by a suitable cluster of interneurons. Therefore it is this cluster that should be sought as the key to the response to a specific stimulus.

4. Having found units that respond, most of the wealth of electrophysiological detail from them seems to be irrelevant, and when changes in the response of a unit are found, there are no rules for distinguishing whether the changes are relevant ones or whether they are secondary effects.

5. Most interneurons can only be studied in relative isolation. In vertebrates especially, an understanding of the integrated behaviour requires knowledge of the actions of groups of neurons.

6. Only stimulus situations known to be relevant need be considered, but we usually do not know what is relevant to an animal that is so unlike ourselves. The same problem applies to machines built to perform like animals; it is usually impossible to predict what they are best suited for.

7. The best measure of whether a stimulus is appropriate is that the next higher-order interneuron, which the observed neuron acts upon, is also giving a healthy response. This is difficult to achieve, and presumably some of the highest interneurons only fire on very particular occasions. Therefore analysis of an ongoing behavioural response, in which motoneurons are the terminal analysers, is always more promising than searching for the receptive field of interneurons that have been randomly encountered.

8. Specificity can always be enhanced by disregarding small responses and by supposing that discriminations exist between patterns of impulses and differences in some measure of the strength of response. Whether the next higher interneuron so discriminates must then be tested.

9. The more stimuli there are employed, the more types of unit there are found; it is feasible that there are no two identical units, including sensory fibres, in any nervous system.

10. The observer tries to correlate the interneuron response with the

Figure 16.2

Specialized arborizations that are restricted in distribution to definite regions of layered neuropile; see also Figures 10.8, 12.3, and 13.9. Note the diversity of types of terminals, which set intriguing problems as to how they grow in this way, the effect and importance of the shape and position, and how they distinguish each other when forming the appropriate synaptic contacts. This section is of the optic medulla of the blowfly. (Cajal and Sánchez, reference 10 on p. 192.)

stimulus and can make use of repeated stimuli and latency; the interneuron, however, has no knowledge of the actual stimulus but merely integrates whatever excitation falls upon it. Therefore latencies, average responses, or histograms based on responses may be useful in analysis but cannot be used by the nervous system.

11. Study of the hormonal control of behaviour has led to the depressing generalization that no single hormone has a specific effect upon an individual action that can be traced to few neurons; on the contrary, hormones act in unison upon the whole CNS or upon units of such high order that they in turn have widespread effects.

C. *Additional problems in studying learning*

1. There is no reason to suppose that learning mechanisms are all of one kind or that the primary elements in learning will be evident in the properties of neuron membranes.

2. The experimental conditions for electrophysiology and for learning are usually antagonistic to each other. Plastic changes usually require highly patterned noninjurious stimuli, free movement, and freedom from anaesthetic or painful distracting stimuli.

3. The first, and perhaps only, use of electrode work in studies of learning is to locate the neurons in which changes can *first* be detected. This means that the constancy of the presynaptic inputs must be demonstrated simultaneously.

4. Habituation and interaction effects can readily be found in interneurons, but small units cannot be held for long, so that it is usually impossible to work on long-term effects. Usually a return to the initial state of affairs shows that a neuron keeps its own properties. Interneurons that change their inputs on stimulation would be a pleasant surprise but difficult to anticipate with a suitable stimulus.

5. There is no general means of telling whether an effect, if discovered, is the primary cause or a secondary effect of a long-term change.

6. When one is searching for units that may change their preferred pattern of input, means must be found for ensuring that the change is seen. But one cannot avoid modifying the relevant unit while tests are fruitlessly applied to another unit that turns out to be of no interest. This is the major problem in the observation of learning in action because at the critical area the crucial change presumably occurs between presentations, or at a single presentation.

7. Apart from morphogenetic changes equivalent to growth, no means has been demonstrated by which long-term adaptive changes in the membrane or in the connections of neurons are controlled by cytoplasmic systems. We have no available mechanisms of learning, and hardly know what to look for within the cell.

8. The ultimate test of whether a change is the crucial one in learning is to see whether learning can be induced by bringing about this change artificially in a naive animal, with no other effect.

D. *Limitations of explanatory models*

1. Electron microscopy reveals that the majority of the fibres in all nervous systems are in the range 0.2 to 2.0 μm and many are 0.1 μm in diameter. Electrodes made to date record only from fibres in the size range 3.0 ± 2.0 μm upwards. Numerous explanations

of what is seen are therefore possible in terms of what is not seen, but such explanations are not testable.

2. A model of physiological pathways can be drawn from results of electrophysiological recording experiments, and comparable fibres can be described anatomically. However, before equating these pathways with the mechanism of a behavioural response, we have to be sure that we know every aspect of the behaviour in its full complexity. Subsequent reappraisal usually reveals aspects that were not taken into account, and the whole model may fall.

3. It is impossible to explain higher-order units in terms of lower-order ones until *all* of the latter have been found. For technical reasons, which have been given, this is never possible.

4. One must necessarily obtain a large variety of information on one animal because every animal has a different history at this level of detail. The same applies to every unit tested, because the same neuron will usually not be encountered again. There is therefore

Figure 16.3

Differences in shape of arborizations in the same region of neuropile, and different types of dendrite on one neuron.

A. Second-order cells of the optic pathway of the bee, which form columnar synaptic regions, or cartridges, in the lamina (1st optic neuropile); see Figures 9.7, 9.10, and 13.2.

B. The same region of the lamina of the bee, as in **A**, showing long ramifying fibres. In contrast to those in **A** these are bound to have large receptive or effective fields, whether afferent or efferent. (Cajal and Sánchez, reference 10 on p. 192.)

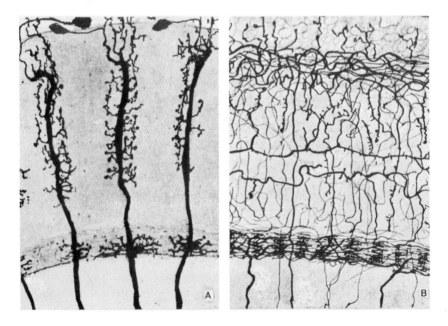

a philosophical problem of reproducibility to tackle. There is an enormous difference between looking at units and the exact analysis of variance in their activity.

5. The occurrence of numerous parallel lines and the existence of their activity in concert, together with the known large overlaps in receptive fields and multimodal units, means that spurious correlations are readily found between activities in any pairs of units. Multitudes of subsets of the most diverse composition interact in all the highest centres in animals with large brains.

6. The possibility of innumerable feedback loops within even the smallest ganglion casts a shadow over any hope of finding a linear sequence whereby one cause has one effect, from sensory neurons through interneurons to motor neurons. Surprisingly, however, and perhaps through ignorance, almost all interneurons and responses in invertebrates have been attributed to straight-line transmission paths, without neural feedback loops.

7. The possibility of persistent effects caused by storage and secretion of chemicals and movements of neuron terminals casts doubt on the possibility of ever evaluating the whole causal influences on any single situation, because long-term changes prevent reproducibility.

E. *Consequences of the filtering action of interneurons*

1. The animal has some means (presumably by its interneuron filters that we are studying) by which it rejects the majority of the vast sensory inflow that is irrelevant, and it operates only on a fraction of importance. Biological systems are not interested in the totality of impinging information—only in certain combinations of detail of relevance to them.

2. Most of the impinging snowstorm of sensory excitation, even in the simplest animals, cannot be satisfactorily defined. We have to rely on the animal's own exclusion of numerous stimuli, which are by definition irrelevant, and look only at changes that it notices.

3. We have faith that the behaviour of an animal depends on the sum of the responses of its neurons to sensory stimuli and to each other. A glance at the responses of individual interneurons reveals an unexpected ambiguity, besides an obscure representation of the stimulus in the higher-order units. The outside world of the animal cannot be reconstructed (by man) when interneurons are examined one at a time. Even if all third-order units were recorded simultaneously, it would still be impossible to interpret the outside world, because a great deal of information has been thrown away be the first- and second-order stages.

4. The reduction in the number of neurons as we pass from sense

organ to motoneuron is paralleled by the throwing away of information as we move from fantastically complex patterns of stimuli from the outside world to a behavioural output with much less information content. It is impossible therefore to infer a unique solution of the mechanism from a quantitative knowledge of the output of any stage. There can never be as many equations as there are unknowns. In contrast, a formal model of the class of mechanism involved can sometimes be inferred by very simple experimental manipulation.

5. In none of the responses of interneurons in any animal, I believe, can the exact nature of the stimulus be reconstructed from the observed pattern of impulses. This ambiguity from the point of view of the outside observer sets a serious problem when we try to explain exact adaptive behaviour in neuronal terms, without reference to the environment to which the behaviour is adapted.

6. Faith in the analytical approach compels us to suppose that the combined activity of all the interneurons in an animal will give a unique picture of those aspects of the stimulus that are relevant, but it remains to be demonstrated that this is in fact so.

F. *Limitations of logical systems that include neural networks*

1. We do not know that all operations of a nervous system are logical. Analysis is successful only so far as we discover regularities. Beyond the firm ground there is always a region where unknown principles may hold.

2. Interneurons are not describable in terms such as "a class of stimuli X excite a class of interneurons Y, *and no other stimuli will do so.*" For all interneurons the situation is open-ended.

3. The total possible interactions of nerve cells cannot be reduced to a limited number of axioms, because these are necessarily inadequate to predict all possible behaviour. Any nervous system can perform actions that are not predictable from a set of descriptive explanations that up to that time is apparently complete.

4. Every property of every interneuron must be unearthed by constructive imaginative experiments. Within the intact nervous system very little can be inferred, because so many alternative interactions are possible.

5. For any region of a nervous system such as an olfactory ganglion we have no certainty that the number of inputs can be described in the time available for experiment.

6. The complete physical state [20] of the nervous system is not determinable, and is influenced by nonnervous factors.

7. Because there is a memory of unknown length, the complete physical state of the nervous system has been determined by events over an unknown period of time.

8. If secretion or any other stored structural feature constitute effective memories, the state of the system is not determinable by observation of excitation that may fail to evoke those memories.

9. There is no reason to suppose that a descriptive method or system adequate for one interneuron will be successfully applied to another. Even the kind of applicable mathematics may be different.

10. Just as the best neuroanatomy is neurophysiologically motivated, a mathematics of multidimensional partial logic suitable for the nervous system may have to be developed by a physiologist.

11. No complex logical system can be complete. If a complete watertight explanation of all brain function could be found, it could not be correct. This is a fundamental theorem of logic and is applicable to other complex systems besides brains.

12. No question as to how a whole nervous system operates in its entirety can be solved. Again, this is a fundamental theorem that applies to all complex systems.

13. There are always combinations of stimuli and interactions of interneurons that have not been tested.

14. As we discover principles of action of neurons, we have no way of knowing whether they will later prove to be inconsistent with each other. This limitation applies to analysis of any complex mechanism.

15. In a system with a memory of unknown extent, there is no telling whether an experimental treatment modifies the state of the system with no immediately observed effect.

16. There is not necessarily a set of principles to explain a brain, because there is no coherent procedure that can test every interneuron for every stimulus.

17. The transformation of stimuli by sensory and then by interneurons must strike a compromise between lacunae and paradoxes. The more reduplication, fragmentation, and eventual integration of the nervous message, the more paradoxes or contrasting inferences will be made by the nervous system; on the other hand, the less integration, the more lacunae or missing abstracting operations there will be.

18. In detail, bearing in mind "noise," we never look at the same nerve cell twice because random fluctuations become significant with even a few neurons. Even the crustacean heart ganglion, of nine neurons, is not a predictable system.

19. The brain describes the brain itself. I quote from Bronowski (1966). "For example, we know (from the work of Kurt Gödel and A. M. Turing) that no machine that uses strict logic can examine its own instructions and prove them consistent. But if it is a question about the measureless future, then it cannot be

answered. A machine is not a natural object; it is a human artefact which mimics and exploits our own understanding of nature; and we cannot foresee how radically we may come to change that understanding. We cannot foresee and we cannot conceive all possible machines—if indeed *all* has any meaning in this sentence."

20. Each neuron and each excitatory event is an individual particularity, but descriptions of neurons and excitation are in terms of classes and systems, none of which corresponds exactly with the real world. The small discrepancies are likely to be crucial.

21. We work in a historical setting, so that tests are orientated along lines that are partly established—for example, switching of lights and movement of edges in the case of visual units. To offset this straightjacket of thought, a repeated reappraisal is required in the light of every new idea and especially when a new anatomical or behavioural detail is discovered. Although they contain no new experimental finding, even these words will influence, however mildly, the attitudes of interneuron seekers and therefore their findings.

G. *Differences between invertebrate and vertebrate interneurons*

1. Invertebrate interneurons are almost always not in homogeneous tracts, do not arise from nuclei or localized areas of definite function in the central nervous system, and do not show ordered arrays that are spatial projections of the periphery. By contrast, many vertebrate interneurons have these features, which have evolved in higher vertebrates from less ordered structures in lower vertebrates.

2. Invertebrate interneurons are often constant in number, constant in receptive field, notably stereotyped, few of each type, accurately duplicated (cell for cell) on the opposite side, and usually with constant layout of main branches. Vertebrate interneurons are numerous, not constant in number, and have dendritic patterns that are not defined for each cell, although recognizable according to their general type.

3. Vertebrates have amacrine cells near the periphery on sensory pathways, and (almost certainly related) the next-stage interneurons have regularly arranged inhibitory surrounds. The receptive fields are controlled at all levels by inhibitory feedback circuits. This organisation is not typical of invertebrates.

4. Vertebrate central circuits have specific feedback arcs to definite small subsystems, as in the visual, auditory, somatic sensory, and proprioceptive pathways. This is not known to be a special feature in invertebrates, even for antagonism of somatic muscles and for coordination of proprioceptors.

5. All central nervous systems have nonspecific systems that ramify everywhere, but in vertebrates the specific systems have neurons with dendritic fields that often are ordered in space, as in most of the nuclei of the central nervous system and in cortical, cerebellar, motor, and sensory regions. Invertebrates have highly ordered dendritic fields in optic lobes but not very obviously anywhere else.

6. Some vertebrate sensory neurons have the feature that when one is excited it may inhibit part of the sensory input. This provides a special form of pattern-selecting mechanism not typical of invertebrates. Even if it doesn't actually learn at this level, such a circuit could be a stage in the evolution of a learning circuit.

H. *General features of interneurons*

1. Interneurons are neither motor nor sensory neurons.

2. All neurons are units of pattern recognition, and every interneuron selects a particular pattern by virtue of the physiologically active connexions of its dendrites.

3. Whether a stimulus is effective or not depends on how nearly it approaches the ideal configuration of input to the neuron. Therefore the relevance of excitation depends on the response of the next stage down the line, and this can be found only by direct observation and testing of all boundary conditions.

4. All configurations of the input that stimulate it will, in general, be treated by the neuron as a single class, although in detail there are differences in firing pattern for a range of different stimuli in that class.

5. The adequate configurations that excite neurons on the sensory pathways are typically broad, so that classes can be quite large, and they overlap (as between neurons at the same level).

6. The nervous system has so evolved that interneurons accept as an adequate sign-stimulus those input configurations that are meaningful in the animal's life.

7. Ambiguity in the response of any neuron is measured by the diversity of stimuli that could have given rise to a response—that is, by the size of the class for that neuron.

8. The central nervous system has so evolved that we find interneurons that are stimulated only by relevant classes of classes of sensory neurons, and so on, as a consequence of the existence of second- and third-order stages.

9. The nervous system has so grown and evolved that motoneurons are excited only by those configurations of interneurons that, when active together, indicate that the movement they cause is environmentally appropriate to the animal's present situation and posture.

A

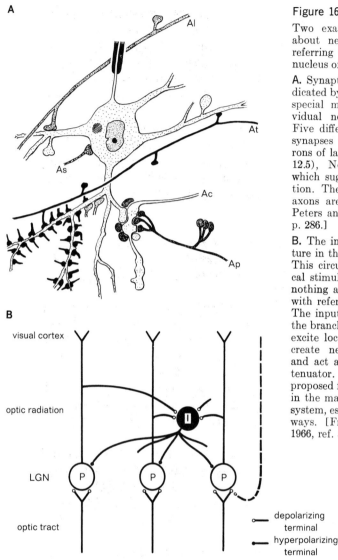

B

Figure 16.4

Two examples of generalizations about neuron connectivity, both referring to the lateral geniculate nucleus of the cat.

A. Synaptic connexions that are indicated by electron microscopy and special methods of staining individual neurons (Golgi method). Five different types of axon form synapses upon the principal neurons of laminae A and A_1 (see Fig. 12.5), Note the serial synapse, which suggests presynaptic inhibition. The origins of the various axons are not all known. [From Peters and Palay, 1966, ref. 29 on p. 286.]

B. The inferred typical unit structure in the lateral geniculate body. This circuit is based upon electrical stimulation and therefore says nothing about the coding of units with reference to peripheral fields. The input is from the optic tract; the branches of the ascending units excite local inhibitory cells, which create new inhibitory surrounds and act as an automatic local attenuator. This circuit has been proposed for numerous other places in the mammalian central nervous system, especially for sensory pathways. [From Burke and Sefton, 1966, ref. 5 on p. 285.]

10. As a result of the rejection of excitation at every stage, the final behaviour contains but a small fraction of the information in the sensory input. Most normal "background" stimuli have no visible effect on an animal.

11. Interneurons and motoneurons do not make decisions on a probabilistic basis. They either respond or not, depending on whether the input excitation exceeds threshold, and by how much.

12. Except in the extreme deterministic systems of some invertebrate

escape responses, there is no *invariant* relationship, like a telephone line, from any part of the nervous system to any other part, since axons always interact with others in their effects.

13. The discrimination in sensory pathways and the choice of action in premotor pathways depend mainly on which neurons are excited (line-labelling) and much less upon frequency-coding, which seems less important further from the sense organs and muscles.

14. Every degree of specificity of response to classes of stimuli can be found, and when one is trying to define the properties of a central unit an enormous range of possibilities has to be worked over.

15. Every individual animal with a central nervous system may feasibly have its own peculiar pattern of dendrites, and consequently a population of interneurons, which in detail is unique to that animal. If so, the interneurons have to adapt themselves to live with each other. It is probable that this is true in detail even though each species has its own fairly predetermined pattern. Perhaps learning evolved as an answer to the problem of interneuron indeterminacy, which, to interneurons further down the line, is inseparable from environmental indeterminacy.

16. At no stage in the nervous system is there an operator or centre upon which the environment is projected. Transformation, collection, comparison, and decision begin at the sense organs.

17. A neuron cannot, as has been suggested, "in a series of transactions compute the probabilities of optimum service to the adaptive needs of the organism" or make any similar calculation or prediction. The response does not depend on whether the incoming signal is significant, new, or familiar. The neuron responds as and when its threshold is exceeded by whatever pattern impinges upon it.

18. An interneuron with wide connections and numerous inputs presumably serves a very basic function, such as reinforcement or arousal.

19. To say that an interneuron responds to the "space structure or time-frequency-dimensionality of its input fibres" (and this has been said) is to suspend one's analytical power on the turn of a plausible phrase. The phrasing will soon be torn to pieces when another investigator defines these parameters more exactly.

20. A pattern-classifying network for a complete discrimination between all combinations of n inputs requires 2^n indicating units, and with increasing number of inputs soon becomes impracticable. Limited classifications adapted to the environment are therefore essential; hence the effectiveness of contours and movement as components of stimulus situations. Ability to learn is a tremendous advantage in survival, so that classificatory or sensory analyser

systems may cope with an environment that has initially unpredictable regularities.

21. Classifying networks that learn can be designed to adapt themselves to the most frequent input patterns and to distinguish about as many patterns as there are units in the system.

22. Careful mapping of receptive fields and quantitative responses reveals numerous irregularities in the properties of interneurons. This variability, together with this unpredictability of normal stimuli, again implies a strong dependence by higher-order interneurons on a mechanism, which may be learning, by which the interneurons adapt themselves to the properties of their inputs and those of their neighbours.

23. Although they cannot make decisions, certain interneurons or groups of them have an activity we call decisive, in that when these are active they cause responses or block the potential activity of rival interneurons. Where such circuits have been described —for example, the either-or properties of Mauthner axons—they are clearly determined genetically, but more subtle ones must also originate by learning.

24. Numerous interneurons can act in parallel and abstract different summaries of the incoming excitation. Each operates on its own time scale. Only those with short time scales have been investigated so far.

25. There is a marked contrast between the period of about 1 msec, which is adequate for the inhibitory surround to sharpen up the localization of a peripheral stimulus at the central endings of nearby receptor fibres, and the period of at least 100 msec, which is necessary for a psychological test using the same stimulus.

26. In a system of interneurons every input experience proceeds into the system along a unique pattern of pathways that it matches. However, in all animals, many parallel pathways perform different aspects of the abstraction process. The over-all behaviour of such a system agrees with the observation that the access into the human recognition system is extremely rapid, considering the total size of the store of memories. If recognition really works in this way, we can infer that terminating excitation has a different local effect from through-passing excitation.

27. As Herrick repeatedly stressed, processes in the brain involving ordinary atoms and molecules occur in an orderly fashion. But the question remains whether the brain is a machine in the sense in which that term is normally used. Machines are known to be mechanical; at every stage they are either determinate with sharply defined inputs and outputs, or probabilistic, with definite probabilities that are estimatable and the result of an engineer's

design considerations. But interneurons are different from machines because the total language in which they operate cannot be expressed for numerous reasons, some of which have been listed.

28. Five principal modes of study are available: morphology of neuron connexions; physiological pathways and their activity; controlled accumulation, localization, and release of active secretions; behaviour of the whole animal; evaluation of theoretical models. No one of these aspects can explain any other aspect, but the information provided by a combination of four of them is sometimes of assistance in the interpretation of the fifth.

GENERAL REFERENCES

1. Ashby, W. R. 1960. *Design for a Brain*. London, Chapman and Hall.
2. Beament, J. W. L. (Ed.). 1962. Biological receptor mechanisms. *Symp. Soc. Exp. Biol.* **16.** Cambridge University Press.
3. Brazier, M. A. B. (Ed.). 1961. *Brain and Behavior*. Washington, D.C., American Institute of Biological Science.
4. Bronowski, J. 1966. *The Identity of Man*. London, Heinemann.
5. Bullock, T. H., and Horridge, G. A. 1965. *Structure and Function in the Nervous Systems of Invertebrates*. San Francisco and London, W. H. Freeman and Company.
6. Burns, B. D. 1958. *The Mammalian Cerebral Cortex*. London, Edward Arnold.
7. Carthy, J. D. 1958. *An Introduction to the Behaviour of Invertebrates*. London, George Allen & Unwin.
8. Coghill, G. A. 1929. *Anatomy and the Problem of Behaviour*. Cambridge University Press.
9. *Comparative Neurophysiology*. 1964. *Amer. Zoologist*, Vol. 2, No. 1.
10. Craik, K. J. W. 1943. *The Nature of Explanation*. Cambridge University Press.
11. Crosby, E. C., Humphrey, T., and Lauer, E. W. 1962. *Correlative Anatomy of the Nervous System*. New York, Macmillan.
12. Deutsch, J. A. 1960. *The Structural Basis of Behaviour*. Cambridge University Press.
13. Eccles, J. C. 1964. *The Physiology of Synapses*. Berlin, Springer-Verlag.
14. Fiegenbaum, E. A., and Feldman, J. (Eds.). 1963. *Computers and Thought*. London, McGraw-Hill.
15. Field, J., Magoun, H. W., and Hall, V. E. (Eds.). 1959–1960. *Handbook of Physiology*. Section 1. *Neurophysiology*. 3 Vols. Washington, D.C., American Physiological Society.
16. Fields, W. S., and Abbot, W. (Eds.). 1963. *Information Storage and Neural Control*. Springfield, Ill., Thomas.
17. Florey, E. (Ed.). 1961. *Nervous Inhibition*. London, Pergamon Press.
18. Gerard, R. W., and Duyff, J. W. (Eds.). 1964. *Information Processing in the Nervous System*. Proceedings of the International Physiological Congress

held at Leiden 1962. Internat. Congress Series, No. 49. Publ. Excerpta Medica Foundation.

19. Gerard, R. 1965. 65th birthday number. *Perspect. Biol. Med.* **9,** No. 1.
20. Gill, A. 1962. *Introduction to the Theory of Finite-state Machines.* New York, McGraw-Hill.
21. Granit, R. 1955. *Receptors and Sensory Perception.* Newhaven, Yale University Press.
22. Granit, R. (Ed.). 1966. *Muscular Afferents and Motor Control.* New York, Wiley.
23. Gutmann, E., and Hnik, P. 1963. *The Effect of Use and Disuse on Neuromuscular Functions.* Amsterdam, Elsevier.
24. Harlow, H. F., and Woolsey, C. N. (Eds.). 1958. *Biological and Biochemical Bases of Behavior.* Madison, University of Wisconsin Press.
25. Herrick, C. J. 1956. *The Evolution of Human Nature.* Evanston, University of Texas Press.
26. Hodgkin, A. L. 1964. *The Conduction of the Nerve Impulse.* Liverpool University Press.
27. Hughes, G. M. (Ed.). 1966. *Nervous and Hormonal Mechanisms of Integration. Symp. Soc. Exp. Biol.* **20.** Cambridge University Press.
28. Nye, P. W. (Ed.). 1966. *Information Processing in Sight-sensory Systems.* Symposium at Pasadena. California Institute of Technology.
29. Ochs, S. 1965. *Elements of Neurophysiology.* New York, Wiley.
30. Reiss, R. F. (Ed.). 1964. *Neural Theory and Modeling.* Stanford University Press.
31. Roe, A., Simpson, G. G. (Eds.). 1958. *Behavior and Evolution.* New Haven, Yale University Press.
32. Roeder, K. D. 1963. *Nerve Cells and Insect Behavior.* Harvard University Press.
33. Rosenblith, W. A. (Ed.). 1959. *Sensory Communication.* New York, Wiley.
34. Ruch, T. H., Patton, H. D., Woodbury, J. W., and Towe, A. C. 1961. *Neurophysiology.* Philadelphia, Saunders.
35. Russell, W. R. 1959. *Brain, Memory, Learning.* Oxford, Clarendon Press.
36. *Sensory Receptors.* 1965. Cold Spring Harbor Symposium on Quantitative Biology **30.**
37. Sherrington, C. S. 1906. *The Integrative Action of the Nervous System.* London, Constable.
38. Sholl, D. A. 1956. *The Organization of the Cerebral Cortex.* London, Methuen.
39. Sutherland, N. S. 1962. *Shape Discrimination by Animals.* Exper. Psychol. Society Mongr. 1. Cambridge, Heffer.
40. Thorpe, W. H., and Zangwill, O. L. (Eds.). 1961. *Current Problems in Animal Behaviour.* Cambridge University Press.
41. Treherne, J. E., and Beament, J. W. L. (Eds.). 1965. *The Physiology of the Insect Central Nervous System.* New York, Academic Press.
42. Wells, M. J. 1962. *Brain and Behaviour in Cephalopods.* London, Heinemann.
43. Wolstenholme, G. E. W., and O'Connor, C. M. (Eds.). 1958. *Neurological Basis of Behaviour.* Ciba Foundation Symposium. London, Churchill.
44. Young, J. Z. 1964. *A Model of the Brain.* Oxford University Press.

Glossary

The following words have been selected for special explanation as being ones that are likely to give the reader some difficulty. Some of them involve important verbal distinctions; others are common words employed as technical terms with a special meaning; many are used elsewhere with a different meaning; most are not defined in the Glossary found on page 1595 of Bullock and Horridge (1965) (*loc. cit.*, p. 18), to which the reader is referred for explanation of other technical terms.

Activity, Spontaneity

Ongoing activity of units in the nervous system may be called "spontaneous" but that usually means that no cause is apparent. Activity in the nervous system does not necessarily imply a behavioural activity of the whole animal.

Afferent, Efferent, Centre

A centre is a small, more or less circumscribed region of the central nervous system which can be conceptually isolated for some functional or anatomical reason. Afferent excitation goes towards the centre; efferent goes away from it after transformation.

Anatomical, Physiological Pathways

The ancient form/function controversy is resolved only when the anatomy or structure is known in sufficient detail that the function becomes self-evident. Usually anatomical and physiological pathways in the nervous system are inferred from quite different types of data and only rarely do they exactly correspond. Similar comments apply to "Centres," Projections," and "Synapses." Each type of concept can be used to reveal deficiencies in the other. A physiological pathway is derived from the observation of signal transmission, and may be represented in many ways—for example, by drawings of neurons or by straight lines in block diagrams. An anatomical pathway is also an idealized or average example, and often derived from a single case with no measure of variability between individuals.

Appraisal

The voluntary maintenance of a stimulus situation until discrimination is achieved. In neuronal terms this implies that some higher order interneurons are not immediately excited but later are, for reasons that are not at all clear.

Central rhythm, Programme, Sequence

An activity pattern, at first in the neurons and then, as a consequence, sometimes observable as a behavioural response, which in some unknown way stems from the structure of the nervous system and is (at least partially) independent of proprioceptive or other sensory feedback. A rhythm is a repeated case; a programme is a spatially and temporally patterned output in many neurons; a sequence is a temporally patterned burst in one neuron.

Conditioning, Learning, Memory, Persistent effect

Any long-term adaptive change is not necessarily learning. "Conditioning" is used in the strict sense (sensory-sensory, operant, and so on) employed in books on learning theory. "Learning" is used where a persistent change is dependent on some element of conditioning. "Memory" is any persistent effect which is part of a reasonable behavioural or neural response, and need involve no reinforcement or conditioning, although it usually does so as ordinarily used. A memory is something stored; learning is the over-all process whereby it is stored when there is conditioning. It is possible therefore to imagine a memory which is not learnt, such as behaviour dependent on dark-adaptation changes or adaptation of a neuron.

Connectivity, Connexion

A connectivity pattern is the actual complete anatomical pattern of connexions between identified neurons. This goal of anatomical studies has been achieved but rarely, and in small regions, but has great explanatory power when achieved. "Connexions" is a word more loosely used for anatomical or physiological points of interaction between neurons. Connexions are not necessarily complete, but are often inferences which are indirect and sometimes tenuous. Usually alternatives and parallel pathways are not ruled out. As a reasonable goal, the most probable pattern of connexions is slowly inferred from a variety of approximate data of different kinds.

Decision

In neuronal terms, the conversion of afferent excitation into efferent excitation, which is then observed as a characteristic response of a neuron, of a centre (q.v.), or of a whole animal.

Discrimination, Line-labelling, Filters, Channelling of stimuli

The selective passage to one set of attributes rather than to another set. Given numerous parallel pathways, the different filtering properties of different neurons lead to line-labelling, so that a different combination of attributes of the stimulus is carried by each. This is thought to be the only neuronal basis of discrimination of stimuli which differ.

Excitational cluster

A set of neurons (usually in parallel pathways) which are normally excited together in a particular temporal and spatial pattern when a normal, biologically significant stimulus occurs.

Interneuron

A neuron (usually of the central nervous system) which is neither sensory nor purely effector-innervating. Interneurons carry on the principal activities of the CNS. The term is sometimes used in a more restricted sense for a small neuron added in a physiological pathway (*q.v.*) to allow for a change from excitatory to inhibitory transmitter.

Interaction, Junction

"Junction" implies fewer assumptions than "Synapse" or "Connexion," the use of which often assumes the very point at issue. In contrast, "Interaction" usually implies no anatomical substrate, and is applicable to results which are entirely physiological.

Model

A representation in any form. Even a two-dimensional anatomical drawing is in some ways a model but the term usually refers to a representation which is a summary of interactions that are inferred from numerous experiments. The representation can be in any form (for example, mathematical or a working model), but models that are most satisfactory as explanations embody the principles of operation of the system which they represent.

Nerve net, Neural network

A nerve net is characteristic of lower animals and is defined as a net of neurons all of which are equivalent and any one of which can act for any other. Neural network is a better term for artificial networks of model neurons.

Pathway (*see* Anatomical, Physiological pathway)

Physiological pathways, Block diagram

Any representation of physiological pathways is likely to be misleading, but deception is minimized by use of several types of representation simultaneously. A block diagram, with straight lines and boxes, leads to quantitative analysis but misleads as to the number of pathways in parallel at every stage. A representation of a physiological pathway by neurons, synapses, or a projection often assumes the very point at issue, but it draws closer attention to the anatomy and unknown connectivity (*q.v.*).

Sign stimulus, Key stimulus, Recognition, Releaser mechanism

An important finding of ethology is that certain features of the environment (including other animals and their behaviour) act as signs which are efficiently recognized and acted upon. In neuronal terms, these stimulus situations are presumably matched to the discrimination or line-labelling by the sensory interneurons, which is achieved by some combination of learning and innate pattern of filtering. Because numerous pathways are excited in parallel, however, no one interneuron necessarily performs the act of recognition, and the system of recognition is not necessarily the same on each occasion that it acts.

Units and Neurons

"Neuron" is an anatomical term for a structure bounded by a cell membrane. "Unit" is a term for a presumed axon, soma, or spiking dendrite, from which recordings are made. When the objective is to explain behaviour in terms of neuron connexions, the concept of units is useful in that it implies physiological entities which are awaiting identification with anatomically described neurons.

Specific

Particular, in contrast to less well distinguished from others of the same kind or in the same area. Applied to centres or connexions when they can be defined rather narrowly anatomically or physiologically.

Uniqueness, Individuality

Every neuron in every nervous system is presumably in some way unique because it occupies a place and has connexions which no other can therefore have. The present course of anatomical and physiological studies is the progressive definition of this individuality and the definition of the extent that it is relevant in the explanation of behaviour in neuronal terms. See, for example, "Discrimination," "Nerve net."

Subject and species index

Index of authors of references